COPYRIGHT

SPECIAL SALES

For more information about buying this book in bulk quantities, or for special sales opportunities (which may include custom cover designs, and content particular to your business or training goals), please send us an email to support@myexcelonline.com

CONNECT WITH US

Website, blog & podcast: https://www.myexcelonline.com

iPhone App: https://www.myexcelonline.com/iphone

Android App: https://www.myexcelonline.com/android

Email Support: support@myexcelonline.com

AUTHOR BIOGRAPHY

John Michaloudis is a Microsoft MVP, and the *Founder* of MyExcelOnline.com. He lives in Vitoria, Spain with his wife and their two beautiful kids. He graduated from La Trobe University in Melbourne, Australia with a Bachelor's Degree in Commerce. John speaks five languages: English, Australian, Greek, Spanish & Excel! In 2001 he started his career as an Accountant & Financial Controller in various big corporates such as Avon Cosmetics & General Electric. In 2014 he founded MyExcelOnline.com, where he passionately teaches thousands of professionals how to use Excel to stand out from the crowd via his blog tutorials, podcasts, webinars and flagship online course – *The MyExcelOnline Academy!*

Bryan Hong is the Content Manager of MyExcelOnline.com. He lives in Canada, where he is happily married to his wonderful wife, Esther. He has a Master's Degree in Computer Science and brings over 10 years of IT and teaching experience. He has a gift for making complex Excel topics simple to understand, whether it be Formulas, Macros, Power Query, Power BI, Pivot Tables or Charts! Bryan is also a Microsoft Certified Systems Engineer.

FREE MICROSOFT EXCEL ONLINE COURSE

As a thank you for your support, we would want to give you a **free Microsoft Excel Online Course** that has 77 video tutorials, 20+ Hours and 10 Modules of different Excel topics such as Excel Functions, Formatting, Tables, Charts, Pivot Tables, Macros, Power Query, Power BI and so much more!

For the **private access link and the password** to this 20+ Hour Excel Course, please go to the **last page of the book**.

TABLE OF CONTENTS

WHAT IS A PIVOT TABLE?

A Pivot Table is an interactive way to quickly summarize large amounts of data with drag and drop ease.

With a Pivot Table you can calculate, summarize, and analyze data to see comparisons, patterns, and trends.

A PivotTable is especially designed for:

- Querying large amounts of data in a user-friendly way.

- Subtotaling and aggregating numeric data, summarizing data by categories and subcategories, and creating custom calculations and formulas.

- Expanding and collapsing levels of data to focus your results.

- Drilling down into the details and areas of interest on the summary data.

- Moving rows to columns, columns to rows, or "pivoting", to see various views and summaries of the source data.

- Filtering, sorting, grouping, and conditionally formatting the most useful and interesting data, enabling you to just focus on the information you want.

- Presenting concise, attractive, and annotated online and printed reports.

Pivot Tables are used daily by Project Managers, Finance Analysts, Accountants, Auditors, CFOs, Sales Analysts, Financial Controllers, Human Resources, Doctors, Statisticians, and various other corporate professionals.

In this book we will show **101 Ways To Master Excel Pivot Tables!** Once you master Pivot Tables, you will dramatically reduce repetition, stress, and hours of daily overtime...

...And exponentially increase your chances of a promotion, pay raise or a new job!

YOUR EXERCISE WORKBOOKS

To get the most value out of this book, **please download the workbooks for each tip** in this book. Follow our step-by-step guide and make sure to practice using the workbook.

Remember...*make mistakes!* You may not get it the first time around. (We certainly didn't!)

When you do get it, you will be a step closer to saving time, reducing stress, and landing that next dream job. But you know what's even better?

You're one step closer to Excel stardom!

For the **download link** that has all the workbooks covered in this book, please go to the **last page of the book**. We are using Microsoft Office 365 for the majority of this book as this version has all the latest features.

Read on and enjoy what the world of Excel Pivot Tables has to offer!

CREATING A PIVOT TABLE

Preparing Data for Pivot Tables

Before you work with Excel Pivot Tables, you will need to **arrange your data set in the correct format**. There are 3 principles which you should follow:

1. **Tabular Format** - Your data must be organized as a list with labelled columns

2. **No Gaps** - No blank columns and no blank rows are allowed

3. **Excel Tables** – Convert your data to Excel Tables (Ctrl + T). Excel Tables automatically expand as more rows and columns are added to your data

You will now be able to harness the full power of Pivot Tables!

Let us go over the principles one by one! Here is our data set:

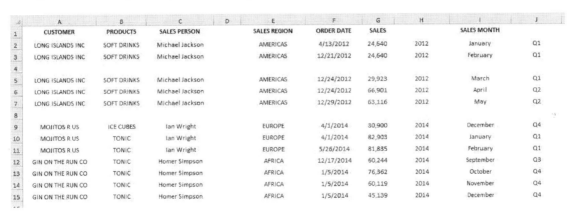

You can see that it has a couple of issues. There are 2 columns without label headers:

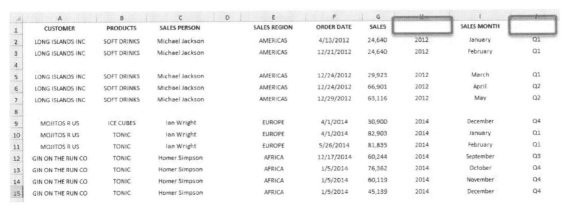

Then we also have 1 blank column and 2 blank rows. Let us get this data cleaned up!

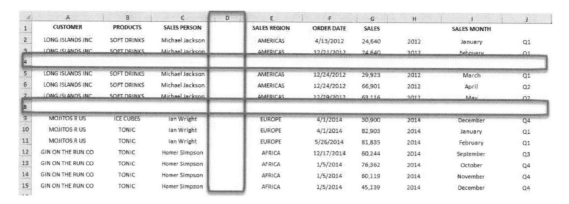

STEP 1: Let me quickly demonstrate to you first that we cannot use this set of data to create a Pivot Table.

Select the entire Table of data and Go to *Insert > Tables > PivotTable*

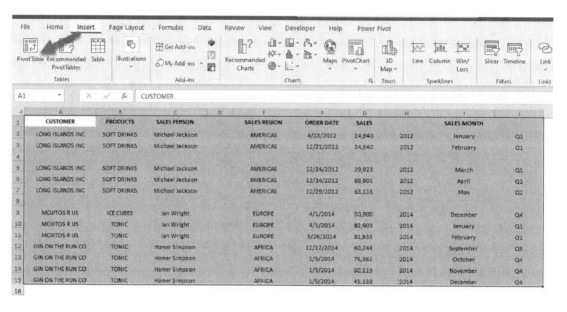

STEP 2: Click **OK**

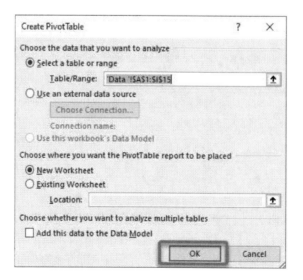

We get this error message because our data is not Pivot Table ready. Let us fix that!

STEP 3: Let us follow the **Tabular Format principle**. For the blank column headers, add **SALES YEAR** and **SALES QTR**:

STEP 4: Now for the **No Gaps principle**, **delete** the blank column D and **delete** the blank rows 4 and 8.

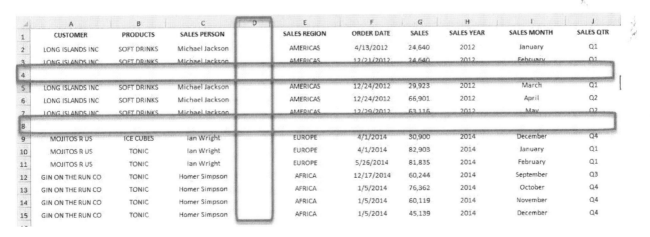

Our data is now looking good!

	CUSTOMER	PRODUCTS	SALES PERSON	SALES REGION	ORDER DATE	SALES	SALES YEAR	SALES MONTH	SALES QTR
1	CUSTOMER	PRODUCTS	SALES PERSON	SALES REGION	ORDER DATE	SALES	SALES YEAR	SALES MONTH	SALES QTR
2	LONG ISLANDS INC	SOFT DRINKS	Michael Jackson	AMERICAS	4/13/2012	24,640	2012	January	Q1
3	LONG ISLANDS INC	SOFT DRINKS	Michael Jackson	AMERICAS	12/21/2012	24,640	2012	February	Q1
4	LONG ISLANDS INC	SOFT DRINKS	Michael Jackson	AMERICAS	12/24/2012	29,923	2012	March	Q1
5	LONG ISLANDS INC	SOFT DRINKS	Michael Jackson	AMERICAS	12/24/2012	66,901	2012	April	Q2
6	LONG ISLANDS INC	SOFT DRINKS	Michael Jackson	AMERICAS	12/29/2012	63,116	2012	May	Q2
7	MOJITOS R US	ICE CUBES	Ian Wright	EUROPE	4/1/2014	30,900	2014	December	Q4
8	MOJITOS R US	TONIC	Ian Wright	EUROPE	4/1/2014	82,903	2014	January	Q1
9	MOJITOS R US	TONIC	Ian Wright	EUROPE	5/26/2014	81,835	2014	February	Q1
10	GIN ON THE RUN CO	TONIC	Homer Simpson	AFRICA	12/17/2014	60,244	2014	September	Q3
11	GIN ON THE RUN CO	TONIC	Homer Simpson	AFRICA	1/5/2014	76,362	2014	October	Q4
12	GIN ON THE RUN CO	TONIC	Homer Simpson	AFRICA	1/5/2014	60,119	2014	November	Q4
13	GIN ON THE RUN CO	TONIC	Homer Simpson	AFRICA	1/5/2014	45,139	2014	December	Q4

STEP 5: Go to **Insert > Table** to convert this into an **Excel Table (Ctrl + T)**

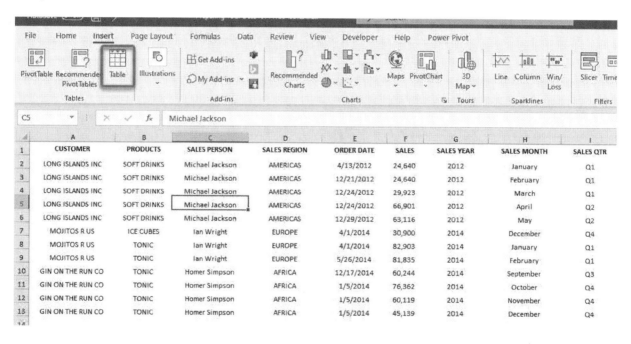

STEP 6: Click **OK**

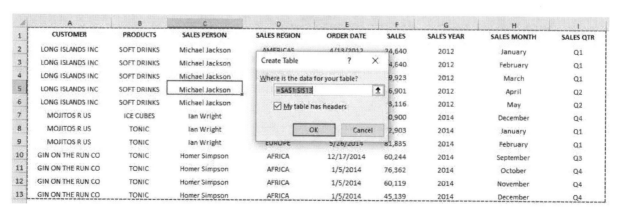

We have our **Excel Table** ready! It's called *Table1* (under **Table Design > Properties)**

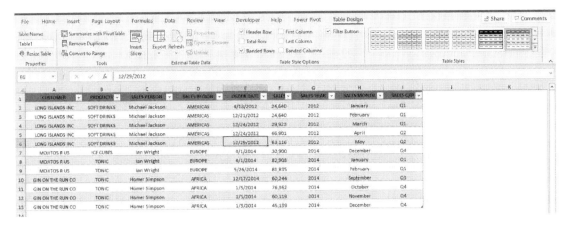

STEP 7: Go to **Insert > PivotTable**

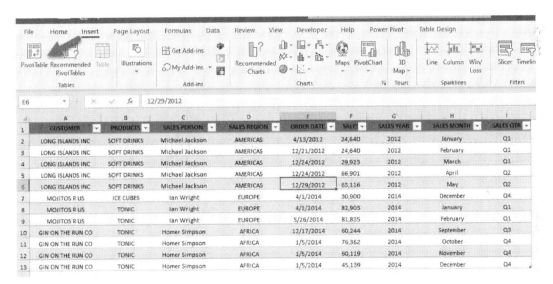

STEP 8: Excel automatically selects the Excel Table – *Table1* as your **Table/Range**. Select **New Worksheet** and click **OK**

We are all set to create our first Pivot Table!

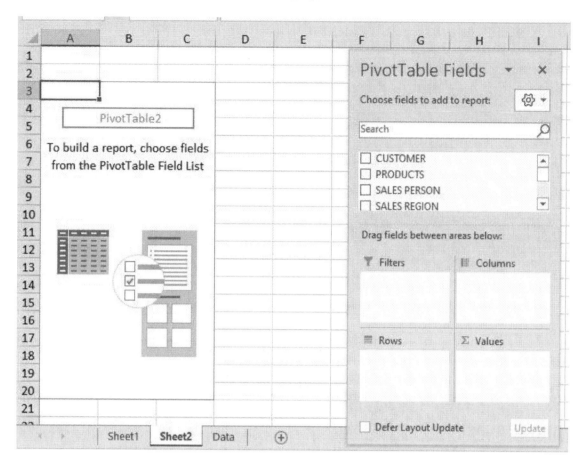

Clean Your Data Set

When working with Excel Pivot Tables, you will need to **ensure your data set is clean**. So, there are 2 things that I want to show you:

1. When your data is not clean

2. How to clean your data

Then you will be able to harness the full power of Pivot Tables!

STEP 1: Here is our data set, select the data and go to *Insert > Tables > PivotTable*

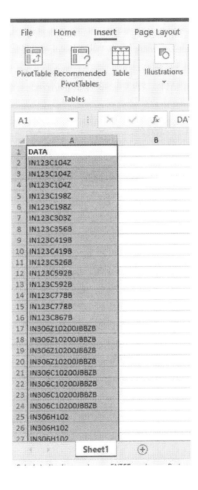

STEP 2: Select **Existing Worksheet** and pick a cell inside the same worksheet to insert our Pivot Table. Click **OK**.

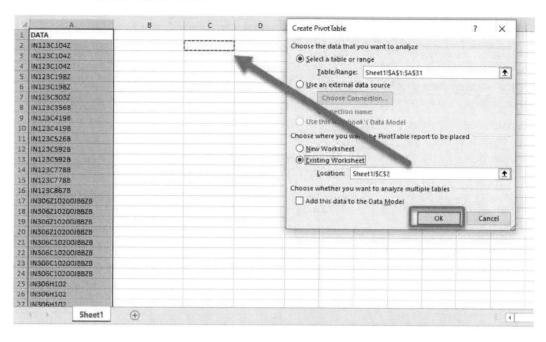

STEP 3: Drag these PivotTable Fields in the following areas below:

Rows: **DATA**
Values: **DATA**

You will notice that **IN123C104Z** is **appearing in 3 rows**? This is caused by our data not being cleaned properly

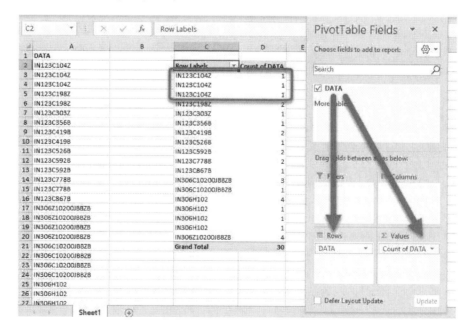

STEP 4: Press **F2 in each cell**. If you inspect the cell closely, you will see that they have **trailing spaces**. This is what's causing our Pivot Table to have weird outputs!

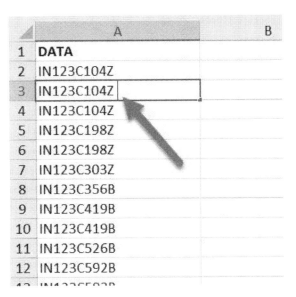

STEP 5: Let us clean those extra spaces! Select the entire column of your data and go to *Data > Data Tools > Text to Columns*

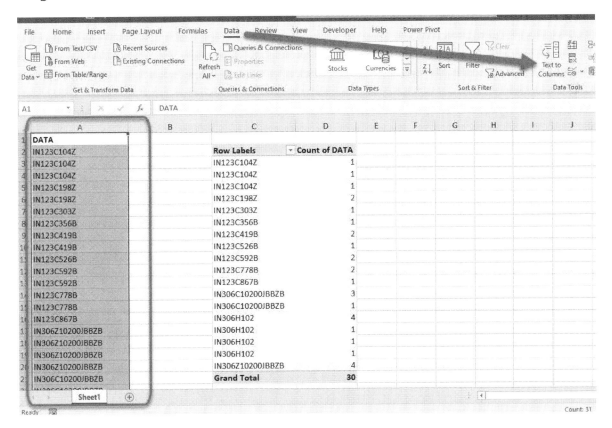

STEP 6: Click **Next**

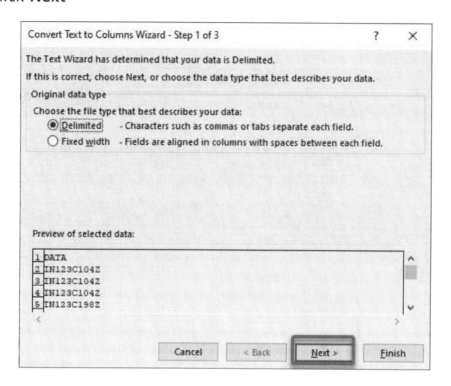

STEP 7: Make sure **Space** is ticked and select **Finish**. This will remove the extra spaces

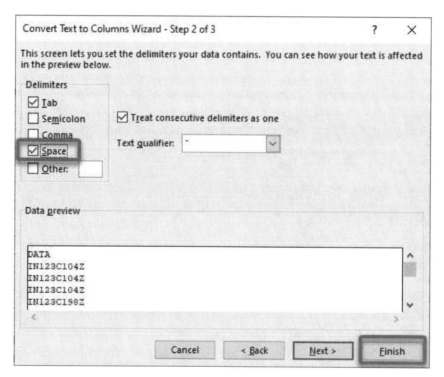

STEP 8: Right click anywhere on your Pivot Table and select **Refresh** to update the data changes in our Pivot Table

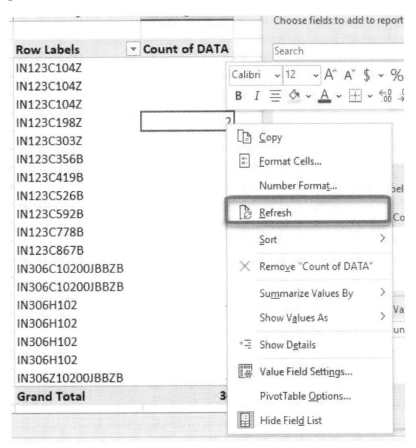

Now that's looking much better!

Row Labels	Count of DATA
IN123C104Z	3
IN123C198Z	2
IN123C303Z	1
IN123C356B	1
IN123C419B	2
IN123C526B	1
IN123C592B	2
IN123C778B	2
IN123C867B	1
IN306C10200JBBZB	4
IN306H102	7
IN306Z10200JBBZB	4
Grand Total	30

Insert a Pivot Table

Pivot Tables allow you to analyze thousands of rows of data with drag and drop ease. Because of its speed-to-output, Pivot Tables are perhaps the most important Excel feature and I'll show you just how easy it is to create one.

Got data to analyze? Then you should always use a Pivot Table. This will enhance your analytical capabilities as well as save lots of time!

When we talk about Pivot Table <u>Fields</u>, these are the headers in your data source e.g., CUSTOMNER, REGION, ORDER DATE, SALES, MONTH & YEAR.

When we talk about Pivot Table <u>Items</u>, these are the unique "items" under each Field e.g. For the REGION Field, the Items are NORTH, SOUTH, EAST & WEST.

STEP 1: Click in your data source. Make sure your data does not have any blank cells, columns or rows!

CUSTOMER	REGION	ORDER DATE	SALES	MONTH	YEAR
Acme, inc.	NORTH	4/13/2014	$24,640	April	2014
Widget Corp	SOUTH	12/21/2014	$24,640	December	2014
123 Warehousing	EAST	2/15/2014	$29,923	February	2014
Demo Company	WEST	5/14/2014	$66,901	May	2014
Smith and Co.	NORTH	6/28/2015	$63,116	June	2015
Foo Bars	SOUTH	1/15/2015	$38,281	January	2015
ABC Telecom	EAST	8/22/2015	$57,650	August	2015
Fake Brothers	WEST	12/31/2015	$90,967	December	2015

STEP 2: Go to *Insert > Pivot Table*

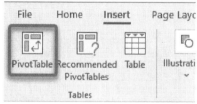

STEP 3: Place the Pivot Table in a **New or Existing Worksheet**

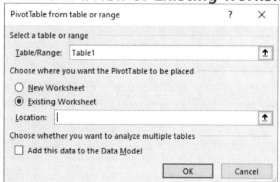

STEP 4: Drag and drop the **PivotTable Fields** in the following areas:

Columns – **YEAR**

Rows – **REGION**

Values - **SALES**

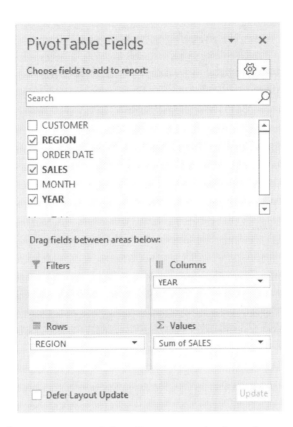

You now have your first Pivot Table. Congratulations!

Sum of SALES	Column Labels		
Row Labels	2014	2015	Grand Total
EAST	29923	57650	87573
NORTH	24640	63116	87756
SOUTH	24640	38281	62921
WEST	66901	90967	157868
Grand Total	**146104**	**250014**	**396118**

If you don't know what PivotTable Fields to put in each of the 4 areas, this explanation will help you:

Rows: Lists the unique values for a given Field as the beginning rows of the Pivot Table

Fields to include: Products, Sales Person, Locations, Business Units

Columns: Shows trending over time (also creates a unique list for a given Field)

Fields to include: Months, Periods and Years

Values: Summarizes Fields you want to quantify with respect to the rows and columns

Fields to include: Revenue, Sales, Costs, Units, Price

Filters: Allows you to filter or drill down on a particular Field

Fields to include: Employees, SKUs, Social Security Numbers

Field List - Customizations

A Pivot Table **Field List** is where the column headings of your data set are stored and these can be dragged into the different areas of a Pivot Table. Looking for your **Field List**? No problem!

STEP 1: Right click on your Pivot Table and select **Show Field List**

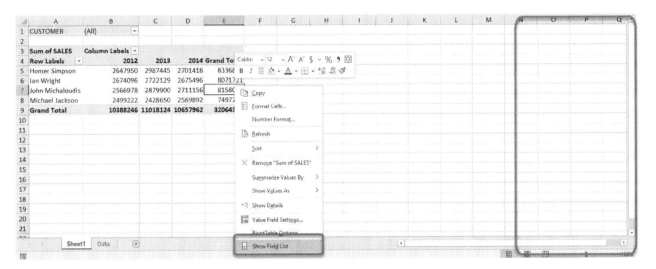

STEP 2: Click on the **down arrow** and you get these options: **Move, Resize** and **Close.**

You can either move it to anywhere on your sheet, expand the panel, or make it hidden again.

STEP 3: Click on the **Gear icon** and you will be able to change the layout of your **Field List**.

The default one we are using is the first one: **Fields Section and Areas Section Stacked.**

Let us have a look at the other layout options!

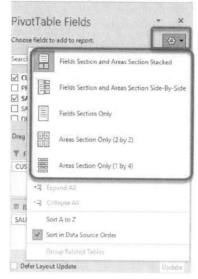

Fields Section and Areas Section Side-By-Side:

Fields Section Only:

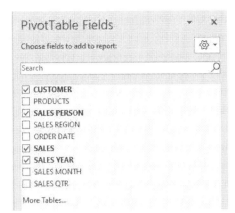

Areas Section Only (2 by 2):

Areas Section Only (1 by 4):

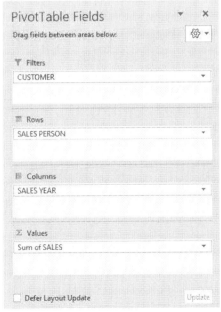

Field List & Areas

When working with Pivot Tables, one of the most crucial concepts is understanding how the Field List and its different Areas work. Knowing these concepts will prevent you from making crucial mistakes and allow you to head straight to your analysis.

Let us go over the different sections:

- Fields

- Rows

- Columns

- Values

- Filters

Here is our initial data Table that we used to create our Pivot Table:

	CUSTOMER	PRODUCTS	SALES PERSON	SALES REGION	ORDER DATE	SALES	SALES YEAR	SALES MONTH	SALES QTR
2	LONG ISLANDS INC	SOFT DRINKS	Michael Jackson	AMERICAS	4/13/2012	51,311	2012	January	Q1
3	LONG ISLANDS INC	SOFT DRINKS	Michael Jackson	AMERICAS	12/21/2012	24,640	2012	February	Q1
4	LONG ISLANDS INC	SOFT DRINKS	Michael Jackson	AMERICAS	12/24/2012	29,923	2012	March	Q1
5	LONG ISLANDS INC	SOFT DRINKS	Michael Jackson	AMERICAS	12/24/2012	66,901	2012	April	Q2
6	LONG ISLANDS INC	SOFT DRINKS	Michael Jackson	AMERICAS	12/29/2012	63,116	2012	May	Q2
7	LONG ISLANDS INC	SOFT DRINKS	Michael Jackson	AMERICAS	6/28/2012	38,281	2012	June	Q2
8	LONG ISLANDS INC	SOFT DRINKS	Michael Jackson	AMERICAS	6/28/2012	57,650	2012	July	Q3
9	LONG ISLANDS INC	SOFT DRINKS	Michael Jackson	AMERICAS	6/29/2012	90,967	2012	August	Q3
10	LONG ISLANDS INC	SOFT DRINKS	Michael Jackson	AMERICAS	6/29/2012	11,910	2012	September	Q3
11	LONG ISLANDS INC	SOFT DRINKS	Michael Jackson	AMERICAS	7/6/2012	53,531	2012	October	Q4
12	LONG ISLANDS INC	SOFT DRINKS	Michael Jackson	AMERICAS	7/6/2012	88,237	2012	November	Q4
13	LONG ISLANDS INC	SOFT DRINKS	Michael Jackson	AMERICAS	9/8/2012	87,868	2012	December	Q4
14	LONG ISLANDS INC	BOTTLES	Michael Jackson	AMERICAS	9/8/2012	95,527	2012	January	Q1
15	LONG ISLANDS INC	BOTTLES	Michael Jackson	AMERICAS	6/30/2012	90,599	2012	February	Q1
16	LONG ISLANDS INC	BOTTLES	Michael Jackson	AMERICAS	12/23/2012	17,030	2012	March	Q1
17	LONG ISLANDS INC	BOTTLES	Michael Jackson	AMERICAS	12/8/2012	65,026	2012	April	Q2
18	LONG ISLANDS INC	BOTTLES	Michael Jackson	AMERICAS	10/28/2012	57,579	2012	May	Q2
19	LONG ISLANDS INC	BOTTLES	Michael Jackson	AMERICAS	10/28/2012	34,338	2012	June	Q2
20	LONG ISLANDS INC	BOTTLES	Michael Jackson	AMERICAS	9/15/2012	90,387	2012	July	Q3
21	LONG ISLANDS INC	BOTTLES	Michael Jackson	AMERICAS	10/28/2012	62,324	2012	August	Q3
22	LONG ISLANDS INC	BOTTLES	Michael Jackson	AMERICAS	10/31/2012	28,871	2012	September	Q3
23	LONG ISLANDS INC	BOTTLES	Michael Jackson	AMERICAS	12/29/2012	34,714	2012	October	Q4
24	LONG ISLANDS INC	BOTTLES	Michael Jackson	AMERICAS	4/15/2012	38,668	2012	November	Q4
25	LONG ISLANDS INC	BOTTLES	Michael Jackson	AMERICAS	12/8/2012	53,810	2012	December	Q4
26	LONG ISLANDS INC	ICE CUBES	Michael Jackson	AMERICAS	12/1/2012	19,058	2012	January	Q1
27	LONG ISLANDS INC	ICE CUBES	Michael Jackson	AMERICAS	12/1/2012	34,096	2012	February	Q1
28	LONG ISLANDS INC	ICE CUBES	Michael Jackson	AMERICAS	10/28/2012	80,441	2012	March	Q1
29	LONG ISLANDS INC	ICE CUBES	Michael Jackson	AMERICAS	8/19/2012	15,306	2012	April	Q2

Sheet1 | **Data** | (+)

STEP 1: Now the first part is the **PivotTable Fields** section, which represents the column headings of our data Table:

STEP 2: The **Row** labels show the unique Fields on the left-hand side of our Pivot Table. Drag **PRODUCTS** to the **Rows** area to see how this looks like.

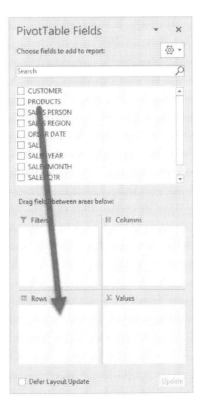

Now you can see our unique Products are listed on the Pivot Table.

STEP 3: The **Column** labels show the trend of your data. For example, this could be periods, time, months, years etc.

Let us drag the **SALES YEAR** to the **Columns** area.

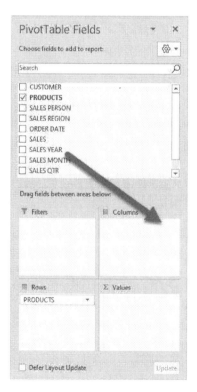

Now you can see the years 2012 - 2014 as the Pivot Table Columns.

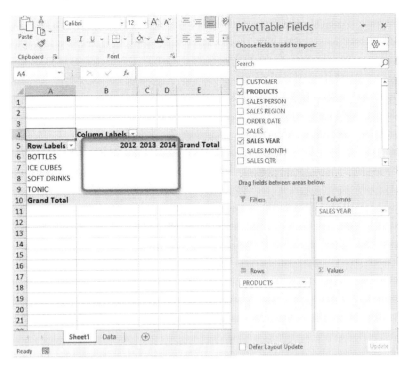

STEP 4: Values are Fields that you want to calculate or quantify. Examples are Sum (for Sales), Count (for Number of Units), Average (for Prices), and Maximum/Minimum (for Sales/Units/Prices etc).

Let us drag **SALES** to **Values.**

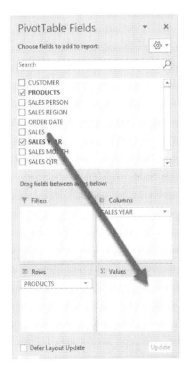

You will get the **Sum of Sales** values here for each Product-Year combination.

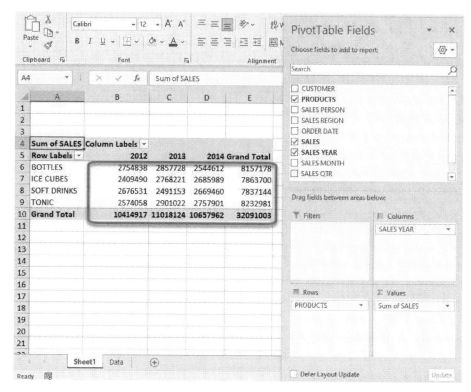

STEP 5: Filters are optional Fields that you want to drill down on or filter, and typically contain lots of entries, e.g., Employees, SKUs, Social Security Numbers.

Drag both **SALES REGION** and **SALES PERSON** to the **Filters** area.

Click on any filter and you will be able to filter your Pivot Table data according to your selection.

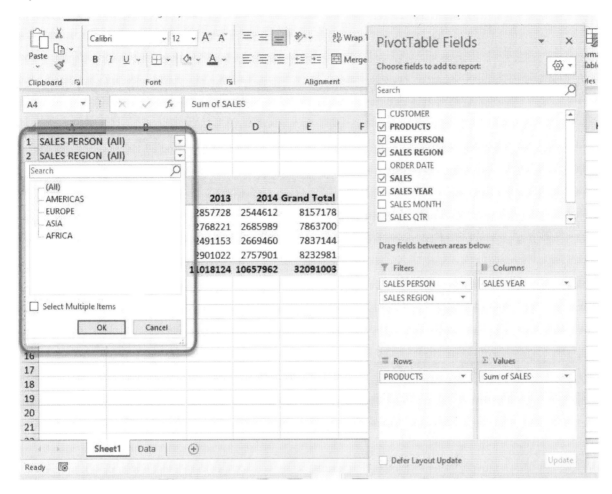

Sort Field List from A to Z

Do you ever get in a situation where your Pivot Table Fields List has over 20 Fields and you spend lots of time trying to locate one?

Well, you can save time by sorting the Pivot Table Field List in alphabetical order!

Our **Field List** is not sorted in alphabetical order as you can see here:

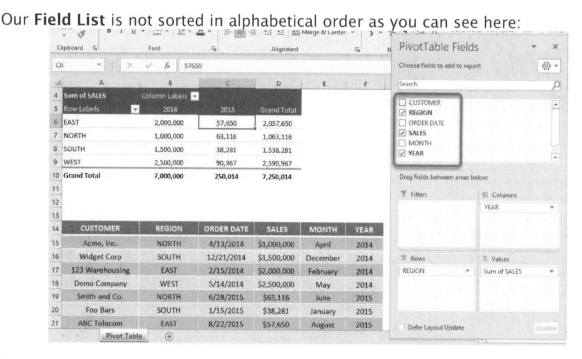

STEP 1: Right click in your Pivot Table and select **PivotTable Options**

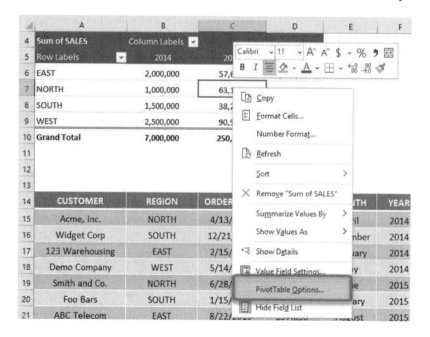

STEP 2: Select *Display > Sort A to Z*. Click **OK**.

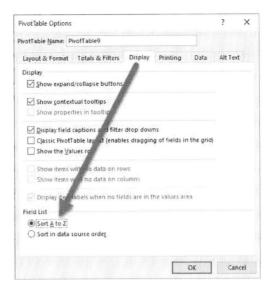

And just like that, our Pivot Table Fields are now **sorted from A to Z**! You can also use the **Search** bar to find your desired Field.

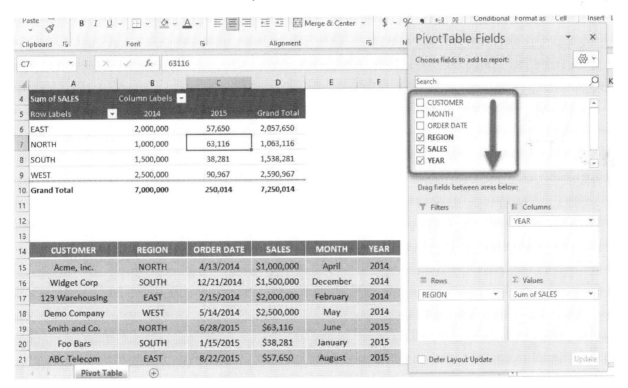

Drill Down To Audit

When you are using a Pivot Table in Excel and want to know what data makes up a certain value, all you have to do is double click on that cell.

This will open up a brand-new Sheet with all the rows of data that make up that value.

Pro Tip: This is an extraction of your data source, so if you edit the information and Refresh your Pivot Table then nothing will happen. Any changes need to be made in your main data source.

If you want to get rid of this sample data, all you have to do is press CTRL+Z and press DELETE in the pop up pox.

So go ahead and double click on any values (including Subtotals and Grand Totals) within your Pivot Table to view the data that makes up your selected value.

STEP 1: Double click on any value cell within the Pivot Table

Row Labels ▼	Sum of SALES
EAST	2,057,650
NORTH	1,063,116
SOUTH	1,538,281
WEST	2,590,967
Grand Total	**7,250,014**

Sum of SALES
Value: 2,590,967
Row: WEST

This opens up a new sheet with the data that makes up the selected cell.

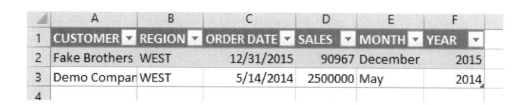

Defer Layout Update

When I use Pivot Tables, I'm used to having all of the updates done instantaneously as I drag Fields between the Pivot Table areas!

But what if you have a lot of rows of data? Generating a live preview on your Pivot Table is going to take time, and you can defer this update! I will show you how it is done below.

This is especially useful for when you're working with really big tables. Sometimes, Excel will slow down when your datasets are super large.

STEP 1: Here is our Pivot Table setup. Select **Defer Layout Update**

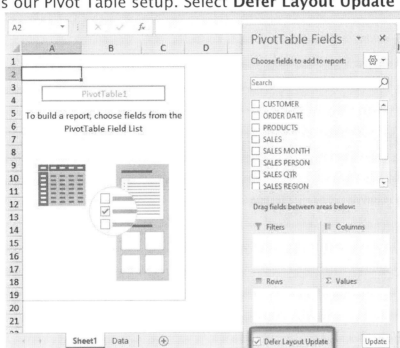

STEP 2: You can setup your Pivot Table in any way that you want. In this example, we have this setup:

Rows: **PRODUCTS**

Columns: **SALES YEAR**

Values: **SALES**

You will notice that we do not have any live preview for our Pivot Table! Because we have deferred this update.

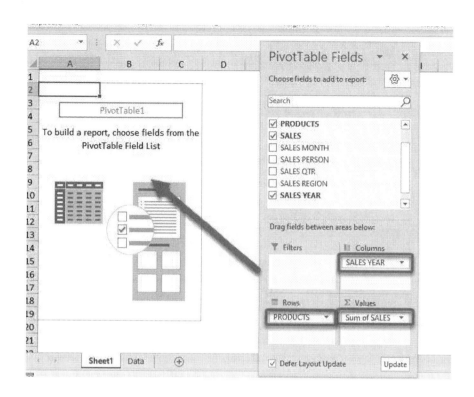

STEP 3: To see how your Pivot Table looks like with this setup, click **Update.**

Now the Pivot Table update has taken place!

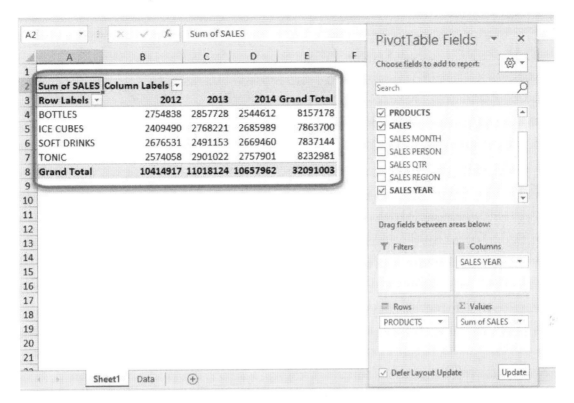

Refresh a Pivot Table

When the information in your data set gets updated, you need to Refresh your Pivot Table to see those changes in your Pivot Table. There are three ways to do this.

First click on your Pivot Table, then do one of the following:

- From the Ribbon select *PivotTable Analyze > Refresh*

- Press the keyboard shortcut: **ALT+F5**

- **Right click** in your Pivot Table and choose Refresh (see this option below)

STEP 1: We have changed the information in the first four SALES rows for 2014.

CUSTOMER	REGION	ORDER DATE	SALES	MONTH	YEAR
Acme, inc.	NORTH	4/13/2014	$1,000,000	April	2014
Widget Corp	SOUTH	12/21/2014	$1,500,000	December	2014
123 Warehousing	EAST	2/15/2014	$2,000,000	February	2014
Demo Company	WEST	5/14/2014	2500000	May	2014
Smith and Co.	NORTH	6/28/2015	$63,116	June	2015
Foo Bars	SOUTH	1/15/2015	$38,281	January	2015
ABC Telecom	EAST	8/22/2015	$57,650	August	2015
Fake Brothers	WEST	12/31/2015	$90,967	December	2015

STEP 2: Click anywhere in the Pivot Table.

Sum of SALES	Column Labels		
Row Labels	2014	2015	Grand Total
EAST	29923	57650	87573
NORTH	24640	63116	87756
SOUTH	24640	38281	62921
WEST	66901	90967	157868
Grand Total	146104	250014	396118

STEP 3: Right click and select **Refresh**.

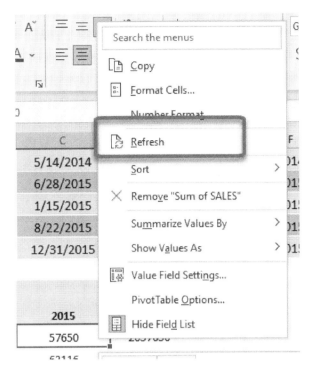

The Pivot Table values are now updated for 2014!

Sum of SALES	Column Labels		
Row Labels	2014	2015	Grand Total
EAST	2000000	57650	2057650
NORTH	1000000	63116	1063116
SOUTH	1500000	38281	1538281
WEST	2500000	90967	2590967
Grand Total	7000000	250014	7250014

Refresh All for Pivot Tables

When the information in your data source gets updated or changed, you need to Refresh your Pivot Table to see those changes.

How about if you have multiple Pivot Tables from the same data source in the same workbook?

How about if you have 2 Pivot Tables that are created from 2 different data sources in the same workbook?

In these scenarios, you can simply select **Data > Refresh All** and all your Pivot Tables will be updated!

STEP 1: We have changed our data set in cell F2 to a large SALES number.

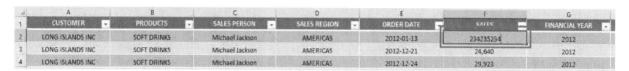

STEP 2: This is our Pivot Table. Take note of the cell that we expect to be updated:

Go to *Data > Refresh All*

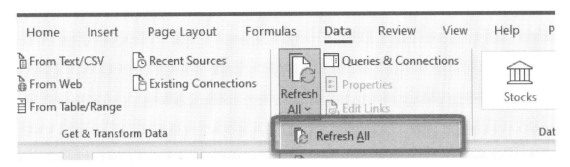

The Pivot Table values are now updated with just one click!

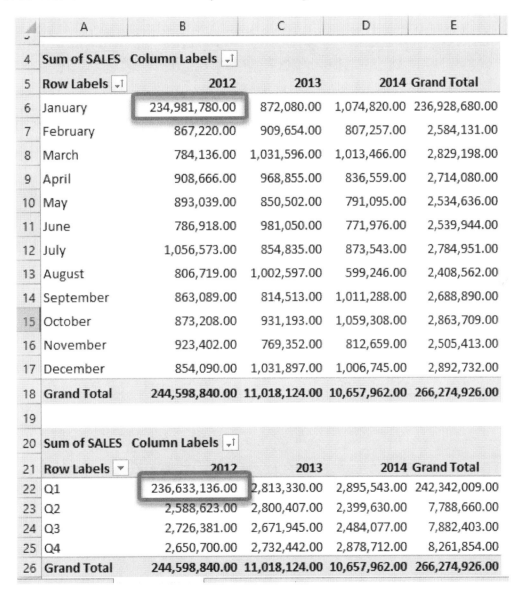

Sum of SALES	Column Labels			
Row Labels	2012	2013	2014	Grand Total
January	234,981,780.00	872,080.00	1,074,820.00	236,928,680.00
February	867,220.00	909,654.00	807,257.00	2,584,131.00
March	784,136.00	1,031,596.00	1,013,466.00	2,829,198.00
April	908,666.00	968,855.00	836,559.00	2,714,080.00
May	893,039.00	850,502.00	791,095.00	2,534,636.00
June	786,918.00	981,050.00	771,976.00	2,539,944.00
July	1,056,573.00	854,835.00	873,543.00	2,784,951.00
August	806,719.00	1,002,597.00	599,246.00	2,408,562.00
September	863,089.00	814,513.00	1,011,288.00	2,688,890.00
October	873,208.00	931,193.00	1,059,308.00	2,863,709.00
November	923,402.00	769,352.00	812,659.00	2,505,413.00
December	854,090.00	1,031,897.00	1,006,745.00	2,892,732.00
Grand Total	244,598,840.00	11,018,124.00	10,657,962.00	266,274,926.00

Sum of SALES	Column Labels			
Row Labels	2012	2013	2014	Grand Total
Q1	236,633,136.00	2,813,330.00	2,895,543.00	242,342,009.00
Q2	2,588,623.00	2,800,407.00	2,399,630.00	7,788,660.00
Q3	2,726,381.00	2,671,945.00	2,484,077.00	7,882,403.00
Q4	2,650,700.00	2,732,442.00	2,878,712.00	8,261,854.00
Grand Total	244,598,840.00	11,018,124.00	10,657,962.00	266,274,926.00

Pivot Cache explained

Whenever you make a change to your data set (updating data, adding more rows or columns), you have to manually refresh your Pivot Table to have your changes reflect.

Why is that?

I'm going to explain to you the concept of the **Pivot Cache**. Join me in understanding this concept with some quick illustrative examples below!

STEP 1: Why is there a need to refresh the Pivot Table each time our data changes? Let us look at the sequence of events below:

1. You initiate the creation of a Pivot Table from your data

2. A snapshot of that data set (in that point in time) is stored in the Pivot Cache (Excel's memory) for quick access

3. Your Pivot Table runs using the Pivot Cache, which is optimized & faster!

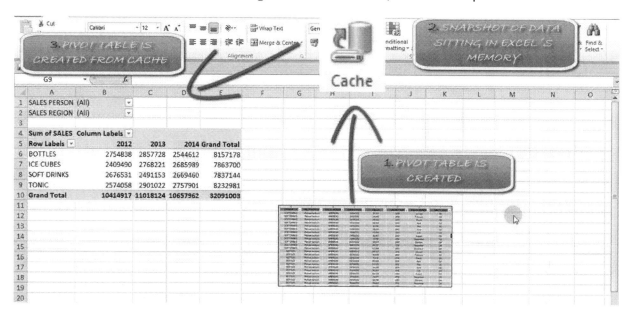

STEP 2: Now what happens when you update the source data?

1. Your source data is updated

2. You Refresh the Pivot Table

3. A snapshot of that data (in that point in time) is stored in the Pivot Cache

4. The Pivot Table is updated instantly using the Pivot Cache

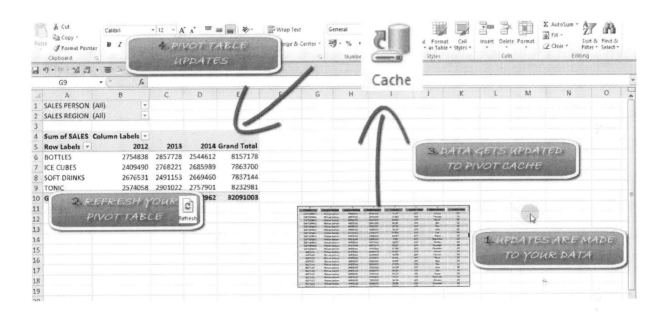

You do not see the **Pivot Cache** as this runs in the background. It's not something you can click on.

Microsoft developed the Pivot Cache technology to optimize changes made to the Pivot Table layout. For most activities, this allows for quick calculations without any lag. Sometimes, however, several large datasets might slow things down. In which case, consider deferring the layout update. This simply tells the **Pivot Cache** to wait until you're ready for an update.

Use External Data Source to Import Data

When creating a **Pivot Table,** what happens if your data source is in another location?

Would you have to copy your data into the same spreadsheet? Well...NO!

You can simply use the **External Data Sources** feature in your Pivot Table and Excel will magically import the data for you!

You can import data into your Pivot Table from the following data sources:

- Another Excel workbook

- Microsoft Access database

- SQL Server

- Analysis Services

- Windows Azure Marketplace

- OData Data Feed

- Plus many more sources!

For our example, we will import data using two data sources, an **Excel workbook** and an **Access file**.

This is our Excel Workbook:

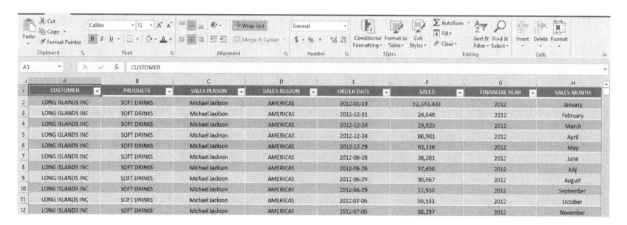

This is our Microsoft Access database:

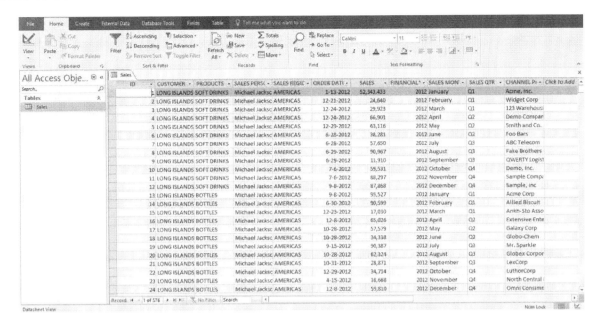

Import from another Excel Workbook:

STEP 1: Go to *Insert > Tables > PivotTable > From External Data Source*

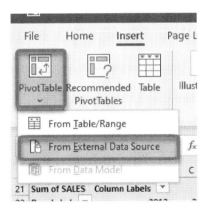

STEP 2: Click **Choose Connection.**

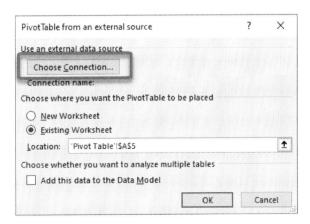

STEP 3: Select **Browse for More.**

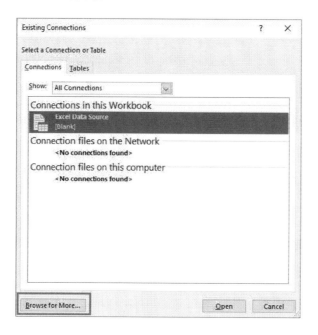

STEP 4: Select the **Excel file** with your data. Click **Open.**

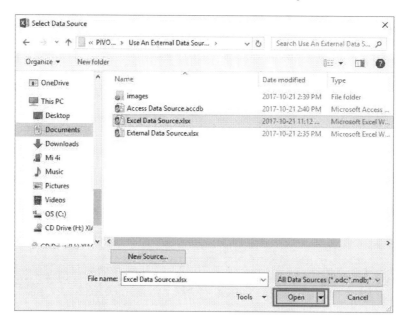

STEP 5: Select the first option and click **OK.**

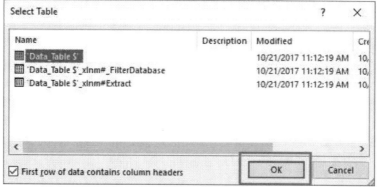

STEP 6: Click **OK.**

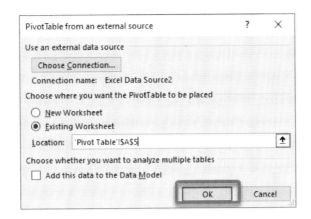

STEP 7: Drag these PivotTable Fields in the following areas below:

Rows: **SALES MONTH**
Columns: **FINANCIAL YEAR**
Values: **SALES**

Your Pivot Table is ready from another Excel workbook!

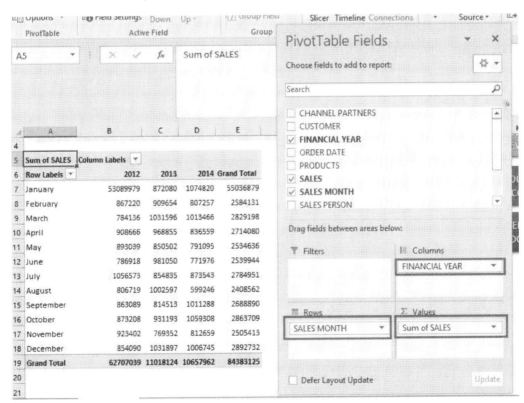

Import From Microsoft Access and into Excel:

STEP 1: Now let us try for an Access database!

Go to *Data > Get Data > From Database > From Microsoft Access Database*

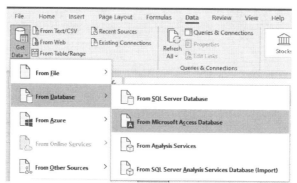

STEP 2: Select the **Access Database Source file in your desktop or company file path.** Click **Open.**

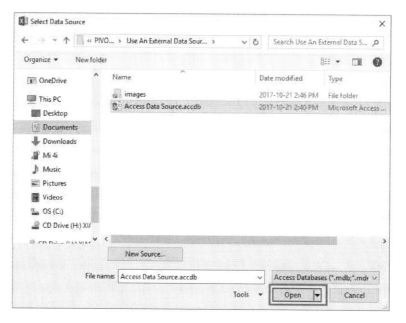

STEP 3: Select **PivotTable Report** and click **OK.**

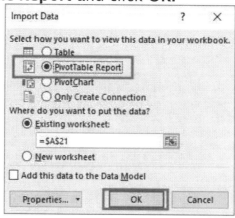

STEP 4: Drag these PivotTable Fields in the following areas below:

Rows: **SALES MONTH**
Columns: **FINANCIAL YEAR**
Values: **SALES**

Your Pivot Table is ready from the Access database!

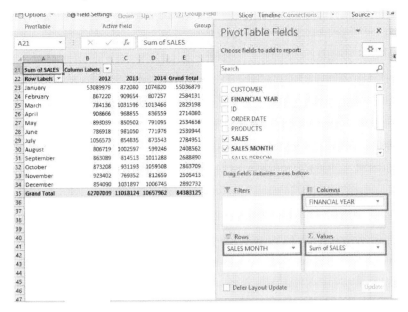

More Ways to Import External Data into a Pivot Table:

You can also use the **Get Data** functionality to import data from other source types: **SQL Server**, **Analysis Services**, **Windows Azure**, **OData Feed plus many more sources.**

Excel is constantly adding to these data sources, so the future is bright!

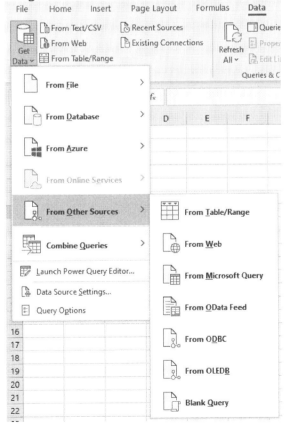

Refresh External Data

The cool thing with Pivot Tables is that you can use a data source that lies outside your current workbook. The external data source could be stored in a shared drive in your company server that your team uses, or it could be in a different location stored on your computer.

Imagine if this external data source gets updated frequently.

How would we ensure that our Pivot Table is refreshed and shows updated data? I have a couple of tips for you below!

Let us check that our Pivot Table is in fact using an External Data

Source. Go to *PivotTable Analyze > Data > Change Data Source*

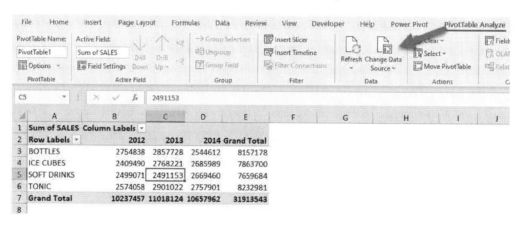

You can see that it is using an external data source called *Shared Data Set3*. **Click OK.**

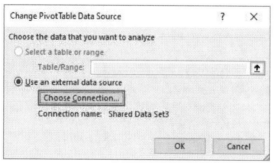

STEP 1: One way is to update this data source by right clicking on the Pivot Table and selecting **Refresh**

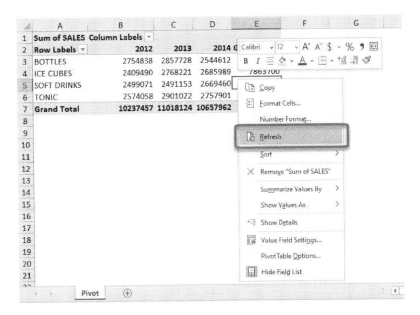

STEP 2: There is another way to ensure your Pivot Table is updated. Go to *PivotTable Analyze > Data > Change Data Source > Connection Properties*

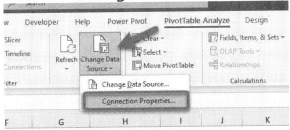

STEP 3: There are two options that you can use:

- **Refresh every X minutes** - this will refresh your Pivot Table automatically after the number of minutes have passed

- **Refresh data when opening the file** - this triggers a Pivot Table update whenever you open the Excel file. This is a good option if you prefer this to happen only once when you open the file.

Change Data Source

After you have finished setting up your Pivot Table, it is very easy to **change the data source** in case you made a mistake or just need to change it. Let me show you how to do it in a couple of steps!

Let us go over our current Pivot Table and select any cell inside it:

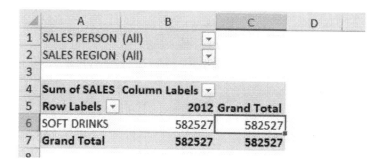

STEP 1: Let us check out the current data source. Go to *PivotTable Analyze > Data > Change Data Source*

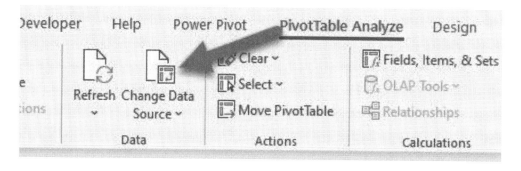

STEP 2: You can see that our current setup is incorrect as it covers only a part of a Data Range. Let us fix that!

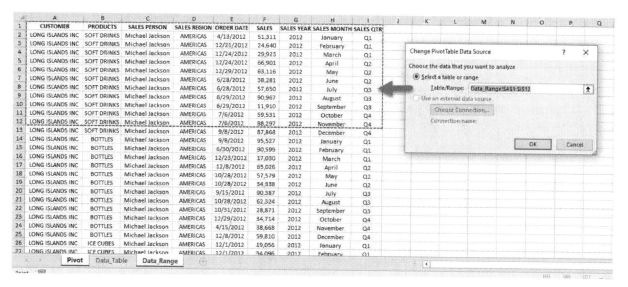

STEP 3: Go to the **Data_Table** worksheet and select the entire data which is in an Excel Table called *Table13* (you can use the **CTRL+A** keyboard shortcut to select this Excel Table).

Click **OK**.

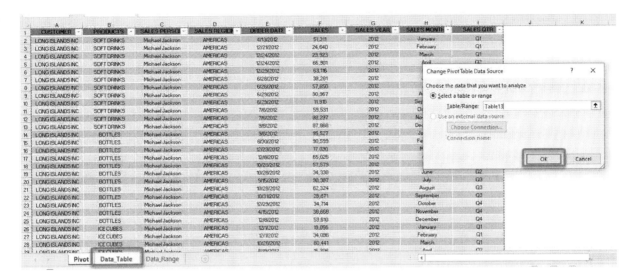

The Pivot Table is now reflecting the **new data source from this Excel Table!**

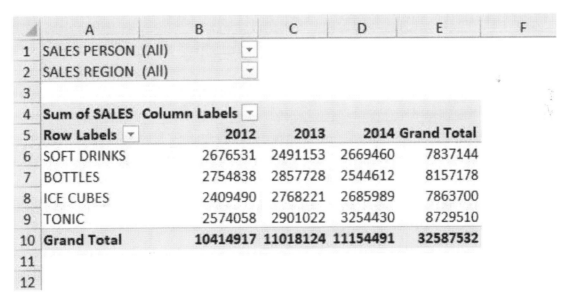

It is better to always use an Excel Table as your data source, so that when you update your data it will always be included inside your data source, due to its structured referencing.

CUSTOMIZING A PIVOT TABLE

Select & format

When it comes to formatting specific sections in your Pivot Table, you can do it the slow manual way—or the fast and easy way! (Which would you rather do?) Thankfully formatting a section in a Pivot Table is very easy to do with the **Enable Selection** feature. I will show you the different ways to use this feature!

Here is our current Pivot Table:

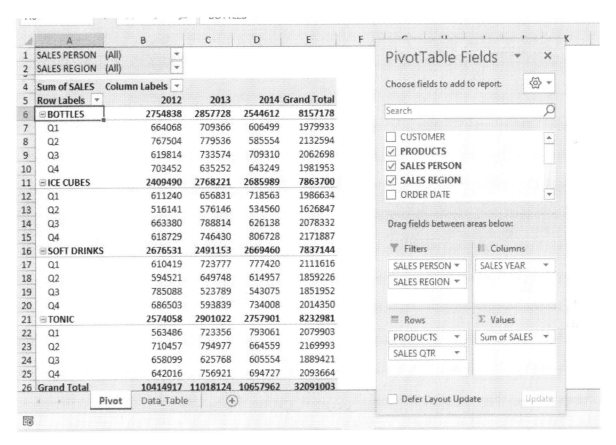

STEP 1: To enable this feature, go to *PivotTable Analyze > Actions > Select > Enable Selection*

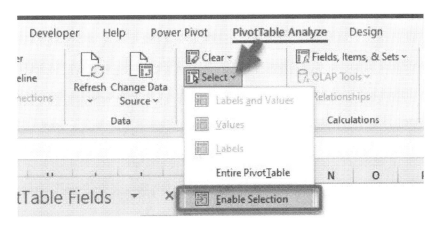

STEP 2: Let us try it out! Select the **Bottles Product** from the left hand side to highlight it.

Sum of SALES	Column Labels			
Row Labels	2012	2013	2014	Grand Total
⊟BOTTLES	2754838	2857728	2544612	8157178
Q1	664068	709366	606499	1979933
Q2	767504	779536	585554	2132594
Q3	619814	733574	709310	2062698
Q4	703452	635252	643249	1981953
⊟ICE CUBES	2409490	2768221	2685989	7863700
Q1	611240	656831	718563	1986634
Q2	516141	576146	534560	1626847
Q3	663380	788814	626138	2078332
Q4	618729	746430	806728	2171887
⊟SOFT DRINKS	2676531	2491153	2669460	7837144
Q1	610419	723777	777420	2111616
Q2	594521	649748	614957	1859226
Q3	785088	523789	543075	1851952
Q4	686503	593839	734008	2014350
⊟TONIC	2574058	2901022	2757901	8232981
Q1	563486	723356	793061	2079903
Q2	710457	794977	664559	2169993
Q3	658099	625768	605554	1889421
Q4	642016	756921	694727	2093664
Grand Total	10414917	11018124	10657962	32091003

Pivot | Data_Table | ⊕

Any formatting change will apply to the entire **Bottles Product**.

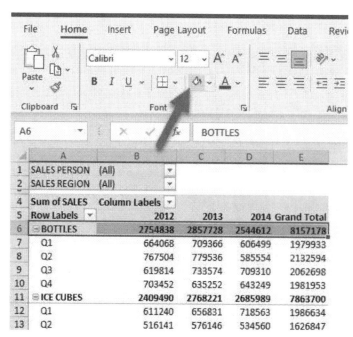

STEP 3: What if we want to apply a formatting change to all **Product items** in one click? Click on the top portion of **Bottles**.

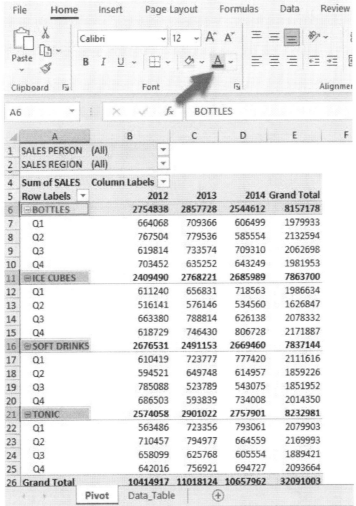

Sum of SALES	Column Labels			
Row Labels	2012	2013	2014	Grand Total
BOTTLES	2754838	2857728	2544612	8157178
Q1	664068	709366	606499	1979933
Q2	767504	779536	585554	2132594
Q3	619814	733574	709310	2062698
Q4	703452	635252	643249	1981953
ICE CUBES	2409490	2768221	2685989	7863700
Q1	611240	656831	718563	1986634
Q2	516141	576146	534560	1626847
Q3	663380	788814	626138	2078332
Q4	618729	746430	806728	2171887
SOFT DRINKS	2676531	2491153	2669460	7837144
Q1	610419	723777	777420	2111616
Q2	594521	649748	614957	1859226
Q3	785088	523789	543075	1851952
Q4	686503	593839	734008	2014350
TONIC	2574058	2901022	2757901	8232981
Q1	563486	723356	793061	2079903
Q2	710457	794977	664559	2169993
Q3	658099	625768	605554	1889421
Q4	642016	756921	694727	2093664
Grand Total	10414917	11018124	10657962	32091003

You will see all of the **Product items** highlighted. Make any formatting change you like.

STEP 4: Let us now try on a specific quarter. Select the left-hand side of **Q1** to select it.

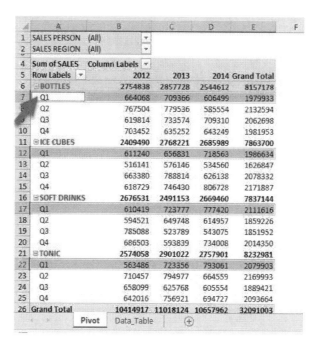

Make any formatting changes. All **Q1 values** will immediately have this formatting change applied.

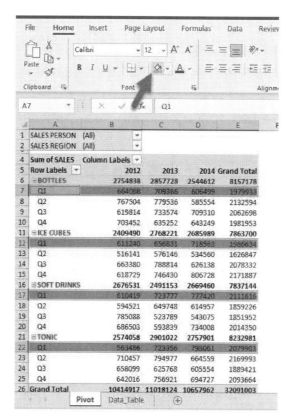

STEP 5: You can do the same for a specific column. Click the 2014 column.

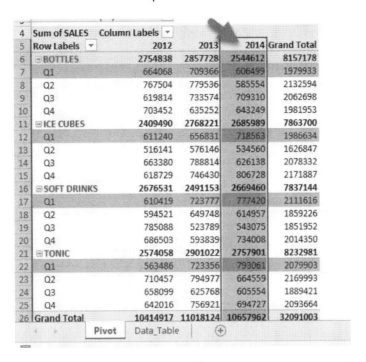

Make the formatting change and see the changes in an instant!

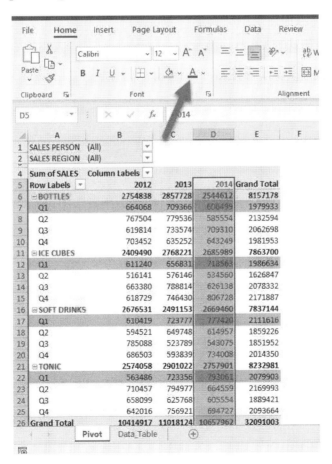

Move a Pivot Table

If you have your Pivot Table ready but it's not in the best location, how do you move this onto another section of your Excel worksheet?

Well, you can simply select **Move PivotTable** and you can move your Excel Pivot Table wherever you like!

For our example, let's move this lovely Pivot Table upwards!

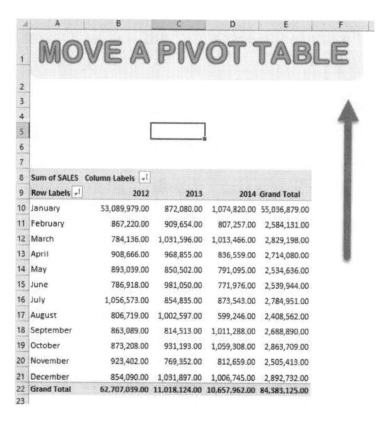

STEP 1: Make sure you have selected your Pivot Table. Go to
PivotTable Analyze > Actions > Move PivotTable

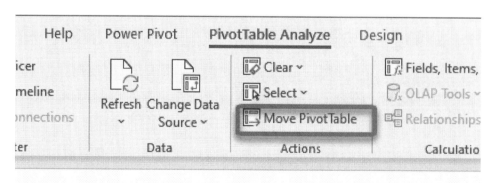

STEP 2: Select the new location where you want to move it. You have the option to move the Pivot Table to a **New Worksheet** or the **Existing Worksheet**.

In our example, we will select the **Existing Worksheet** and cell **A4** and click **OK.**

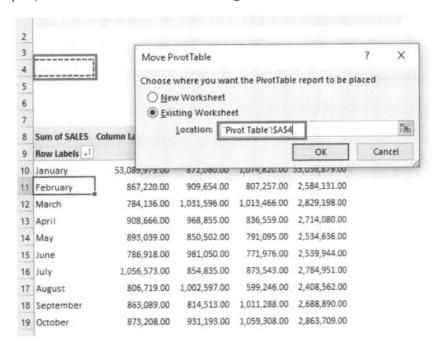

Voila! You have successfully moved your Pivot Table!

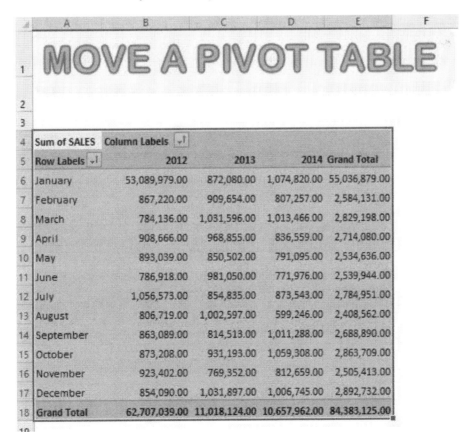

Pivot Table Styles

The default Pivot Table style in Excel is very bland and boring, stemming from a lack of creativity from the nerds over at Microsoft!

You can give some life to your Pivot Table by simply **changing the Pivot Table Style!**

For our example, this is our default **Pivot Table**:

Sum of SALES	Column Labels			
Row Labels	2012	2013	2014	Grand Total
January	53,089,979.00	872,080.00	1,074,820.00	55,036,879.00
February	867,220.00	909,654.00	807,257.00	2,584,131.00
March	784,136.00	1,031,596.00	1,013,466.00	2,829,198.00
April	908,666.00	968,855.00	836,559.00	2,714,080.00
May	893,039.00	850,502.00	791,095.00	2,534,636.00
June	786,918.00	981,050.00	771,976.00	2,539,944.00
July	1,056,573.00	854,835.00	873,543.00	2,784,951.00
August	806,719.00	1,002,597.00	599,246.00	2,408,562.00
September	863,089.00	814,513.00	1,011,288.00	2,688,890.00
October	873,208.00	931,193.00	1,059,308.00	2,863,709.00
November	923,402.00	769,352.00	812,659.00	2,505,413.00
December	854,090.00	1,031,897.00	1,006,745.00	2,892,732.00
Grand Total	62,707,039.00	11,018,124.00	10,657,962.00	84,383,125.00

STEP 1: Make sure you have your Pivot Table selected. Go to *Design > PivotTable Styles*

STEP 2: Expand the styles list and have fun selecting your preferred style! You can see I selected the orange style below, as today is a hot day :)

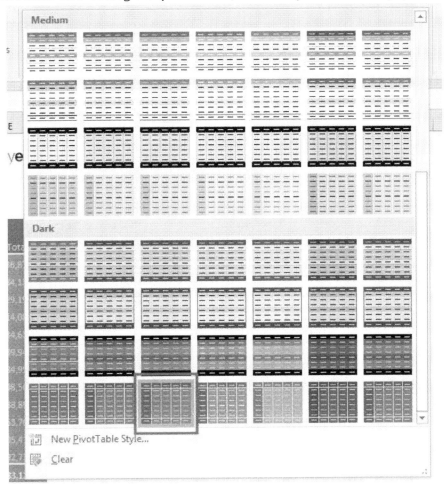

You now have your **Pivot Table** with your new warm style!

Sum of SALES	Column Labe ▾			
Row Labels ▾	2012	2013	2014	Grand Total
January	53,089,979.00	872,080.00	1,074,820.00	55,036,879.00
February	867,220.00	909,654.00	807,257.00	2,584,131.00
March	784,136.00	1,031,596.00	1,013,466.00	2,829,198.00
April	908,666.00	968,855.00	836,559.00	2,714,080.00
May	893,039.00	850,502.00	791,095.00	2,534,636.00
June	786,918.00	981,050.00	771,976.00	2,539,944.00
July	1,056,573.00	854,835.00	873,543.00	2,784,951.00
August	806,719.00	1,002,597.00	599,246.00	2,408,562.00
September	863,089.00	814,513.00	1,011,288.00	2,688,890.00
October	873,208.00	931,195.00	1,059,308.00	2,863,709.00
November	923,402.00	769,352.00	812,659.00	2,505,413.00
December	854,090.00	1,031,897.00	1,006,745.00	2,892,732.00
Grand Total	62,707,039.00	11,018,124.00	10,657,962.00	84,383,125.00

Customizing a Style

There are a lot of **Pivot Table Styles** to choose from when you want to change the look and feel of your Pivot Table. What if even with this multitude of options, you still want to make your own style? There are a couple of ways to do this!

Here is our Pivot Table:

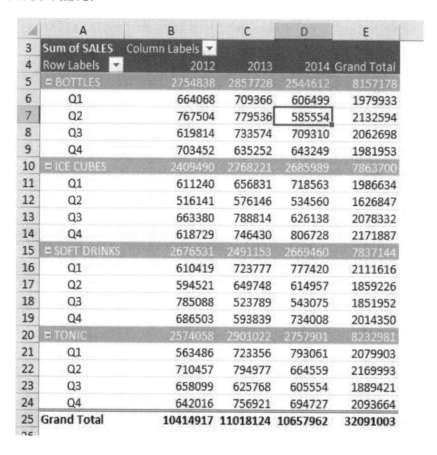

	A	B	C	D	E
3	Sum of SALES	Column Labels			
4	Row Labels	2012	2013	2014	Grand Total
5	⊟ BOTTLES	2754838	2857728	2544612	8157178
6	Q1	664068	709366	606499	1979933
7	Q2	767504	779536	585554	2132594
8	Q3	619814	733574	709310	2062698
9	Q4	703452	635252	643249	1981953
10	⊟ ICE CUBES	2409490	2768221	2685989	7863700
11	Q1	611240	656831	718563	1986634
12	Q2	516141	576146	534560	1626847
13	Q3	663380	788814	626138	2078332
14	Q4	618729	746430	806728	2171887
15	⊟ SOFT DRINKS	2676531	2491153	2669460	7837144
16	Q1	610419	723777	777420	2111616
17	Q2	594521	649748	614957	1859226
18	Q3	785088	523789	543075	1851952
19	Q4	686503	593839	734008	2014350
20	⊟ TONIC	2574058	2901022	2757901	8232981
21	Q1	563486	723356	793061	2079903
22	Q2	710457	794977	664559	2169993
23	Q3	658099	625768	605554	1889421
24	Q4	642016	756921	694727	2093664
25	Grand Total	10414917	11018124	10657962	32091003

STEP 1: Go to *Design > PivotTable Styles* and click the **down arrow** to open the options

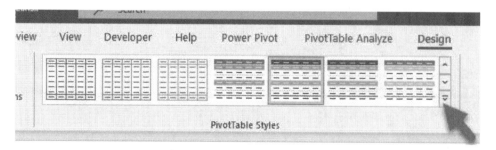

If you want to create a new custom style from scratch, select **New PivotTable Style**

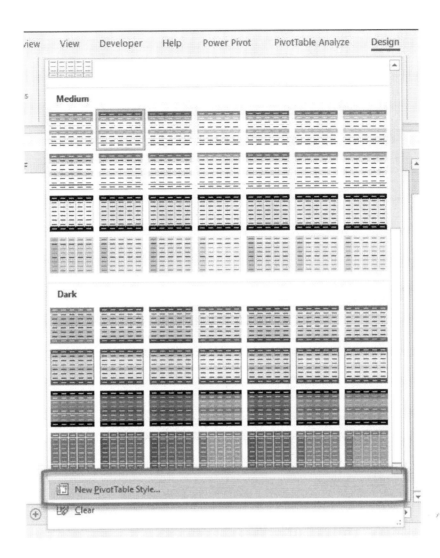

STEP 2: If you have a starting point in mind, you can **right click** on any style and select **Duplicate**....

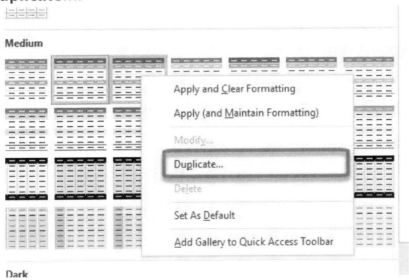

STEP 3: Change the **Name** into your own preference. There are a lot of elements you can format!

For our example, let us edit the **First Column**. Select that and click **Format.**

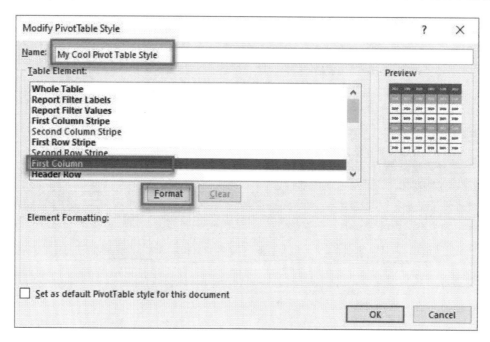

STEP 4: Try out any formatting that you want. We can try to change the **Fill color to green.** Click **OK**

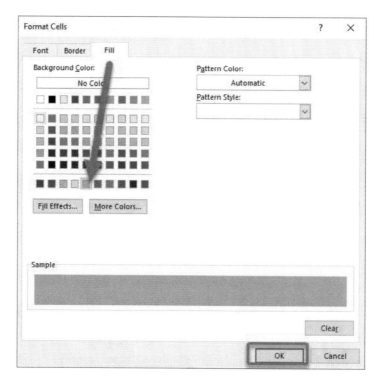

STEP 5: You can see a preview of how it will look. Our first column changed its fill color to green! Click **OK**

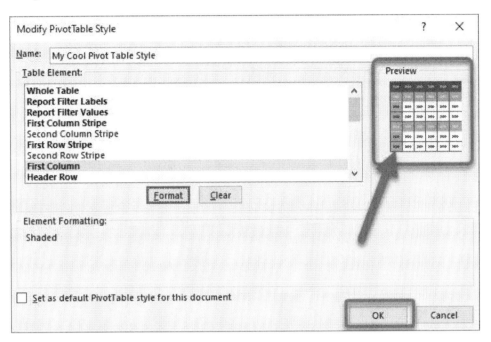

STEP 6: The new Style that we created is not applied yet.

To apply it to the Pivot Table, go to **Design > PivotTable Styles** and select the new Style that we have created.

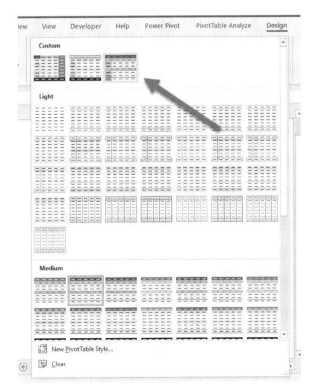

And there you have it!

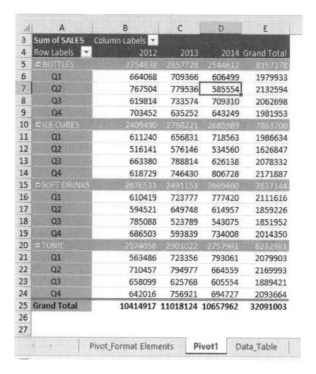

I have also created this diagram for you to see the different Pivot Table Style elements that you can format. Have fun creating your awesome styles!

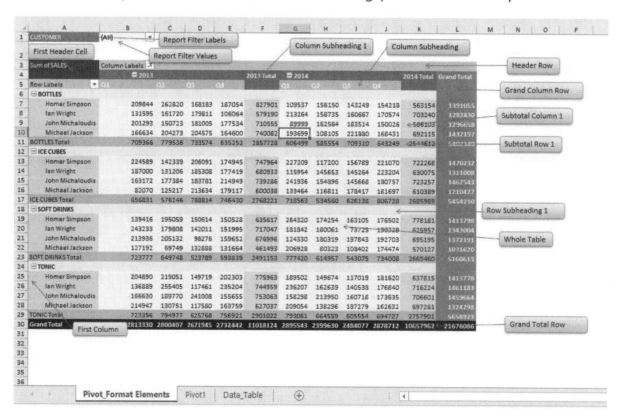

Insert Subtotals

When you create a Pivot Table that has multiple Fields in the Row Labels, Excel will automatically add a Subtotal to the top of the Group.

What about if you want to move the Subtotals to the bottom of the Group or take the Subtotals out all together?

Well, you have that flexibility when you are dealing with Subtotals, here is how:

STEP 1: Enter at least **two FIELDS** in the **Rows** area

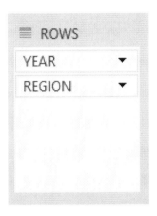

STEP 2: Click in your Pivot Table and go to *Design > Subtotals*

STEP 3: You can choose **either of the 3 options available:**

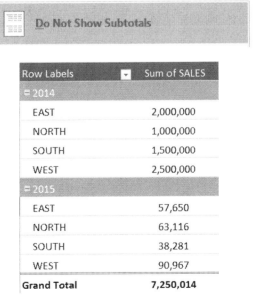

Show all Subtotals at Bottom of Group

Row Labels	Sum of SALES
⊟ 2014	
EAST	2,000,000
NORTH	1,000,000
SOUTH	1,500,000
WEST	2,500,000
2014 Total	**7,000,000**
⊟ 2015	
EAST	57,650
NORTH	63,116
SOUTH	38,281
WEST	90,967
2015 Total	**250,014**
Grand Total	**7,250,014**

 Show all Subtotals at Top of Group

Row Labels	Sum of SALES
⊟ 2014	7,000,000
EAST	2,000,000
NORTH	1,000,000
SOUTH	1,500,000
WEST	2,500,000
⊟ 2015	250,014
EAST	57,650
NORTH	63,116
SOUTH	38,281
WEST	90,967
Grand Total	**7,250,014**

Insert Grand Totals

When you insert a Pivot Table and drop a Field in the Row/Column Labels, you will automatically get a Grand Total.

How about if you want to remove this Grand Total or show it only for a Row or Column?

Well you have that flexibility and this is how...

STEP 1: Click in your Pivot Table and go to *Design > Grand Totals.*

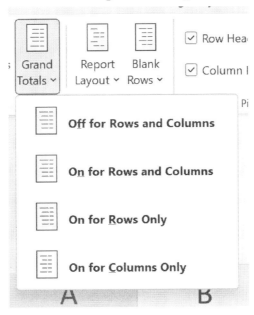

STEP 2: Choose any of the options below:

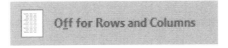

Sum of SALES	Column Labels	
Row Labels	2014	2015
EAST	2,000,000	57,650
NORTH	1,000,000	63,116
SOUTH	1,500,000	38,281
WEST	2,500,000	90,967

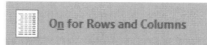

Sum of SALES	Column Labels		
Row Labels	2014	2015	Grand Total
EAST	2,000,000	57,650	2,057,650
NORTH	1,000,000	63,116	1,063,116
SOUTH	1,500,000	38,281	1,538,281
WEST	2,500,000	90,967	2,590,967
Grand Total	**7,000,000**	**250,014**	**7,250,014**

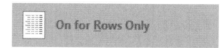

Sum of SALES	Column Labels		
Row Labels	2014	2015	Grand Total
EAST	2,000,000	57,650	2,057,650
NORTH	1,000,000	63,116	1,063,116
SOUTH	1,500,000	38,281	1,538,281
WEST	2,500,000	90,967	2,590,967

Sum of SALES	Column Labels	
Row Labels	2014	2015
EAST	2,000,000	57,650
NORTH	1,000,000	63,116
SOUTH	1,500,000	38,281
WEST	2,500,000	90,967
Grand Total	**7,000,000**	**250,014**

Report Layouts

Pivot Tables have 3 different layouts that you can choose from: *Compact, Outline and Tabular Form.*

You can select each layout by clicking in the Pivot Table and going to ***Design > Report Layouts.***

They each have their advantages and disadvantages and I explain each below:

COMPACT LAYOUT (default layout)

Advantages:

- Optimizes for readability

- Keeps related data in one column

Disadvantages: If you copy and paste the data into a new worksheet it will be harder to do further analysis

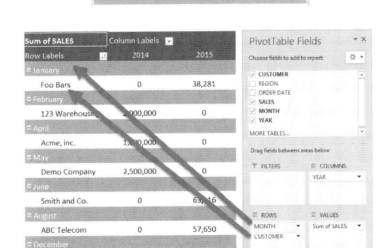

OUTLINE LAYOUT

Advantages:

- Includes Field headers in each Column

- Can Repeat All Item Labels

- Can reuse the data of the Pivot Table to a new location for further analysis

- This is the classic Pivot Table style in older versions of Excel

Disadvantages: Takes up too much horizontal space

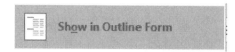

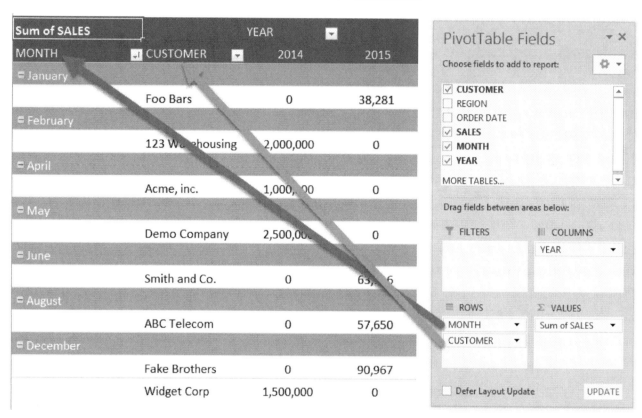

TABULAR LAYOUT

Advantages:

- Includes Field headers in each Column

- Can Repeat All Item Labels

- See all data in a traditional Table format

- Can reuse the data of the Pivot Table to a new location for further analysis

Disadvantages:

- Takes too much horizontal space

- Subtotals can never appear at the top of the group

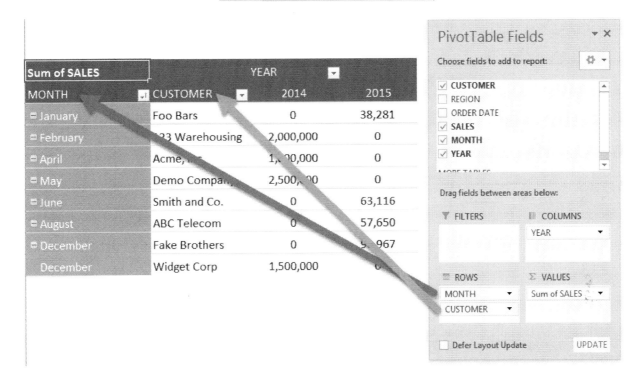

Show in Tabular Form

Sum of SALES		YEAR ▼	
MONTH ↓	CUSTOMER ▼	2014	2015
January	Foo Bars	0	38,281
February	23 Warehousing	2,000,000	0
April	Acme,	1, 0,000	0
May	Demo Compan,	2,500, 0	0
June	Smith and Co.	0	63,116
August	ABC Telecom	0	57,650
December	Fake Brothers	0	967
December	Widget Corp	1,500,000	

PivotTable Fields ▼ ✕

Choose fields to add to report: ⚙ ▼

- ☑ **CUSTOMER**
- ☐ REGION
- ☐ ORDER DATE
- ☑ **SALES**
- ☑ **MONTH**
- ☑ **YEAR**

Drag fields between areas below:

▼ FILTERS	▦ COLUMNS
	YEAR ▼

▦ ROWS	Σ VALUES
MONTH ▼	Sum of SALES ▼
CUSTOMER ▼	

☐ Defer Layout Update   UPDATE

Insert Blank Rows

Pivot Table reports are shown in a Compact Layout format as a default and if you have **two or more Items in the Row Labels** (e.g. Month & Customer), then the **Pivot Table report can look very clunky**...

Sum of SALES	Column Labels	
Row Labels	2014	2015
January	53,586	56,959
Acme, inc.	0	56,959
Smith and Co.	53,586	0
February	14,333	47,189
Foo Bars	14,333	0
Widget Corp	0	47,189
March	29,570	37,544
123 Warehousing	0	37,544
ABC Telecom	29,570	0

There is a cool little trick that most Excel users do not know about that **adds a blank row after each item,** making the Pivot Table report look more appealing

STEP 1: Click any cell in the Pivot Table

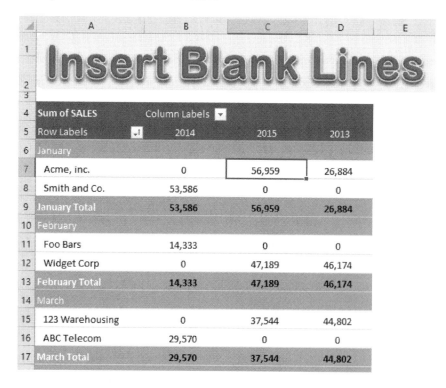

STEP 2: Go to *Design > Blank Rows*

STEP 3: You will need to click on the **Blank Rows** button and select *Insert Blank Line After Each Item*

Pro Tip: *For this to work you will need at least two Pivot Table Items in the Rows Labels*

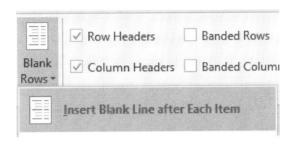

You will then get the following Pivot Table report which is easier on the eye:

Sum of SALES	Column Labels		
Row Labels	2014	2015	2013
January			
Acme, inc.	0	56,959	26,884
Smith and Co.	53,586	0	0
January Total	**53,586**	**56,959**	**26,884**
February			
Foo Bars	14,333	0	0
Widget Corp	0	47,189	46,174
February Total	**14,333**	**47,189**	**46,174**
March			
123 Warehousing	0	37,544	44,802
ABC Telecom	29,570	0	0
March Total	**29,570**	**37,544**	**44,802**
April			
Demo Company	0	53,413	49,049
Fake Brothers	83,468	0	0
April Total	**83,468**	**53,413**	**49,049**

You can easily remove this blank row from the Pivot Table as well!

METHOD 1: Simply press CTRL + Z if you have recently inserted a blank row.

METHOD 2: Go to *Design > Blank Row dropdown > Remove Blank Line After Each Item.*

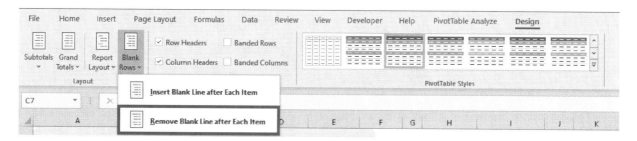

This will remove the blank rows after each item!

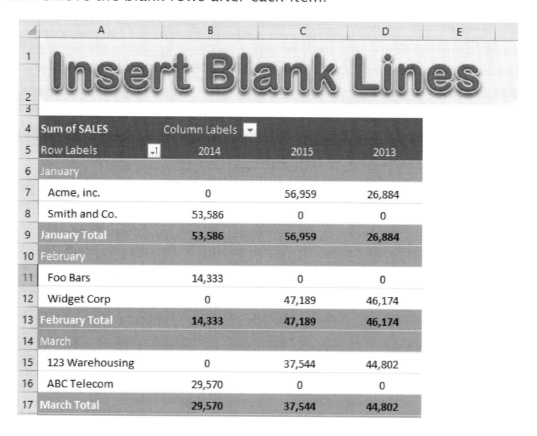

Classic Pivot Table Layout View

For all of you Excel old schoolers out there who have used the drag and drop Pivot Table option in Excel 2003 or prior, guess what? You *still* have that option in Excel 2010 and onwards.

This is our starting Pivot Table showing our Sales totals:

Sum of SALES	YEAR		
REGION	2014	2015	Grand Total
EAST	2,000,000	57,650	2,057,650
NORTH	1,000,000	63,116	1,063,116
SOUTH	1,500,000	38,281	1,538,281
WEST	2,500,000	90,967	2,590,967
Grand Total	7,000,000	250,014	7,250,014

STEP 1: Right click in the Pivot Table and select **PivotTable Options**

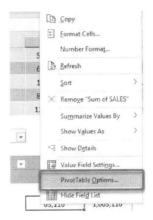

STEP 2: Go to *Display > Classic PivotTable Layout* and check that option

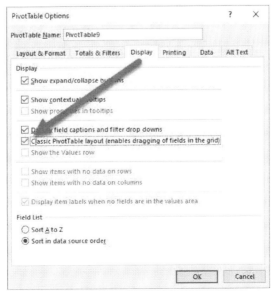

STEP 3: Now you can drag the Fields in or out of the Pivot Table where the blue outline is highlighted.

Drag the **YEAR** away to remove it from the Pivot Table

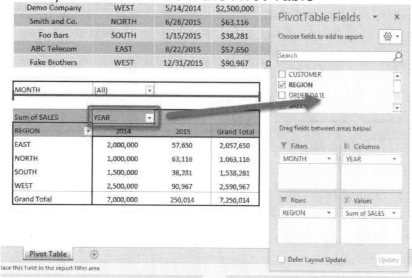

STEP 4: You can now drag the **CUSTOMER** Field into your Pivot Table

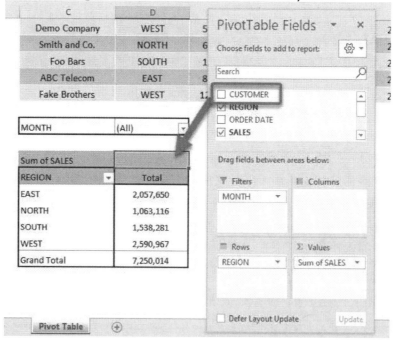

You have now customized your Pivot Table the **good ol' classic way!**

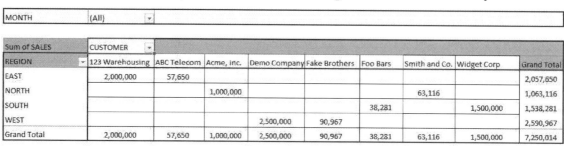

Sum of SALES	CUSTOMER								
REGION	123 Warehousing	ABC Telecom	Acme, inc.	Demo Company	Fake Brothers	Foo Bars	Smith and Co.	Widget Corp	Grand Total
EAST	2,000,000	57,650							2,057,650
NORTH			1,000,000				63,116		1,063,116
SOUTH						38,281		1,500,000	1,538,281
WEST				2,500,000	90,967				2,590,967
Grand Total	2,000,000	57,650	1,000,000	2,500,000	90,967	38,281	63,116	1,500,000	7,250,014

Move & Remove Fields and Items

There are lots of ways to customize the Field arrangement in your Pivot Table. This gives you full control on how you want your Pivot Table to look like.

Here is how our Pivot Table is currently set up:

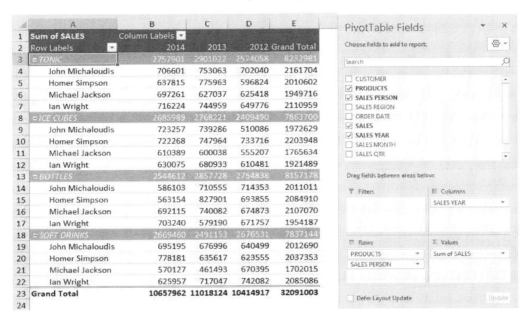

STEP 1: Let us work with the Rows first. Let's move the **TONIC** item down one spot. Right click on the **TONIC** name and go to *Move > Move "TONIC" Down*

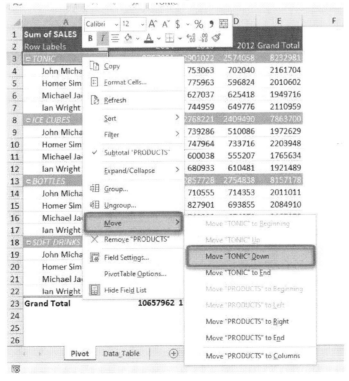

It now moved one spot below

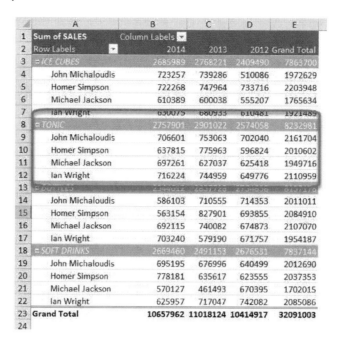

STEP 2: You can also move it by typing the value as well!

Let us move it to the last Product row where **SOFT DRINKS** resides. Type in **TONIC** over the name **SOFT DRINKS**.

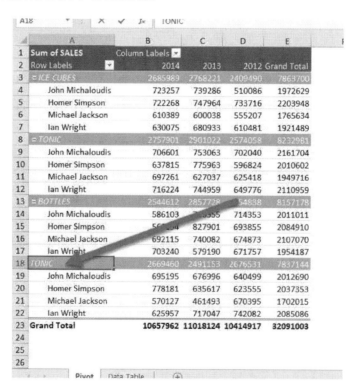

And just like that it has magically moved to the bottom of the Pivot Table!

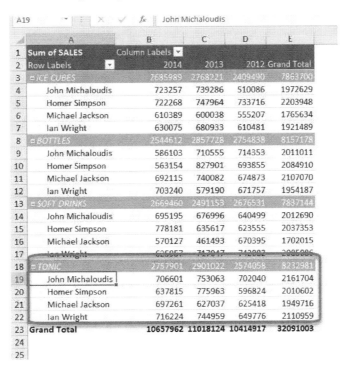

STEP 3: What if we want to update the hierarchy of our Fields? Right click on any PRODUCTS item and go to *Move > Move "PRODUCTS" To End*

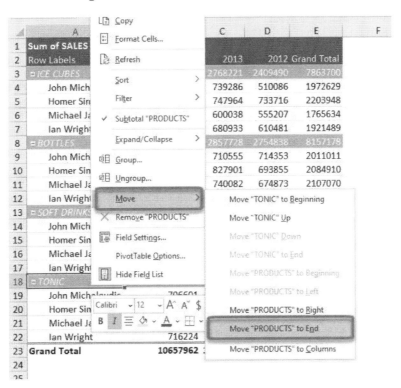

Now it's the **SALES PERSON** that is at the top of the hierarchy.

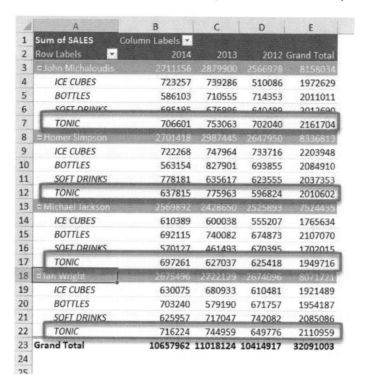

STEP 4: The same tips apply for the Columns as well. Let's move the **2014** item to the very end.

Right click on the **2014** item and go to *Move > Move "2014" to End*

And there you have it!

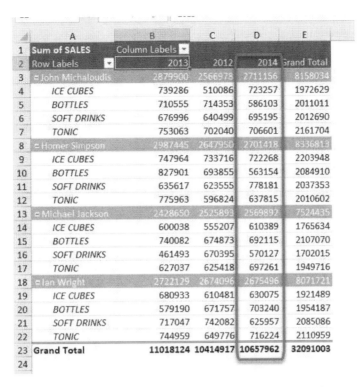

Bonus Tip: Use your mouse to drag & move items inside the Pivot Table.

STEP 5: To remove a Field, you simply **right click on an item** and select **Remove.**

In our scenario, right click on **BOTTLES** and select **Remove "PRODUCTS"**

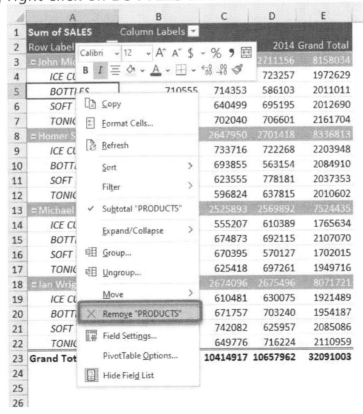

You are now left with only the **SALES PERSON** Field!

Sum of SALES	Column Labels			
Row Labels	2013	2012	2014	Grand Total
John Michaloudis	2879900	2566978	2711156	8158034
Homer Simpson	2987445	2647950	2701418	8336813
Michael Jackson	2428650	2525893	2569892	7524435
Ian Wright	2722129	2674096	2675496	8071721
Grand Total	**11018124**	**10414917**	**10657962**	**32091003**

Show & Hide Field List

Have you ever had the scenario where you are working on your Pivot Table and the Field List disappears? The Field List looks like the image below:

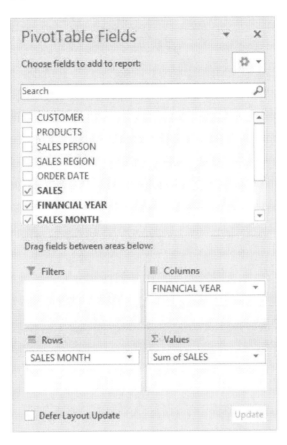

Lots of Excel users get annoyed with this but luckily, I'm here to help you out with two ways to show/hide a Field List.

Using Right Click

If your Pivot Table Field List disappears, you can easily bring it back as I show you below!

For our example, this is our **Pivot Table**:

Sum of SALES	Column Labels			
Row Labels	2012	2013	2014	Grand Total
January	53,089,979.00	872,080.00	1,074,820.00	55,036,879.00
February	867,220.00	909,654.00	807,257.00	2,584,131.00
March	784,136.00	1,031,596.00	1,013,466.00	2,829,198.00
April	908,666.00	968,855.00	836,559.00	2,714,080.00
May	893,039.00	850,502.00	791,095.00	2,534,636.00
June	786,918.00	981,050.00	771,976.00	2,539,944.00
July	1,056,573.00	854,835.00	873,543.00	2,784,951.00
August	806,719.00	1,002,597.00	599,246.00	2,408,562.00
September	863,089.00	814,513.00	1,011,288.00	2,688,890.00
October	873,208.00	931,193.00	1,059,308.00	2,863,709.00
November	923,402.00	769,352.00	812,659.00	2,505,413.00
December	854,090.00	1,031,897.00	1,006,745.00	2,892,732.00
Grand Total	62,707,039.00	11,018,124.00	10,657,962.00	84,383,125.00

STEP 1: To show the Field List, **Right Click on your Pivot Table** and select **Show Field List.**

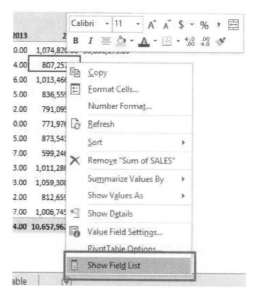

Your *PivotTable Field List* is now showing!

Let us show in the next step how to hide this.

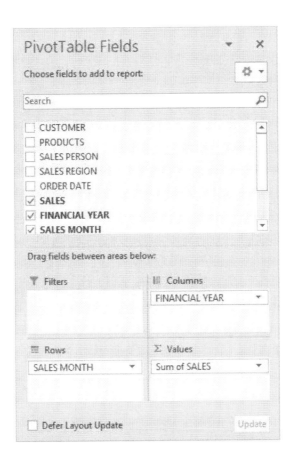

STEP 2: To hide the Field List, **Right Click on your Pivot Table** and select **Hide Field List.**

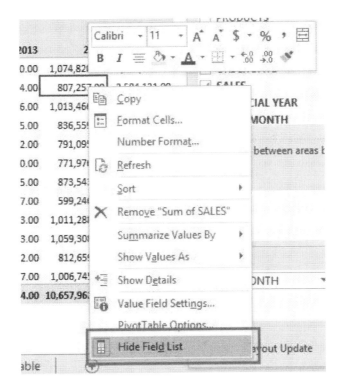

Your Pivot Table Field List is now hidden!

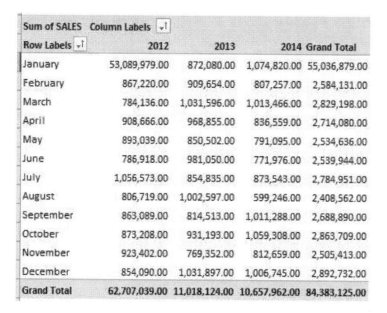

Sum of SALES	Column Labels ▾			
Row Labels ▾	2012	2013	2014	Grand Total
January	53,089,979.00	872,080.00	1,074,820.00	55,036,879.00
February	867,220.00	909,654.00	807,257.00	2,584,131.00
March	784,136.00	1,031,596.00	1,013,466.00	2,829,198.00
April	908,666.00	968,855.00	836,559.00	2,714,080.00
May	893,039.00	850,502.00	791,095.00	2,534,636.00
June	786,918.00	981,050.00	771,976.00	2,539,944.00
July	1,056,573.00	854,835.00	873,543.00	2,784,951.00
August	806,719.00	1,002,597.00	599,246.00	2,408,562.00
September	863,089.00	814,513.00	1,011,288.00	2,688,890.00
October	873,208.00	931,193.00	1,059,308.00	2,863,709.00
November	923,402.00	769,352.00	812,659.00	2,505,413.00
December	854,090.00	1,031,897.00	1,006,745.00	2,892,732.00
Grand Total	62,707,039.00	11,018,124.00	10,657,962.00	84,383,125.00

Using the Ribbon

The Field List for Pivot Table can easily be toggled on and off using the ribbon menu.

STEP 1: Click on any cell in the Pivot Table.

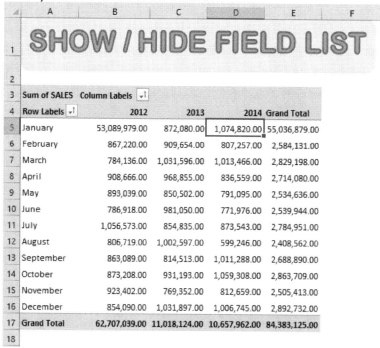

STEP 2: Go to **PivotTable Analyze > Field List**.

STEP 3: The Field List will appear next to the Pivot Table!

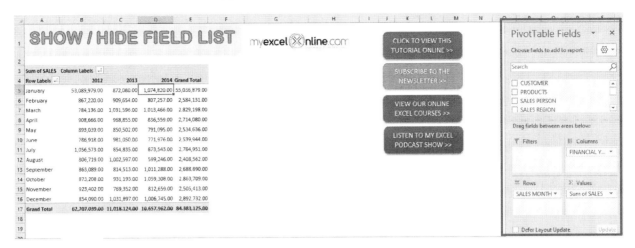

You can hide the Field List using the same steps.

STEP 4: Go to **PivotTable Analyze** > **Field List**.

This will hide the Field List section from the worksheet!

Sum of SALES	Column Labels			
Row Labels	2012	2013	2014	Grand Total
January	53,089,979.00	872,080.00	1,074,820.00	55,036,879.00
February	867,220.00	909,654.00	807,257.00	2,584,131.00
March	784,136.00	1,031,596.00	1,013,466.00	2,829,198.00
April	908,666.00	968,855.00	836,559.00	2,714,080.00
May	893,039.00	850,502.00	791,095.00	2,534,636.00
June	786,918.00	981,050.00	771,976.00	2,539,944.00
July	1,056,573.00	854,835.00	873,543.00	2,784,951.00
August	806,719.00	1,002,597.00	599,246.00	2,408,562.00
September	863,089.00	814,513.00	1,011,288.00	2,688,890.00
October	873,208.00	931,193.00	1,059,308.00	2,863,709.00
November	923,402.00	769,352.00	812,659.00	2,505,413.00
December	854,090.00	1,031,897.00	1,006,745.00	2,892,732.00
Grand Total	62,707,039.00	11,018,124.00	10,657,962.00	84,383,125.00

Show & Hide Field Headers

Whenever you work with Pivot Tables, you can see the **Row Labels** and **Column Labels** being generated on top of the Pivot Table. This is handy as they can be used to filter your records.

But what if you want to hide them to make your Pivot Table more presentable? Or, what if you want to show your results to a coworker but don't want them clicking around and changing your stuff?! It's easy to show & hide Field Headers with a button click!

This is our Pivot Table. You can see the two Field Headers on the top corner:

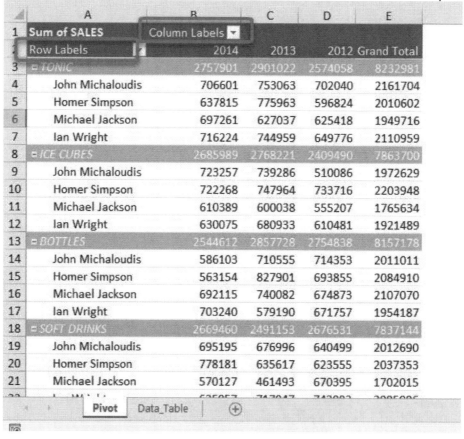

STEP 1: Go to *PivotTable Analyze > Show > Field Headers*

Click on it to hide the Field Headers:

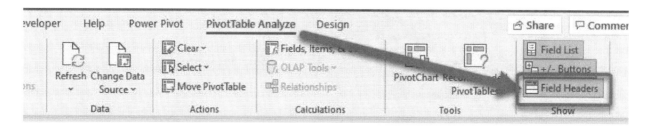

They are now hidden! You can click on the same button to show them again.

Sum of SALES	2014	2013	2012	Grand Total
⊟ TON...	2757901	290...	2574058	8232981
John Michaloudis	706601	753063	702040	2161704
Homer Simpson	637815	775963	596824	2010602
Michael Jackson	697261	627037	625418	1949716
Ian Wright	716224	744959	649776	2110959
⊟ ICE CUBES	2685989	2768221	2409490	7863700
John Michaloudis	723257	739286	510086	1972629
Homer Simpson	722268	747964	733716	2203948
Michael Jackson	610389	600038	555207	1765634
Ian Wright	630075	680933	610481	1921489
⊟ BOTTLES	2544612	2857728	2754838	8157178
John Michaloudis	586103	710555	714353	2011011
Homer Simpson	563154	827901	693855	2084910
Michael Jackson	692115	740082	674873	2107070
Ian Wright	703240	579190	671757	1954187
⊟ SOFT DRINKS	2669460	2491153	2676531	7837144
John Michaloudis	695195	676996	640499	2012690
Homer Simpson	778181	635617	623555	2037353
Michael Jackson	570127	461493	670395	1702015

Pivot | Data_Table | ⊕

Change Count of to Sum of

When setting up your Pivot Table, sometimes your Values show up as a **Count of** instead of a **Sum of**. What gives?

This typically happens when you use categorical data. But sometimes Excel confuses numeric data with categorical data. The good news is that you can easily change this calculation in your Pivot Table Value Field Settings!

Here is our Pivot Table and the Values calculation shows a **Count of SALES** rather than a **Sum of SALES.** This is how we can change this around.

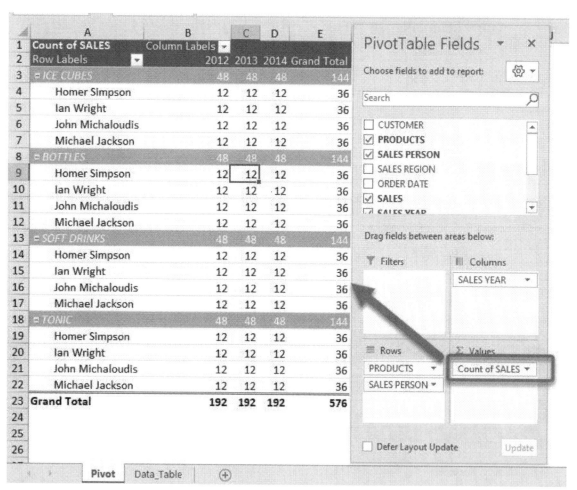

STEP 1: Click on the arrow beside **Count of SALES** and select **Value Field Settings**

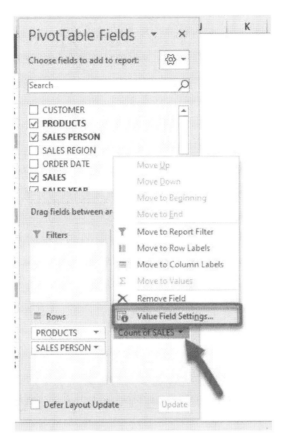

STEP 2: Select **Sum** and click **OK**

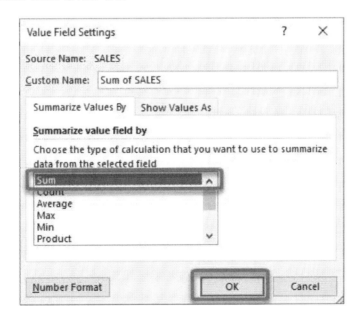

Now your **SALES** Values are being calculated as a **Sum** instead of **Count**!

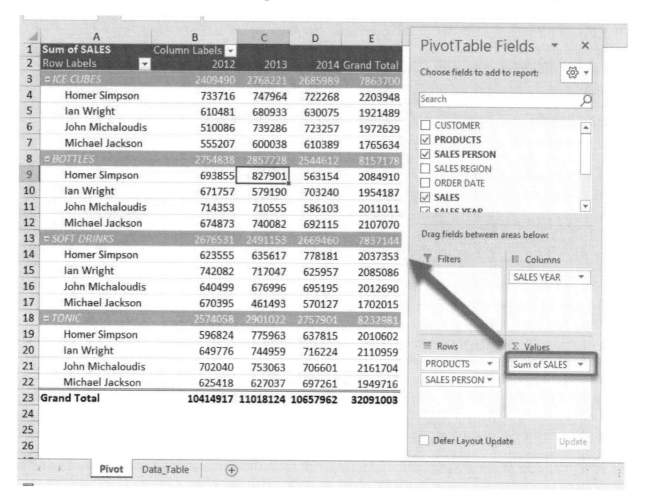

Bonus Tip: You can right click on any value inside the Pivot Table and select **Value Field Settings** from there to make your calculation changes!

Number Formatting

You can easily change the formatting of your Pivot Table values. You have lots of options to choose from. Let's see!

STEP 1: Right click in a Pivot Table value and choose **Number Format....**

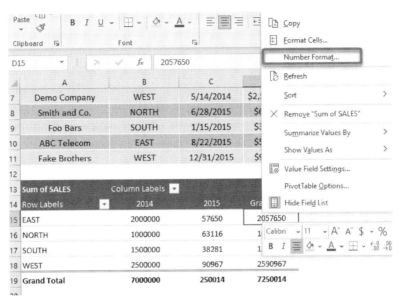

STEP 2: Choose your desired format from the Category list, like **Number, Currency, Accounting, Date, Time, Percentage, Fraction, Scientific, Text, Special or Custom.**

We will select a Number format with **0 decimal places** and for the negative numbers we will select the **negative red numbers**.

The Pivot Table is now updated with your new number formatting!

Sum of SALES	Column Labels ▾		
Row Labels ▾	2014	2015	Grand Total
EAST	2,000,000	57,650	2,057,650
NORTH	1,000,000	63,116	1,063,116
SOUTH	1,500,000	38,281	1,538,281
WEST	2,500,000	90,967	2,590,967
Grand Total	7,000,000	250,014	7,250,014

Bonus Tip: From the **PivotTable Fields**, you can click on the **Values area drop down** and select **Value Field Settings** > **Number Format** to make your formatting changes!

Field Name Formatting

When you drop a values Field in the Values area, the Field Name gets generated automatically to either a *Sum of…* or a *Count of…*

What if you had a better name in mind? After all, the default name isn't very descriptive. I will show you how to set up custom Field Names!

Here is our Pivot Table. We want to change **Sum of SALES** to **Total Sales** for better readability.

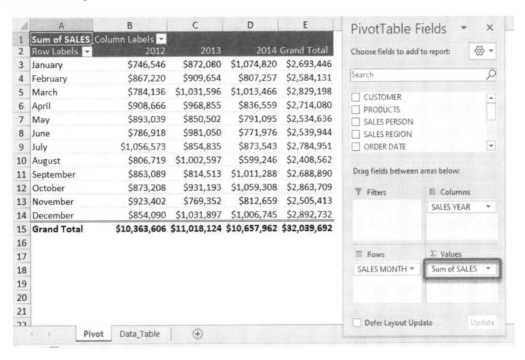

STEP 1: Click on the arrow beside **Sum of SALES** and select **Value Field Settings**

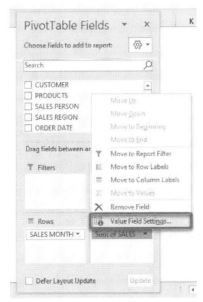

STEP 2: Type **Total Sales** in the **Custom Name** area and click **OK**

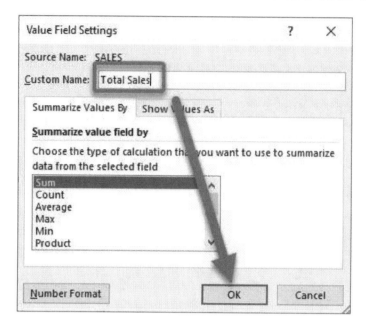

Now you have **Total Sales** as your **Field Name!**

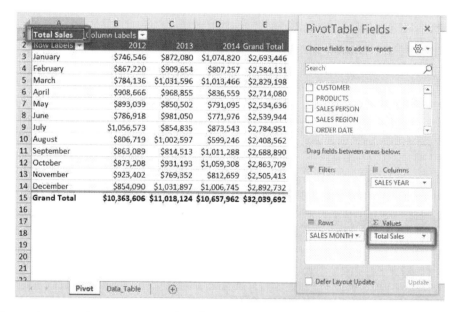

STEP 3: There is another way to do this. Now we want to change **SALES YEAR** to **Financial Year.**

Select any **SALES YEAR** item in your Pivot Table and go to *PivotTable Analyze > Active Field > Active Field.*

Type in **Financial Year** as the new name.

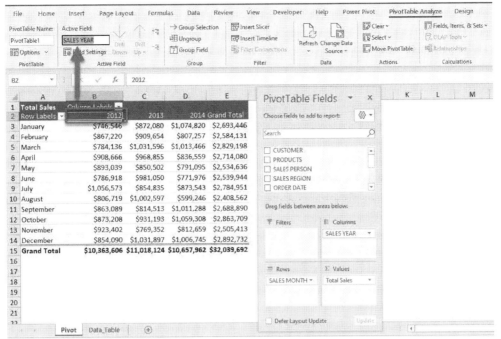

Now you can see your new Field Name take effect!

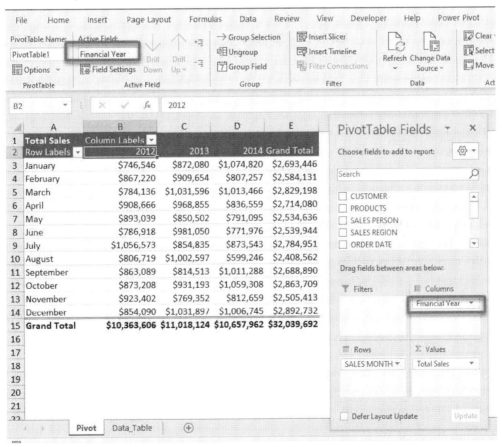

This name change is reflected in your PivotTable Fields only. That means the data source name does NOT get updated. This is very important. No matter what changes are made to the frontend of your Pivot Table, the underlying integrity of the raw data is always protected.

Predetermined Number Formatting

Let us say you have one **Sum of SALES** value that you've formatted as a number with commas.

When you drop the **SALES** Field a second time in the Values area, you would expect to get the same numerical format but instead the format doesn't apply for **Sum of SALES2**:

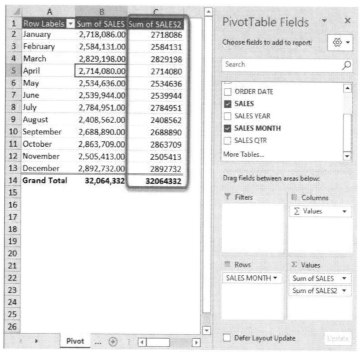

What happened? Your formatting does not take effect on the second SALES Field. I have the perfect workaround for this. Here is our current Pivot Table setup:

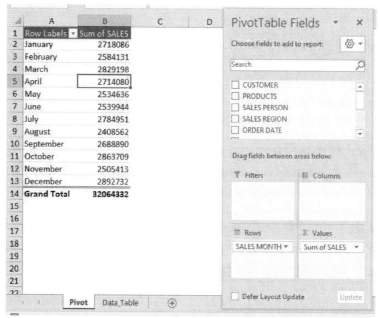

STEP 1: We need to select the entire Pivot Table. Go to *PivotTable Analyze > Actions > Select > Entire PivotTable*

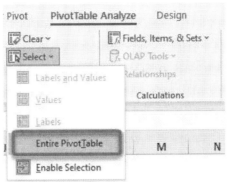

STEP 2: Now to select the SALES Field, go to *PivotTable Analyze > Actions > Select > Values*

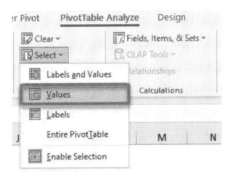

STEP 3: Let us apply our number formatting! Open the **Format Cells** dialog by pressing **CTRL + 1.**

Select **Number** and tick the **Use 1000 Separator (,) box.**

Click **OK.**

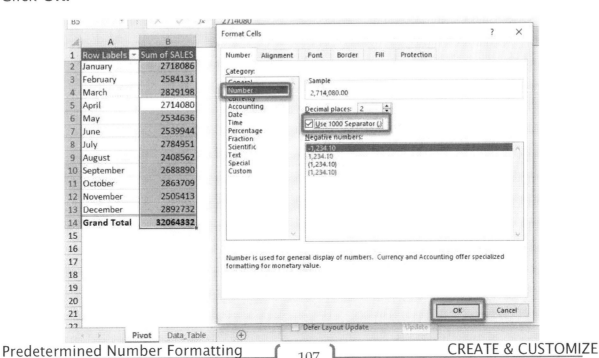

STEP 4: The number formatting is applied on our first SALES Field called **Sum of SALES.** Now drag the **SALES Field a second time** to the **Values area.**

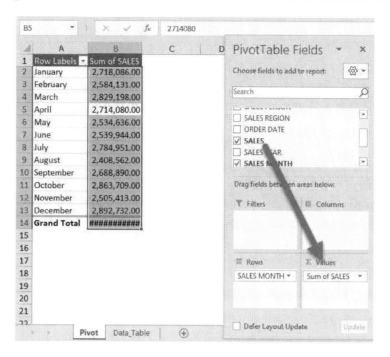

The formatting is also applied to our second SALES Field **Sum of SALES2**!

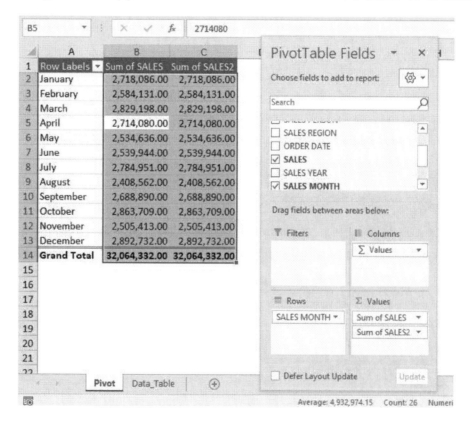

Change Sum Views in Fields Areas

Did you know that you can achieve different views in your Pivot Table just by moving the Values Field. Let us explore the different views that you can achieve!

STEP 1: Here is our Pivot Table. Drag the **SALES** Field to the **Values** area a second time.

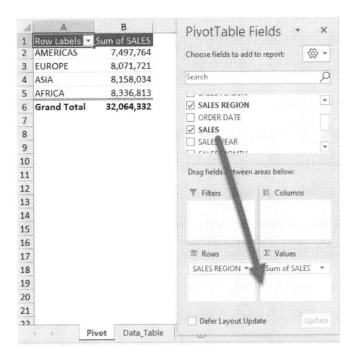

Notice that we have an Σ **Values** Field added to the **Columns** area. This happens because we have more than one metric in our **Values** area.

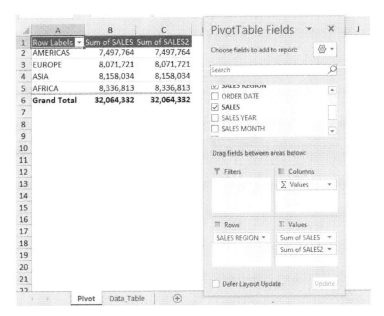

STEP 2: Let us change the second **Sum of SALES** Field into a **Count** calculation. Click on the arrow and select **Value Field Settings**

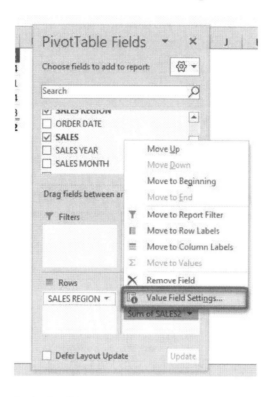

STEP 3: Select **Count** and click **OK**

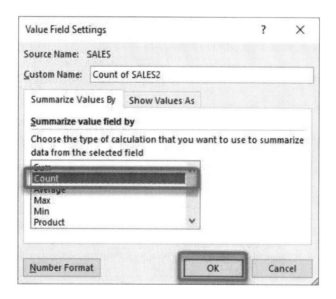

STEP 4: Now that we have our Count calculation, drag the **Σ Values** Field to the **Rows** area and see what happens to the Pivot Table layout!

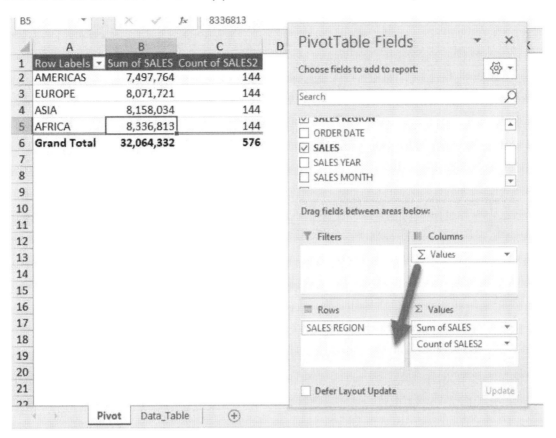

STEP 5: We have a completely different view. Now try moving the **Σ Values** Field above the **SALES REGION** Field in the **Rows** area

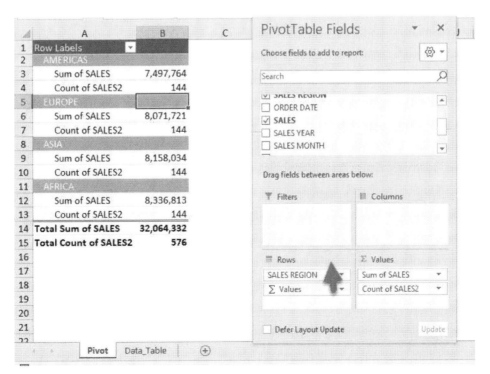

So you can see how many different views you can achieve just by moving the Σ **Values** Field around in the Pivot Table areas!

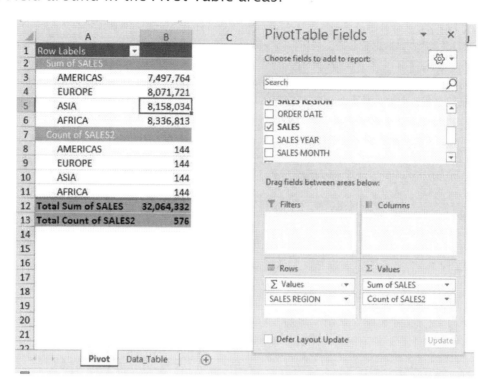

Change Layout of a Filter

The Filter is very useful when it comes to drilling down on your Pivot Table data. There is a hidden option that allows you to customize the Filter layout to different views.

Here is our Pivot Table and you can see the layout of our Filters:

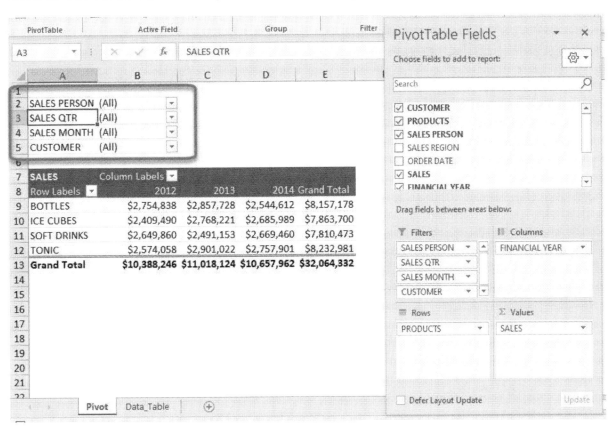

STEP 1: Let us change that! Go to *PivotTable Analyze > PivotTable > Options*

STEP 2: Select **Over, Then Down** and click **OK**

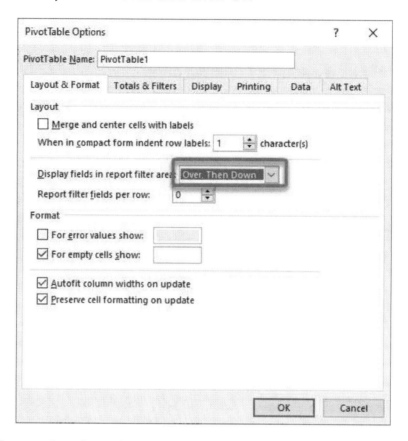

The layout of our Filter has changed!

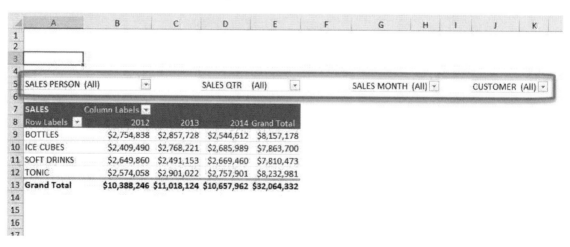

STEP 3: Let us try another setup. Go back to *PivotTable Analyze > PivotTable > Options*

STEP 4: Set it to **Down, Then Over** and set the **Report filter Fields per column** to **2**.

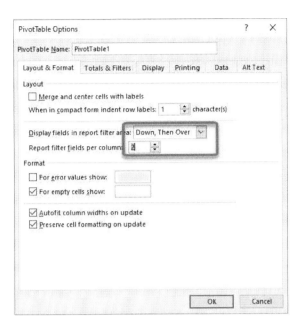

You now have a **2-column layout** for your filters!

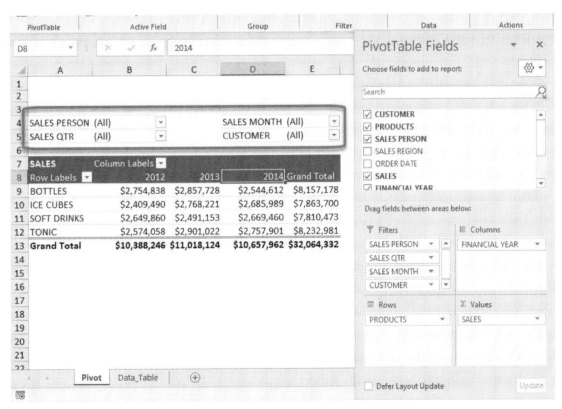

Format Error Values

Whenever you do a calculation in a Pivot Table you may get an error value like a **#DIV/0!**

This looks ugly when you are presenting important information but luckily you can override this with a custom value or text.

STEP 1: We have an error in our Pivot Table calculation.

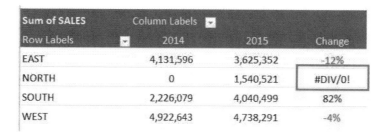

STEP 2: Right click on any value and Go to *Pivot Table Options.*

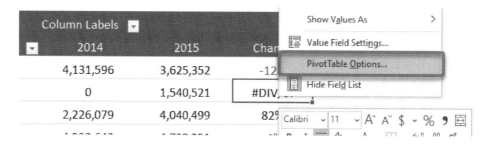

STEP 3: Check the Box: *For Error Values Show*

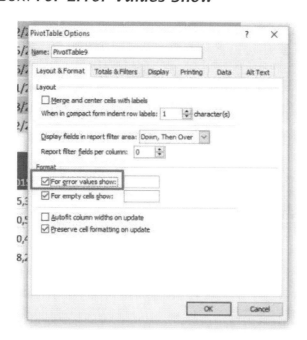

STEP 4: Enter any **text or value.** We will enter **na.**

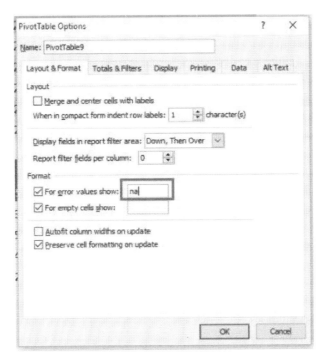

Now your error values are properly formatted!

Sum of SALES	Column Labels		
Row Labels	2014	2015	Change
EAST	4,131,596	3,625,352	-12%
NORTH	0	1,540,521	na
SOUTH	2,226,079	4,040,499	82%
WEST	4,922,643	4,738,291	-4%

Fill Blank Cells

I am sure that you have come across a Pivot Table which has empty cell values and thought...

"Why is my Pivot Table showing blanks instead of value?"

This is because your data source has no value for certain Items, which can happen. The **default setting in a Pivot Table** is to display the values of those Items as **blank cells**.

In this tutorial, you will learn how to fill blank cells in a Pivot Table with a custom text.

Example 1:

Suppose you have this data set containing **SALES data** as shown below:

CUSTOMER	REGION	ORDER DATE	SALES	MONTH	YEAR
Acme, inc.	NORTH	4/13/2014		April	2014
Widget Corp	SOUTH	12/21/2014	$1,500,000	December	2014
123 Warehousing	EAST	2/15/2014	$2,000,000	February	2014
Demo Company	WEST	5/14/2014	$2,500,000	May	2014
Smith and Co.	NORTH	6/28/2015		June	2015
Foo Bars	SOUTH	1/15/2015	$38,281	January	2015
ABC Telecom	EAST	8/22/2015	$57,650	August	2015
Fake Brothers	WEST	12/31/2015	$90,967	December	2015

Drag these PivotTable Fields in the following areas below:

Rows: **REGION**
Values: **SALES**

The resultant Pivot Table is shown below.

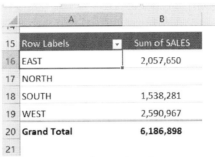

Row Labels	Sum of SALES
EAST	2,057,650
NORTH	
SOUTH	1,538,281
WEST	2,590,967
Grand Total	**6,186,898**

As you can see the value for North REGION is blank! Let's fix this.

STEP 1: Click on any cell in the Pivot Table.

	A	B
15	Row Labels	Sum of SALES
16	EAST	2,057,650
17	NORTH	
18	SOUTH	1,538,281
19	WEST	2,590,967
20	Grand Total	6,186,898
21		

STEP 2: Go to *PivotTable Analyze Tab > Options*

STEP 3: In the PivotTable Options dialog box, set *For empty cells show* with your preferred value. We will enter a **0**. Press **OK**.

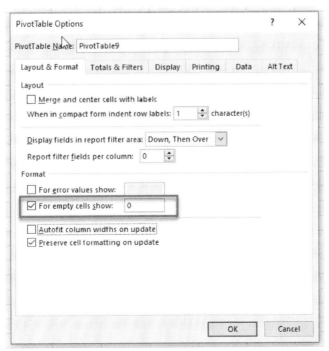

All of your **blank values** are now replaced with a **0**!

Row Labels	Sum of SALES
EAST	2,057,650
NORTH	0
SOUTH	1,538,281
WEST	2,590,967
Grand Total	**6,186,898**

Let's look at another example on how to fill blank cells in a Pivot Table with a custom text.

Example 2:

In this example, we have different departments and job numbers related to that department. A budget has been assigned to these items.

	A	B	C
4	**Department**	**Job Number**	**Budget**
5	HR	A7586	$ 47,723
6	IT	A8169	$ 21,938
7	Finance	A8955	$ 14,983
8	Finance	A8452	$ 58,259
9	Finance	A5760	$ 31,630
10	IT	A5267	$ 61,684
11	IT	A8801	$ 52,320
12	IT	A6005	$ 52,419
13	Operations	A4015	$ 51,329
14	Finance	A8970	$ 18,393
15	IT	A3946	$ 48,231
16	HR	A7084	$ 17,695
17	IT	A9092	$ 24,443

A Pivot Table is created with **Job Number** in the **Rows** area, **Department** in the **Columns** area and **Budget** in the **Values** area. The result is shown below:

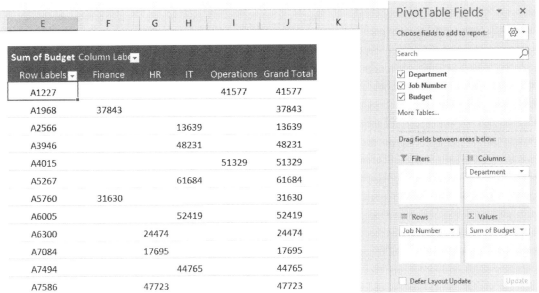

You might see there are blank cells in this Pivot Table. This is because there are no records for that row/column combination.

For example, there is no budget assigned for job number A1227 in Finance, IT and HR.

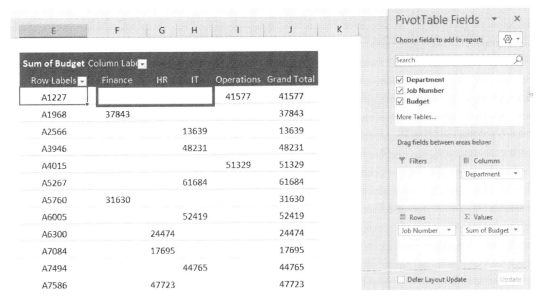

You can easily replace this blank cell with the text "NA".

STEP 1: Right click on any cell in the Pivot Table.

Sum of Budget	Column Labels				
Row Labels	Finance	HR	IT	Operations	Grand Total
A1227				41577	41577
A1968	37843				37843
A2566			13639		13639
A3946			48231		48231
A4015				51329	51329
A5267			61684		61684
A5760	31630				31630
A6005			52419		52419
A6300		24474			24474
A7084		17695			17695
A7494			44765		44765

STEP 2: Select **PivotTable Options** from the list.

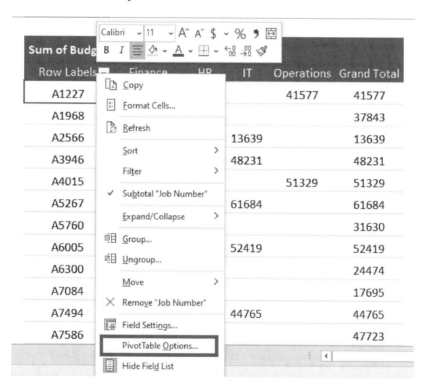

STEP 3: In the PivotTable Options dialog box, enter **NA** in the **For empty cells show** section:

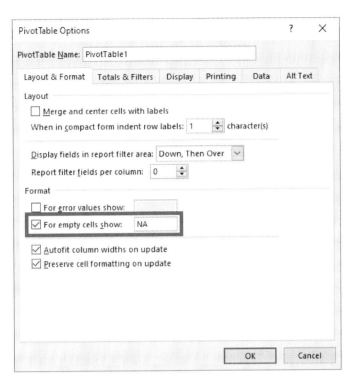

That's it! All the blank cells will now show **NA**.

Sum of Budget	Column Labels				
Row Labels	Finance	HR	IT	Operations	Grand Total
A1227	NA	NA	NA	41577	41577
A1968	37843	NA	NA	NA	37843
A2566	NA	NA	13639	NA	13639
A3946	NA	NA	48231	NA	48231
A4015	NA	NA	NA	51329	51329
A5267	NA	NA	61684	NA	61684
A5760	31630	NA	NA	NA	31630
A6005	NA	NA	52419	NA	52419
A6300	NA	24474	NA	NA	24474
A7084	NA	17695	NA	NA	17695
A7494	NA	NA	44765	NA	44765
A7586	NA	47723	NA	NA	47723

Fix Column Width

Each time you Refresh a Pivot Table you will most likely get annoyed at the fact that the column widths that you worked so hard to align return back to their incorrect default width.

Do not fear, Pivot Table Options is here!

STEP 1: Right click in the Pivot Table and select **Pivot Table Options**

STEP 2: Uncheck **Autofit Column Widths on Update**

STEP 3: Update your data

CUSTOMER	REGION	ORDER DATE	SALES	MONTH	YEAR
Acme, inc.	NORTH	4/13/2014	$387,082	April	2014
Widget Corp	SOUTH	12/21/2014	$331,581	December	2014
23 Warehousir	EAST	2/15/2014	568444	February	2014
Demo Compan	WEST	5/14/2014	$100,173	May	2014
Smith and Co.	NORTH	6/28/2015	$386,462	June	2015
Foo Bars	SOUTH	1/15/2015	$403,764	January	2015
ABC Telecom	EAST	8/22/2015	$346,513	August	2015
Fake Brothers	WEST	12/31/2015	$292,243	December	2015

STEP 4: Refresh your Pivot Table

Sum of SALES	Column Labels ▾		
Row Labels ▾	2014	2015	
EAST	485,772	346,51	
NORTH	387,082	386,46	
SOUTH	331,581	403,76	
WEST	100,173	292,24	
Grand Total	**1,304,608**	**1,428,982**	**2,733,590**

Our Pivot Table column widths do not change anymore!

Sum of SALES	Column Labels ▾		
Row Labels ▾	2014	2015	Grand Total
EAST	568,444	346,513	914,957
NORTH	387,082	386,462	773,544
SOUTH	331,581	403,764	735,345
WEST	100,173	292,243	392,416
Grand Total	**1,387,280**	**1,428,982**	**2,816,262**

Automatically Refresh a Pivot Table

Most Excel users forget that each time your data source gets updated, you will also need to manually Refresh your Pivot Table in order to show changes.

Here, I show you a couple of ways that you can automatically Refresh a Pivot Table.

REFRESH PIVOT TABLE UPON OPENING:
This is a great feature and one that most people don't know about.

It allows you to Refresh your Pivot Tables as soon as you open your Excel workbook.

This is great if your workbook is shared, and the data gets updated by your colleagues in the evening.

STEP 1: Right Click in your Pivot Table and choose **Pivot Table Options**:

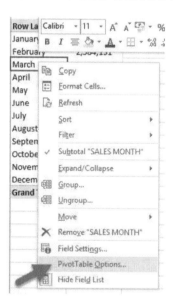

STEP 2: Select the **Data** tab and **check the "Refresh data when opening the file"** checkbox and **OK.**

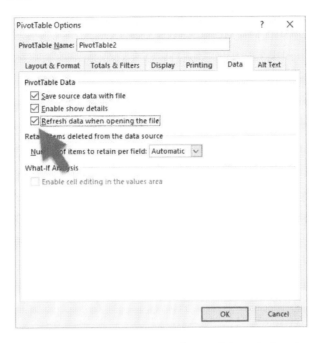

Now each time that you open up your Excel workbook in the morning, you can be sure that the Pivot Table is refreshed with the new changes!

AUTOMATIC REFRESH EVERY *X* **MINUTES**:

If you have your data set linked in an external data source, you can Auto-Refresh every **X** minutes.

Your data can be stored in an external data source such as an Excel workbook, Access, a Website, SQL Server, Azure Marketplace etc

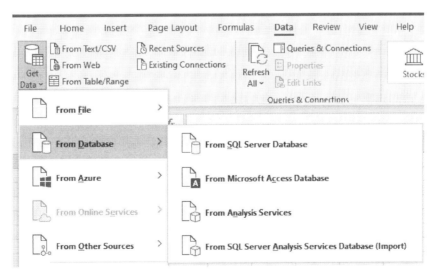

STEP 1: If your data is stored externally, you will need to **click in your Pivot Table** and go to **Properties** (this will only be enabled for selection if you have an external data source linked)

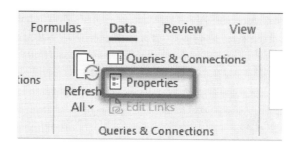

STEP 2: This will open up the **Connection Properties** and you will need to select the **Refresh every** checkbox and **manually set the time & press OK.**

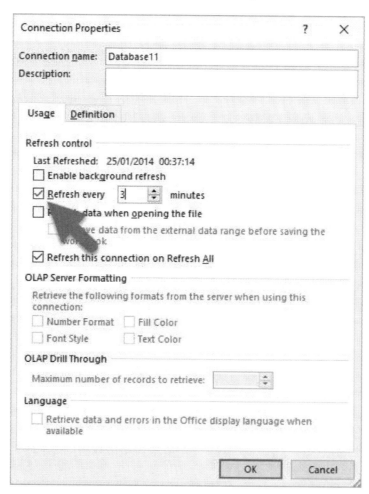

You can now sit back and enjoy a cup of coffee whilst your Pivot Table gets updated every few minutes!

Printing a Pivot Table on Two Pages

When you need to print out your Pivot Table, Excel has you covered when it comes to how you want to print it out. There are levels of customization such as being able to set how you want pagination to occur!

Here is our Pivot Table that we want to print in 2 separate pages. Say for **page 1**, we want the **years 2012 and 2013**, then on **page 2**, we are going to show **year 2014**.

STEP 1: Let us select the entire Pivot Table. Go to *PivotTable Analyze >*
Actions > Select > Entire PivotTable

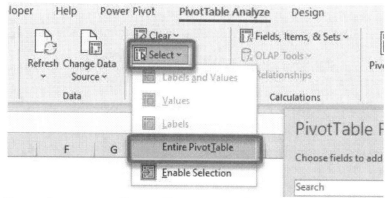

STEP 2: Go to *Page Layout > Page Setup > Print Area > Set Print Area*

Our print area based on the whole Pivot Table is now set.

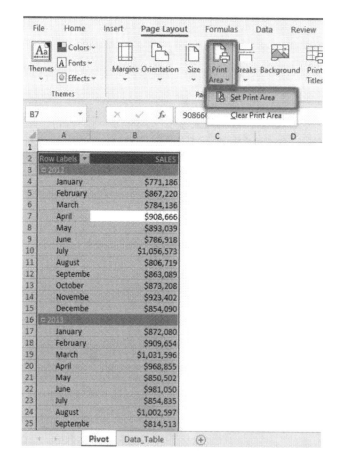

STEP 3: Select the 2014 row, then go to *Page Layout > Page Setup > Breaks > Insert Page Break*

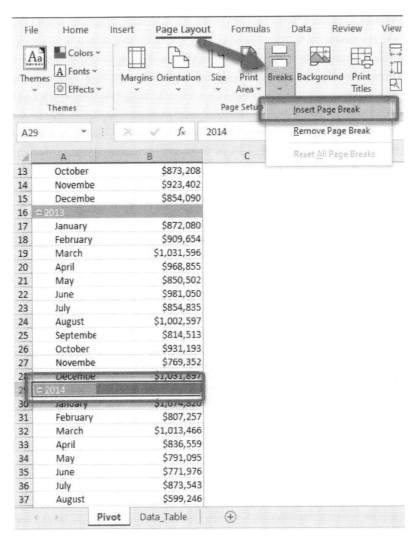

STEP 4: Now with our page break all set, go to *PivotTable Analyze > PivotTable > Options*

We will make sure that the Row Labels are shown on every printed page.

Go to **Printing** and check **Repeat row labels on each printed page.** Click **OK**

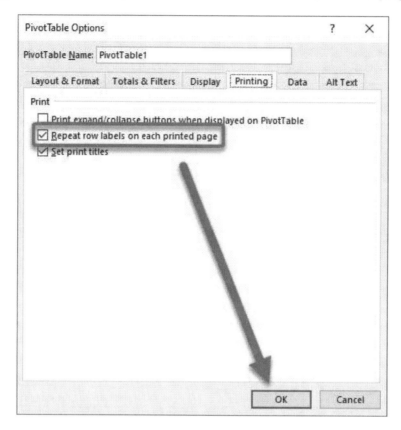

STEP 5: Go to *File > Print*

You can now see the first page showing the years 2012 and 2013! Click on the next page.

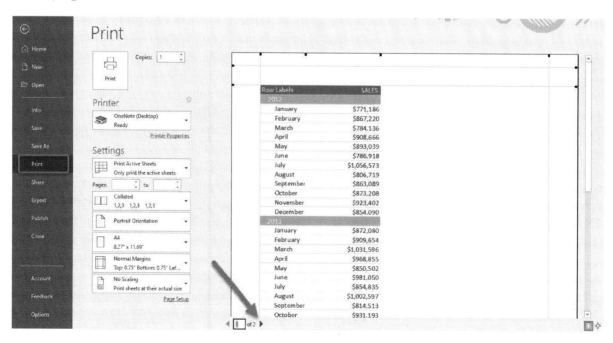

On the second page, you will see the year 2014 because that is where we placed the **page break** from Step 3.

Now press Print!

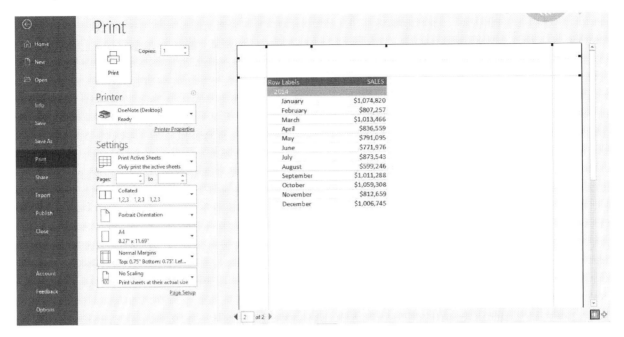

Show Report Filter Pages

When you are using a Pivot Table, you can show the Items within the Filter on separate sheets inside your workbook.

This is great if you have set up an awesome Pivot Table and want to duplicate that Pivot Table on various sheets for each Customer.

Here is our Pivot Table:

CUSTOMER	REGION	ORDER DATE	SALES	MONTH	YEAR
Acme, inc.	NORTH	4/13/2014	$1,000,000	April	2014
Widget Corp	SOUTH	12/21/2014	$1,500,000	December	2014
123 Warehousing	EAST	2/15/2014	$2,000,000	February	2014
Demo Company	WEST	5/14/2014	$2,500,000	May	2014
Smith and Co.	NORTH	6/28/2015	$63,116	June	2015
Foo Bars	SOUTH	1/15/2015	$38,281	January	2015

Row Labels	Sum of SALES	Count of SALES2
EAST	2,000,000	1
NORTH	1,063,116	2
SOUTH	1,538,281	2
WEST	2,500,000	1
Grand Total	**7,101,397**	**6**

STEP 1: Drop the **CUSTOMER** Field in the **Filters area.**

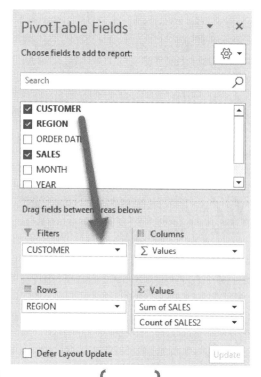

STEP 2: Go to *Options > Options Drop Down > Show Report Filter Pages*

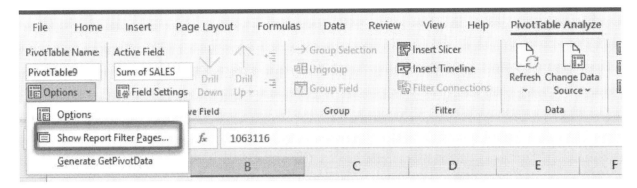

STEP 3: Press **OK.**

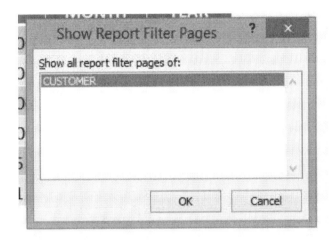

Each customer's Pivot Table will be shown in a unique sheet that is named after each Customer.

How cool is that!

Repeat All Item Labels

Whenever you create a Pivot Table, the default layout is in a **Compact Form**, which puts all the data in one column.

Many people do not like this layout as you cannot copy and paste the data and do further analysis in another worksheet.

The best layout to use is the **Tabular** layout. You can then select to **Repeat All Item Labels** which will fill in any gaps and allow you to take the data of the Pivot Table to a new location for further manual analysis.

STEP 1: Click in the Pivot Table and choose **Design > Report Layouts > Show in Tabular Form**

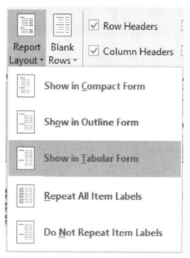

STEP 2: Now to fill in the empty cells in the Row Labels you need to select **Design > Report Layouts > Repeat All Item Labels**

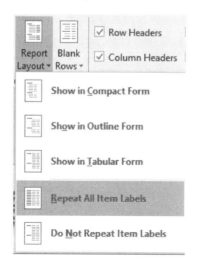

STEP 3: Your Pivot Table will show all the Item Labels and you can now copy & paste it into a new area to do further analysis!

Sum of SALES	
MONGH	CUSTOMER
January	Acme, inc.
	Foo Bars
February	123 Warehousing
	Widget Corp
March	123 Warehousing
April	Acme, inc.
	Demo Company
May	Demo Company
	Smith and Co.
June	Foo Bars
	Smith and Co.
July	ABC Telecom
August	ABC Telecom
	Fake Brothers
December	Fake Brothers

Sum of SALES	
MONTH	CUSTOMER
January	Acme, inc.
January	Foo Bars
February	123 Warehousing
February	Widget Corp
March	123 Warehousing
April	Acme, inc.
April	Demo Company
May	Demo Company
May	Smith and Co.
June	Foo Bars
June	Smith and Co.
July	ABC Telecom
August	ABC Telecom
August	Fake Brothers
December	Fake Brothers

VALUE FIELD SETTINGS > SUMMARIZE VALUES BY

Create Multiple Subtotals

When using Pivot Table Subtotals, we have become accustomed to using the **Sum**, as this is the default function used.

Did you know that you can create multiple subtotals and use different functions?

This is the full list of the subtotal functions:

- **Sum** – this adds everything up

- **Count** – this counts the amount of items

- **Average** – this applies the arithmetic mean to the data

- **Max** – this finds the maximum in a list of numeric items

- **Min** – this finds the minimum in a list of numeric items

- **Product** – this multiplies items

- **Count Numbers** – this counts ONLY the numbers in a list of data

- **StdDev** – this applies the standard deviation calculation to a list of numbers pulled from a statistical sample when the population is not known

- **StdDevp** – this applies the standard deviation calculation to a list of numbers when the population is known

- **Var** – this applies the variance calculation to a list of numbers pulled from a statistical sample when the population is not known

- **Varp** – this applies the variance calculation to a list of numbers when the population is known

Let us easily add these calculations as subtotals so that we can compare results!

STEP 1: This is our Pivot Table. Click on the arrow beside **PRODUCTS.**

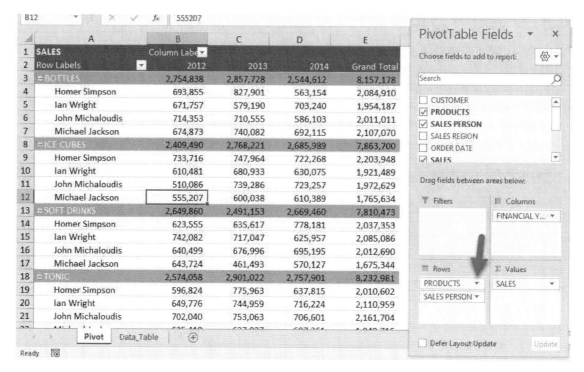

Select **Field Settings**

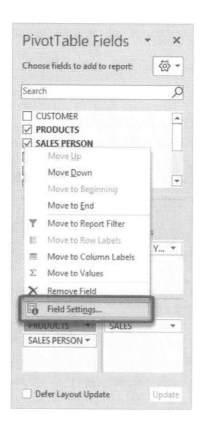

STEP 2: Select **Custom** for the Subtotals option. Then you can select **Sum, Count, Average, Max, Min** to see what happens!

Click **OK.**

Now you have the different Subtotals for each **PRODUCT**! You can see that for **Bottles**, the **Sum, Count, Average, Max and Min** are all being shown!

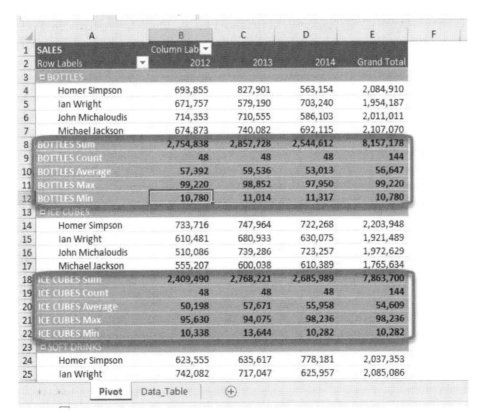

Pro Tip: This tip will only work when you have multiple items in the **ROWS** section of your **Field List.** Otherwise, Excel will not know what to subtotal.

Count Transactions

The default Value Field Setting when analyzing data with a Pivot Table is to *Sum* but you can also analyze a Pivot Table with a *Count*.

This is useful when you want to see how many sales transactions took place within a Region, a Month, a Year or per Business Unit.

Here is the current setup of our Pivot Table where it's showing the **Sum of SALES:**

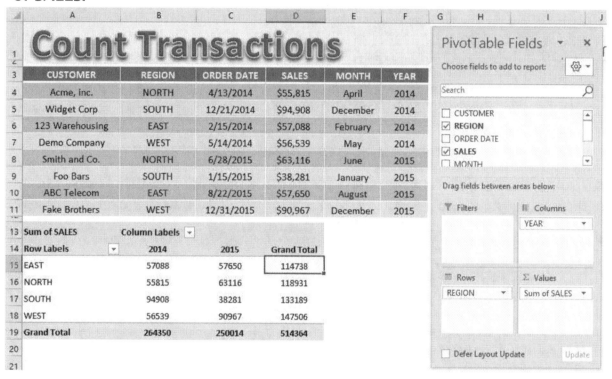

STEP 1: Right click on a Pivot Table value and select *Summarize Values By > Count*

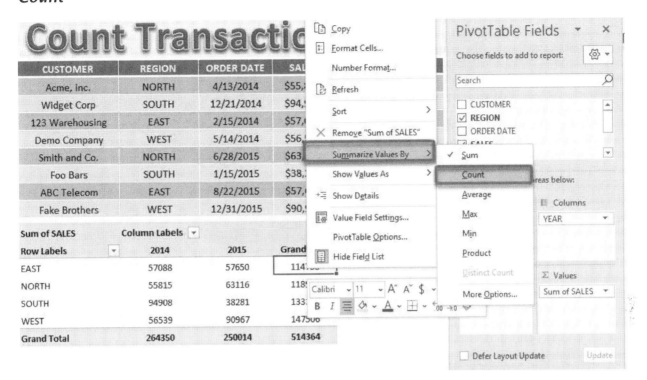

With that, the **Counts** of each transaction are now being shown!

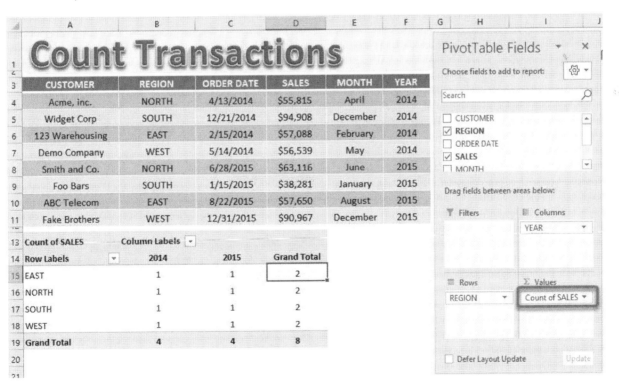

Show Averages

The default Value Field Setting when analyzing data with a Pivot Table is to *Sum*, but you can also analyze a Pivot Table with *Averages*.

STEP 1: Here is the current setup of our Pivot Table where it shows the **Sum of SALES:**

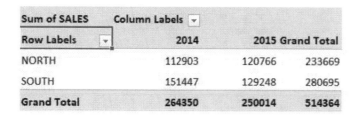

STEP 2: Now that your Pivot Table is set up, you need to **Right Click** in any of the Pivot Table values and choose ***Summarize Values By > Average***

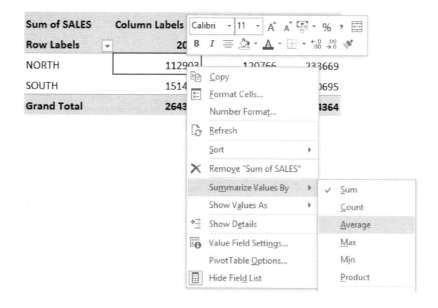

Another method is to **click on the arrow next to the Sum of SALES** Field in the Values area and select **Value Field Setting.**

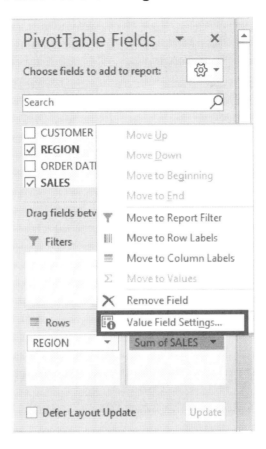

In the Value Field Setting dialog box, **Select Average** in the **Summarize value by** tab and Click **OK**.

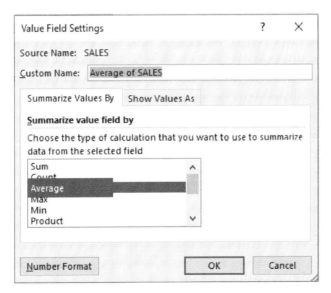

STEP 3: Now you have your Pivot Table report showing the **Average SALES** values per Region for each year:

Average of SALES	Column Labels		
Row Labels	2014	2015	Grand Total
NORTH	56451.5	60383	58417.25
SOUTH	75723.5	64624	70173.75
Grand Total	66087.5	62503.5	64295.5

Sometimes, when you are dealing with averages the result may end up with **a different mixture of decimal places** for different values, as you can see from the image above.

It would be ideal to format the result for a better presentation. To do this:

STEP 4: Right Click on any value cell and select **Value Field Setting.**

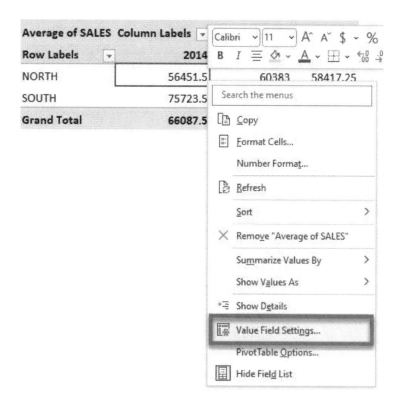

STEP 5: In the Value Field Setting dialog box, select **Number Format**.

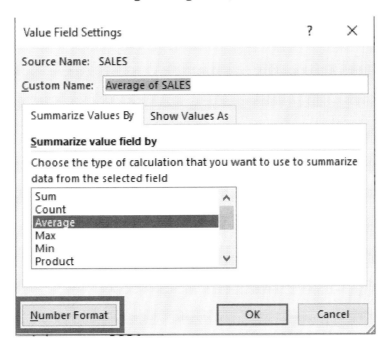

STEP 6: In the Format Cells dialog box, select **Number** under Category and type **2 for Decimal Places**. Click OK.

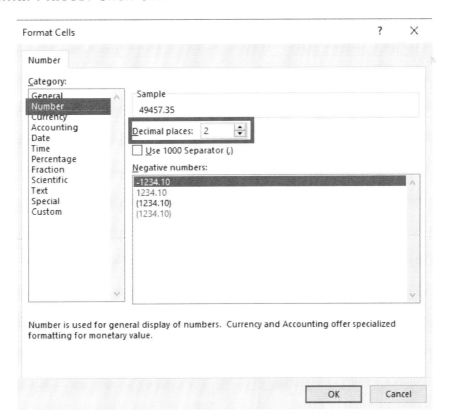

STEP 7: Click OK.

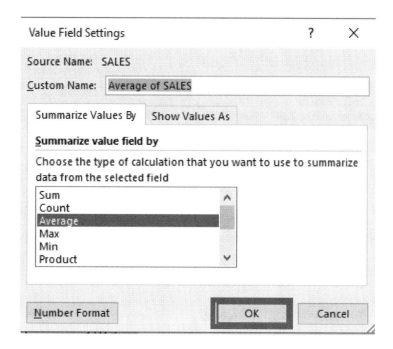

All values in the Pivot Table will now **have 2 decimal points**.

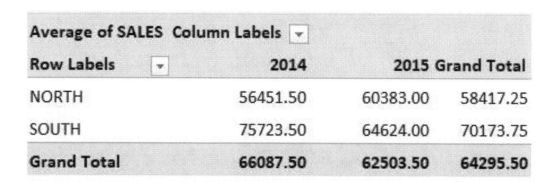

Average of SALES	Column Labels		
Row Labels	2014	2015	Grand Total
NORTH	56451.50	60383.00	58417.25
SOUTH	75723.50	64624.00	70173.75
Grand Total	**66087.50**	**62503.50**	**64295.50**

Maximum

With Pivot Tables, you can add a new column in your report that displays the maximum value in just a few clicks. In our example, we want to show the maximum sales amount for each salesperson!

This is our Pivot Table:

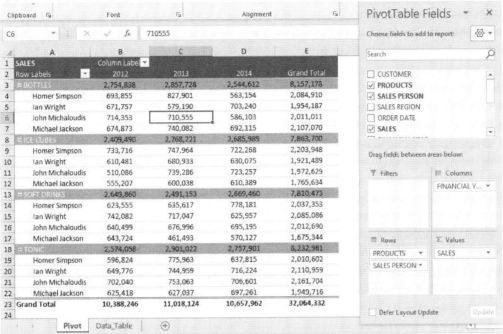

STEP 1: Drag the **SALES** Field to the **Values** area a second time. This will default to become **Sum of SALES**

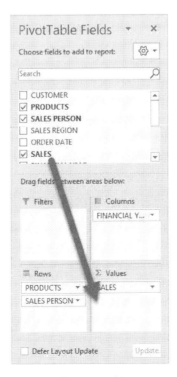

STEP 2: Click on the arrow beside **Sum of SALES** and select **Value Field Settings**

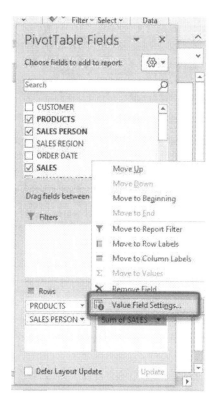

STEP 3: Select **Max** under **Summarize value Field by**. Click **OK**

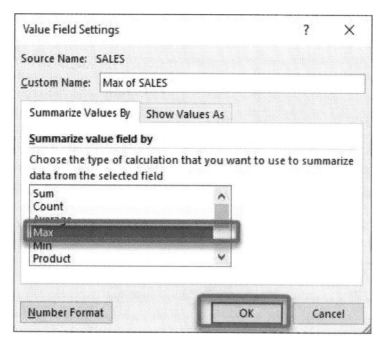

Now you have the **maximum sales value for that specific YEAR, PRODUCT and SALES PERSON**.

You can quickly check the maximum values here and determine who will get that sweet bonus!

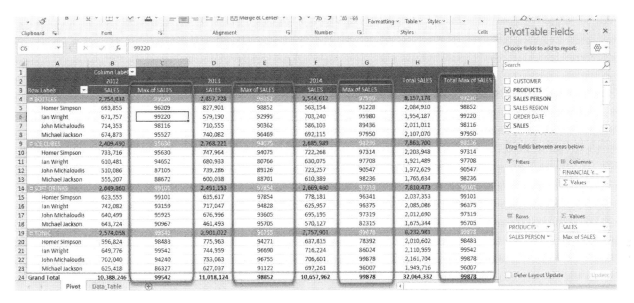

Product

The **Product function** is used to multiply values together in a Pivot Table but how will we ever use this?

I will show you a cool trick that will be able to track defects in our transactions.

Here is our data set. Notice that I have added a **DEFECTS column.** If there is a defect that day, we simply mark it as 1. This will be crucial once we use the **Product function** later.

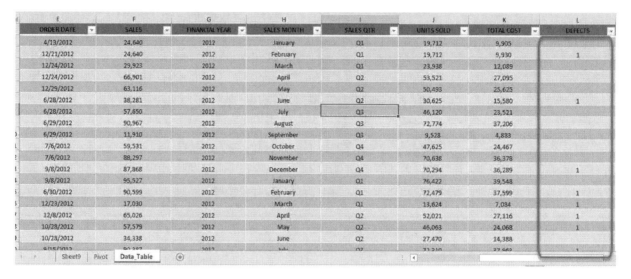

STEP 1: This is our Pivot Table setup. Drag **DEFECTS** to the **Values** area:

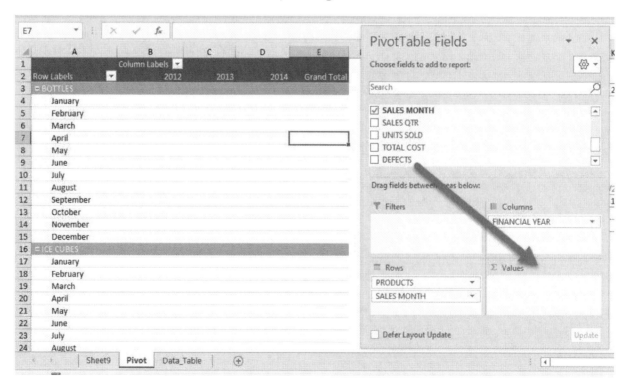

STEP 2: It will default as **Sum of DEFECTS**. Click on the arrow and select **Value Field Settings**

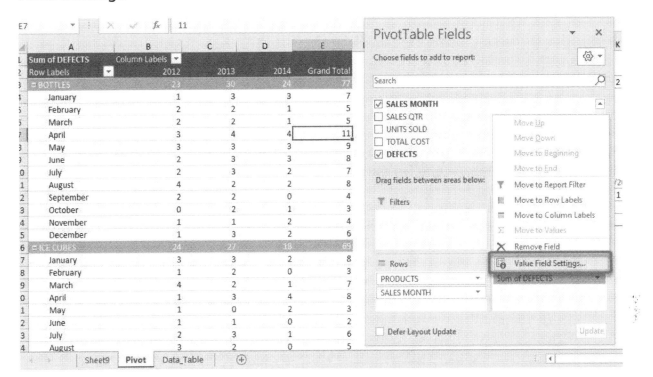

Select **Product** and click **OK.**

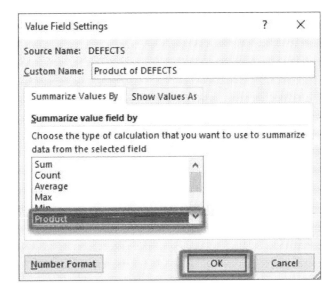

STEP 3: Now what Excel has done is for each Month it has multiplied all the DEFECT values. So, if any row for that specific Month has a 1, then the result in this Pivot Table will be a 1 as well.

We love the cells that show a 0 because that means there are no defects!

For example, a 0 defect occurred for the **BOTTLES** during the month of **September 2014.** Double click on it to see more details!

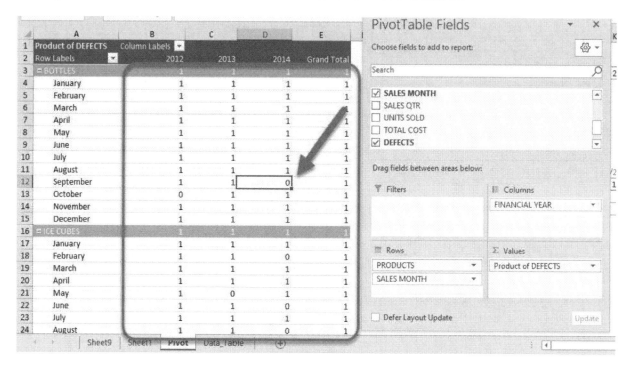

You can see that in the data breakdown for **September 2014**, there are no defects! Which is why the **Product** result is **0**.

Now try double clicking on **ICE CUBES** during the month of **March 2013**:

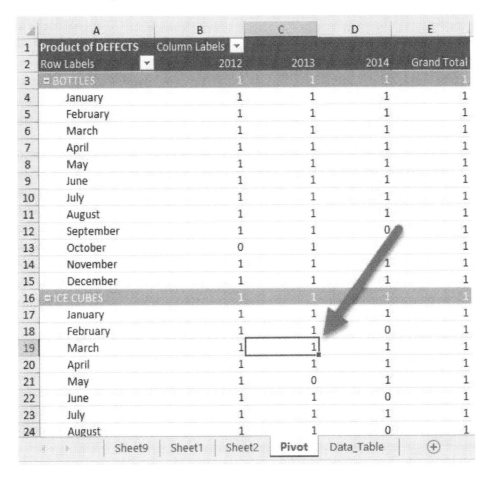

You can see that it has two defects, which is why the **Product function** result when you multiply them together is **1**.

Sum Vs Count

Ever faced this problem?

The values show as a **Count of** rather than a **Sum of** in a Pivot Table?

This is one of the most common complaints encountered when dealing with Pivot Tables and I will show you why this happens and how to fix the underlying issue.

Why the Pivot Table values show as Count instead of Sum

When you drag and drop a **values Field** in the Values area, it automatically shows the **Sum of**.

But sometimes it shows the **Count of**. Well, there are **3 reasons** why this is the case:

1. There are **blank cells** in your values Field within your data set; or

2. There are **"text" cells** in your values Field within your data set; or

3. A **Values Field is Grouped** within your Pivot Table.

BLANK CELL(S):

If you have at least one blank cell in your data source for a **values Field**, like SALES, Excel automatically thinks that the whole column is text-based and gives you a **Count of**.

TEXT CELL(S):

If you have at least one cell in your data source that is formatted as "text" for a **values Field**, like SALES, then it will also cause it to **Count** rather than **Sum**.

This usually happens when you download data from your ERP or external system and it throws in numbers that are formatted as text e.g. **382821P**

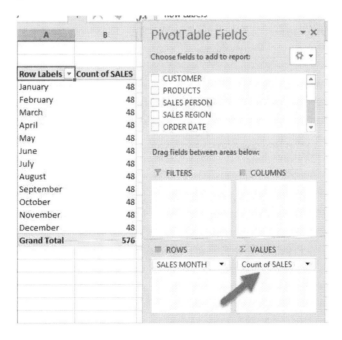

We get the annoying **Count of SALES** in our Pivot Table below:

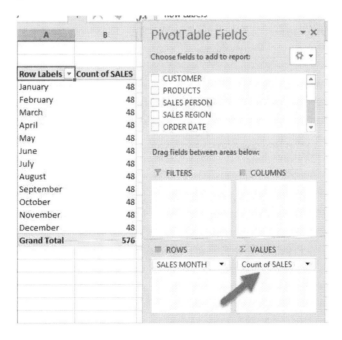

GROUPED VALUES:

Let's say that you put a **values Field,** like SALES, in the Row area and then you Group it (more on how to Group your data in later chapters).

When you drop in the same **values Field** in the Values area, you will also get a **Count of...**

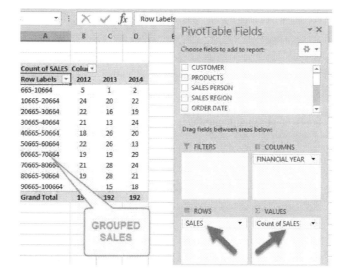

A Pivot Table basically has very simple rules. If all the cells in the selected Field are numeric, the calculation type will default to SUM.

Now that you know the reason for the error, let's learn how to fix it!

How to fix this issue

You need to clean up your data and make sure there are no cells that contain a blank or text.

There are 3 ways to make sure that the calculation type shows a **Sum of**:
METHOD 1 -_Replace Blanks with a Zero

STEP 1: Select the **entire column** that contains a blank. Press **Ctrl + Space Bar** to select the entire column.

CUSTOMER	PRODUCTS	SALES PERSON	SALES	FINANCIAL YEAR
MOJITOS R US	ICE CUBES	Ian Wright	61,386	2012
GIN ON THE RUN CO	ICE CUBES	Homer Simpson	95,630	2012
TEQUILA TACOS LTD	TONIC	John Michaloudis	13,307	2012
TEQUILA TACOS LTD	TONIC	John Michaloudis	61,439	2012
TEQUILA TACOS LTD	BOTTLES	John Michaloudis		2012
MOJITOS R US	SOFT DRINKS	Ian Wright	46,788	2012
TEQUILA TACOS LTD	BOTTLES	John Michaloudis	70,149	2012
GIN ON THE RUN CO	SOFT DRINKS	Homer Simpson	71,644	2012
GIN ON THE RUN CO	TONIC	Homer Simpson	35,366	2012
LONG ISLANDS INC	ICE CUBES	Michael Jackson	11,347	2012
TEQUILA TACOS LTD	ICE CUBES	John Michaloudis		2012
MOJITOS R US	BOTTLES	Ian Wright	20,650	2012
TEQUILA TACOS LTD	SOFT DRINKS	John Michaloudis	95,925	2012
GIN ON THE RUN CO	SOFT DRINKS	Homer Simpson	20,166	2012
GIN ON THE RUN CO	SOFT DRINKS	Homer Simpson	57,670	2012
MOJITOS R US	BOTTLES	Ian Wright	51,708	2012
MOJITOS R US	SOFT DRINKS	Ian Wright	73,163	2012
GIN ON THE RUN CO	SOFT DRINKS	Homer Simpson	44,719	2012
GIN ON THE RUN CO	BOTTLES	Homer Simpson	71,006	2012

STEP 2: Press **Ctrl + H** to open the **Find and Replace** dialog box.

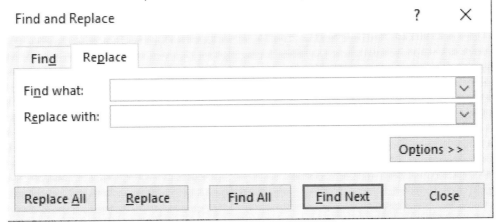

STEP 3: Delete everything in the **Find what** box and type **0** in **Replace with** box.

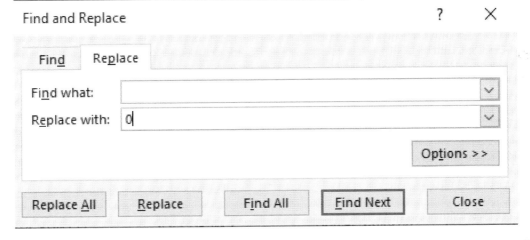

STEP 4: Press **Replace All**. This will replace all the blank cells with **0**.

CUSTOMER	PRODUCTS	SALES PERSON	SALES	FINANCIAL YEAR
MOJITOS R US	ICE CUBES	Ian Wright	61,386	2012
GIN ON THE RUN CO	ICE CUBES	Homer Simpson	95,630	2012
TEQUILA TACOS LTD	TONIC	John Michaloudis	15,307	2012
TEQUILA TACOS LTD	TONIC	John Michaloudis	61,439	2012
TEQUILA TACOS LTD	BOTTLES	John Michaloudis	0	2012
MOJITOS R US	SOFT DRINKS	Ian Wright	46,788	2012
TEQUILA TACOS LTD	BOTTLES	John Michaloudis	70,149	2012
GIN ON THE RUN CO	SOFT DRINKS	Homer Simpson	71,644	2012
GIN ON THE RUN CO	TONIC	Homer Simpson	35,366	2012
LONG ISLANDS INC	ICE CUBES	Michael Jackson	11,347	2012
TEQUILA TACOS LTD	ICE CUBES	John Michaloudis	0	2012
MOJITOS R US	BOTTLES	Ian Wright	20,650	2012
TEQUILA TACOS LTD	SOFT DRINKS	John Michaloudis	95,925	2012
GIN ON THE RUN CO	SOFT DRINKS	Homer Simpson	20,166	2012
GIN ON THE RUN CO	SOFT DRINKS	Homer Simpson	57,670	2012
MOJITOS R US	BOTTLES	Ian Wright	51,708	2012
MOJITOS R US	SOFT DRINKS	Ian Wright	73,163	2012
GIN ON THE RUN CO	SOFT DRINKS	Homer Simpson	44,719	2012
GIN ON THE RUN CO	BOTTLES	Homer Simpson	71,006	2012

Now you can create a Pivot Table as all the values will contain a number! If you have a Pivot Table already created, make sure to **Refresh the Pivot Table** so the data can be updated in your Pivot Table report.

METHOD 2 - Convert Text to Numbers

If a cell contains numbers but is stored as text, you will have to convert it to a value.

To do that click on the **small yellow icon** on the left and select **Convert to Number**.

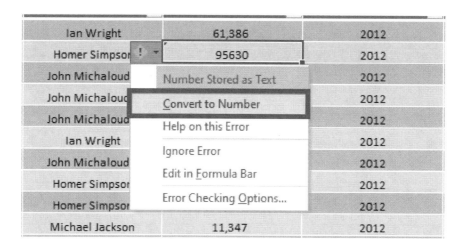

METHOD 3 - Ungroup values in the Pivot Table

STEP 1: Right Click on the Grouped values in the Pivot Table and choose **Ungroup**:

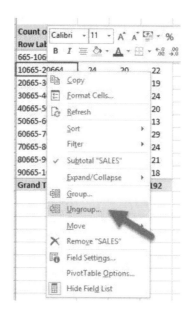

STEP 2: Drag the **Count of SALES** out of the **Values** area and let go to remove it

STEP 3: Drop in the **SALES** Field in the **Values** area. Once again, it will now show a **Sum of SALES!**

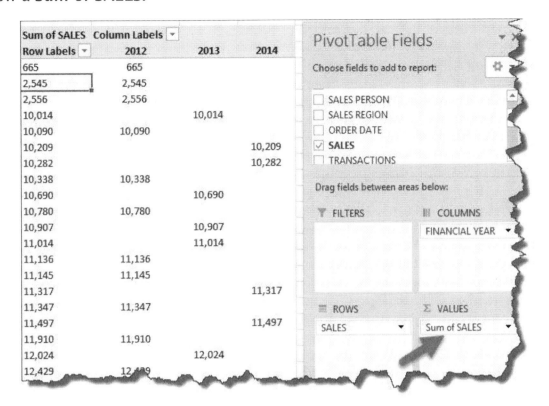

Pro tip: Sometimes you will need to locate the Pivot Table Field that has the Grouped values. It's not always clear which fields are Grouped, especially if they are not selected in the Row/Column areas.

You may need to drag and drop unselected Fields into the Row/Column areas to confirm that they are Grouped.

Then you can proceed with ungrouping them.

Std Dev

It is very easy to use a Pivot Table to summarize data using the Sum, Count, or Average calculations. But did you know it can also calculate the **Standard Deviation (Std Dev)** as well?

The **Standard Deviation** is a measure of how widely values are dispersed from the average value (the mean). This is crucial if you want to understand how volatile your data is!

STEP 1: Here is our Pivot Table. Drag **UNITS SOLD** to the **Values** area

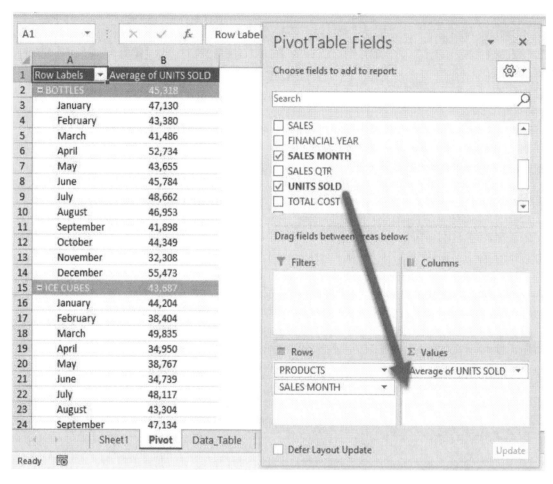

STEP 2: This will default to **Sum of UNITS SOLD**. Let us change that by clicking on the arrow and selecting **Value Field Settings**

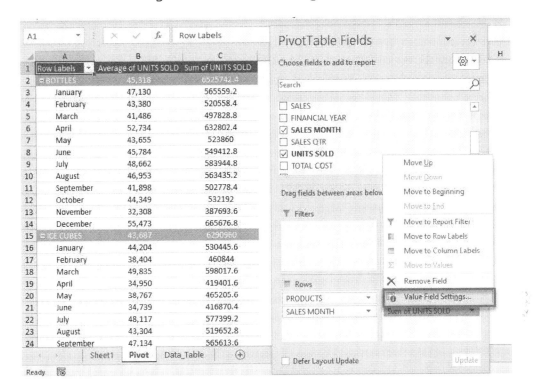

STEP 3: Select **StdDevp** and click **OK**.

We will use the **StdDevp** function as we have the complete data (population) used in the calculation. When only a portion of the data is used, then **StdDev** should be used instead.

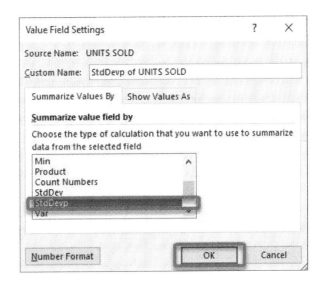

Now you have your Standard Deviation for each PRODUCT!

You can see for **ICE CUBES** in the month of **June** the Standard Deviation is quite low.

This means that the individual **UNITS SOLD** values for June is close to its average of 34,739, meaning the deviation of the values from its average is low.

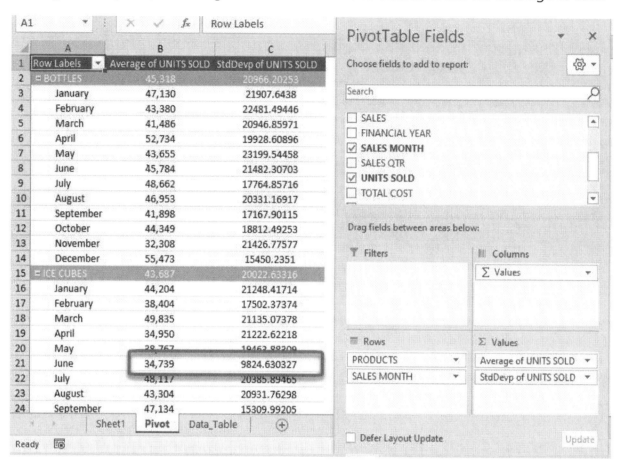

Var

The **Var** calculates variance based on the entire population. This shows the variability from the average or mean value of the group.

This is crucial if you want to understand how volatile your data is!

STEP 1: Here is our Pivot Table. Drag **UNITS SOLD** to the **Values** area

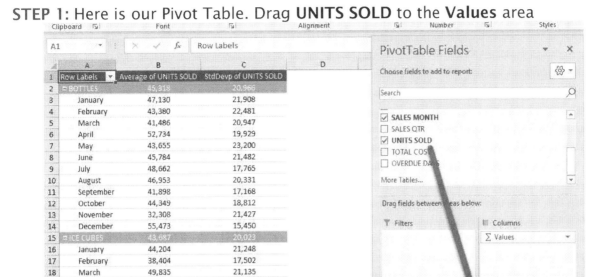

STEP 2: This will default to **Sum of UNITS SOLD**. Let us change that by clicking on the arrow and selecting **Value Field Settings**

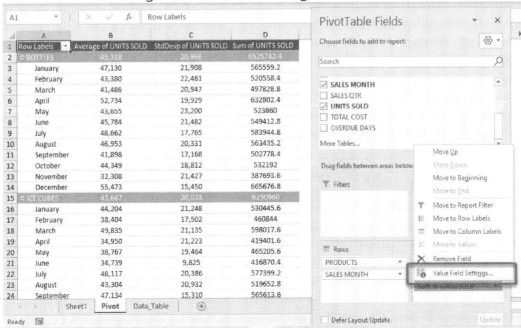

STEP 3: Select **Varp** and click **OK**.

We will use the **Varp** function as we have the complete data (population) used in the calculation. When only a portion of the data is used, then **Var** should be used instead.

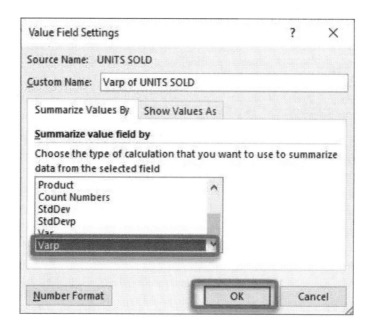

Now you have your Variance.

Did you know that the square root of the **variance** will give you the **standard deviation** value? Give it a try with the values below!

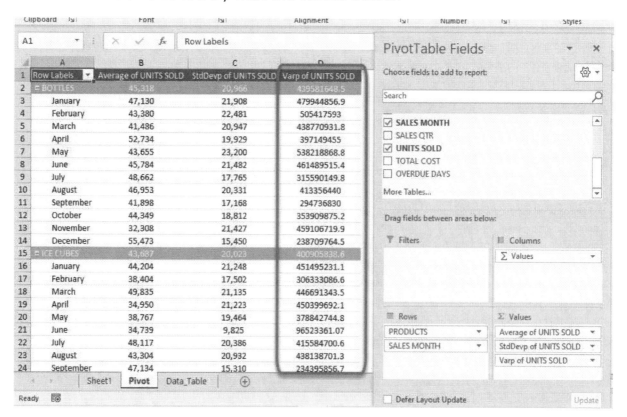

Show Various Grand Totals

With a Pivot Table you can only have one Grand Total In this tip I have a quick hack that allows me to have multiple Grand Totals! Read on to see how...

STEP 1: Here is our Pivot Table with multiple Subtotals. However, notice that we only have one **Grand Total** in row 31.

Row Labels	2012	2013	2014	Grand Total
BOTTLES				
Homer Simpson	693,855	827,901	563,154	2,084,910
Ian Wright	671,757	579,190	703,240	1,954,187
John Michaloudis	714,353	710,555	586,103	2,011,011
Michael Jackson	674,873	740,082	692,115	2,107,070
BOTTLES Sum	2,754,838	2,857,728	2,544,612	8,157,178
BOTTLES Average	57,392	59,536	53,013	56,647
ICE CUBES				
Homer Simpson	733,716	747,964	722,268	2,203,948
Ian Wright	610,481	680,933	630,075	1,921,489
John Michaloudis	510,086	739,286	723,257	1,972,629
Michael Jackson	555,207	600,038	610,389	1,765,634
ICE CUBES Sum	2,409,490	2,768,221	2,685,989	7,863,700
ICE CUBES Average	50,198	57,671	55,958	54,609
SOFT DRINKS				
Homer Simpson	623,555	635,617	778,181	2,037,353
Ian Wright	742,082	717,047	625,957	2,085,086
John Michaloudis	640,499	676,996	695,195	2,012,690
Michael Jackson	643,724	461,493	570,127	1,675,344
SOFT DRINKS Sum	2,649,860	2,491,153	2,669,460	7,810,473
SOFT DRINKS Average	55,205	51,899	55,614	54,239
TONIC				
Homer Simpson	596,824	775,963	637,815	2,010,602
Ian Wright	649,776	744,959	716,224	2,110,959
John Michaloudis	702,040	753,063	706,601	2,161,704
Michael Jackson	625,418	627,037	697,261	1,949,716
TONIC Sum	2,574,058	2,901,022	2,757,901	8,232,981
TONIC Average	53,626	60,438	57,456	57,173
Grand Total	10,388,246	11,018,124	10,657,962	32,064,332

Pivot   Data_Table   (+)

STEP 2: Go to the data source and add a blank column called **GRAND TOTAL**.

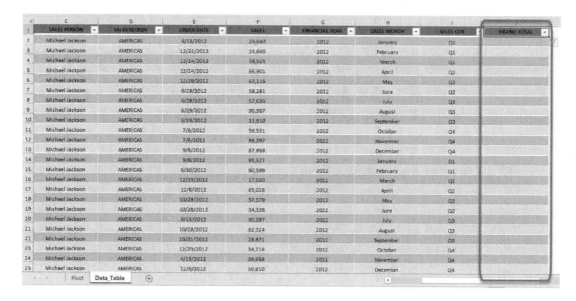

STEP 3: Now right click anywhere on your Pivot Table and select **Refresh**

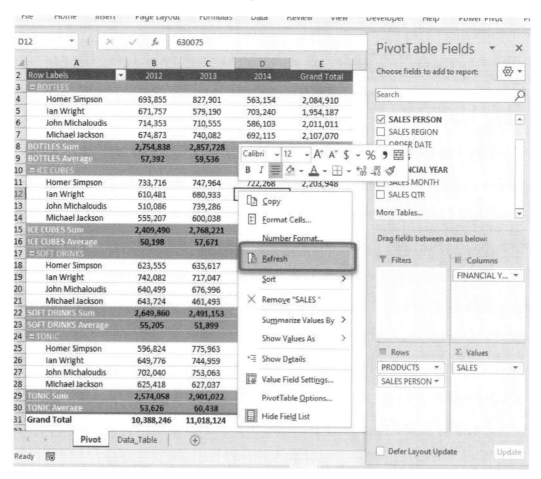

Drag the new **GRAND TOTAL** Field to the **Rows** area.

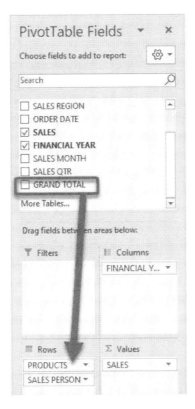

You will see a new row being added on the top left-hand corner called **(blank).**

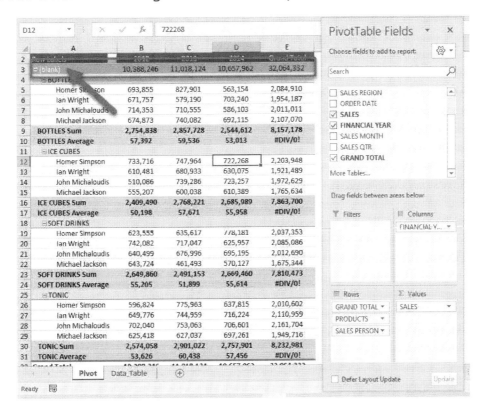

STEP 4: Now let's do our magic! Right click on (blank) and select **Field Settings**

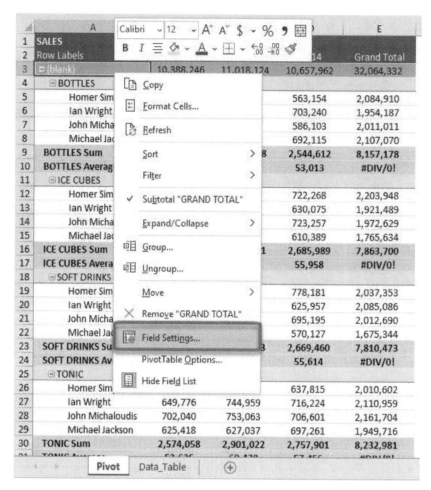

Select **Custom** and pick the functions that you want to display. Click **OK.**

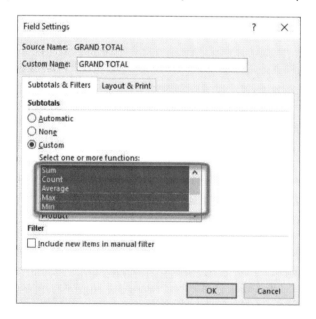

STEP 5: We do not need our original **Grand Total** row anymore. Right click on it and select **Remove Grand Total**

21	John Michaloudis	640,499	676,996	695,195	2,012,690
22	Michael Jackson	643.724	461.493	570,127	1,675,344
23	**SOFT DRINKS Sum**	Copy		2,669,460	7,810,473
24	**SOFT DRINKS Average**			55,614	54,239
25	⊟TONIC	Format Cells...			
26	Homer Simpson	Number Format...		637,815	2,010,602
27	Ian Wright			716,224	2,110,959
28	John Michaloudis	Refresh		706,601	2,161,704
29	Michael Jackson			697,261	1,949,716
30	**TONIC Sum**	Remove Grand Total		2,757,901	8,232,981
31	**TONIC Average**	Summarize Values By >		57,456	57,173
32	(blank) Sum			10,657,962	32,064,332
33	(blank) Count	Value Field Settings...		192	576
34	(blank) Average			55,510	55,667
35	(blank) Max	PivotTable Options...		99,878	99,878
36	(blank) Min	Hide Field List		10,209	10,014
37	**Grand Total**			10,657,962	32,064,332

Now you have your multiple **Grand Totals!**

	A	B	C	D	E	F
7	John Michaloudis	714,353	710,555	586,103	2,011,011	
8	Michael Jackson	674,873	740,082	692,115	2,107,070	
9	**BOTTLES Sum**	**2,754,838**	**2,857,728**	**2,544,612**	**8,157,178**	
10	**BOTTLES Average**	57,392	59,536	53,013	56,647	
11	⊟ICE CUBES					
12	Homer Simpson	733,716	747,964	722,268	2,203,948	
13	Ian Wright	610,481	680,933	630,075	1,921,489	
14	John Michaloudis	510,086	739,286	723,257	1,972,629	
15	Michael Jackson	555,207	600,038	610,389	1,765,634	
16	**ICE CUBES Sum**	**2,409,490**	**2,768,221**	**2,685,989**	**7,863,700**	
17	**ICE CUBES Average**	50,198	57,671	55,958	54,609	
18	⊟SOFT DRINKS					
19	Homer Simpson	623,555	635,617	778,181	2,037,353	
20	Ian Wright	742,082	717,047	625,957	2,085,086	
21	John Michaloudis	640,499	676,996	695,195	2,012,690	
22	Michael Jackson	643,724	461,493	570,127	1,675,344	
23	**SOFT DRINKS Sum**	**2,649,860**	**2,491,153**	**2,669,460**	**7,810,473**	
24	**SOFT DRINKS Average**	55,205	51,899	55,614	54,239	
25	⊟TONIC					
26	Homer Simpson	596,824	775,963	637,815	2,010,602	
27	Ian Wright	649,776	744,959	716,224	2,110,959	
28	John Michaloudis	702,040	753,063	706,601	2,161,704	
29	Michael Jackson	625,418	627,037	697,261	1,949,716	
30	**TONIC Sum**	**2,574,058**	**2,901,022**	**2,757,901**	**8,232,981**	
31	**TONIC Average**	53.626	60.438	57.456	57.173	
32	(blank) Sum	10,388,246	11,018,124	10,657,962	32,064,332	
33	(blank) Count	192	192	192	576	
34	(blank) Average	54,105	57,386	55,510	55,667	
35	(blank) Max	99,542	98,852	99,878	99,878	
36	(blank) Min	10,090	10,014	10,209	10,014	

| Pivot | Data_Table | ⊕ |

Show Field and Value Settings

With Excel Pivot Tables you can do a lot of stuff with your data. But did you know that you can edit your **Field and Value Settings** in multiple places?

Let me show you the different shortcuts available in your **Pivot Table**!

STEP 1: Let us have a look at the existing Pivot Table. To view the Field Settings, we can do the following:

Under *PivotTable Fields > Rows Field > Field Settings*

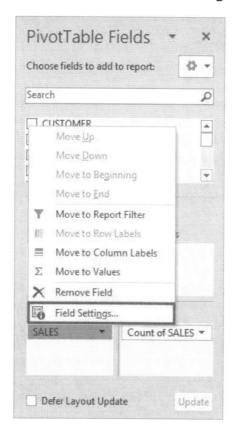

You can also **Right Click** on a **Row Label** and select **Field Settings.**

Or while having a Row Label selected, you can go to *PivotTable Analyze > Field Settings*

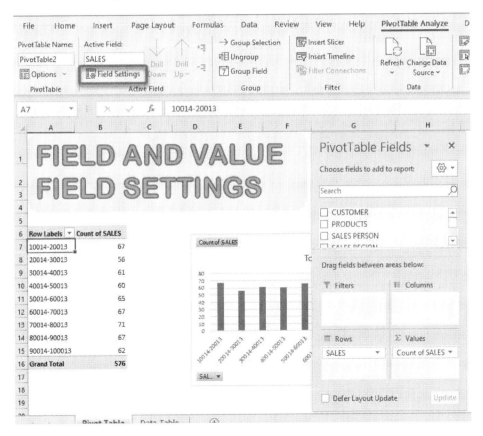

And now you have your Field Settings open!

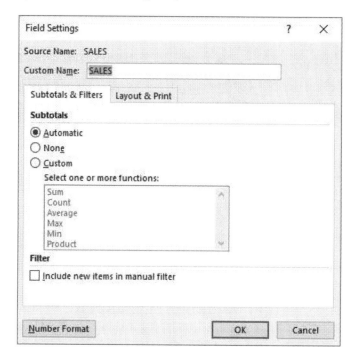

STEP 2: Now let us see how to access the **Value Field Settings**.

Go to *PivotTable Fields > Values Field > Value Field Settings*

You can also **Right Click** on a **Value** and select **Value Field Settings.**

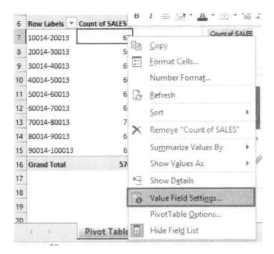

Or while having a value selected in your Pivot Table, you can go to *PivotTable Analyze > Field Settings*

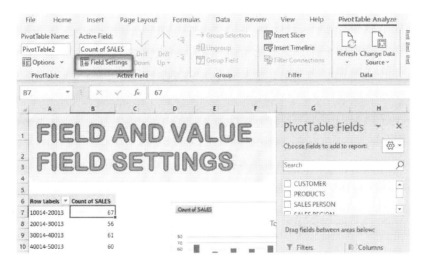

You now have your **Value Field Settings!**

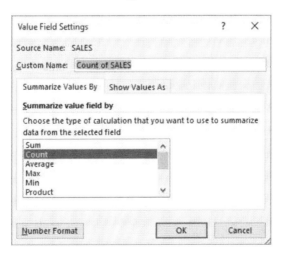

Distinct or Unique Count

Excel added some new features to its arsenal and one that has been well overdue was the Unique Count (aka "Distinct Count").

Previously when we created a Pivot Table and dropped a CUSTOMERS Field in the Row area and then again in the Values area, we got the **"Total Number of Transactions"** for each customer.

But what about if we want to show the Total Distinct or Unique customers?

Starting in Excel 2013 we can, by using the newly created Pivot Table **Data Model**.

This is our data set:

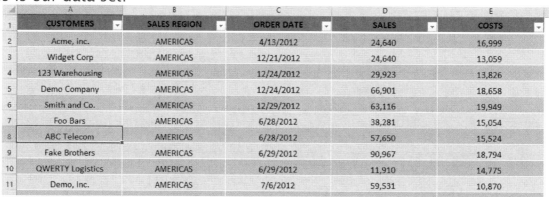

	CUSTOMERS	SALES REGION	ORDER DATE	SALES	COSTS
1	CUSTOMERS	SALES REGION	ORDER DATE	SALES	COSTS
2	Acme, inc.	AMERICAS	4/13/2012	24,640	16,999
3	Widget Corp	AMERICAS	12/21/2012	24,640	13,059
4	123 Warehousing	AMERICAS	12/24/2012	29,923	13,826
5	Demo Company	AMERICAS	12/24/2012	66,901	18,658
6	Smith and Co.	AMERICAS	12/29/2012	63,116	19,949
7	Foo Bars	AMERICAS	6/28/2012	38,281	15,054
8	ABC Telecom	AMERICAS	6/28/2012	57,650	15,524
9	Fake Brothers	AMERICAS	6/29/2012	90,967	18,794
10	QWERTY Logistics	AMERICAS	6/29/2012	11,910	14,775
11	Demo, inc.	AMERICAS	7/6/2012	59,531	10,870

STEP 1: Click in your data source and go to ***Insert > Pivot Table***

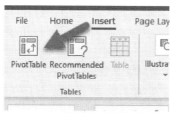

STEP 2: The important step here is to **"check"** the **Add this data to the Data Model** box and press **OK**

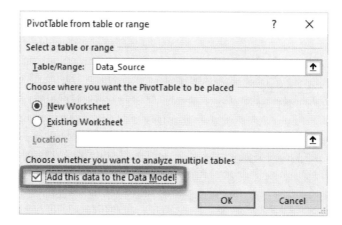

STEP 3: This will create a Pivot Table. Drag these PivotTable Fields in the following areas below which will give you the "Total Transactions" for each customer:

Rows: **CUSTOMERS**
Values: **CUSTOMERS**

STEP 4: To get a Distinct Count, you need to click on the **Values drop down** for the **Count of CUSTOMERS** and select the **Value Field Settings**

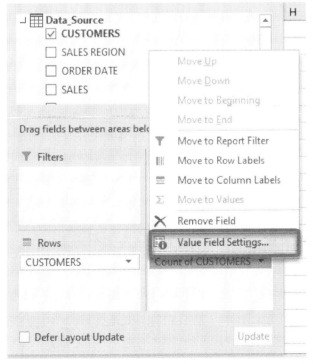

STEP 5: Under the tab **Summarize Values By**, select the last option, **Distinct Count** and press **OK**

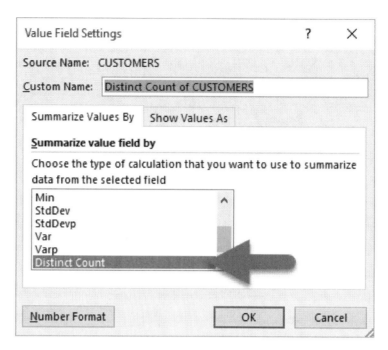

You now have your Distinct Counts!

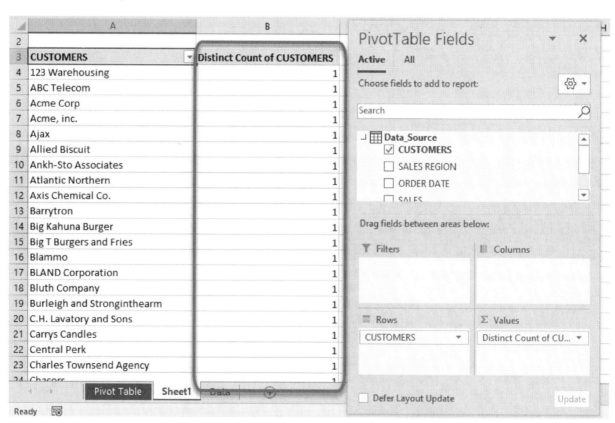

VALUE FIELD SETTINGS > SHOW VALUES AS

Percent % of Grand Total

Pivot Tables have a lot of useful calculations under the **Show Values As** option and one of the most useful ones is the **Percentage of Grand Total** calculation.

This option displays values as a percentage of the Grand Total of all the values or data points in the report.

STEP 1: Select any cell in our Excel Table data source.

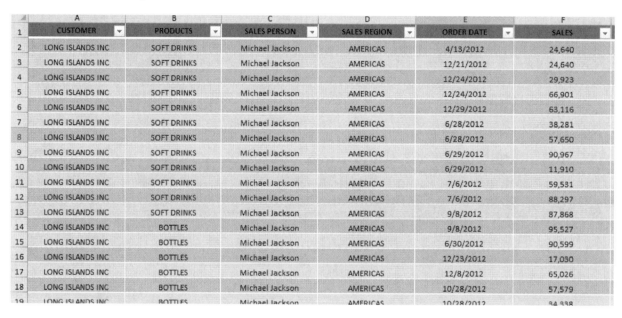

	A	B	C	D	E	F
1	CUSTOMER	PRODUCTS	SALES PERSON	SALES REGION	ORDER DATE	SALES
2	LONG ISLANDS INC	SOFT DRINKS	Michael Jackson	AMERICAS	4/13/2012	24,640
3	LONG ISLANDS INC	SOFT DRINKS	Michael Jackson	AMERICAS	12/21/2012	24,640
4	LONG ISLANDS INC	SOFT DRINKS	Michael Jackson	AMERICAS	12/24/2012	29,923
5	LONG ISLANDS INC	SOFT DRINKS	Michael Jackson	AMERICAS	12/24/2012	66,901
6	LONG ISLANDS INC	SOFT DRINKS	Michael Jackson	AMERICAS	12/29/2012	63,116
7	LONG ISLANDS INC	SOFT DRINKS	Michael Jackson	AMERICAS	6/28/2012	38,281
8	LONG ISLANDS INC	SOFT DRINKS	Michael Jackson	AMERICAS	6/28/2012	57,650
9	LONG ISLANDS INC	SOFT DRINKS	Michael Jackson	AMERICAS	6/29/2012	90,967
10	LONG ISLANDS INC	SOFT DRINKS	Michael Jackson	AMERICAS	6/29/2012	11,910
11	LONG ISLANDS INC	SOFT DRINKS	Michael Jackson	AMERICAS	7/6/2012	59,531
12	LONG ISLANDS INC	SOFT DRINKS	Michael Jackson	AMERICAS	7/6/2012	88,297
13	LONG ISLANDS INC	SOFT DRINKS	Michael Jackson	AMERICAS	9/8/2012	87,868
14	LONG ISLANDS INC	BOTTLES	Michael Jackson	AMERICAS	9/8/2012	95,527
15	LONG ISLANDS INC	BOTTLES	Michael Jackson	AMERICAS	6/30/2012	90,599
16	LONG ISLANDS INC	BOTTLES	Michael Jackson	AMERICAS	12/23/2012	17,030
17	LONG ISLANDS INC	BOTTLES	Michael Jackson	AMERICAS	12/8/2012	65,026
18	LONG ISLANDS INC	BOTTLES	Michael Jackson	AMERICAS	10/28/2012	57,579
19	LONG ISLANDS INC	BOTTLES	Michael Jackson	AMERICAS	10/28/2012	34,338

STEP 2: Insert a new Pivot Table by clicking on your data and going to *Insert > Pivot Table.*

STEP 3: Select **New Worksheet,** and then click **OK**.

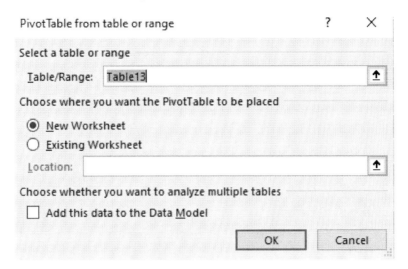

STEP 4: Drag these PivotTable Fields in the following areas below:

Rows: **SALES MONTH**
Columns: **FINANCIAL YEAR**
Values: **SALES** (drag it here twice, I explain why below)

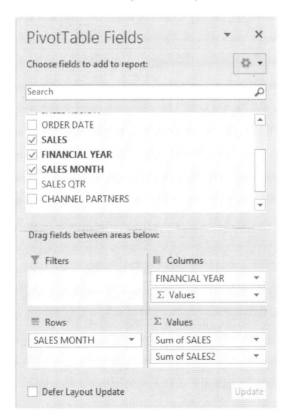

The Pivot Table will look like this:

Row Labels	2012		2013		2014		Total Sum of SALES	Total Percent of Grand Total
	Sum of SALES	Percent of Grand Total	Sum of SALES	Percent of Grand Total	Sum of SALES	Percent of Grand Total		
January	771186	771186	872080	872080	1074820	1074820	2718086	2718086
February	867220	867220	909654	909654	807257	807257	2584131	2584131
March	784136	784136	1031596	1031596	1013466	1013466	2829198	2829198
April	908666	908666	968855	968855	836559	836559	2714080	2714080
May	893039	893039	850502	850502	791095	791095	2534636	2534636
June	786918	786918	981050	981050	771976	771976	2539944	2539944
July	1056573	1056573	854835	854835	873543	873543	2784951	2784951
August	806719	806719	1002597	1002597	599246	599246	2408562	2408562
September	863089	863089	814513	814513	1011288	1011288	2688890	2688890
October	873208	873208	931193	931193	1059308	1059308	2863709	2863709
November	923402	923402	769352	769352	812659	812659	2505413	2505413
December	854090	854090	1031897	1031897	1006745	1006745	2892732	2892732
Grand Total	10388246	10388246	11018124	11018124	10657962	10657962	32064332	32064332

STEP 5: Click the **Sum of SALES2** drop down and choose **Value Field Settings**

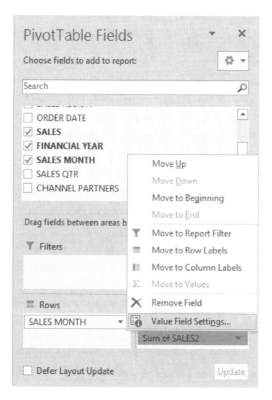

STEP 6: Select the **Show Values As** tab and from the drop down choose *% of Grand Total.*

Also, change the **Custom Name** into *Percent of Grand Total* to make it more presentable. Click **OK.**

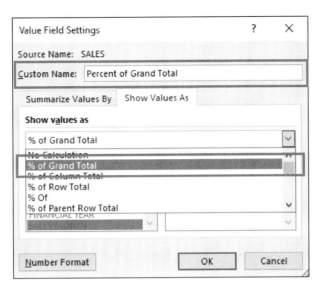

STEP 7: Notice that the *Percent of Grand Total* data is in a decimal format and it is hard to read it:

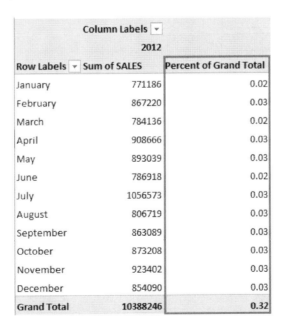

To format the *Percent of Grand Total* column, click the second SALES Field's *Percent of Grand Total* drop down and choose **Value Field Settings.**

The goal here is for us to transform numbers from a decimal format (e.g., 0.23), into a percentage format that is more readable (e.g., 23%).

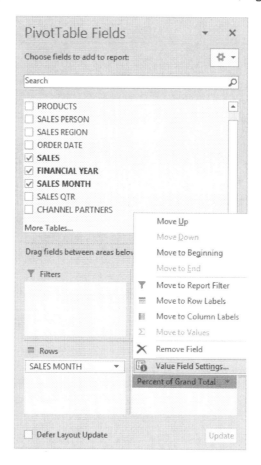

STEP 8: Click the **Number Format** button.

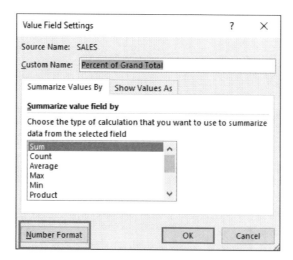

STEP 9: Inside the *Format Cells* dialog box, make your formatting changes and press **OK** twice.

In this example, we used the **Percentage** category to make our *Percent of Grand Total* numbers become more readable.

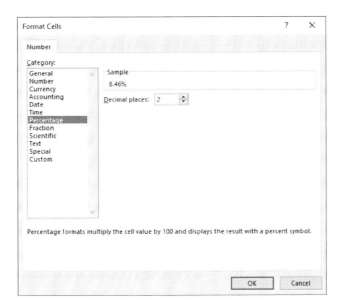

You now have your Pivot Table showing the sales proportion for each Month and Year to the **Grand Total of SALES**.

All of the sales numbers are represented as a Percentage of the Grand Total of $32,064,332.00, which you can see on the lower right corner is represented as **100%** in totality.

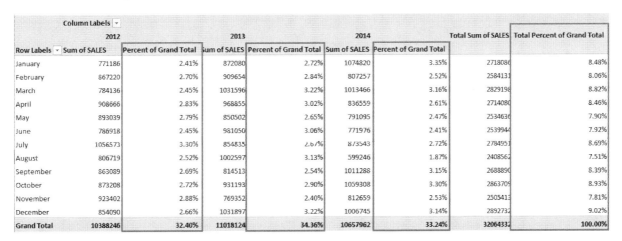

Column Labels								
	2012		2013		2014		Total Sum of SALES	Total Percent of Grand Total
Row Labels	Sum of SALES	Percent of Grand Total	Sum of SALES	Percent of Grand Total	Sum of SALES	Percent of Grand Total		
January	771186	2.41%	872080	2.72%	1074820	3.35%	2718086	8.48%
February	867220	2.70%	909654	2.84%	807257	2.52%	2584131	8.06%
March	784136	2.45%	1031596	3.22%	1013466	3.16%	2829198	8.82%
April	908666	2.83%	968855	3.02%	836559	2.61%	2714080	8.46%
May	893039	2.79%	850502	2.65%	791095	2.47%	2534636	7.90%
June	786918	2.45%	981050	3.06%	771976	2.41%	2539944	7.92%
July	1056573	3.30%	854835	2.67%	873543	2.72%	2784951	8.69%
August	806719	2.52%	1002597	3.13%	599246	1.87%	2408562	7.51%
September	863089	2.69%	814513	2.54%	1011288	3.15%	2688890	8.39%
October	873208	2.72%	931193	2.90%	1059308	3.30%	2863709	8.93%
November	923402	2.88%	769352	2.40%	812659	2.53%	2505413	7.81%
December	854090	2.66%	1031897	3.22%	1006745	3.14%	2892732	9.02%
Grand Total	**10388246**	**32.40%**	**11018124**	**34.36%**	**10657962**	**33.24%**	**32064332**	**100.00%**

Percent % of Column Total

The **Percent of Column Total** displays all the values in each column as a percentage of the Total for the column.

STEP 1: Insert a new Pivot Table by clicking on your data and going to *Insert > Pivot Table > New Worksheet or Existing Worksheet*

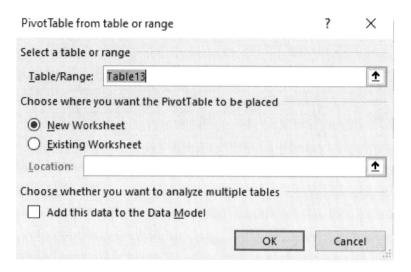

STEP 2: Drag these PivotTable Fields in the following areas below:

Rows: **SALES MONTH**
Columns: **FINANCIAL YEAR**
Values: **SALES** (drag it here twice, I explain why below)

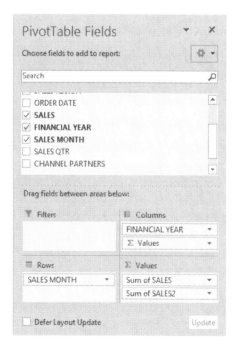

STEP 3: Click the second **Sum of SALES2** drop down and choose **Value Field Settings.**

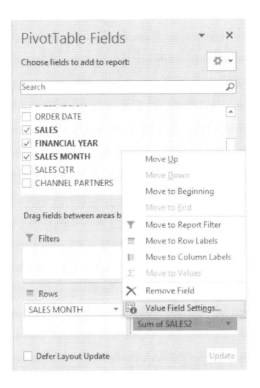

STEP 4: Select the **Show Values As** tab and from the drop down choose **% of Column Total.**

Also change the **Custom Name** into *Percent of Column Total* to make it more presentable. Click **OK.**

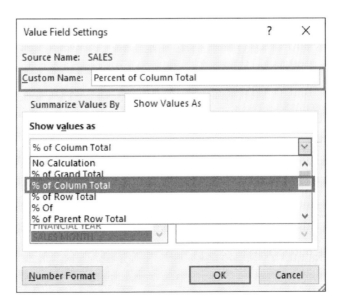

STEP 5: Notice that the *Percent of Column Total* data is in a decimal format that is hard to read:

	2012	
Row Labels ▾	Sum of SALES	Percent of Column Total
January	771186	0.07
February	867220	0.08
March	784136	0.08
April	908666	0.09
May	893039	0.09
June	786918	0.08
July	1056573	0.10
August	806719	0.08
September	863089	0.08
October	873208	0.08
November	923402	0.09
December	854090	0.08
Grand Total	10388246	1.00

To format the *Percent of Column Total* column, click the second Sales Field's *Percent of Column Total* drop down and choose **Value Field Settings.**

The goal here is for us to transform numbers from a decimal format (e.g., 0.23), into a percentage format that is more readable (e.g., 23%).

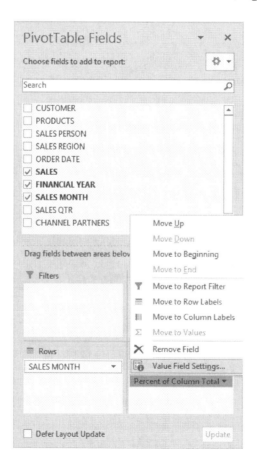

STEP 6: Click the **Number Format** button.

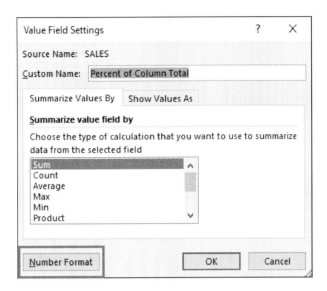

STEP 7: Inside the *Format Cell*s dialog box, make your formatting changes within here and press **OK** twice.

In this example, we used the **Percentage** category to make our *Percent of Column Total* numbers become more readable.

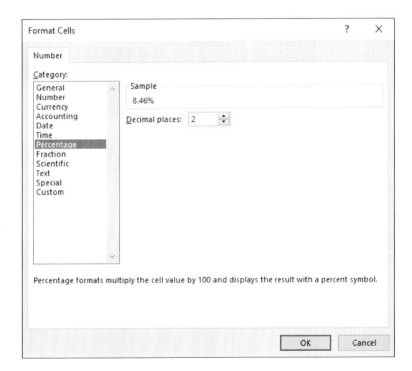

You now have your Pivot Table showing the sales proportion of each Month to its respective Year.

Row Labels	2012		2013		2014		Total Sum of SALES	Total Percent of Column Total
	Sum of SALES	Percent of Column Total	Sum of SALES	Percent of Column Total	Sum of SALES	Percent of Column Total		
January	771186	7.42%	872080	7.91%	1074820	10.08%	2718086	8.48%
February	867220	8.35%	909654	8.26%	807257	7.57%	2584131	8.06%
March	784136	7.55%	1031596	9.36%	1013466	9.51%	2829198	8.82%
April	908666	8.75%	968855	8.79%	836559	7.85%	2714080	8.46%
May	893039	8.60%	850502	7.72%	791095	7.42%	2534636	7.90%
June	786918	7.58%	981050	8.90%	771976	7.24%	2539944	7.92%
July	1056573	10.17%	854835	7.76%	873543	8.20%	2784951	8.69%
August	806719	7.77%	1002597	9.10%	599246	5.62%	2408562	7.51%
September	863089	8.31%	814513	7.39%	1011288	9.49%	2688890	8.39%
October	873208	8.41%	931193	8.45%	1059308	9.94%	2863709	8.93%
November	923402	8.89%	769352	6.98%	812659	7.62%	2505413	7.81%
December	854090	8.22%	1031897	9.37%	1006745	9.45%	2892732	9.02%
Grand Total	10388246	100.00%	11018124	100.00%	10657962	100.00%	32064332	100.00%

Percent % of Row Total

The **Percent of Row Total** displays all the values in each row as a percentage
of the Total for the row.

STEP 1: Select any cell in the Excel Table

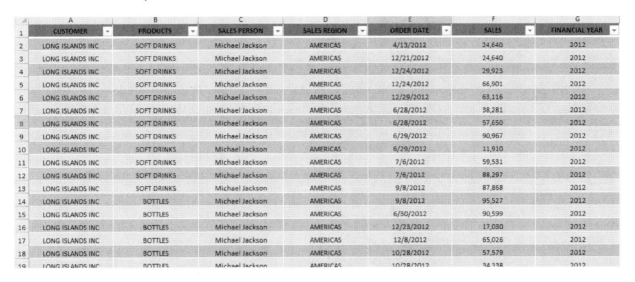

	A	B	C	D	E	F	G
1	CUSTOMER	PRODUCTS	SALES PERSON	SALES REGION	ORDER DATE	SALES	FINANCIAL YEAR
2	LONG ISLANDS INC	SOFT DRINKS	Michael Jackson	AMERICAS	4/13/2012	24,640	2012
3	LONG ISLANDS INC	SOFT DRINKS	Michael Jackson	AMERICAS	12/21/2012	24,640	2012
4	LONG ISLANDS INC	SOFT DRINKS	Michael Jackson	AMERICAS	12/24/2012	29,923	2012
5	LONG ISLANDS INC	SOFT DRINKS	Michael Jackson	AMERICAS	12/24/2012	66,901	2012
6	LONG ISLANDS INC	SOFT DRINKS	Michael Jackson	AMERICAS	12/29/2012	63,116	2012
7	LONG ISLANDS INC	SOFT DRINKS	Michael Jackson	AMERICAS	6/28/2012	38,281	2012
8	LONG ISLANDS INC	SOFT DRINKS	Michael Jackson	AMERICAS	6/28/2012	57,650	2012
9	LONG ISLANDS INC	SOFT DRINKS	Michael Jackson	AMERICAS	6/29/2012	90,967	2012
10	LONG ISLANDS INC	SOFT DRINKS	Michael Jackson	AMERICAS	6/29/2012	11,910	2012
11	LONG ISLANDS INC	SOFT DRINKS	Michael Jackson	AMERICAS	7/6/2012	59,531	2012
12	LONG ISLANDS INC	SOFT DRINKS	Michael Jackson	AMERICAS	7/6/2012	88,297	2012
13	LONG ISLANDS INC	SOFT DRINKS	Michael Jackson	AMERICAS	9/8/2012	87,868	2012
14	LONG ISLANDS INC	BOTTLES	Michael Jackson	AMERICAS	9/8/2012	95,527	2012
15	LONG ISLANDS INC	BOTTLES	Michael Jackson	AMERICAS	6/30/2012	90,599	2012
16	LONG ISLANDS INC	BOTTLES	Michael Jackson	AMERICAS	12/23/2012	17,030	2012
17	LONG ISLANDS INC	BOTTLES	Michael Jackson	AMERICAS	12/8/2012	65,026	2012
18	LONG ISLANDS INC	BOTTLES	Michael Jackson	AMERICAS	10/28/2012	57,579	2012
19	LONG ISLANDS INC	BOTTLES	Michael Jackson	AMERICAS	10/28/2012	34,338	2012

STEP 2: Go to **Insert** > **PivotTable**.

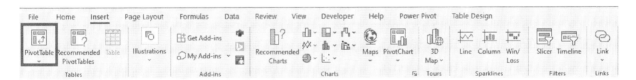

STEP 3: Select a **New/Existing Worksheet** and then Click **OK**.

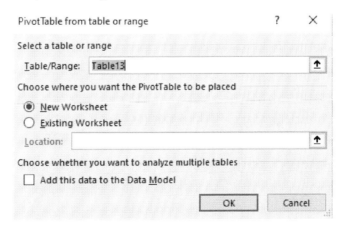

STEP 4: Drag these PivotTable Fields in the following areas below:

Rows: **SALES PERSON**
Columns: **FINANCIAL YEAR**
Values: **SALES** (drag it here twice, I explain why below)

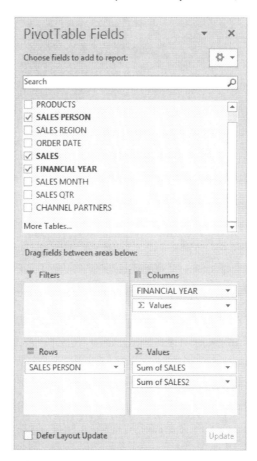

A Pivot Table will be created and looks like this:

Row Labels	2012 Sum of SALES	2012 Sum of SALES2	2013 Sum of SALES	2013 Sum of SALES2	2014 Sum of SALES	2014 Sum of SALES2	Total Sum of SALES	Total Sum of SALES2
Homer Simpson	2647950	2647950	2987445	2987445	2701418	2701418	8336813	8336813
Ian Wright	2674096	2674096	2722129	2722129	2675496	2675496	8071721	8071721
John Michaloudis	2566978	2566978	2879900	2879900	2711156	2711156	8158034	8158034
Michael Jackson	2499222	2499222	2428650	2428650	2569892	2569892	7497764	7497764
Grand Total	10388246	10388246	11018124	11018124	10657962	10657962	32064332	32064332

STEP 5: Click the **Sum of SALES2** drop down and choose **Value Field Settings.**

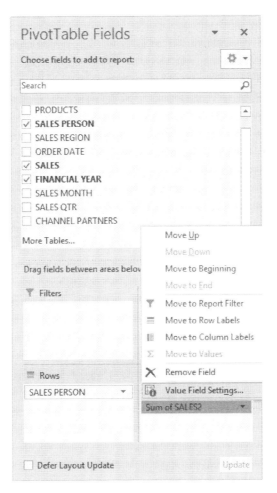

STEP 6: Select the **Show Values As** tab and from the drop down choose *% of Row Total.*

Also, change the **Custom Name** into *Percent of Row Total* to make it more presentable. Click **OK.**

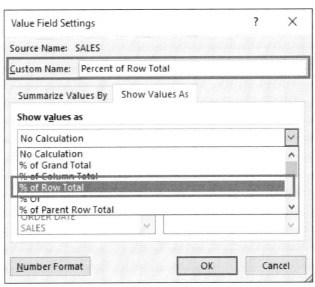

STEP 7: Notice that the *Percent of Row Total* data is in a decimal format that is hard to read:

Row Labels	Sum of SALES	Percent of Row Total
	2012	
Homer Simpson	2647950	0.32
Ian Wright	2674096	0.33
John Michaloudis	2566978	0.31
Michael Jackson	2499222	0.33
Grand Total	10388246	0.32

To format the *Percent of Row Total* column, click the second Sales Field's *Percent of Row Total* drop down and choose **Value Field Settings.**

The goal here is for us to transform numbers from a decimal format (e.g., 0.23), into a percentage format that is more readable (e.g., 23%).

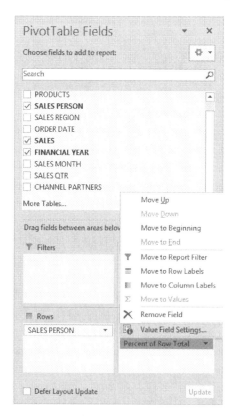

STEP 8: Click the **Number Format** button.

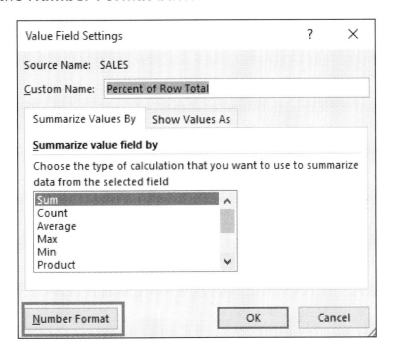

STEP 9: Inside the *Format Cell*s dialog box, make your formatting changes within here and press **OK** twice.

In this example, we used the **Percentage** category to make our *Percent of Row Total* numbers become more readable.

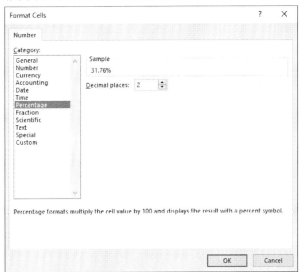

You now have your Pivot Table showing the sales proportion of each SALES PERSON over the three years.

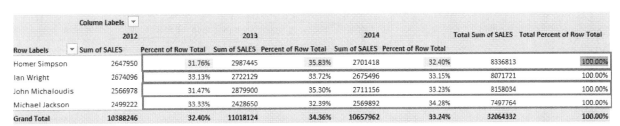

Row Labels	Sum of SALES	Percent of Row Total	Sum of SALES	Percent of Row Total	Sum of SALES	Percent of Row Total	Total Sum of SALES	Total Percent of Row Total
	2012		**2013**		**2014**			
Homer Simpson	2647950	31.76%	2987445	35.83%	2701418	32.40%	8336813	100.00%
Ian Wright	2674096	33.13%	2722129	33.72%	2675496	33.15%	8071721	100.00%
John Michaloudis	2566978	31.47%	2879900	35.30%	2711156	33.23%	8158034	100.00%
Michael Jackson	2499222	33.33%	2428650	32.39%	2569892	34.28%	7497764	100.00%
Grand Total	10388246	32.40%	11018124	34.36%	10657962	33.24%	32064332	100.00%

Percent % of

The **Percent of** calculation displays the value of one item (**the Base Field**) as the percentage of another item (**the Base Item**).

I will show you two separate examples to understand this concept more clearly.

% of Year

In the example below I will show you how to get the *Percent of the Previous Year's Sales* i.e., each Year's **SALES** will be compared to the **SALES** for the previous Year in form of a percentage!

STEP 1: Insert a new Pivot Table by clicking on your data and going to *Insert > Pivot Table > New Worksheet or Existing Worksheet*

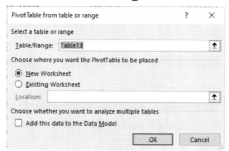

STEP 2: Drag these PivotTable Fields in the following areas below:
Rows: **SALES PERSON**
Columns: **FINANCIAL YEAR**
Values: **SALES** (drag it here twice, I explain why below)

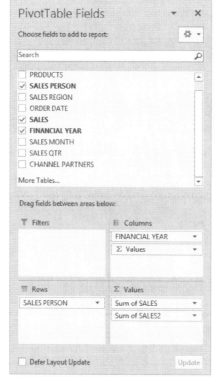

Here is how the Pivot Table looks like:

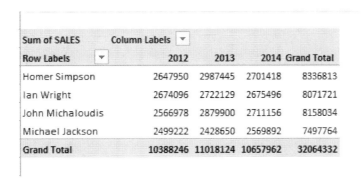

STEP 3: Click the **Sum of SALES2** drop down and choose **Value Field Settings.**

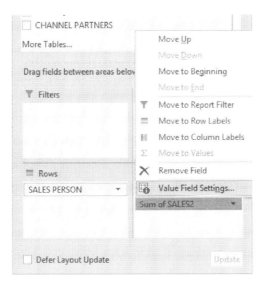

STEP 4: Select the following inside **Show Values As:**

Show values as: **% Of**

Base Field: **FINANCIAL YEAR**

Base Item: **(previous)**

This means we want to get the **% of** values based on the **previous FINANCIAL YEAR.**

Also, change the **Custom Name** into *Percent of Previous Year* to make it more presentable. Click **OK.**

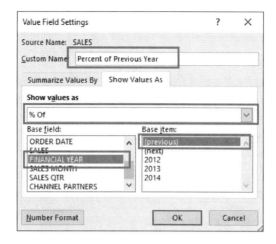

STEP 5: Notice that the *Percent of Previous Year* data is in a decimal format that is hard to read:

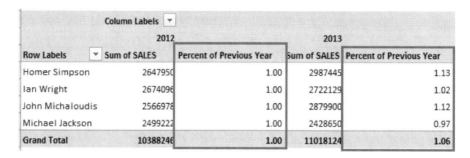

		2012		2013	
Row Labels	Sum of SALES	Percent of Previous Year	Sum of SALES	Percent of Previous Year
Homer Simpson	2647950	1.00	2987445	1.13
Ian Wright	2674096	1.00	2722129	1.02
John Michaloudis	2566978	1.00	2879900	1.12
Michael Jackson	2499222	1.00	2428650	0.97
Grand Total	**10388246**	**1.00**	**11018124**	**1.06**

To format the *Percent of Previous Year* column, click the second Sales Field's *(Percent of Previous Year)* drop down and choose **Value Field Settings.**

The goal here is for us to transform numbers from a decimal format (e.g., 0.23), into a percentage format that is more readable (e.g., 23%).

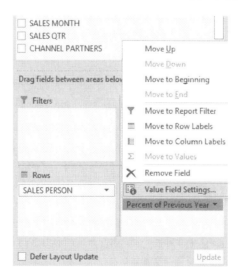

STEP 6: Click the **Number Format** button.

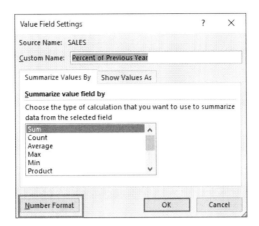

STEP 7: Inside the *Format Cell*s dialog box, make your formatting changes within here and press **OK** twice.

In this example, we used the **Percentage** category to make our *Percent of Previous Year* numbers become more readable.

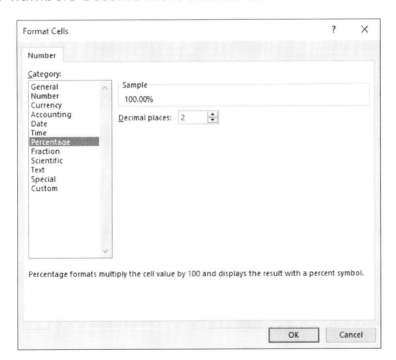

All of the SALES numbers are now represented as a **Percentage of the Previous Year.** For instance, **Year 2013** is represented as a **Percentage of Year 2012**, and **Year 2014** is represented as a **Percentage of Year 2013**.

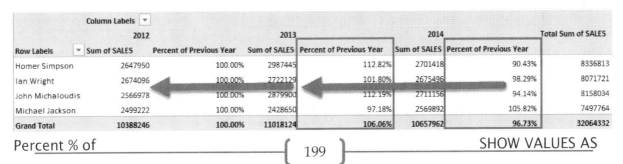

	2012		2013		2014		Total Sum of SALES
Row Labels	Sum of SALES	Percent of Previous Year	Sum of SALES	Percent of Previous Year	Sum of SALES	Percent of Previous Year	
Homer Simpson	2647950	100.00%	2987445	112.82%	2701418	90.43%	8336813
Ian Wright	2674096	100.00%	2722129	101.80%	2675496	98.29%	8071721
John Michaloudis	2566978	100.00%	2879900	112.19%	2711156	94.14%	8158034
Michael Jackson	2499222	100.00%	2428650	97.18%	2569892	105.82%	7497764
Grand Total	10388246	100.00%	11018124	106.06%	10657962	96.73%	32064332

Percent % of

SHOW VALUES AS

% of Sales Person's Sales

Now we are going to display **% of Sales Person's Sales** in the Pivot Table.

STEP 1: Click on any cell in the Excel Table.

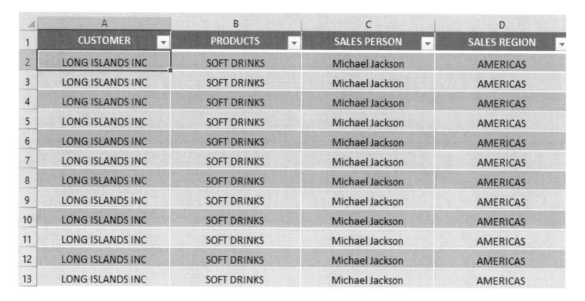

STEP 2: Go to **Insert > Pivot Table.**

STEP 3: Select **New/Existing Worksheet** and then click **OK.**

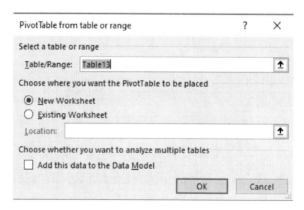

STEP 4: Drag these PivotTable Fields in the following areas below:
Rows: **SALES PERSON**
Columns: **FINANCIAL YEAR**
Values: **SALES**

This is the Pivot Table that we will be working with!

Sum of SALES	Column Labels			
Row Labels	2012	2013	2014	Grand Total
Homer Simpson	2647950	2987445	2701418	8336813
Ian Wright	2674096	2722129	2675496	8071721
John Michaloudis	2566978	2879900	2711156	8158034
Michael Jackson	2499222	2428650	2569892	7497764
Grand Total	10388246	11018124	10657962	32064332

STEP 5: Right Click on any value in the Pivot Table and select **Value Field Settings**.

STEP 6: Select the following inside **Show Values As:**

Show values as: **% Of**

Base Field: **SALES PERSON**

Base Item: **Homer Simpson**

This means we want to get the **% of Homer Simpson's** values compared to the other **SALES PERSON**. Click **OK.**

This will add percentages to our Pivot Table!

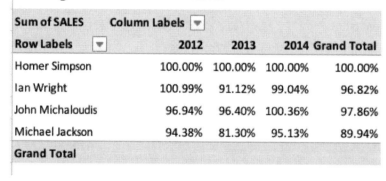

Sum of SALES	Column Labels			
Row Labels	2012	2013	2014	Grand Total
Homer Simpson	100.00%	100.00%	100.00%	100.00%
Ian Wright	100.99%	91.12%	99.04%	96.82%
John Michaloudis	96.94%	96.40%	100.36%	97.86%
Michael Jackson	94.38%	81.30%	95.13%	89.94%
Grand Total				

Excel will display 100% for all values for Homer Simpson as it is be compared to itself.

For the other **SALES PERSON**, Excel will show the **SALES** amount as a percentage of Homer's **SALES** for that particular **Year**.

Pretty cool!

Percent % of Parent Row Total

The **Percent of Parent Row Total** calculates the values as

follows: (value for the item) / (value for the parent item on rows)

STEP 1: Insert a new Pivot Table by clicking on your data and going to *Insert > Pivot Table > New Worksheet or Existing Worksheet*

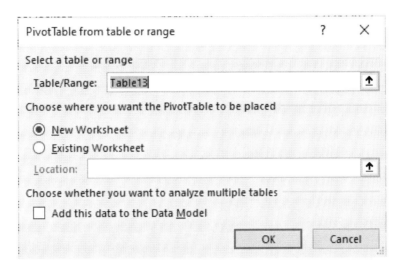

STEP 2: Drag these PivotTable Fields in the following areas below:

Rows: **SALES PERSON** and **SALES QTR**
Columns: **FINANCIAL YEAR**
Values: **SALES** (drag it here twice, I explain why below)

STEP 3: Click the **Sum of SALES2** drop down and choose **Value Field Settings.**

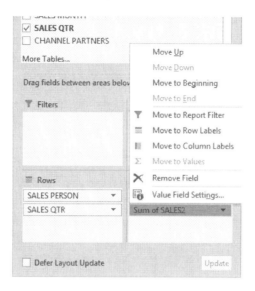

STEP 4: Select the **Show Values As** tab and from the drop down choose *% of Parent Row Total.*

Also change the **Custom Name** into *% of Parent Row Total* to make it more presentable. Click **OK.**

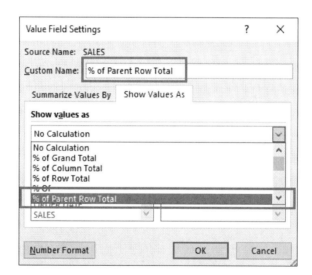

STEP 5: Notice that the **_% of Parent Row Total_** data is in a decimal format that is hard to read:

Row Labels	Sum of SALES	% of Parent Row Total
	Column Labels	
	2012	
⊟ Homer Simpson	2647950	0.25
Q1	776782	0.29
Q2	659919	0.25
Q3	585325	0.22
Q4	625924	0.24
⊟ Ian Wright	2674096	0.26
Q1	591445	0.22
Q2	758121	0.28
Q3	657629	0.25
Q4	666901	0.25
⊟ John Michaloudis	2566978	0.25
Q1	560250	0.22
Q2	658377	0.26
Q3	693252	0.27
Q4	655099	0.26
⊟ Michael Jackson	2499222	0.24
Q1	494065	0.20
Q2	512206	0.20
Q3	790175	0.32
Q4	702776	0.28
Grand Total	**10388246**	**1.00**

To format the **_% of Parent Row Total_** column, click the second Sales Field's **_% of Parent Row Total_** drop down and choose **Value Field Settings.**

The goal here is for us to transform numbers from a decimal format (e.g., 0.23), into a percentage format that is more readable (e.g., 23%).

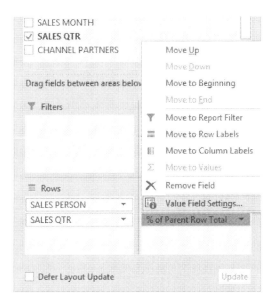

STEP 6: Click the **Number Format** button.

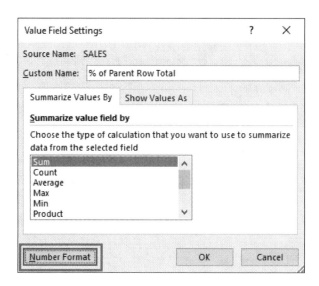

STEP 7: Inside the *Format Cell*s dialog box, make your formatting changes within here and press **OK** twice.

In this example, we used the **Percentage** category to make our **% *of Parent Row Total*** numbers become more readable.

All of the SALES numbers are now represented as a **Percentage of its Parent's Total.**

You can see that each red box is represented as **100%** in totality and all the blue boxes are represented as **100%** in totality, that is:

Quarterly SALES as a percentage of each Sales Person´s Total Sales.

Sales Person's SALES as a percentage of Grand Total SALES.

Row Labels	2012 Sum of SALES	2012 % of Parent Row Total	2013 Sum of SALES	2013 % of Parent Row Total	2014 Sum of SALES	2014 % of Parent Row Total	Total Sum of SALES	Total % of Parent Row Total
⊟Homer Simpson	2647950	25.49%	2987445	27.11%	2701418	25.35%	8336813	26.00%
Q1	776782	29.34%	778739	26.07%	790568	29.26%	2346089	28.14%
Q2	659919	24.92%	819269	27.42%	597278	22.11%	2076466	24.91%
Q3	585325	22.10%	674607	22.58%	580162	21.48%	1840094	22.07%
Q4	625924	23.64%	714830	23.93%	733410	27.15%	2074164	24.88%
⊟Ian Wright	2674096	25.74%	2722129	24.71%	2675496	25.10%	8071721	25.17%
Q1	591445	22.12%	698717	25.67%	747267	27.93%	2037429	25.24%
Q2	758121	28.35%	728139	26.75%	647088	24.19%	2133348	26.43%
Q3	657629	24.59%	624591	22.94%	520194	19.44%	1802414	22.33%
Q4	666901	24.94%	670682	24.64%	760947	28.44%	2098530	26.00%
⊟John Michaloudis	2566978	24.71%	2879900	26.14%	2711156	25.44%	8158034	25.44%
Q1	560250	21.83%	745031	25.87%	614563	22.67%	1919844	23.53%
Q2	658377	25.65%	723009	25.11%	711729	26.25%	2093115	25.66%
Q3	693252	27.01%	704070	24.45%	687743	25.37%	2085065	25.56%
Q4	655099	25.52%	707790	24.58%	697121	25.71%	2060010	25.25%
⊟Michael Jackson	2499222	24.06%	2428650	22.04%	2569892	24.11%	7497764	23.38%
Q1	494065	19.77%	590843	24.33%	743145	28.92%	1828053	24.38%
Q2	512206	20.49%	529990	21.82%	443535	17.26%	1485731	19.82%
Q3	790175	31.62%	668677	27.53%	695978	27.08%	2154830	28.74%
Q4	702776	28.12%	639140	26.32%	687234	26.74%	2029150	27.06%
Grand Total	10388246	100.00%	11018124	100.00%	10657962	100.00%	32064332	100.00%

Percent % of Parent Column Total

The **Percent of Parent Column Total** calculates the values as

follows: (value for the item) / (value for the parent item on columns)

STEP 1: Insert a new Pivot Table by clicking on your data and going to *Insert > Pivot Table > New Worksheet or Existing Worksheet*

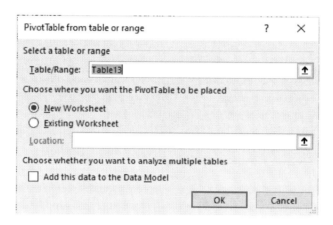

STEP 2: Drag these PivotTable Fields in the following areas

below: Rows: **SALES PERSON**
Columns: **SALES QTR** and **FINANCIAL YEAR**
Values: **SALES** (drag it here twice, I explain why below)

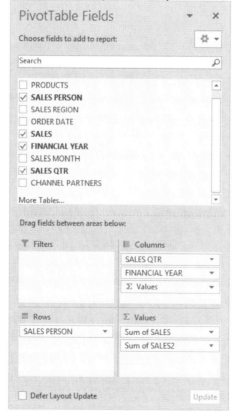

STEP 3: Click the **Sum of SALES2** drop down and choose **Value Field Settings.**

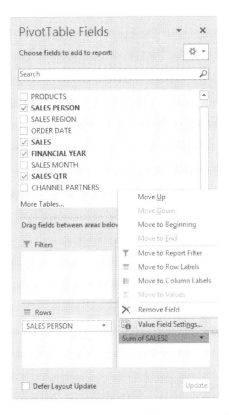

STEP 4: Select the **Show Values As** tab and from the drop down choose *% of Parent Column Total.*

Also change the **Custom Name** into *% of Parent Column Total* to make it more presentable. Click **OK.**

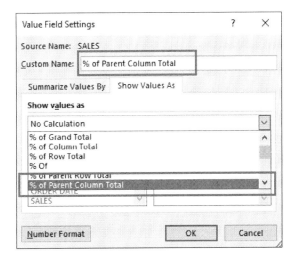

STEP 5: Notice that the *% of Parent Column Total* data is in a decimal format that is hard to read:

Row Labels	2012 Sum of SALES	2012 % of Parent Column Total	2013 Sum of SALES	2013 % of Parent Column Total	2014 Sum of SALES	2014 % of Parent Column Total	Q1 Sum of SALES
Homer Simpson	776782	0.33	778739	0.33	790568	0.34	2346089
Ian Wright	591445	0.29	698717	0.34	747267	0.37	2037429
John Michaloudis	560250	0.29	745031	0.39	614563	0.32	1919844
Michael Jackson	494065	0.27	590843	0.32	743149	0.41	1828053
Grand Total	2422542	0.30	2813330	0.35	2895543	0.36	8131415

To format the *% of Parent Column Total* column, click the second Sales Field's *% of Parent Column Total* drop down and choose **Value Field Settings.**

The goal here is for us to transform numbers from a decimal format (e.g., 0.23), into a percentage format that is more readable (e.g., 23%).

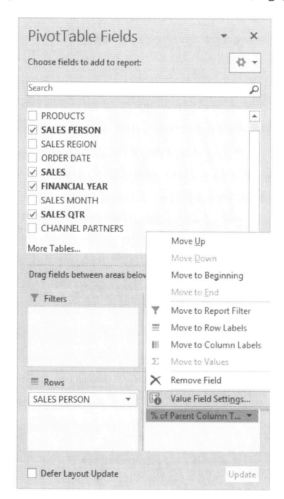

STEP 6: Click the **Number Format** button:

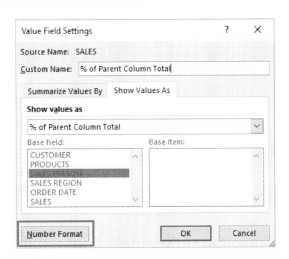

STEP 7: Inside the ***Format Cells*** dialogue box, make your formatting changes within here and press **OK** twice. In this example, we used the **Percentage** category to make our *% of Parent Column Total* numbers become more readable.

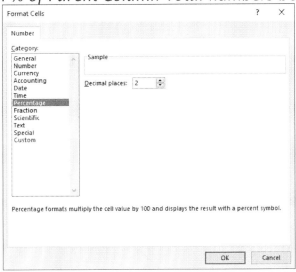

All of the SALES numbers are now represented as a **Percentage of its Parent's Total.** You can see that each red box is represented as **100%** in totality and all the blue boxes are represented as **100%** in totality, that is:

Yearly SALES as a percentage of each Sales Person´s Total Sales for each Quarter.
Quarterly SALES as a percentage of each Sales Person's Grand Total SALES.

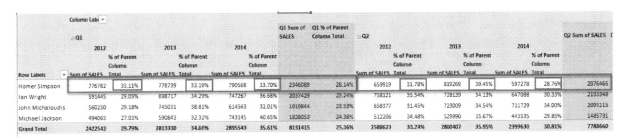

Percent % of Parent Total

The **Percent of Parent Total** calculates the values as follows:

(value for the item) / (value for the parent item of the selected **Base field**)

In the example below I show you how to get the **Percent of a Product Total** i.e., *The % Sales of each Product broken down by Sales Rep and Quarter.*

STEP 1: Insert a new Pivot Table by clicking on your data and going to ***Insert > Pivot Table > New Worksheet or Existing Worksheet***

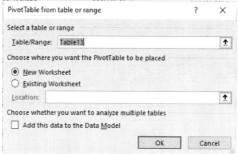

STEP 2: Drag these PivotTable Fields in the following areas below: Rows:

PRODUCTS, SALES PERSON and **SALES QTR**
Columns: **FINANCIAL YEAR**
Values: **SALES** (drag it here twice, I explain why below)

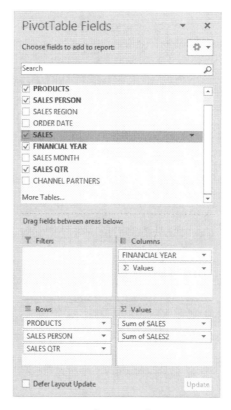

STEP 3: Click the **Sum of SALES2** drop down and choose **Value Field Settings.**

STEP 4: Select the following inside **Show Values As:**

Show values as: **% of Parent Total**

Base Field: **PRODUCTS**

Also change the **Custom Name** into *% of Product Total* to make it more presentable. Click **OK.**

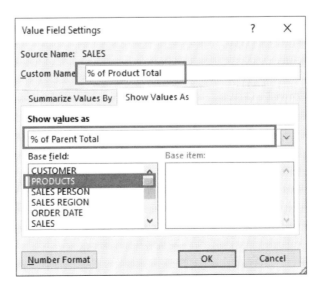

STEP 5: Notice that the *% of Product Total* data is in a decimal format that is hard to read:

Row Labels	Sum of SALES (2012)	% of Product Total (2012)	Sum of SALES (2013)
⊟ BOTTLES	2754838	1.00	2857728
⊟ Homer Simpson	693855	0.25	827901
Q1	150215	0.05	209844
Q2	246834	0.09	262820
Q3	125122	0.05	168183
Q4	171684	0.06	187054
⊟ Ian Wright	671757	0.24	579190
Q1	136980	0.05	131595
Q2	185611	0.07	161720
Q3	101050	0.04	179811
Q4	248116	0.09	106064
⊟ John Michaloudis	714353	0.26	710555
Q1	173717	0.06	201293
Q2	178116	0.06	150723
Q3	212060	0.08	181005
Q4	150460	0.05	177534

To format the *% of Product Total* column, click the second Sales Field's *% of Product Total* drop down and choose **Value Field Settings.**

The goal here is for us to transform numbers from a decimal format (e.g., 0.23), into a percentage format that is more readable (e.g., 23%).

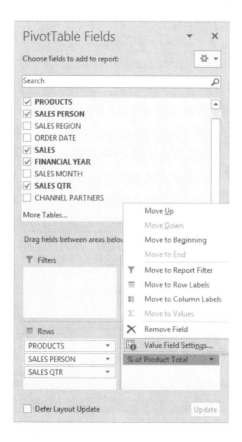

STEP 6: Click the **Number Format** button.

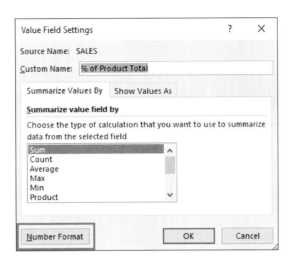

STEP 7: Inside the *Format Cells* dialog box, make your formatting changes within here and press **OK** twice.

In this example, we used the **Percentage** category to make our *% of Product Total* numbers become more readable.

All of the sales numbers are now represented as a **Percentage of its Parent** *i.e the Product Field.*

You can see that each red box is represented as **100%** in totality and all the blue boxes are represented as **100%** in totality, that is:

Quarterly SALES of each Sales Person as a percentage of each Product's Total Sales.

Sales Person's SALES as a percentage of each Product's Total Sales.

Row Labels	2012 Sum of SALES	2012 % of Product Total	2013 Sum of SALES	2013 % of Product Total	2014 Sum of SALES	2014 % of Product Total	Total Sum of SALES	Total % of Product Total
⊟ BOTTLES	2754838	100.00%	2857728	100.00%	2544612	100.00%	8157178	100.00%
⊟ Homer Simpson	693855	25.19%	827901	28.97%	563154	22.13%	2084910	25.56%
Q1	150215	5.45%	209844	7.34%	109537	4.30%	469596	5.76%
Q2	246834	8.96%	262820	9.20%	156150	6.14%	665804	8.16%
Q3	125122	4.54%	168183	5.89%	143249	5.63%	436554	5.35%
Q4	171684	6.23%	187054	6.55%	154218	6.06%	512956	6.29%
⊟ Ian Wright	671757	24.38%	579190	20.27%	703240	27.64%	1954187	23.96%
Q1	136980	4.97%	131595	4.60%	213264	8.38%	481839	5.91%
Q2	185611	6.74%	161720	5.66%	158735	6.24%	506066	6.20%
Q3	101050	3.67%	179811	6.29%	160667	6.31%	441528	5.41%
Q4	248116	9.01%	106064	3.71%	170574	6.70%	524754	6.43%
⊟ John Michaloudis	714353	25.93%	710555	24.86%	586103	23.03%	2011011	24.65%
Q1	173717	6.31%	201293	7.04%	89999	3.54%	465009	5.70%
Q2	178116	6.47%	150723	5.27%	162564	6.39%	491403	6.02%
Q3	212060	7.70%	181005	6.33%	183514	7.21%	576579	7.07%
Q4	150460	5.46%	177534	6.21%	150026	5.90%	478020	5.86%
⊟ Michael Jackson	674873	24.50%	740082	25.90%	692115	27.20%	2107070	25.83%
Q1	203156	7.37%	166634	5.83%	193699	7.61%	563489	6.91%
Q2	156943	5.70%	204273	7.15%	108105	4.25%	469321	5.75%
Q3	181582	6.59%	204575	7.16%	221880	8.72%	608037	7.45%
Q4	133192	4.83%	164600	5.76%	168431	6.62%	466223	5.72%

Difference From

The **Difference From** calculation displays values as the difference from the value of the **Base item** in the **Base field**.

This is just great when your boss asks you how the business is tracking to the previous *months, years, days...*

Show The Difference From Previous Months

STEP 1: Select any cell in the Excel Table data source.

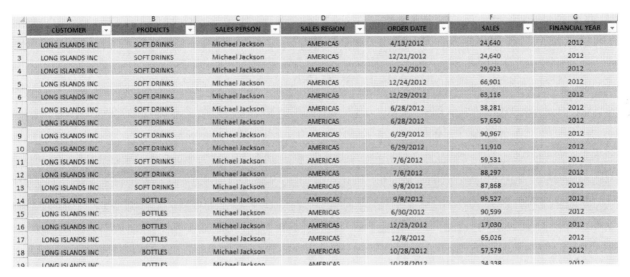

STEP 2: Insert a new Pivot Table by clicking on your data and going to *Insert > Pivot Table.*

STEP 3: Insert a new Pivot Table in the Create PivotTable dialog box, select the **Table range** and **New Worksheet,** and then click **OK.**

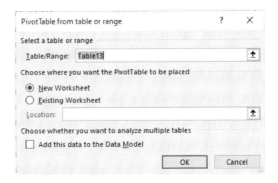

STEP 4: Drag these PivotTable Fields in the following areas below:

Rows: **SALES MONTH**
Columns: **FINANCIAL YEAR**
Values: **SALES** (drag it here twice, I explain why below)

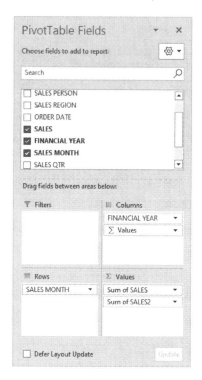

The Pivot Table will look like this:

Row Labels	2012 Sum of SALES	2012 Sum of SALES2	2013 Sum of SALES	2013 Sum of SALES2	2014 Sum of SALES	2014 Sum of SALES2	Total Sum of SALES	Total Sum of SALES2
January	771186	771186	872080	872080	1074820	1074820	2718086	2718086
February	867220	867220	909654	909654	807257	807257	2584131	2584131
March	784136	784136	1031596	1031596	1013466	1013466	2829198	2829198
April	908666	908666	968855	968855	836559	836559	2714080	2714080
May	893039	893039	850502	850502	791095	791095	2534636	2534636
June	786918	786918	981050	981050	771976	771976	2539944	2539944
July	1056573	1056573	854835	854835	873543	873543	2784951	2784951
August	806719	806719	1002597	1002597	599246	599246	2408562	2408562
September	863089	863089	814513	814513	1011288	1011288	2688890	2688890
October	873208	873208	931193	931193	1059308	1059308	2863709	2863709
November	923402	923402	769352	769352	812659	812659	2505413	2505413
December	854090	854090	1031897	1031897	1006745	1006745	2892732	2892732
Grand Total	**10388246**	**10388246**	**11018124**	**11018124**	**10657962**	**10657962**	**32064332**	**32064332**

STEP 5: Now click on the **Sum of SALES2** drop down and choose **Value Field Settings.**

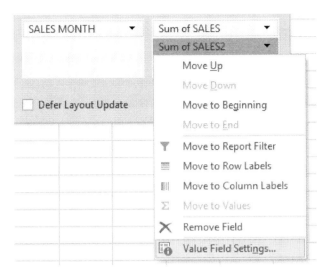

STEP 6: Now you need to select the **Show Values As** tab and from the drop-down choose the **Difference From**

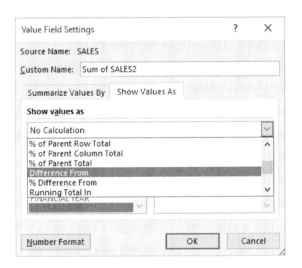

STEP 7: Select the following inside **Show Values As:**

Show values as: **Difference From**

Base Field: **SALES MONTH**

Base Item: **(previous)**

So it will read the "*Difference from the previous Sales Month*". Press OK.

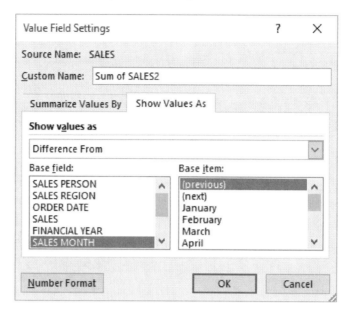

STEP 8: You can do some cosmetic changes by going back into the **Values Field Settings** (from step 5) and changing the **Custom Name** to show whatever you like e.g. *Diff. From Previous Month or Monthly Variance.*

From here, you can also click on the **Number Format** (bottom left-hand corner) to change the way the numbers are shown:

Row Label	2012 Sum of SALES	2012 Diff From Previous Month	2013 Sum of SALES	2013 Diff From Previous Month	2014 Sum of SALES	2014 Diff From Previous Month
January	771,186		872,080		1,074,820	
February	867,220	96,034	909,654	37,574	807,257	-267,563
March	784,136	-83,084	1,031,596	121,942	1,013,466	206,209
April	908,666	124,530	968,855	-62,741	836,559	-176,907
May	893,039	-15,627	850,502	-118,353	791,095	-45,464
June	786,918	-106,121	981,050	130,548	771,976	-19,119
July	1,056,573	269,655	854,835	-126,215	873,543	101,567
August	806,719	-249,854	1,002,597	147,762	599,246	-274,297
September	863,089	56,370	814,513	-188,084	1,011,288	412,042
October	873,208	10,119	931,193	116,680	1,059,308	48,020
November	923,402	50,194	769,352	-161,841	812,659	-246,649
December	854,090	-69,312	1,031,897	262,545	1,006,745	194,086
Grand Total	**10,388,246**		**11,018,124**		**10,657,962**	

Show the Difference From Previous Month with Directional Icons

Now that we have our Pivot Table report below, we can show the variances per Month using an up/down or directional icons with **Conditional Formatting**.

Column Labels	2012		2013		2014	
Row Label	Sum of SALES	Diff From Previous Month	Sum of SALES	Diff From Previous Month	Sum of SALES	Diff From Previous Month
January	771,186		872,080		1,074,820	
February	867,220	96,034	909,654	37,574	807,257	-267,563
March	784,136	-83,084	1,031,596	121,942	1,013,466	206,209
April	908,666	124,530	968,855	-62,741	836,559	-176,907
May	893,039	-15,627	850,502	-118,353	791,095	-45,464
June	786,918	-106,121	981,050	130,548	771,976	-19,119
July	1,056,573	269,655	854,835	-126,215	873,543	101,567
August	806,719	-249,854	1,002,597	147,762	599,246	-274,297
September	863,089	56,370	814,513	-188,084	1,011,288	412,042
October	873,208	10,119	931,193	116,680	1,059,308	48,020
November	923,402	50,194	769,352	-161,841	812,659	-246,649
December	854,090	-69,312	1,031,897	262,545	1,006,745	194,086
Grand Total	10,388,246		11,018,124		10,657,962	

STEP 1: Click on any variance value in the Pivot Table and go to *Home > Conditional Formatting > Icon Sets > Directional*

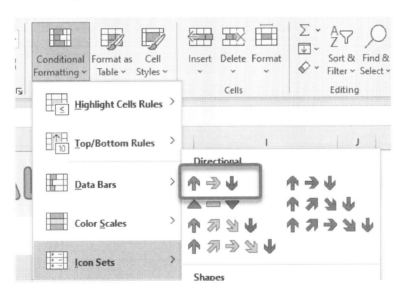

STEP 2: This will bring up the **Apply Formatting Rule to** dialogue box. **Choose the 3rd option** as this will apply the Conditional Format on all the values except the Subtotals.

9,654	⇨	37,574	807,257	⬇	-267,563

Apply formatting rule to ...

○ Selected cells

○ All cells showing "Diff From Previous Month" values

◉ All cells showing "Diff From Previous Month" values for "SALES MONTH" and "FINANCIAL YEAR"

Your Pivot Table will look like this:

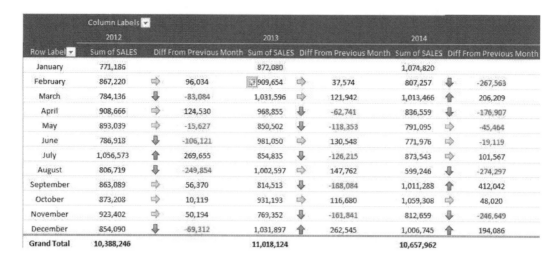

	2012			2013			2014		
Row Labels	Sum of SALES		Diff From Previous Month	Sum of SALES		Diff From Previous Month	Sum of SALES		Diff From Previous Month
January	771,186			872,080			1,074,820		
February	867,220	⇨	96,034	909,654	⇨	37,574	807,257	⬇	-267,563
March	784,136	⬇	-83,084	1,031,596	⇨	121,942	1,013,466	⬆	206,209
April	908,666	⇨	124,530	968,855	⬇	-62,741	836,559	⬇	-176,907
May	893,039	⇨	-15,627	850,502	⬇	-118,353	791,095	⇨	-45,464
June	786,918	⬇	-106,121	981,050	⇨	130,548	771,976	⇨	-19,119
July	1,056,573	⬆	269,655	854,835	⬇	-126,215	873,543	⇨	101,567
August	806,719	⬇	-249,854	1,002,597	⇨	147,762	599,246	⬇	-274,297
September	863,089	⇨	56,370	814,513	⬇	-188,084	1,011,288	⬆	412,042
October	873,208	⇨	10,119	931,193	⇨	116,680	1,059,308	⇨	48,020
November	923,402	⇨	50,194	769,352	⬇	-161,841	812,659	⬇	-246,649
December	854,090	⬇	-69,312	1,031,897	⬆	262,545	1,006,745	⬆	194,086
Grand Total	10,388,246			11,018,124			10,657,962		

STEP 3: Now we need to make some edits in the Conditional Formatting Rule to get the icons right.

Go to *Home > Conditional Formatting > Manage Rules > Edit Rule*

STEP 4: Inside the **Edit Formatting Rule** box you need to make the following changes:

Value = 0
Type = Number
"Check" the Show Icon Only box and press **OK to** confirm the changes:

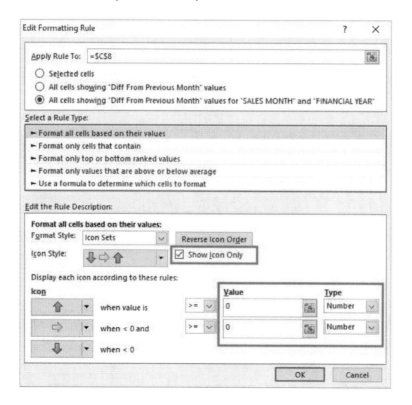

STEP 5: In the next screen you will get the **Conditional Formatting Rules Manager**. Hit **Apply** to see the changes and **OK** to confirm them:

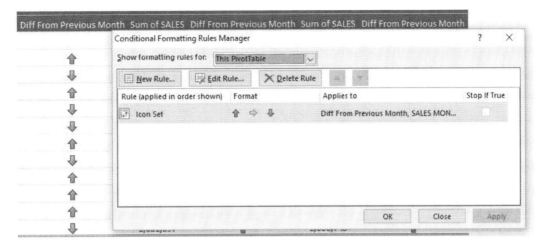

Now you have your Pivot Table showing the differences from the previous Months with directional icons only!

Row Label	2012 Sum of SALES	2012 Diff From Previous Month	2013 Sum of SALES	2013 Diff From Previous Month	2014 Sum of SALES	2014 Diff From Previous Month
January	771,186		872,080		1,074,820	
February	867,220	⇧	909,654	⇧	807,257	⇩
March	784,136	⇩	1,031,596	⇧	1,013,466	⇧
April	908,666	⇧	968,855	⇩	836,559	⇩
May	893,039	⇩	850,502	⇩	791,095	⇩
June	786,918	⇩	981,050	⇧	771,976	⇩
July	1,056,573	⇧	854,835	⇩	873,543	⇧
August	806,719	⇩	1,002,597	⇧	599,246	⇩
September	863,089	⇧	814,513	⇩	1,011,288	⇧
October	873,208	⇧	931,193	⇧	1,059,308	⇧
November	923,402	⇧	769,352	⇩	812,659	⇩
December	854,090	⇩	1,031,897	⇧	1,006,745	⇧
Grand Total	10,388,246		11,018,124		10,657,962	

Show The Difference From Previous Years

In this example you will learn how to show the difference from the previous Year.

Below is the data that we will be using to create our Pivot Table:

	A CUSTOMER	B PRODUCTS	C SALES PERSON	D SALES REGION	E ORDER DATE	F SALES	G FINANCIAL YEAR
2	LONG ISLANDS INC	SOFT DRINKS	Michael Jackson	AMERICAS	4/13/2012	24,640	2012
3	LONG ISLANDS INC	SOFT DRINKS	Michael Jackson	AMERICAS	12/21/2012	24,640	2012
4	LONG ISLANDS INC	SOFT DRINKS	Michael Jackson	AMERICAS	12/24/2012	29,923	2012
5	LONG ISLANDS INC	SOFT DRINKS	Michael Jackson	AMERICAS	12/24/2012	66,901	2012
6	LONG ISLANDS INC	SOFT DRINKS	Michael Jackson	AMERICAS	12/29/2012	63,116	2012
7	LONG ISLANDS INC	SOFT DRINKS	Michael Jackson	AMERICAS	6/28/2012	38,281	2012
8	LONG ISLANDS INC	SOFT DRINKS	Michael Jackson	AMERICAS	6/28/2012	57,650	2012
9	LONG ISLANDS INC	SOFT DRINKS	Michael Jackson	AMERICAS	6/29/2012	90,967	2012
10	LONG ISLANDS INC	SOFT DRINKS	Michael Jackson	AMERICAS	6/29/2012	11,910	2012
11	LONG ISLANDS INC	SOFT DRINKS	Michael Jackson	AMERICAS	7/6/2012	59,531	2012
12	LONG ISLANDS INC	SOFT DRINKS	Michael Jackson	AMERICAS	7/6/2012	88,297	2012
13	LONG ISLANDS INC	SOFT DRINKS	Michael Jackson	AMERICAS	9/8/2012	87,868	2012
14	LONG ISLANDS INC	BOTTLES	Michael Jackson	AMERICAS	9/8/2012	95,527	2012
15	LONG ISLANDS INC	BOTTLES	Michael Jackson	AMERICAS	6/30/2012	90,599	2012
16	LONG ISLANDS INC	BOTTLES	Michael Jackson	AMERICAS	12/23/2012	17,030	2012
17	LONG ISLANDS INC	BOTTLES	Michael Jackson	AMERICAS	12/8/2012	65,026	2012
18	LONG ISLANDS INC	BOTTLES	Michael Jackson	AMERICAS	10/28/2012	57,379	2012
19	LONG ISLANDS INC	BOTTLES	Michael Jackson	AMERICAS	10/28/2012	34,338	2012

STEP 1: Insert a Pivot Table by clicking on your data and going to *Insert > Pivot Table*

STEP 2: In the Create PivotTable dialog box, Select **Table range** and then click on **New Worksheet**. Click **OK**.

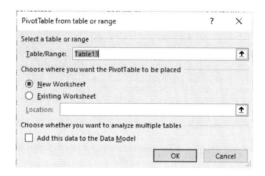

STEP 3: Drag these PivotTable Fields in the following areas below:

Rows: **SALES MONTH**
Columns: **FINANCIAL YEAR**
Values: **SALES** (drag it here twice, I explain why below)

STEP 4: Now click on the **Sum of SALES2** drop down and choose **Value Field Settings.**

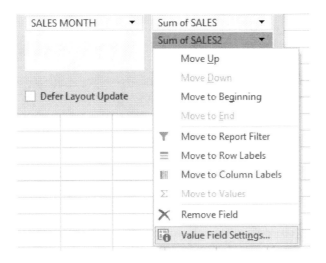

STEP 5: Now you need to select the **Show Values As** tab and from the drop-down choose the *Difference From*

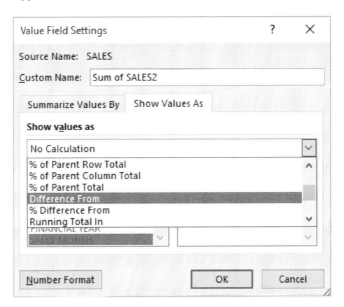

STEP 6: Select the following inside **Show Values As:**

Show values as: **Difference From**

Base Field: **FINANCIAL YEAR**

Base Item: **(previous)**

So it will read the "***Difference from the previous Financial Year***". Press OK.

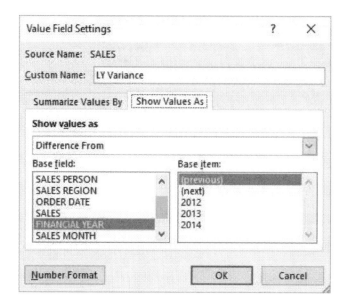

STEP 7: To format the values you need to select the Pivot Table and go to ***Pivot Table Analyze > Select > Entire Pivot Table***

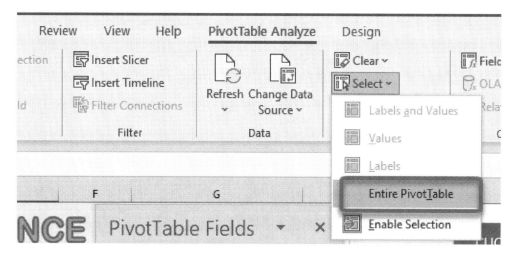

Then you need to once again go to ***Pivot Table Analyze > Select*** but this time select the ***Values***

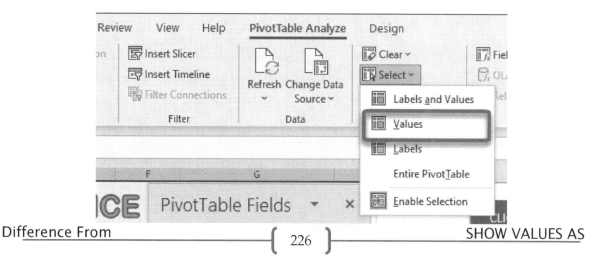

Now press **CTRL+1 to** bring up the ***Format Cell****s* dialogue box and make your formatting changes within here and press **OK.**

Pro tip: This will fix the number format permanently and any new Field that get added into the Pivot Table will have this format.

Format Cells
Number
Alignment
Font
Border
Fill
Protection
Category:
General
Number
Currency
Accounting
Date
Time
Percentage
Fraction
Scientific
Text
Special
Custom
Sample
836,559.00
Decimal places: 2
Symbol: None
Negative numbers:
-1,234.10
1,234.10
-1,234.10
-1,234.10
Currency formats are used for general monetary values. Use Accounting formats to align decimal points in a column.
OK
Cancel

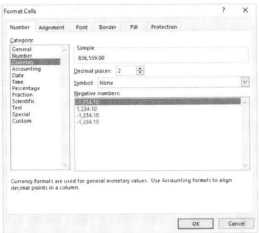

STEP 8: To change the **Sum of SALES2** name within the Pivot Table, you need to **click on a cell in the Pivot Table** that contains **Sum of SALES2** and manually make the change, and press **Enter**

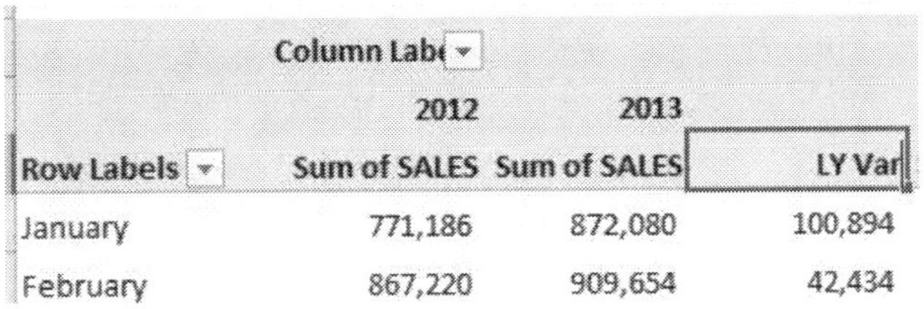

Column Labe
2012
2013
Row Labels
Sum of SALES
Sum of SALES
LY Var
January
771,186
872,080
100,894
February
867,220
909,654
42,434

STEP 9: You need to **select the whole column** that contains the empty values and **Right Click** and select **Hide.**

This column is empty as there are no previous values it can compare with. For example, the Year 2012 is the first year and has no data from the previous year to compare to.

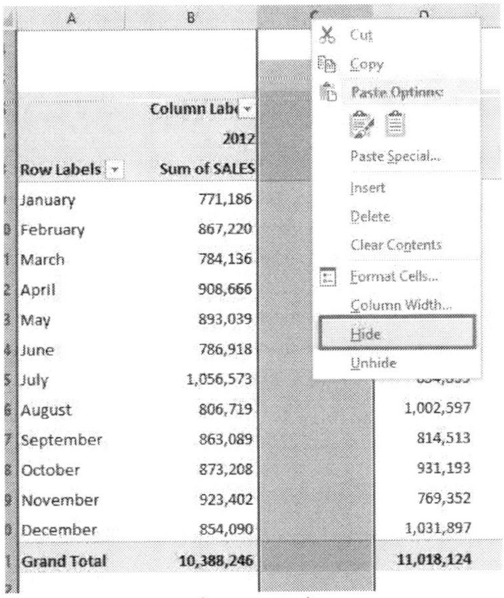

Cut
Copy
Paste Options:
Paste Special...
Insert
Delete
Clear Contents
Format Cells...
Column Width...
Hide
Unhide
Column Labe
2012
Row Labels
Sum of SALES
January
771,186
February
867,220
March
784,136
April
908,666
May
893,039
June
786,918
July
1,056,573
August
806,719
1,002,597
September
863,089
814,513
October
873,208
931,193
November
923,402
769,352
December
854,090
1,031,897
Grand Total
10,388,246
11,018,124

You now have your Pivot Table, all formatted and showing the **Difference from the previous Year (LY Variance)**:

Row Labels	2012 Sum of SALES	2013 Sum of SALES	LY Variance	2014 Sum of SALES	LY Variance
January	771,186	872,080	100,894	1,074,820	202,740
February	867,220	909,654	42,434	807,257	-102,397
March	784,136	1,031,596	247,460	1,013,466	-18,130
April	908,666	968,855	60,189	836,559	-132,296
May	893,039	850,502	-42,537	791,095	-59,407
June	786,918	981,050	194,132	771,976	-209,074
July	1,056,573	854,835	-201,738	873,543	18,708
August	806,719	1,002,597	195,878	599,246	-403,351
September	863,089	814,513	-48,576	1,011,288	196,775
October	873,208	931,193	57,985	1,059,308	128,115
November	923,402	769,352	-154,050	812,659	43,307
December	854,090	1,031,897	177,807	1,006,745	-25,152
Grand Total	10,388,246	11,018,124	629,878	10,657,962	-360,162

Percent % of Difference From

The **Percentage Difference From** calculation displays values as the percentage difference from the value of the **Base item** in the **Base field**.

I am sure that your boss has asked you to come up with a Year on Year variance or other type of time-based comparison. There are a couple of ways to deliver the answer – read on to see!

We *could* use formulas but that will take time to set up and you are exposed to errors!

The other method is the Pivot Table way—it's quicker and reduces errors!

Let's go!

STEP 1: Insert a new Pivot Table by clicking on your data and going to *Insert > Pivot Table > New Worksheet or Existing Worksheet*

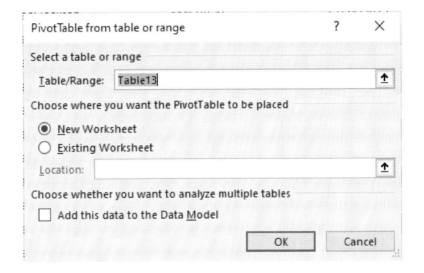

STEP 2: Drag these PivotTable Fields in the following areas below:

Rows: **SALES MONTH**
Columns: **FINANCIAL YEAR**
Values: **SALES** (drag it here twice, I explain why below)

STEP 3: Click the **Sum of SALES2** drop down and choose **Value Field Settings.**

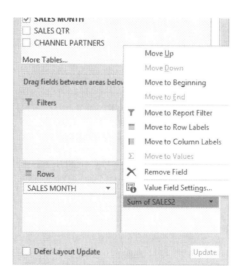

STEP 4: Select the following inside **Show Values As:**

Show values as: **% Difference From**

Base Field: **FINANCIAL YEAR**

Base Item: **(previous)**

This means that we will compute the Percentage Difference from the Previous Year.

Also change the **Custom Name** into *% Difference from Previous Year* to make it more presentable. Click **OK.**

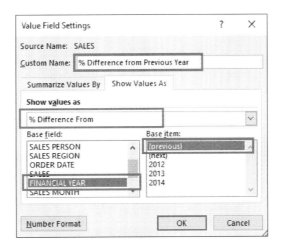

STEP 5: Notice that the *% Difference from Previous Year* data is in a decimal format that is hard to read:

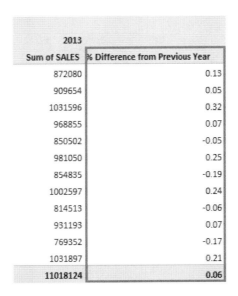

2013	
Sum of SALES	% Difference from Previous Year
872080	0.13
909654	0.05
1031596	0.32
968855	0.07
850502	-0.05
981050	0.25
854835	-0.19
1002597	0.24
814513	-0.06
931193	0.07
769352	-0.17
1031897	0.21
11018124	**0.06**

To format the *% Difference from Previous Year* column, click the second Sales Field's *% Difference from Previous Year* drop down and choose **Value Field Settings.**

The goal here is for us to transform numbers from a decimal format (e.g., 0.23), into a percentage format that is more readable (e.g., 23%).

STEP 6: Click the **Number Format** button.

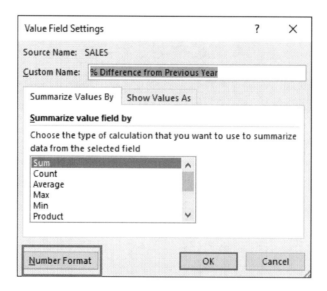

STEP 7: Inside the *Format Cells* dialog box, make your formatting changes within here and press **OK** twice.

In this example, we used the **Percentage** category to make our *% Difference from Previous Year* numbers become more readable.

STEP 8: Right click on the columns with the empty columns and click **Hide**.

This column is empty as there are no previous values it can compare with. For example, the Year 2012 is the first year and has no previous year to compare to.

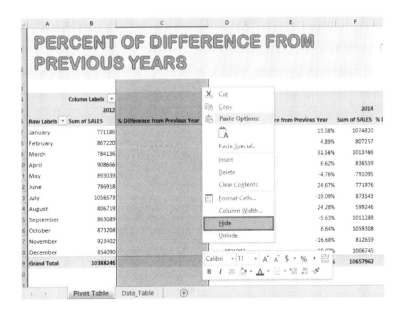

You now have your Pivot Table, showing the **% Difference from Previous Year** (e.g., 2013 vs. 2012, 2014 vs. 2013).

You can see that each red box is the percentage of difference computed against the previous year (e.g., Year 2013 vs. Year 2012, and Year 2014 vs. Year 2013).

Column Labels						
	2012	2013		2014		Total Sum of SALES
Row Labels	Sum of SALES	Sum of SALES	% Difference from Previous Year	Sum of SALES	% Difference from Previous Year	
January	771186	872080	13.08%	1074820	23.25%	2718086
February	867220	909654	4.89%	807257	-11.26%	2584131
March	784136	1031596	31.56%	1013466	-1.76%	2829198
April	908666	968855	6.62%	836559	-13.65%	2714080
May	893039	850502	-4.76%	791095	-6.98%	2534636
June	786918	981050	24.67%	771976	-21.31%	2539944
July	1056573	854835	-19.09%	873543	2.19%	2784951
August	806719	1002597	24.28%	599246	-40.23%	2408562
September	863089	814513	-5.63%	1011288	24.16%	2688890
October	873208	931193	6.64%	1059308	13.76%	2863709
November	923402	769352	-16.68%	812659	5.63%	2505413
December	854090	1031897	20.82%	1006745	-2.44%	2892732
Grand Total	10388246	11018124	6.06%	10657962	-3.27%	32064332

Running Total In

The **Running Total In** calculation displays the value for successive items in the **Base field** as a running total.

A Running Total In is the accumulation of values over a certain period, like days, months, and years. It is sometimes referred to as to-Date analysis.

A Running Total In takes a period's values, then adds a second period, then a third and so forth, successively accumulating values up to the end of the defined time period (or interval).

In this example we will show you the Running Total In using a values format.

Here is our current Pivot Table setup, with the Sum of SALES being shown for each Month-Year combination.

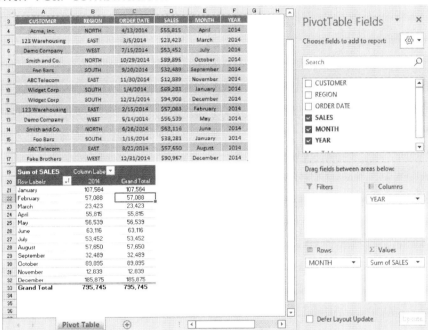

STEP 1: Click on **Sum of Sales** and select **Value Field Settings**

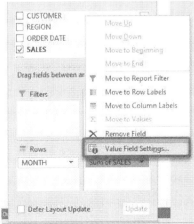

STEP 2: Select the following inside **Show Values As**:

Show values as: **Running Total in**

Base Field: **MONTH**

Click **OK**.

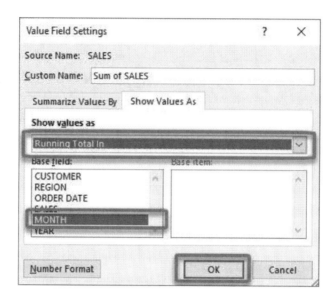

The values are now shown as **Running Totals** throughout the months!

Sum of SALES	Column Labels	
Row Labels	2014	Grand Total
January	107,564	107,564
February	164,652	164,652
March	188,075	188,075
April	243,890	243,890
May	300,429	300,429
June	363,545	363,545
July	416,997	416,997
August	474,647	474,647
September	507,136	507,136
October	597,031	597,031
November	609,870	609,870
December	795,745	795,745
Grand Total		

Running Total in %

The **Running Total In** calculation displays the value as a percentage for successive items in the **Base field** that are displayed as a running total.

A Running Total In is the accumulation of values over a certain period, like days, months, and years. It is sometimes referred to as to-Date analysis.

A Running Total In takes a period's values, then adds a second period, then a third and so forth, successively accumulating values up to the end of the defined time period (or interval).

In this example we will show you the Running Total In using a percentage format.

STEP 1: Insert a Pivot Table by clicking in your data and going to *Insert > Pivot Table* and choose to insert it in a **New or Existing Worksheet**

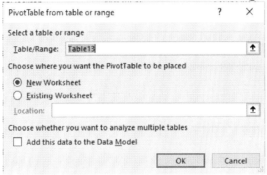

STEP 2: Drag these PivotTable Fields in the following areas below:
Rows: **SALES MONTH**
Columns: **FINANCIAL YEAR**
Values: **SALES** (drag it here twice, I explain why below)

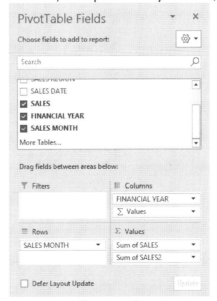

STEP 3: Right Click on a Totals cell and choose **Remove Grand Total**

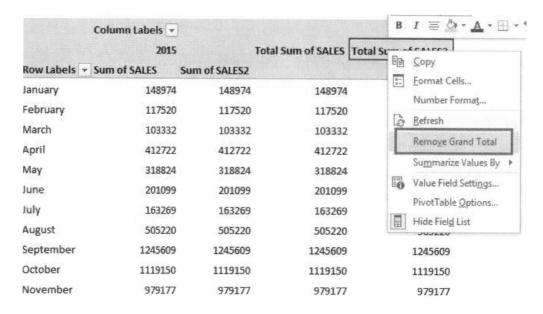

STEP 4: Right Click on a **Sum of SALES2 value** in the Pivot Table and select *Show Values As > % Running Total In > Base Field: SALES MONTH*

STEP 5: You can manually change the name of the **Sum of SALES2** Field by clicking in the cell's title within the Pivot Table and typing **YTD%.**

YTD%
2.20%
3.93%

You now have your % Running Total In values in a separate column, all the way to 100%.

Row Labels	Sum of SALES	YTD%
	Column Labels	
	2015	
January	148974	2.20%
February	117520	3.93%
March	103332	5.45%
April	412722	11.54%
May	318824	16.24%
June	201099	19.20%
July	163269	21.61%
August	505220	29.06%
September	1245609	47.42%
October	1119150	63.92%
November	979177	78.36%
December	1468002	100.00%
Grand Total	**6782898**	

Rank Smallest to Largest

The **Rank Smallest to Largest** calculation displays the rank of selected values in a specific Field. The smallest value will rank as 1 with each number thereafter successively ranked in order from smallest to largest.

This allows you to quickly eyeball your data and clearly see the smallest value(s) in your Pivot Table.

STEP 1: Insert a new Pivot Table by clicking on your data and going to *Insert > Pivot Table > New Worksheet or Existing Worksheet*

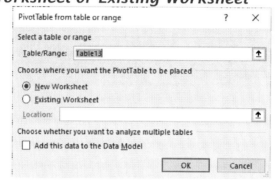

STEP 2: Drag these PivotTable Fields in the following areas below:
Rows: **SALES MONTH**
Columns: **FINANCIAL YEAR**
Values: **SALES** (drag it here twice, I explain why below)

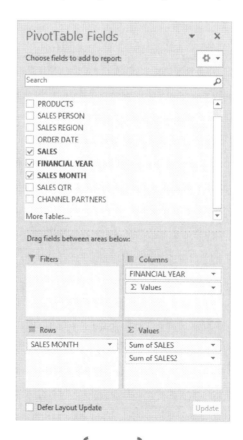

STEP 3: Click on the **Sum of SALES2** drop down and choose **Value Field Settings.**

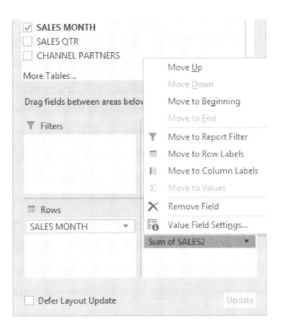

STEP 4: Select the following inside **Show Values As:**

Show values as: **Rank Smallest to Largest**

Base Field: **SALES MONTH**

This means that we will rank the Sales Values by the Sales Month (where Rank 1 is the Smallest).

Also change the **Custom Name** into *Rank Smallest to Largest* to make it more presentable. Click **OK.**

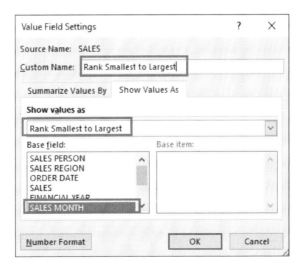

You now have your Pivot Table, showing the **Smallest to Largest Rankings for each Month.**

You can see that each red box highlights the ranking for each individual year (for Years 2012, 2013, and 2014) and the Total Rankings.

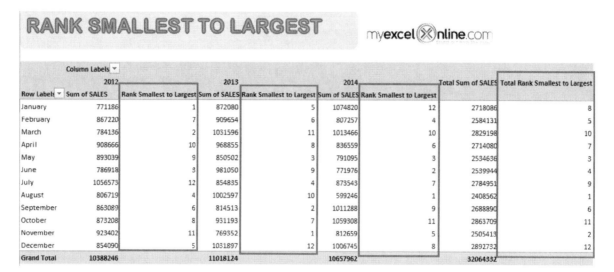

Row Labels	2012 Sum of SALES	Rank Smallest to Largest	2013 Sum of SALES	Rank Smallest to Largest	2014 Sum of SALES	Rank Smallest to Largest	Total Sum of SALES	Total Rank Smallest to Largest
January	771186	1	872080	5	1074820	12	2718086	8
February	867220	7	909654	6	807257	4	2584131	5
March	784136	2	1031596	11	1013466	10	2829198	10
April	908666	10	968855	8	836559	6	2714080	7
May	893039	9	850502	3	791095	3	2534636	3
June	786918	3	981050	9	771976	2	2539944	4
July	1056573	12	854835	4	873543	7	2784951	9
August	806719	4	1002597	10	599246	1	2408562	1
September	863089	6	814513	2	1011288	9	2688890	6
October	873208	8	931193	7	1059308	11	2863709	11
November	923402	11	769352	1	812659	5	2505413	2
December	854090	5	1031897	12	1006745	8	2892732	12
Grand Total	10388246		11018124		10657962		32064332	

Rank Largest to Smallest

The **Rank Largest to Smallest** calculation displays the rank of selected values in a specific field. The largest item in the field starts with a rank of 1, with each successive value increasing in rank thereafter.

This allows you to quickly eyeball your data and clearly see the largest value(s) in your Pivot Table.

STEP 1: Insert a new Pivot Table by clicking on your data and going to *Insert > Pivot Table > New Worksheet or Existing Worksheet*

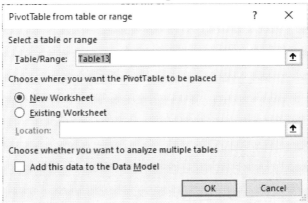

STEP 2: Drag these Pivot Table Fields in the following areas below:
Rows: **SALES MONTH**
Columns: **FINANCIAL YEAR**
Values: **SALES** (drag it here twice, I explain why below)

STEP 3: Click the second **SALES** Field's (**Sum of SALES2**) drop down and choose **Value Field Settings**

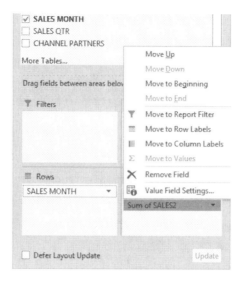

STEP 4: Select the following inside **Show Values As:**

Show values as: **Rank Largest to Smallest**

Base Field: **SALES MONTH**

This means that we will rank the Sales Values by the Sales Month (where Rank 1 is the Largest).

Also change the **Custom Name** into *Rank Largest to Smallest* to make it more presentable. Click **OK.**

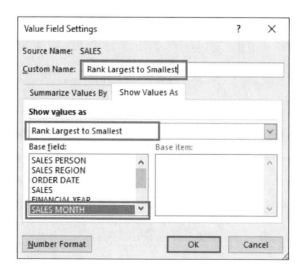

You now have your Pivot Table, showing the **Rank Largest to Smallest.**

You can see that each red box is the ranking for each year (for Years 2012, 2013, and 2014) and the Total Rankings.

RANK LARGEST TO SMALLEST

myexcel(X)nline.com

Row Labels	2012 Sum of SALES	2012 Rank Largest to Smallest	2013 Sum of SALES	2013 Rank Largest to Smallest	2014 Sum of SALES	2014 Rank Largest to Smallest	Total Sum of SALES	Total Rank Largest to Smallest
January	771186	12	872080	8	1074820	1	2718086	5
February	867220	6	909654	7	807257	9	2584131	8
March	784136	11	1031596	2	1013466	3	2829198	3
April	908666	3	968855	5	836559	7	2714080	6
May	893039	4	850502	10	791095	10	2534636	10
June	786918	10	981050	4	771976	11	2539944	9
July	1056573	1	854835	9	873543	6	2784951	4
August	806719	9	1002597	3	599246	12	2408562	12
September	863089	7	814513	11	1011288	4	2688890	7
October	873208	5	931193	6	1059308	2	2863709	2
November	923402	2	769352	12	812659	8	2505413	11
December	854090	8	1031897	1	1006745	5	2892732	1
Grand Total	10388246		11018124		10657962		32064332	

Column Labels ▼

Index

The Index calculates values as follows:

((value in cell) x (Grand Total of Grand Totals)) / ((Grand Row Total) x (Grand Column Total))

The Index tells you the **relative importance of a cell within a column**.

It can help you make decisions if, for example, you want to increase the price of your product. The Index will be able to identify the item that will be most impacted. In other words, the greater the index, the greater the impact.

STEP 1: Here is our Pivot Table. The two tables are identical.

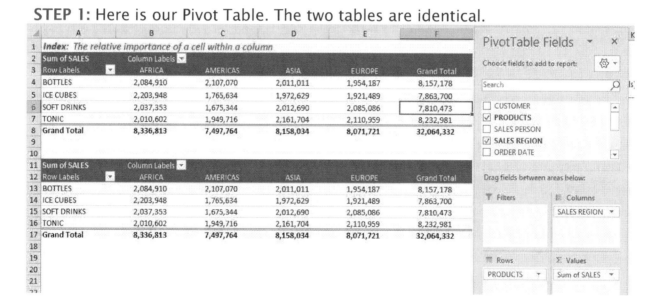

STEP 2: Go to the second Pivot Table, and click on the arrow of **Sum of SALES** and select **Value Field Settings**

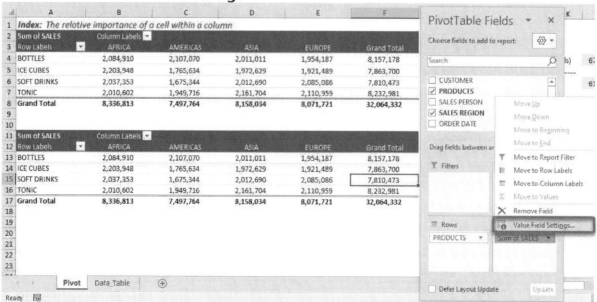

STEP 3: Select *Show values as > Index.* Click **OK**

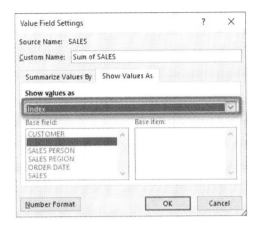

STEP 4: Now we have our **Index** values!

The higher value means that it is the most important value for that column.

For example, **ICE CUBES** have the greatest impact for the **AFRICA** region in terms of sales, as do **BOTTLES** for the **AMERICAS** region....

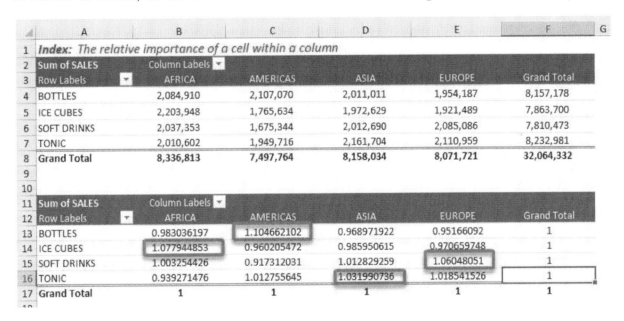

	A	B	C	D	E	F	G
1	*Index: The relative importance of a cell within a column*						
2	Sum of SALES	Column Labels					
3	Row Labels	AFRICA	AMERICAS	ASIA	EUROPE	Grand Total	
4	BOTTLES	2,084,910	2,107,070	2,011,011	1,954,187	8,157,178	
5	ICE CUBES	2,203,948	1,765,634	1,972,629	1,921,489	7,863,700	
6	SOFT DRINKS	2,037,353	1,675,344	2,012,690	2,085,086	7,810,473	
7	TONIC	2,010,602	1,949,716	2,161,704	2,110,959	8,232,981	
8	Grand Total	8,336,813	7,497,764	8,158,034	8,071,721	32,064,332	
9							
10							
11	Sum of SALES	Column Labels					
12	Row Labels	AFRICA	AMERICAS	ASIA	EUROPE	Grand Total	
13	BOTTLES	0.983036197	1.104662102	0.968971922	0.95166092	1	
14	ICE CUBES	1.077944853	0.960205472	0.985950615	0.970659748	1	
15	SOFT DRINKS	1.003254426	0.917312031	1.012829259	1.06048051	1	
16	TONIC	0.939271476	1.012755645	1.031990736	1.018541526	1	
17	Grand Total	1	1	1	1	1	

Now let's do a quick manual calculation to show you how Index is calculated.

First you need to turn off the GETPIVOTDATA feature by clicking on the Pivot Table and selecting **PivotTable Analyze > Options > uncheck Generate GetPivotData.**

STEP 5: In cell L4 enter the = sign and select the **BOTTLES Sales for AMERICAS** then multiply it by the **Grand Total**.

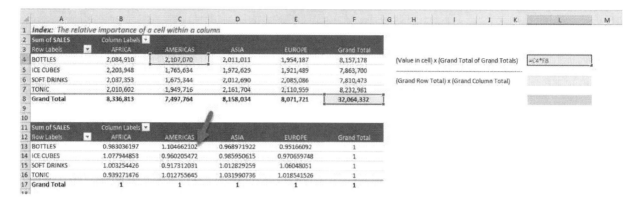

STEP 6: Multiply the **Grand Row Total of BOTTLES** and the **Grand Column Total of AMERICAS**.

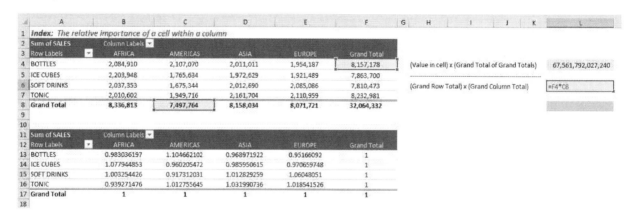

STEP 7: Divide them and you will get the Index!

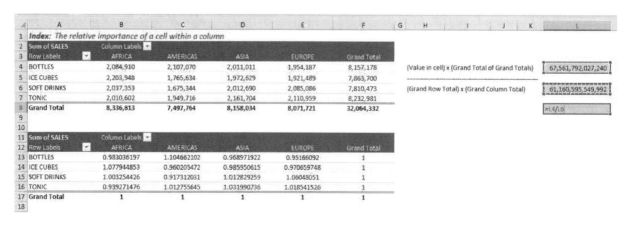

The values are exactly the same!

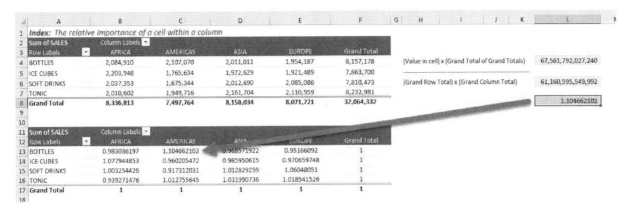

Index: The relative importance of a cell within a column					
Sum of SALES	Column Labels				
Row Labels	AFRICA	AMERICAS	ASIA	EUROPE	Grand Total
BOTTLES	2,084,910	2,107,070	2,011,011	1,954,187	8,157,178
ICE CUBES	2,203,948	1,765,634	1,972,629	1,921,489	7,863,700
SOFT DRINKS	2,037,353	1,675,344	2,012,690	2,085,086	7,810,473
TONIC	2,010,602	1,949,716	2,161,704	2,110,959	8,232,981
Grand Total	8,336,813	7,497,764	8,158,034	8,071,721	32,064,332

Sum of SALES	Column Labels				
Row Labels	AFRICA	AMERICAS	ASIA	EUROPE	Grand Total
BOTTLES	0.983036197	1.104662102	0.968971922	0.95166092	1
ICE CUBES	1.077944853	0.960205472	0.985950615	0.970659748	1
SOFT DRINKS	1.003254426	0.917312031	1.012829259	1.06048051	1
TONIC	0.939271476	1.012755645	1.031990736	1.018541526	1
Grand Total	1	1	1	1	1

(Value in cell) x (Grand Total of Grand Totals)   67,561,792,027,240

(Grand Row Total) x (Grand Column Total)   61,160,595,549,992

1.104662102

GROUPING

Group Dates by Month & Year

Before I was a Pivot Table guru, I used to download rows of daily sales and group them into a report using Formulas.

Grouping dates would take a ton of effort using Formulas, as I would have to:

- Extract the Month and Year from each transactional date; AND

- Manually group them together to get the Total Sales for each Month and Year. It was PAINFUL & SLOW!

Thankfully, Pivot Tables have a way to do this, which is much quicker and reduces the risks of making errors! (I wish I had known this back then.)

In this example we will group our **ORDER DATE** by Month and Years and then drop our **SALES** to get the Total Sales for each Month & Year.

STEP 1: Insert a new Pivot Table by clicking on your data and going to *Insert > Pivot Table > New Worksheet.* Press OK.

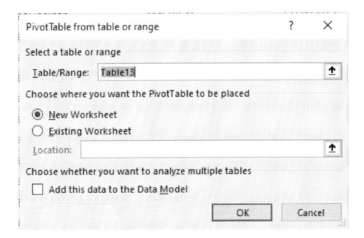

STEP 2: In the **Rows** section put in the **ORDER DATE** Field.

Notice that in Microsoft 365 it will automatically Group the **ORDER DATE** into **Years & Quarters**.

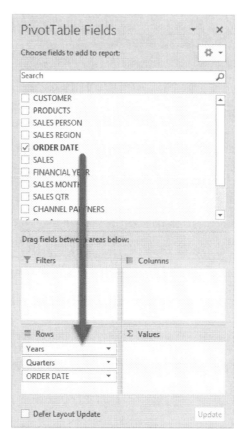

STEP 3: Right-click on any row in your Pivot Table and select **Group**.

STEP 4: We need to deselect **Quarters** and make sure only **Months** and **Years** are selected (which will be highlighted in blue).

This will group our dates by the **Months** and **Years** only. Click **OK.**

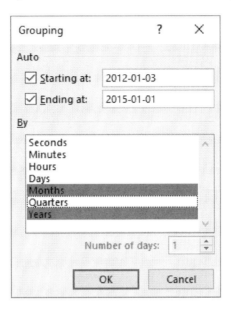

STEP 5: In the **VALUES** area put in the **SALES** Field. This will now show the **Total Sales** for each Month & Year.

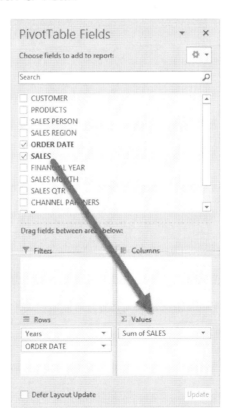

This is how you can easily create a Pivot Table grouping dates by Month & Year!

Row Labels	Sum of SALES
⊟ 2012	
Jan	303393
Feb	470022
Mar	549089
Apr	346341
May	452180
Jun	878102
Jul	729880
Aug	573632
Sep	1546863
Oct	1756156
Nov	1629628
Dec	1152960
⊟ 2013	
Jan	548468
Feb	612361
Mar	362942
Apr	1520822

Group Dates by Weeks

There are many possibilities when grouping dates in Pivot Tables. Did you know you can group dates by weeks?!

To group dates by weeks, follow the steps below:

STEP 1: Right click on one of the dates in the Pivot Table and select **Group**.

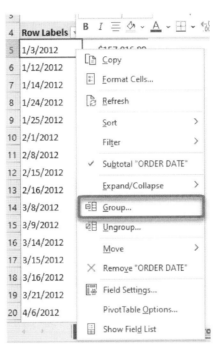

STEP 2: Select the **Days** option (highlighted in blue) from the list and deselect any other options.

STEP 3: In the **Number of days** section, type 7. Press OK.

The dates will be grouped into weeks.

Row Labels ▾	Sum of SALES
1/3/2012 - 1/9/2012	$157,016.00
1/10/2012 - 1/16/2012	$74,746.00
1/24/2012 - 1/30/2012	$71,631.00
1/31/2012 - 2/6/2012	$177,159.00
2/7/2012 - 2/13/2012	$98,452.00
2/14/2012 - 2/20/2012	$194,411.00
3/6/2012 - 3/12/2012	$240,596.00
3/13/2012 - 3/19/2012	$242,589.00
3/20/2012 - 3/26/2012	$65,904.00
4/3/2012 - 4/9/2012	$272,943.00
4/10/2012 - 4/16/2012	$73,398.00
5/1/2012 - 5/7/2012	$26,804.00
5/8/2012 - 5/14/2012	$244,506.00
5/15/2012 - 5/21/2012	$180,870.00
5/29/2012 - 6/4/2012	$128,060.00
6/5/2012 - 6/11/2012	$131,514.00

Group Sales by Weeks Starting on a Monday

Ever faced a situation when you were asked to prepare a **Weekly Sales Report**?

Creating a Weekly Report is super easy in Excel by using **Pivot Table**

Grouping. What if your boss wanted **all the weeks to start on a Monday**?

I will show you how easy this report is to create.

STEP 1: Insert a new Pivot Table by clicking on your data and going to *Insert > Pivot Table > New Worksheet.*

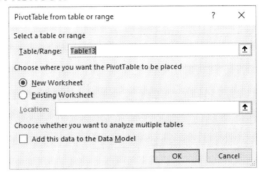

STEP 2: In the **Rows** area put in the **ORDER DATE** field.

Notice that in Microsoft 365 it automatically groups dates into Years & Quarters.

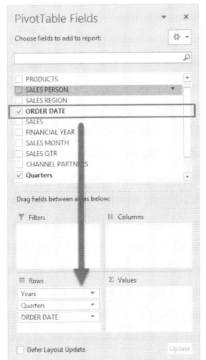

STEP 3: Right-click on any date in your Pivot Table and select **Group.**

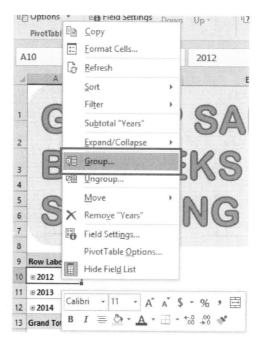

STEP 4: Notice that it was able to determine our minimum and maximum dates based on our ORDER DATE data source. However, we need our weeks to start on a **Monday**.

Our starting date is **January 3, 2012**. Let us have a quick check in our calendar:

We can see that the nearest Monday before that date is **January 2, 2012**.

Deselect **Months, Quarters,** and **Years** and make sure only **Days** is selected (highlighted in blue).

Set the **Number of days** to 7.

Set the **Start Date** to **2012-01-02** i.e. On a Monday.

Click **OK.**

STEP 5: In the **Values** area put in the **SALES** Field.

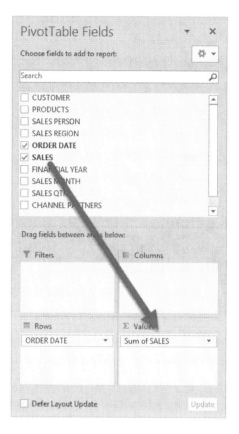

STEP 6: This will give us the Total Sales for each 7-day date range we have defined starting every Monday.

We can now **format our Sales numbers** into something more presentable.

Row Labels	Sum of SALES
2012-01-02 - 2012-01-08	157016
2012-01-09 - 2012-01-15	74746
2012-01-23 - 2012-01-29	71631
2012-01-30 - 2012-02-05	177159
2012-02-06 - 2012-02-12	98452
2012-02-13 - 2012-02-19	194411
2012-03-05 - 2012-03-11	240596
2012-03-12 - 2012-03-18	242589
2012-03-19 - 2012-03-25	65904
2012-04-02 - 2012-04-08	272943
2012-04-09 - 2012-04-15	73398
2012-04-30 - 2012-05-06	26804
2012-05-07 - 2012-05-13	244506
2012-05-14 - 2012-05-20	180870
2012-05-28 - 2012-06-03	128060
2012-06-04 - 2012-06-10	131514

Click the **Sum of SALES** drop down and select **Value Field Settings.**

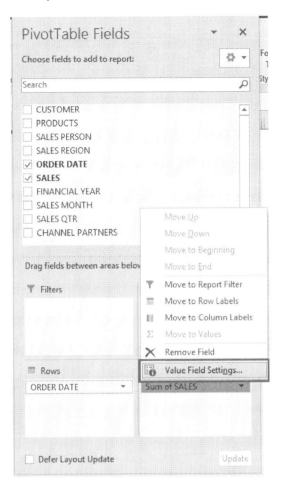

STEP 7: Select **Number Format**

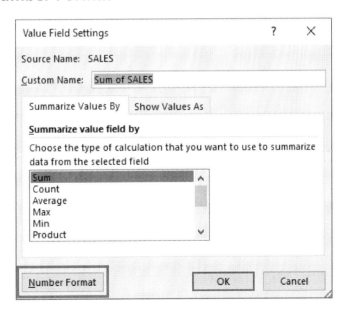

STEP 8: Select **Currency.** Click **OK.**

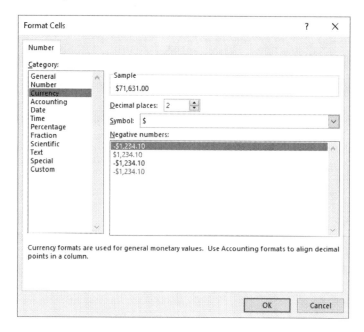

We now have our **Total Sales for each 7-day period starting on Mondays**!

Row Labels	Sum of SALES
2012-01-02 - 2012-01-08	$157,016.00
2012-01-09 - 2012-01-15	$74,746.00
2012-01-23 - 2012-01-29	$71,631.00
2012-01-30 - 2012-02-05	$177,159.00
2012-02-06 - 2012-02-12	$98,452.00
2012-02-13 - 2012-02-19	$194,411.00
2012-03-05 - 2012-03-11	$240,596.00
2012-03-12 - 2012-03-18	$242,589.00
2012-03-19 - 2012-03-25	$65,904.00
2012-04-02 - 2012-04-08	$272,943.00
2012-04-09 - 2012-04-15	$73,398.00
2012-04-30 - 2012-05-06	$26,804.00
2012-05-07 - 2012-05-13	$244,506.00
2012-05-14 - 2012-05-20	$180,870.00
2012-05-28 - 2012-06-03	$128,060.00
2012-06-04 - 2012-06-10	$131,514.00
2012-06-11 - 2012-06-17	$142,867.00
2012-06-18 - 2012-06-24	$126,802.00
2012-06-25 - 2012-07-01	$348,859.00
2012-07-02 - 2012-07-08	$244,037.00
2012-07-09 - 2012-07-15	$283,849.00
2012-07-23 - 2012-07-29	$201,994.00
2012-07-30 - 2012-08-05	$162,220.00
2012-08-06 - 2012-08-12	$259,825.00
2012-08-13 - 2012-08-19	$103,309.00

Control Automatic Grouping

In Excel 2016, a new feature was introduced where automatic grouping of Date/Time fields was enforced.

This feature will group your Date field into Months, Quarters and Years automatically.

You can easily turn off this automatic grouping feature in Excel. To do that, follow the steps below:

STEP 1: Go to **File Tab** > **Options**

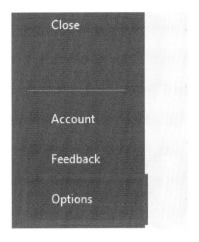

STEP 2: In the Excel Options dialog box, click **Data** in the categories on the left.

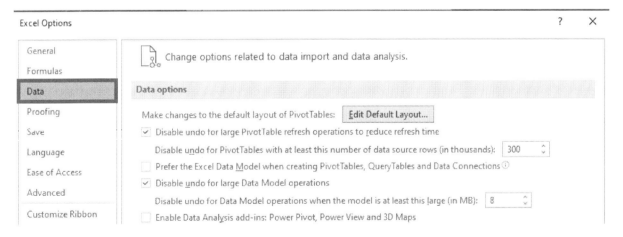

STEP 3: Check **Disable automatic grouping of Date/Time columns in PivotTables** checkbox. Click **OK**.

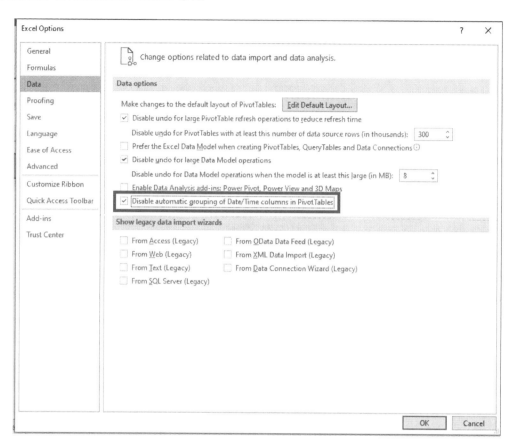

Next time you drag a Date field to a Rows/Columns area in the Pivot Table, you will have to manually group these Dates.

If you'd like to go back to the default grouping behavior, simply deselect this option from the Excel Options dialog box.

Group by Sales Ranges

With Pivot Tables you can group your Sales figures, which will aggregate your data and give you more analytical power!

STEP 1: Let us start with an empty Pivot Table. Drag the **SALES Field** to the **Rows area**

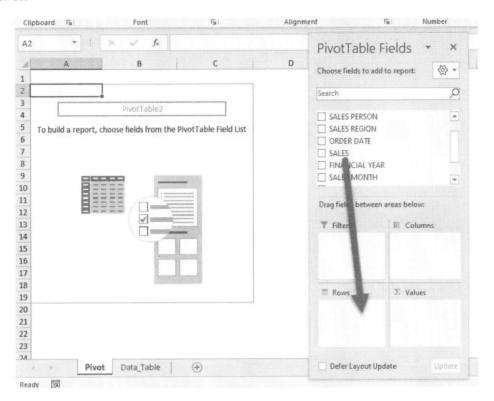

STEP 2: Right click on any **SALES** value and select **Group**

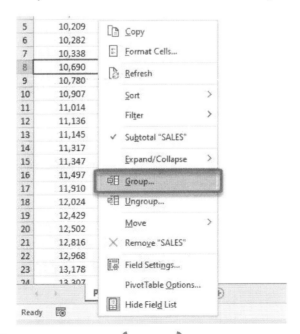

STEP 3: Let us set our **Grouping** to:

Starting at: 10,000

Ending at: 100,000

By: 10,000

Click **OK.**

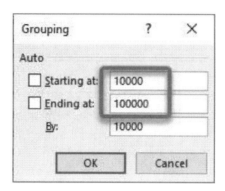

STEP 4: Now drag the **SALES** Field to the **Values** area twice.

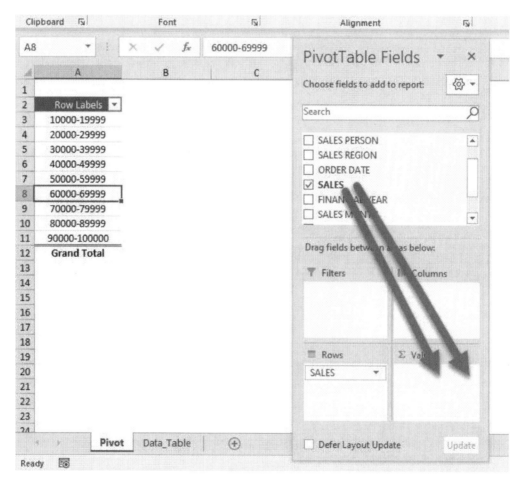

STEP 5: We will get 2 similar columns but we want to show the **Sum** and **Count**.

Select the first **Count of SALES** drop down pick **Value Field Settings.**

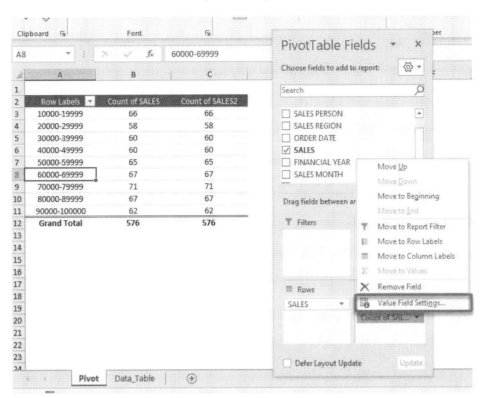

STEP 6: Select **Sum** and click **OK.**

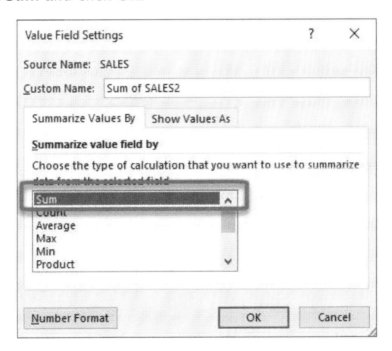

Now we can analyze the data based on the grouped sales figures!

We can see that for the Sales group between $10,000-$19,999 there were a total of 66 Sales transactions which totaled $991,398.

The most Sales transactions occurred for the Sales group between $70,000-$79,999 with 71.

The most Sales occurred for the Sales group between $90,000-$99,999 with $5,875,427.

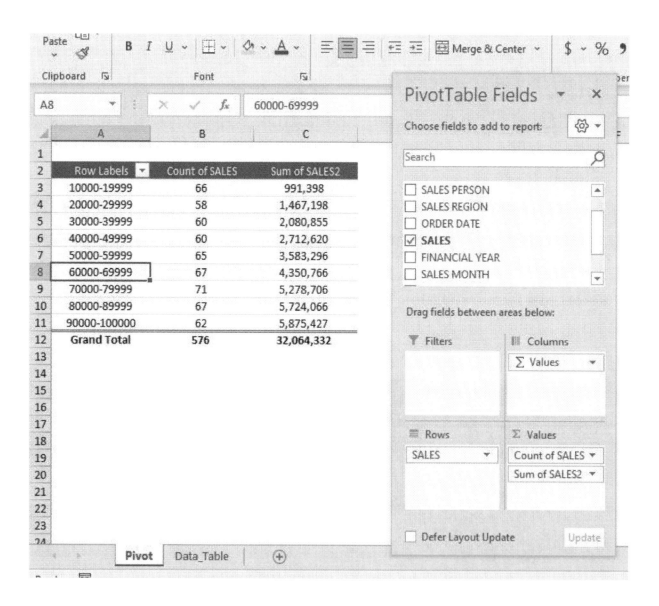

Group by Text Fields

Grouping by numerical data or dates is straightforward to do in Pivot Tables as we have shown in previous tips within this chapter.

Most Excel users don't know that you can also group text Fields as

well! For example, we want to create these groupings:

- **West** - Americas
- **East** - Asia
- **Central** – Africa, Europe

Here is our current Pivot Table setup:

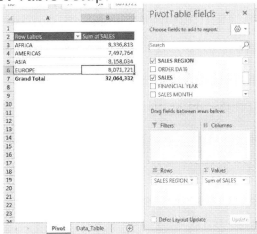

STEP 1: Let us group **Africa** and **Europe** together.

Hold the **CTRL** key while clicking on both AFRICA and EUROPE. **Right-click** on any of the two items and select **Group.**

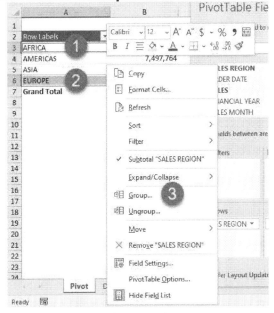

STEP 2: Now we have our grouping by Text.

Click on each of the group headers and rename each one of them to: **Central, West, East** and press **ENTER** after each name change.

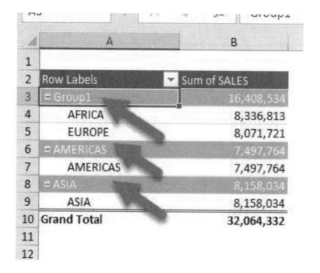

We have the updated group names! Notice that the **SALES REGION2** was added automatically in the **Rows area** because of this new grouping.

Click on the arrow beside the **SALES REGION2** so that we can give this a better name.

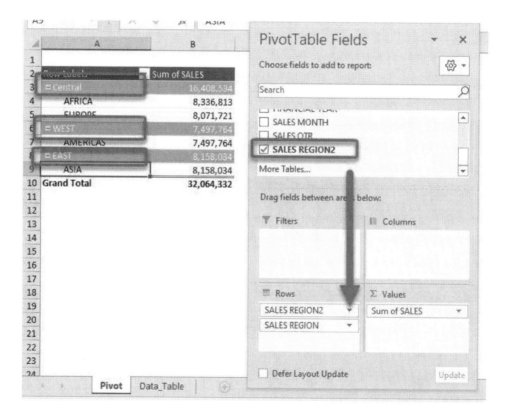

STEP 3: Set the **Custom Name** to *NEW REGIONS*. Click **OK**

Your new text groups are now all set!

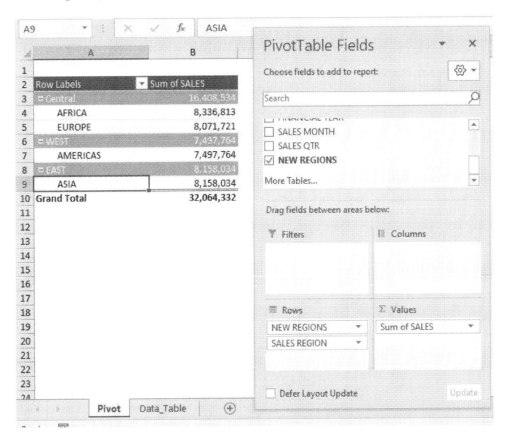

Group by Time

If you ever want to show the Sales numbers by the hour, so that you can understand which **part of the day had the best sales and which had the worst**, you can using Grouping by Time.

Below I will give you a detailed guide on the following methods:

- Group by hour

- Group by custom time interval

Let's look at each one of these methods using a real-life example!

Group by Hour

In the example below we have Sales data. We want to get the **SALES** grouped by **TIME OF SALE**.

	C	D	E	F	G	H	I	J
	SALES PERSON	SALES REGION	ORDER DATE	SALES	FINANCIAL YEAR	SALES MONTH	SALES QTR	TIME OF SALE
2	Michael Jackson	AMERICAS	4/13/2012	24,640	2012	January	Q1	09:36:00
3	Michael Jackson	AMERICAS	12/21/2012	24,640	2012	February	Q1	11:31:12
4	Michael Jackson	AMERICAS	12/24/2012	29,923	2012	March	Q1	13:49:26
5	Michael Jackson	AMERICAS	12/24/2012	66,901	2012	April	Q2	16:35:20
6	Michael Jackson	AMERICAS	12/29/2012	63,116	2012	May	Q2	19:54:24
7	Michael Jackson	AMERICAS	6/28/2012	38,281	2012	June	Q2	23:53:16
8	Michael Jackson	AMERICAS	6/28/2012	57,650	2012	July	Q3	09:36:00
9	Michael Jackson	AMERICAS	6/29/2012	90,967	2012	August	Q3	11:31:12
10	Michael Jackson	AMERICAS	6/29/2012	11,910	2012	September	Q3	13:49:26
11	Michael Jackson	AMERICAS	7/6/2012	59,531	2012	October	Q4	16:35:20
12	Michael Jackson	AMERICAS	7/6/2012	88,297	2012	November	Q4	12:54:24
13	Michael Jackson	AMERICAS	9/8/2012	87,868	2012	December	Q4	23:53:16
14	Michael Jackson	AMERICAS	9/8/2012	95,527	2012	January	Q1	09:36:00
15	Michael Jackson	AMERICAS	6/30/2012	90,599	2012	February	Q1	11:31:12
16	Michael Jackson	AMERICAS	12/23/2012	17,030	2012	March	Q1	12:49:26

STEP 1: Insert a new Pivot Table by clicking on your data and going to *Insert > Pivot Table > New Worksheet or Existing Worksheet*

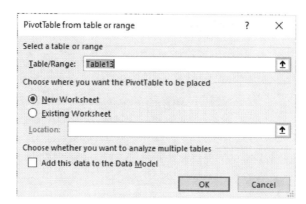

STEP 2: In the **Rows** area put in the **TIME OF SALE** Field.

Notice Excel will automatically Group the **TIME OF SALE** Field into **Hours & Minutes.**

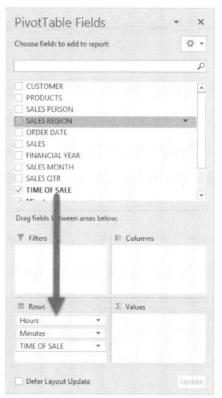

STEP 3: Right-click on any Row item in your Pivot Table and select **Group.**

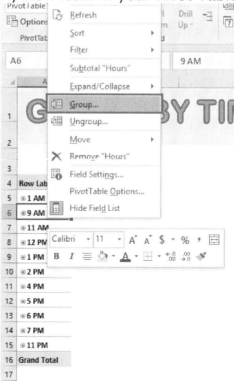

STEP 4: Excel was able to determine our time range (minimum time and maximum time).

Make sure only **Hours** is selected (blue highlight). Click **OK**.

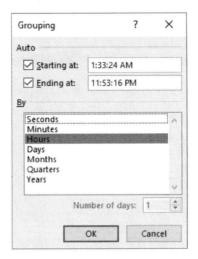

STEP 5: In the **Values** area put in the **SALES** Field. This will give us the Total Sales for each Hourly range we defined in the previous step:

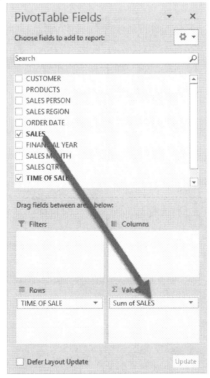

Now we have our Pivot Table grouped by Hours. So around 1 AM there were $1,182,194 of Sales. There were no sales between 2 AM and 8 AM.

Row Labels	Sum of SALES
1 AM	1182194
9 AM	4186208
11 AM	3724823
12 PM	2634464
1 PM	4206843
2 PM	1502861
4 PM	4074928
5 PM	1316829
6 PM	1267870
7 PM	2534636
11 PM	5432676
Grand Total	**32064332**

STEP 6: Click the **Sum of SALES** and select **Value Field Settings** to improve the formatting.

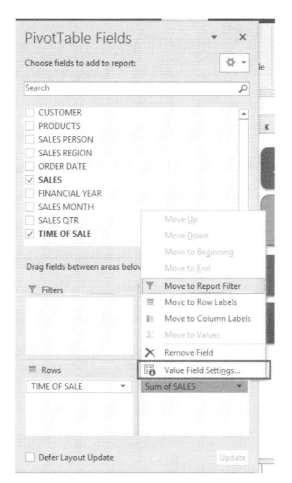

STEP 7: Select **Number Format**

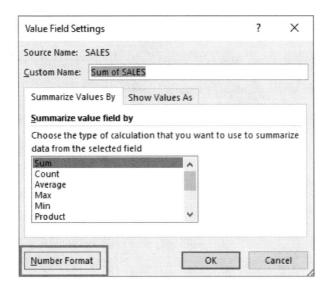

STEP 8: Select **Currency.** Click **OK.**

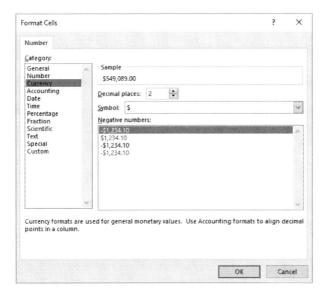

We now have our **Total Sales** for each hourly period formatted as currency!

Row Labels	Sum of SALES
1 AM	$1,182,194.00
9 AM	$4,186,208.00
11 AM	$3,724,823.00
12 PM	$2,634,464.00
1 PM	$4,206,843.00
2 PM	$1,502,861.00
4 PM	$4,074,928.00
5 PM	$1,316,829.00
6 PM	$1,267,870.00
7 PM	$2,534,636.00
11 PM	$5,432,676.00
Grand Total	**$32,064,332.00**

Bonus Tip: You can Right Click on any **SALES** value in the Pivot Table and select **Sort > Largest to Smallest**. This will show you the part of the day that has the most sales at the top. Give it a try!

Group by Custom Time Interval

There might be a time when you want to review the **data based on a specific time block instead of a standard 1-hour interval.**

For example, you want the Pivot Table data to **be grouped by 15 minutes or 2 hours** or any other custom time interval.

You can easily do that using Excel's **FLOOR function.**

Before we learn how to group by 15 minutes, let's first understand the FLOOR function and its use!

The FLOOR Function can be **used to round a number down to the nearest multiple of significance.**

The Syntax of the FLOOR function is :

=FLOOR (number, significance)

where

- **number** - The numeric value you want to round
- **significance** - The multiple to which you want to round.

Luckily, Excel treats dates and times as numbers.

The integer portion of the number represents the day and the decimal portion represents the time.

The FLOOR function also **accepts an argument in "hh: mm" format** and it easily converts them to decimal values.

For example, Excel converts 00:15 into 0.0104166666666667, which is the decimal value of 15 minutes, and rounds it using that value.

Now, let's take the same example and create an Excel Pivot Table group by 15 minutes.

STEP 1: Insert a new column in the data set. Name the column **FLOOR**.

	CUSTOMER	PRODUCTS	SALES PERSON	SALES REGION	ORDER DATE	SALES	FINANCIAL YEAR	SALES MONTH	SALES QTR	TIME OF SALE	FLOOR
2	LONG ISLANDS INC	SOFT DRINKS	Michael Jackson	AMERICAS	4/13/2012	24,640	2012	January	Q1	09:36:00	
3	LONG ISLANDS INC	SOFT DRINKS	Michael Jackson	AMERICAS	12/21/2012	24,640	2012	February	Q1	11:31:12	
4	LONG ISLANDS INC	SOFT DRINKS	Michael Jackson	AMERICAS	12/24/2012	29,923	2012	March	Q1	13:49:26	
5	LONG ISLANDS INC	SOFT DRINKS	Michael Jackson	AMERICAS	12/24/2012	66,901	2012	April	Q2	16:35:20	
6	LONG ISLANDS INC	SOFT DRINKS	Michael Jackson	AMERICAS	12/29/2012	63,116	2012	May	Q2	19:54:24	
7	LONG ISLANDS INC	SOFT DRINKS	Michael Jackson	AMERICAS	6/28/2012	38,281	2012	June	Q2	23:53:16	
8	LONG ISLANDS INC	SOFT DRINKS	Michael Jackson	AMERICAS	6/28/2012	57,650	2012	July	Q3	09:36:00	
9	LONG ISLANDS INC	SOFT DRINKS	Michael Jackson	AMERICAS	6/29/2012	90,967	2012	August	Q3	11:31:12	
10	LONG ISLANDS INC	SOFT DRINKS	Michael Jackson	AMERICAS	6/29/2012	11,910	2012	September	Q3	13:49:26	
11	LONG ISLANDS INC	SOFT DRINKS	Michael Jackson	AMERICAS	7/6/2012	59,531	2012	October	Q4	16:35:20	
12	LONG ISLANDS INC	SOFT DRINKS	Michael Jackson	AMERICAS	7/6/2012	88,297	2012	November	Q4	12:54:24	
13	LONG ISLANDS INC	SOFT DRINKS	Michael Jackson	AMERICAS	9/8/2012	87,868	2012	December	Q4	23:53:16	

STEP 2: Insert the function FLOOR.

=FLOOR (

FLOOR ▼		× ✓ fx	=FLOOR(	
	G	**H**	**I**	**J**	**K**
1	FINANCIAL YEAR	SALES MONTH	SALES QTR	TIME OF SALE	FLOOR
2	2012	January	Q1	09:36:00	=FLOOR(
					FLOOR(**number**, significance)
3	2012	February	Q1	11:31:12	
4	2012	March	Q1	13:49:26	
5	2012	April	Q2	16:35:20	
6	2012	May	Q2	19:54:24	
7	2012	June	Q2	23:53:16	
8	2012	July	Q3	09:36:00	
9	2012	August	Q3	11:31:12	
10	2012	September	Q3	13:49:26	
11	2012	October	Q4	16:35:20	
12	2012	November	Q4	12:54:24	
13	2012	December	Q4	23:53:16	
14	2012	January	Q1	09:36:00	
15	2012	February	Q1	11:31:12	
16	2012	March	Q1	12:49:26	
17	2012	April	Q2	14:35:20	

STEP 3: Insert the first argument - **Time of Sales**.

=FLOOR ([@TIME OF SALES]

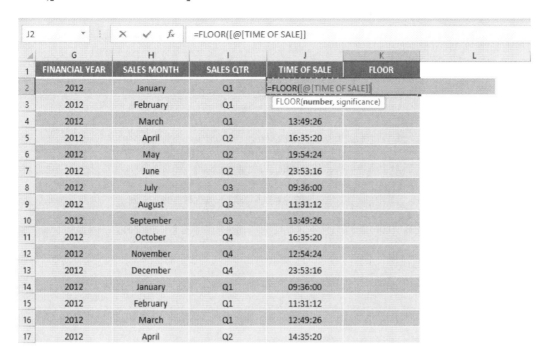

STEP 4: Insert the second argument - significance. Enter 15 minutes as **"00:15"**.

=FLOOR ([@TIME OF SALES],"00:15")

	G	H	I	J	K	L
K2		× ✓ fx	=FLOOR([@[TIME OF SALE]],"00:15")			
1	FINANCIAL YEAR	SALES MONTH	SALES QTR	TIME OF SALE	FLOOR	
2	2012	January	Q1	=FLOOR([@[TIME OF SALE]],"00:15")		
3	2012	February	Q1	11:31:12		
4	2012	March	Q1	13:49:26		
5	2012	April	Q2	16:35:20		
6	2012	May	Q2	19:54:24		
7	2012	June	Q2	23:53:16		
8	2012	July	Q3	09:36:00		
9	2012	August	Q3	11:31:12		
10	2012	September	Q3	13:49:26		
11	2012	October	Q4	16:35:20		
12	2012	November	Q4	12:54:24		
13	2012	December	Q4	23:53:16		
14	2012	January	Q1	09:36:00		
15	2012	February	Q1	11:31:12		
16	2012	March	Q1	12:49:26		
17	2012	April	Q2	14:35:20		
18	2012	May	Q2	19:54:24		

STEP 5: Copy-paste the formula down the column.

As you can see, the FLOOR function has rounded the TIME OF SALE in intervals of 15 minutes.

STEP 6: In the PivotTable Fields, drag and drop the **FLOOR** Field in the **Rows** area and **SALES Field** in the **Values** area.

STEP 7: Below is our Pivot Table with time intervals of 15 minutes.

Row Labels	Sum of SALES
01:30:00	627314
01:45:00	554880
09:00:00	1113616
09:30:00	3072592
11:15:00	927405
11:30:00	2797418
12:00:00	870421
12:45:00	1764043
13:15:00	852221
13:45:00	3354622
14:00:00	617835
14:30:00	885026
16:15:00	578833
16:30:00	3496095
17:30:00	631393
17:45:00	685436
18:00:00	600675
18:30:00	667195
19:30:00	693420
19:45:00	1841216

Pro Tip: If you ever come across a situation where you have **data containing date and time together,** for example **11/13/3022 9:16,** you can easily extract the time, **9:16,** from that column and then perform the grouping feature.

Before we move forward, let's first understand how to remove a decimal from a number in Excel.

The **TRUNC function** can be used to truncate a number by **removing the decimal portion of a number**.

It **does not round off** the number, it simply truncates the number.

For example, TRUNC(11.8) will return 11, and TRUNC(-9.2) will return -9.

In cell E2 we have **11/13/3022 9:36**, which in a number format   is **410120.4** – where:

11/13/3022 = 410120

9:36 = 0.4

By using the formula below, we can move 0.4 to the **TIME OF SALE** column and get the time **09:36:00**.

J2 | =[@[ORDER DATE & TIME]]-TRUNC([@[ORDER DATE & TIME]])

	CUSTOMER	PRODUCTS	SALES PERSON	SALES REGION	ORDER DATE & TIME	SALES	FINANCIAL YEAR	SALES MONTH	SALES QTR	TIME OF SALE
2	LONG ISLANDS INC	SOFT DRINKS	Michael Jackson	AMERICAS	11/13/3022 9:36	24,640	2012	January	Q1	09:36:00
3	LONG ISLANDS INC	SOFT DRINKS	Michael Jackson	AMERICAS	10/7/3029 11:31	24,640	2012	February	Q1	11:31:12
4	LONG ISLANDS INC	SOFT DRINKS	Michael Jackson	AMERICAS	11/6/3029 13:49	29,923	2012	March	Q1	13:49:26
5	LONG ISLANDS INC	SOFT DRINKS	Michael Jackson	AMERICAS	11/6/3029 16:35	66,901	2012	April	Q2	16:35:20
6	LONG ISLANDS INC	SOFT DRINKS	Michael Jackson	AMERICAS	12/26/3029 19:54	63,116	2012	May	Q2	19:54:24
7	LONG ISLANDS INC	SOFT DRINKS	Michael Jackson	AMERICAS	12/12/3024 23:53	38,281	2012	June	Q2	23:53:16
8	LONG ISLANDS INC	SOFT DRINKS	Michael Jackson	AMERICAS	12/12/3024 9:36	57,650	2012	July	Q3	09:36:00
9	LONG ISLANDS INC	SOFT DRINKS	Michael Jackson	AMERICAS	12/22/3024 11:31	90,967	2012	August	Q3	11:31:12
10	LONG ISLANDS INC	SOFT DRINKS	Michael Jackson	AMERICAS	12/22/3024 13:49	11,910	2012	September	Q3	13:49:26
11	LONG ISLANDS INC	SOFT DRINKS	Michael Jackson	AMERICAS	3/2/3025 16:35	59,531	2012	October	Q4	16:35:20
12	LONG ISLANDS INC	SOFT DRINKS	Michael Jackson	AMERICAS	3/2/3025 12:54	88,297	2012	November	Q4	12:54:24

Group by Half Years

Let us take grouping by Months up another notch and group it by **Half Years!**

In the example below I show you how to get the Sales grouped by
Half Years: **January to June and July to December**

STEP 1: Insert a new Pivot Table by clicking on your data and going to **Insert >
Pivot Table > New Worksheet or Existing Worksheet**

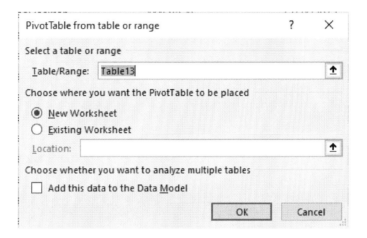

STEP 2: In the **Rows** area put in the **SALES MONTH** Field.

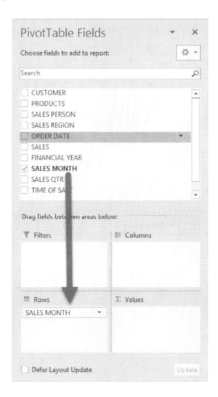

STEP 3: Highlight the first 6 months (**January - June**). Right click on the highlighted area and select **Group.**

STEP 4: Highlight the next 6 months (**July - December**). Right click on this highlighted area and select **Group.**

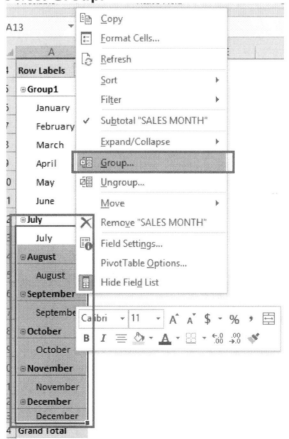

STEP 5: Rename the groups to make them more readable by manually typing over the cell's headers.

Rename **"Group1"** header to **"1st Half"**, then rename **"Group2"** header to **"2nd Half"**.

Notice that a new Field **SALES MONTH2** was created in the Rows area. This contains our new Half-Year groupings.

STEP 6: We do not need the SALES MONTH anymore. Remove the **SALES MONTH** by dragging it back to the Field List.

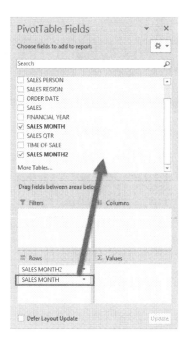

STEP 7: In the **Values** area put in the **SALES** Field. This will get the Total Sales for each Half-Year range we have defined.

In the **Rows** area put in the **FINANCIAL YEAR** Field on top of the **SALES MONTH2** Field:

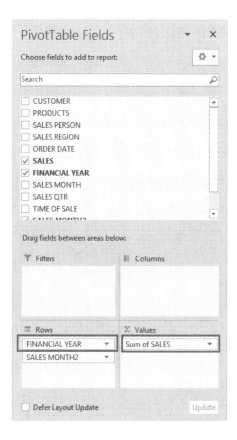

STEP 8: Click the **Sum of SALES** drop down and select **Value Field Settings.**

STEP 9: Select **Number Format**

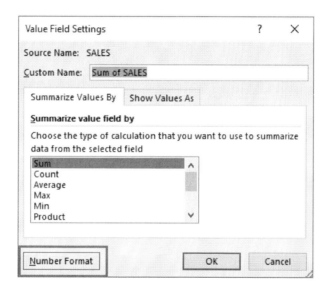

STEP 10: Select **Currency**. Click **OK**.

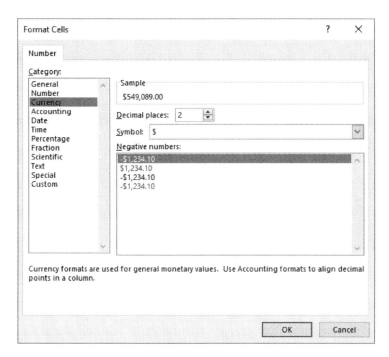

We now have our Pivot Table grouped by Half Years!

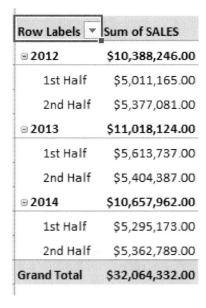

Row Labels	Sum of SALES
⊟ 2012	$10,388,246.00
1st Half	$5,011,165.00
2nd Half	$5,377,081.00
⊟ 2013	$11,018,124.00
1st Half	$5,613,737.00
2nd Half	$5,404,387.00
⊟ 2014	$10,657,962.00
1st Half	$5,295,173.00
2nd Half	$5,362,789.00
Grand Total	$32,064,332.00

Group by Custom Dates

At the start of this chapter we showed you how to group Dates.

We can take this concept a step further and Group Dates based on a custom date range.

STEP 1: Insert a new Pivot Table by clicking on your data and going to *Insert > Pivot Table > New Worksheet or Existing Worksheet*

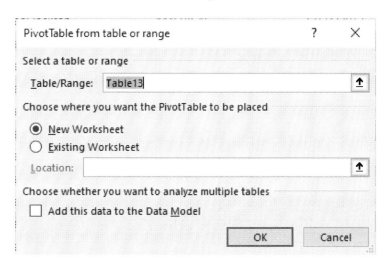

STEP 2: In the **Rows** area put in the **ORDER DATE** Field.

Notice that in Microsoft 365 it will **automatically Group** the **ORDER DATE** into years and quarters:

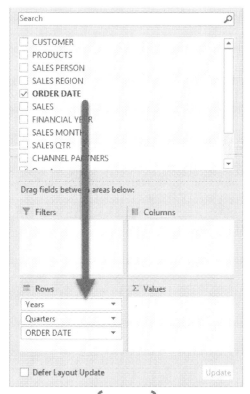

STEP 3: Right-click on any date in your Pivot Table and select **Group** so we can select our Group order that we want:

STEP 4: We need to deselect **Quarters, Years** and make sure only **Months** are selected (which will be highlighted in blue). This will group our Dates by *Months* only.

We can now define a custom date range! Our data source has **ORDER DATES** ranging from 2012-03-01 up to 2014-12-31.

We want to group anything that is before 2014-01-01together and anything that is after 2014-09-30 together. Anything in between those dates we want to group into individual months.

To do this we need to set the following:

Starting at: 2014-01-01

Ending at: 2014-09-30

Click **OK.**

STEP 5: In the **Values** area put in the **SALES** Field. This will show the Total Sales for each Month:

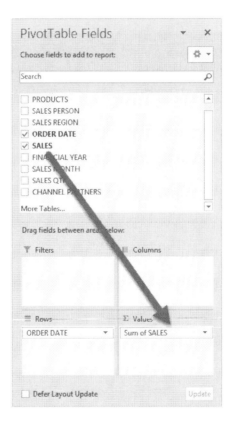

We can see that everything that does not fall in before January 2014 and after September 2014 is Grouped into its own month.

STEP 6: Now we have our sales numbers grouped by onth & Years, notice that we can improve the formatting.

Click on the **Sum of SALES** drop down and select **Value Field Settings.**

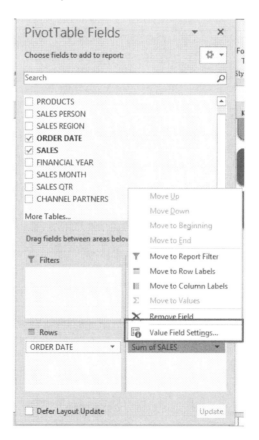

STEP 7: Select **Number Format**

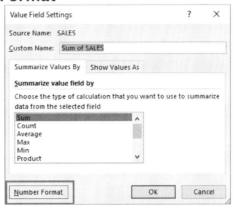

STEP 8: Select **Currency.** Click **OK.**

We now have your Total Sales for each Monthly period based on our custom dates!

Row Labels	Sum of SALES
<2014-01-01	$21,406,370.00
Jan	$670,523.00
Feb	$336,683.00
Mar	$141,655.00
Apr	$1,429,966.00
May	$830,498.00
Jun	$865,977.00
Jul	$606,762.00
Aug	$532,421.00
Sep	$882,080.00
>2014-09-30	$4,361,397.00
Grand Total	$32,064,332.00

Group by Fiscal Years & Quarters

Grouping by calendar years and quarters is straightforward as this is provided out of the box. However, when it comes to grouping data by fiscal years (e.g., Starting in July for Australia) and quarters, it's a different story.

We will show this setup in our Pivot Table data:

- Fiscal Year starts in July
- Fiscal Quarters:
    - 1st Quarter - July, August, September
    - 2nd Quarter - October, November, December
    - 3rd Quarter - January, February, March
    - 4th Quarter - April, May, June

We will be using the help of formulas to add two columns to our data source: **Fiscal Year and Fiscal Quarter**.

STEP 1: Let us start with the **Fiscal Year** first. Since our Fiscal Year starts in July, then our formula will be:

$$=YEAR(E2) + (MONTH(E2) >= 7)$$

If the month is July or later, then we add 1 to the year. That will give us the following Fiscal Year.

For example, **December 21, 2012** will have a Fiscal Year of **2013**, as it is July or later.

E	F	G
ORDER DATE	FISCAL YEAR	FISCAL QUARTER
4/13/2012	=YEAR(E2)+(MONTH(E2)>=7)	
12/21/2012	2013	
12/24/2012	2013	
12/24/2012	2013	
12/29/2012	2013	
6/28/2012	2012	
6/28/2012	2012	
6/29/2012	2012	
6/29/2012	2012	
7/6/2012	2013	
7/6/2012	2013	
9/8/2012	2013	

STEP 2: Let us work on the **Fiscal Quarter** next. Since our first Fiscal Quarter starts in July, then our formula will be:

$$=CHOOSE(MONTH(E2),3,3,3,4,4,4,1,1,1,2,2,2)$$

This formula will simply match the Month number to the sequence of:

- 3rd Quarter - January (3), February (3), March (3)
- 4th Quarter - April (4), May (4), June (4)
- 1st Quarter - July (1), August (1), September (1)
- 2nd Quarter - October (2), November (2), December (2)

For example, **December 21, 2012** will have a Fiscal Quarter of **2** as it will match the last part of the formula:

$$=CHOOSE(MONTH(E2),3,3,3,4,4,4,1,1,1,2,2,2)$$

=CHOOSE(MONTH(E2),3,3,3,4,4,4,1,1,1,2,2,2)					
B	C	D	E	F	G
ODUCTS	SALES PERSON	SALES REGION	ORDER DATE	FISCAL YEAR	FISCAL QUARTER
FT DRINKS	Michael Jackson	AMERICAS	4/13/2012	=CHOOSE(MONTH(E2),3,3,3,4,4,4,1,1,1,2,2,2)	
FT DRINKS	Michael Jackson	AMERICAS	12/21/2012	2013	2
FT DRINKS	Michael Jackson	AMERICAS	12/24/2012	2013	2
FT DRINKS	Michael Jackson	AMERICAS	12/24/2012	2013	2
FT DRINKS	Michael Jackson	AMERICAS	12/29/2012	2013	2
FT DRINKS	Michael Jackson	AMERICAS	6/28/2012	2012	4
FT DRINKS	Michael Jackson	AMERICAS	6/28/2012	2012	4
FT DRINKS	Michael Jackson	AMERICAS	6/29/2012	2012	4
FT DRINKS	Michael Jackson	AMERICAS	6/29/2012	2012	4
FT DRINKS	Michael Jackson	AMERICAS	7/6/2012	2013	1
FT DRINKS	Michael Jackson	AMERICAS	7/6/2012	2013	1
FT DRINKS	Michael Jackson	AMERICAS	9/8/2012	2013	1
OTTLES	Michael Jackson	AMERICAS	9/8/2012	2013	1
OTTLES	Michael Jackson	AMERICAS	6/30/2012	2012	4
OTTLES	Michael Jackson	AMERICAS	12/23/2012	2013	2
OTTLES	Michael Jackson	AMERICAS	12/8/2012	2013	2
OTTLES	Michael Jackson	AMERICAS	10/28/2012	2013	2
OTTLES	Michael Jackson	AMERICAS	10/28/2012	2013	2
OTTLES	Michael Jackson	AMERICAS	9/15/2012	2013	1
OTTLES	Michael Jackson	AMERICAS	10/28/2012	2013	2

Data_Table

STEP 3: Insert a new Pivot Table by clicking on your data and going to *Insert > Pivot Table > New Worksheet or Existing Worksheet*

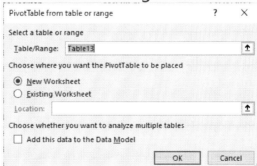

STEP 4: Drag these PivotTable Fields in the following areas below:

Rows: **FISCAL YEAR** and **FISCAL QUARTER**
Values: **SALES**

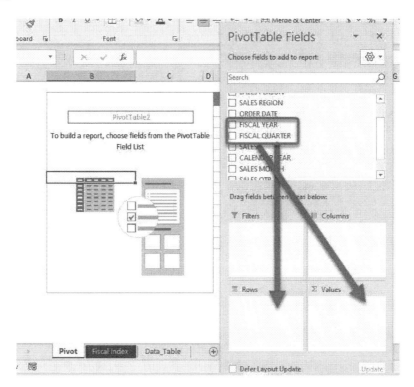

We now have our data setup using **Fiscal Years and Quarters**!

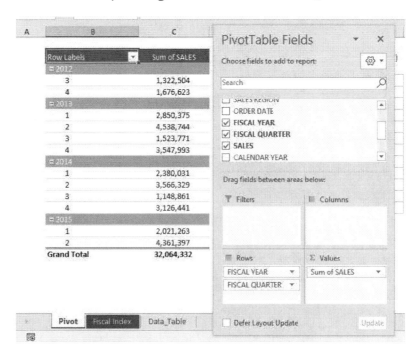

Errors when Grouping by Dates

I am sure that you have tried to group your Pivot Table data and get this dreaded error message:

What gives? I will explain why this error occurs and how you can fix it.

This is our current Pivot Table setup:

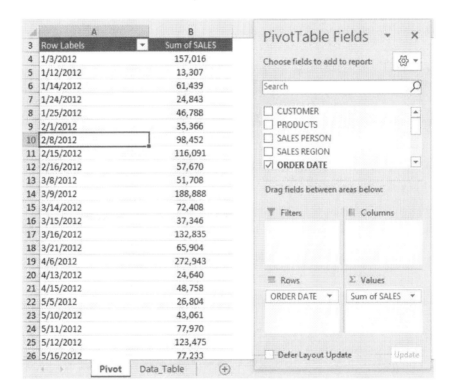

STEP 1: Right click on any Date in the Pivot Table and select **Group**

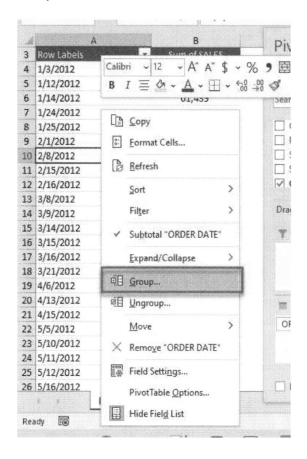

We get the "**Cannot group that selection**" error message. There is something wrong with our Dates in the data.

In most cases, the Dates in the data source are formatted incorrectly or they are formatted as text.

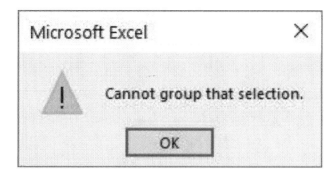

STEP 2: Let us look for the errors!

Select the **ORDER DATE** column in your data source and press **CTRL + G** then click on **Special.**

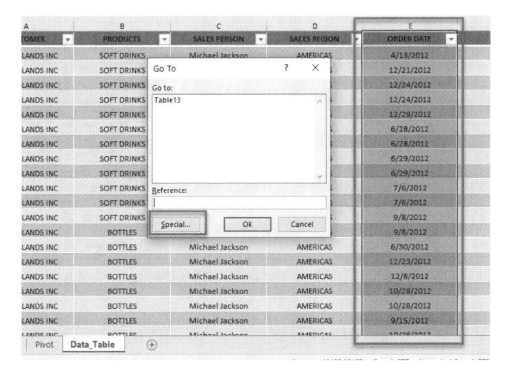

STEP 3: Select **Constants, Text**, and **Errors.**

This will show the Dates that have errors. Click **OK.**

STEP 4: The errors are now selected although we cannot see them. Click on the **Fill Color** and select the **yellow** color.

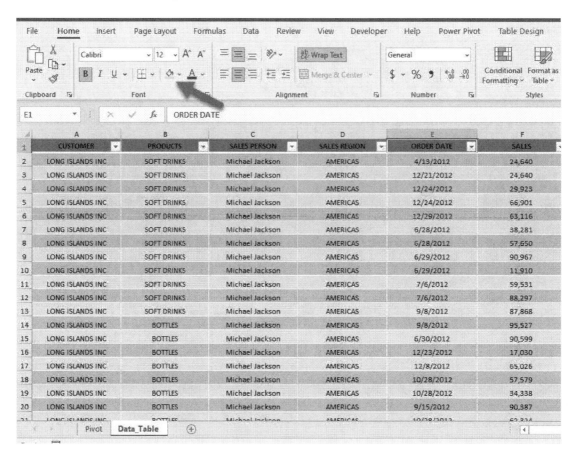

STEP 5: Click on the **ORDER DATE** drop down and select **Filter by Color** and select **yellow.**

You will now see the Dates that have errors.

There is a cell with **N/A,** which is being treated as a text format.

Also there cannot be 31 days in February, hence our error for **02/31/2012**.

	CUSTOMER	PRODUCTS	SALES PERSON	SALES REGION	ORDER DATE	SALES	FINANCIAL YEAR	SALES MONTH
53	LONG ISLANDS INC	SOFT DRINKS	Michael Jackson	AMERICAS	N/A	17,100	2015	April
440	GIN ON THE RUN CO	SOFT DRINKS	Homer Simpson	AFRICA	2/31/2012	71,644	2012	July
562	GIN ON THE RUN CO	ICE CUBES	Homer Simpson	AFRICA	2/31/2012	65,439	2014	September
568	GIN ON THE RUN CO	TONIC	Homer Simpson	AFRICA	2/31/2012	50,033	2014	March
578	Total					4		

Let's manually enter the correct these Dates.

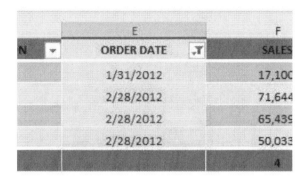

N	ORDER DATE	SALES
	1/31/2012	17,100
	2/28/2012	71,644
	2/28/2012	65,439
	2/28/2012	50,033
		4

STEP 6: Right click anywhere on your Pivot Table and select **Refresh.**

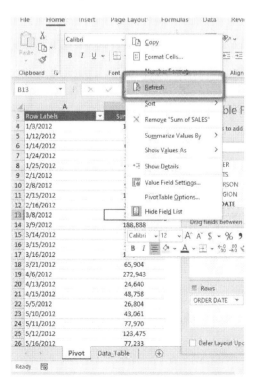

STEP 7: Right click on any Date in the Pivot Table and select **Group**

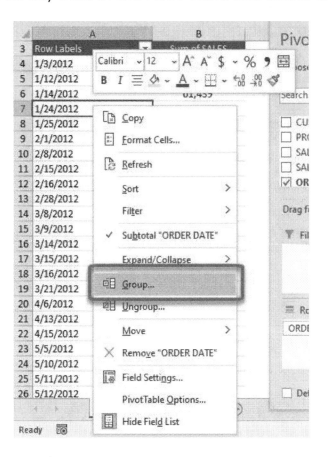

Our Grouping is now working!

Group Two Pivot Tables Independently

When you duplicate a Pivot Table, the same grouping will apply to both Pivot Tables.

But what if you want to group 2 Pivot Tables independently?

I will show you how you can achieve independent Pivot Tables but first let me show you what happens when you duplicate 2 Pivot Tables and then go to group one of them.

Here is our Pivot Table setup:

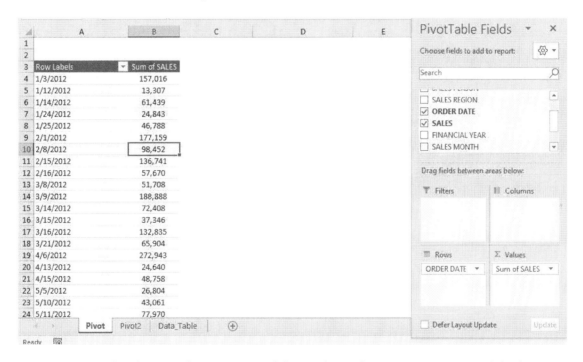

STEP 1: Let us duplicate this Pivot Table. Select the entire Pivot Table by pressing **CTRL + A, right click** and select **Copy.**

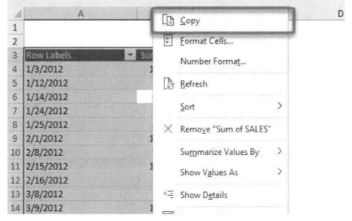

Pick any cell right next to the original Pivot Table and select **Paste**.

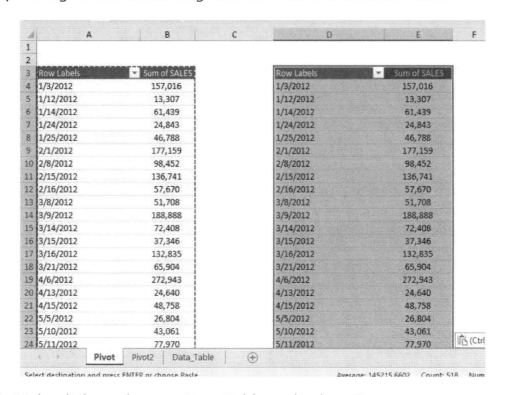

STEP 2: Right click on the new Pivot Table and select **Group**

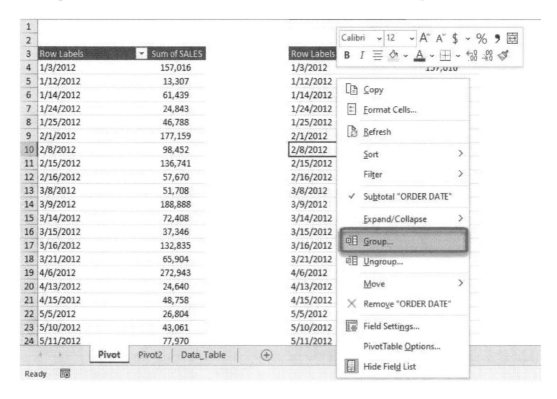

Make any grouping selection that you prefer and click **OK.**

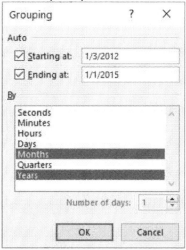

STEP 3: Notice that the grouping is applied to **both Pivot Tables!**

We do not want that to happen as we want the grouping to only occur on one Pivot Table.

Click the **Undo button** and let us work on the workaround for this.

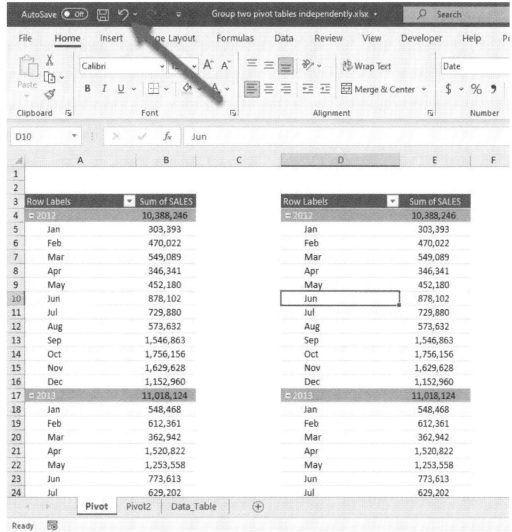

STEP 4: Select the new Pivot Table and click the **Cut** icon

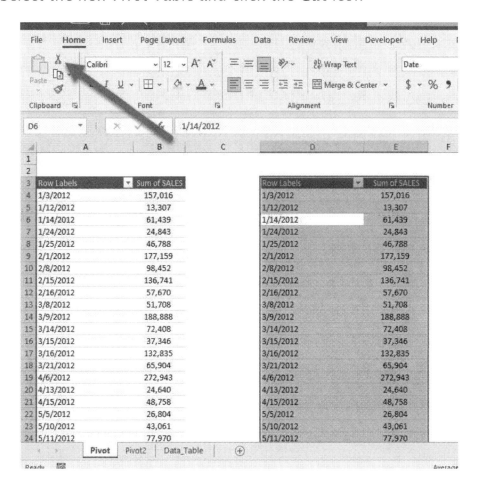

STEP 5: Open a new Excel workbook by pressing **CTRL + N** and select **Paste**

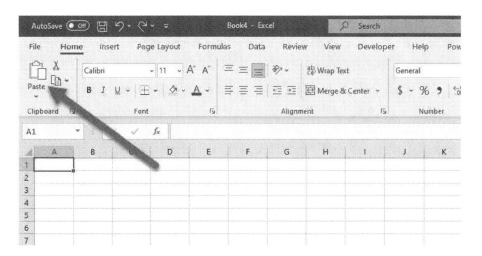

STEP 6: Now right click on this Pivot Table in the new Excel workbook, select **Group** and pick the groupings that you prefer. Click **OK**

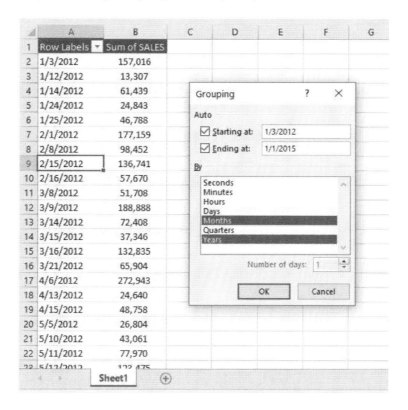

STEP 7: Select this Pivot Table and click the **Cut** icon again.

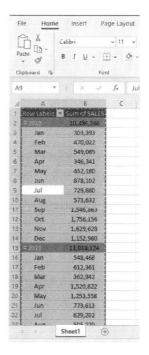

STEP 8: Paste this back on the original workbook.

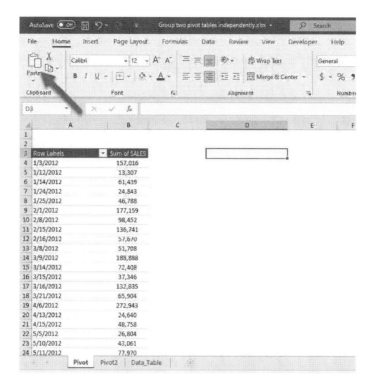

You will notice that the grouping is now applied only to this Pivot Table!

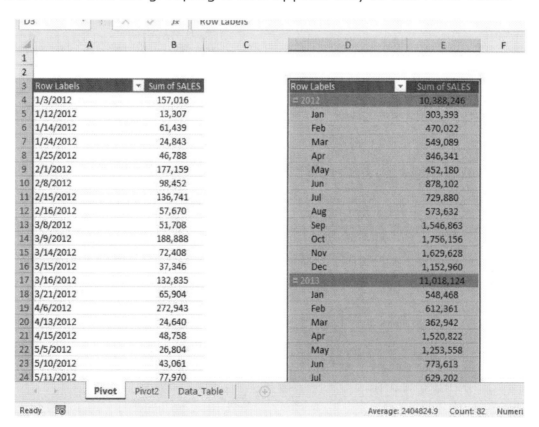

Ungroup Data

Grouping data is very easy in Pivot Tables as we have shown in the previous tips.

But what if you didn't like the Pivot Table grouping and wanted to get rid of it?

I will show you how you can do this below.

Below we have our grouped ORDER DATES as shown in our previous tip called **Group Dates by Month & Year**.

To ungroup these dates, simply **right-click** on any grouped date and select **Ungroup**.

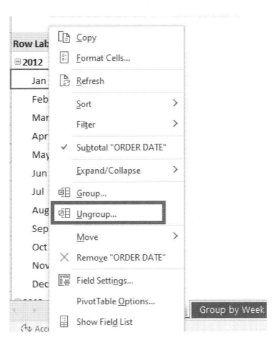

Another way is to select a grouped date inside the Pivot Table and go to the **PivotTable Analyze tab** and select **Ungroup**.

Once this is done, the data will be ungrouped again into individual dates.

	A	B
4	Row Labels ▾	Sum of SALES
5	1/3/2012	$157,016
6	1/12/2012	$13,307
7	1/14/2012	$61,439
8	1/24/2012	$24,843
9	1/25/2012	$46,788
10	2/1/2012	$177,159
11	2/8/2012	$98,452
12	2/15/2012	$136,741
13	2/16/2012	$57,670
14	3/8/2012	$51,708
15	3/9/2012	$188,888
16	3/14/2012	$72,408
17	3/15/2012	$37,346
18	3/16/2012	$132,835
19	3/21/2012	$65,904
20	4/6/2012	$272,943

Expand & Collapse Buttons

The magic with Pivot Tables is that it's very easy to "expand" and show additional data for your analysis, then to quickly "collapse" and hide that data. Here is how:

Here is our Pivot Table.

	A	B	C	D	E	F
1	Sum of SALES	Column Labels				
2	Row Labels	2012	2013	2014	Grand Total	
3	☐ ICE CUBES	2409490	2768221	2685989	7863700	
4	Homer Simpson	733716	747964	722268	2203948	
5	Ian Wright	610481	680933	630075	1921489	
6	John Michaloudis	510086	739286	723257	1972629	
7	Michael Jackson	555207	600038	610389	1765634	
8	☐ BOTTLES	2754838	2857728	2544612	8157178	
9	☐ SOFT DRINKS	2676531	2491153	2669460	7837144	
10	☐ TONIC	2574058	2901022	2757901	8232981	
11	Grand Total	10414917	11018124	10657962	32091003	
12						

STEP 1: You can click on the - **button** to collapse each Product's item, or the + **button** to expand the Product's item. Give it a try!

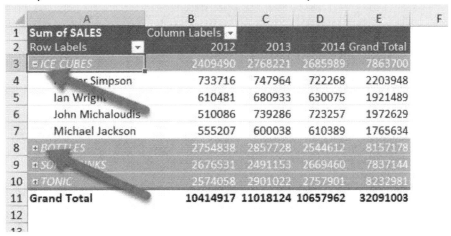

You can see the **ICE CUBES** is now collapsed, while **BOTTLES** has expanded.

	A	B	C	D	E
1	Sum of SALES	Column Labels			
2	Row Labels	2012	2013	2014	Grand Total
3	☐ ICE CUBES	2409490	2768221	2685989	7863700
4	☐ BOTTLES	2754838	2857728	2544612	8157178
5	Homer Simpson	693855	827901	563154	2084910
6	Ian Wright	671757	579190	703240	1954187
7	John Michaloudis	714353	710555	586103	2011011
8	Michael Jackson	674873	740082	692115	2107070
9	☐ SOFT DRINKS	2676531	2491153	2669460	7837144
10	☐ TONIC	2574058	2901022	2757901	8232981
11	Grand Total	10414917	11018124	10657962	32091003

STEP 2: If you want this change to happen for all of the Products, **right click** on a Product Field (Bottles) and select *Expand/Collapse > Expand Entire Field.*

You can select the **Collapse Entire Field** option if you want to collapse all the Product Fields.

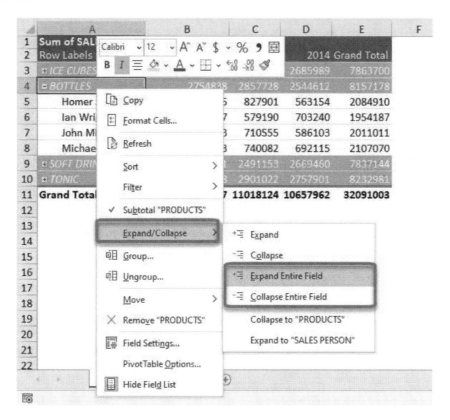

All of the Products are now expanded!

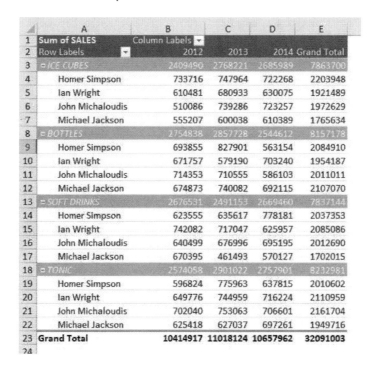

STEP 3: What if we want to expand the Salesperson Field? **Right click** on any Salesperson and select *Expand/Collapse > Expand Entire Field*

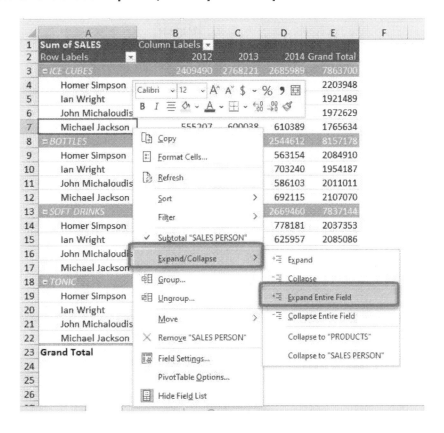

STEP 4: You will be given the option to **add a new Field** under the Salesperson Field. Select **SALES QTR** and click **OK**

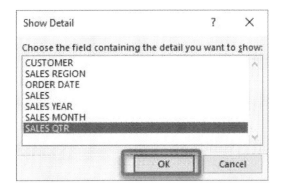

STEP 5: Now you have an additional level of detail (SALES QTR) under Salesperson for your analysis!

	A	B	C	D	E
1	**Sum of SALES**	Column Labels			
2	Row Labels	2012	2013	2014	Grand Total
3	⊟ *ICE CUBES*	2409490	2768221	2685989	7863700
4	⊟ Homer Simpson	733716	747964	722268	2203948
5	Q1	275704	224589	227209	727502
6	Q2	169263	142339	117200	428802
7	Q3	88508	206091	156789	451388
8	Q4	200241	174945	221070	596256
9	⊟ Ian Wright	610481	680933	630075	1921489
10	Q1	133127	187000	115954	436081
11	Q2	152463	131206	145653	429322
12	Q3	201707	185308	145264	532279
13	Q4	123184	177419	223204	523807
14	⊟ John Michaloudis	510086	739286	723257	1972629
15	Q1	68816	163172	241936	473924
16	Q2	156626	177384	154896	488906
17	Q3	131811	183781	145668	461260
18	Q4	152833	214949	180757	548539
19	⊟ Michael Jackson	555207	600038	610389	1765634
20	Q1	133593	82070	133464	349127
21	Q2	37789	125217	116811	279817
22	Q3	241354	213634	178417	633405
23	Q4	142471	179117	181697	503285
24	⊟ *BOTTLES*	2754838	2857728	2544612	8157178
25	⊟ Homer Simpson	693855	827901	563154	2084910
26	Q1	150215	209844	109537	469596

Pivot | Data_Table | (+)

You have the same functionality for Columns as well. Drag the **SALES QTR** Field from **Rows** to **Columns.**

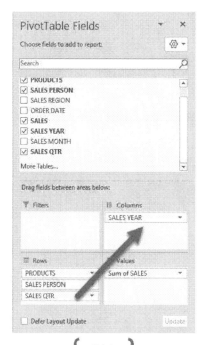

STEP 6: Now our Column of **SALES YEAR** has the additional details of **SALES QTR.**

You can quickly click on the - **button** to collapse the SALES YEAR Field, or the + **button** to expand the SALES YEAR Field.

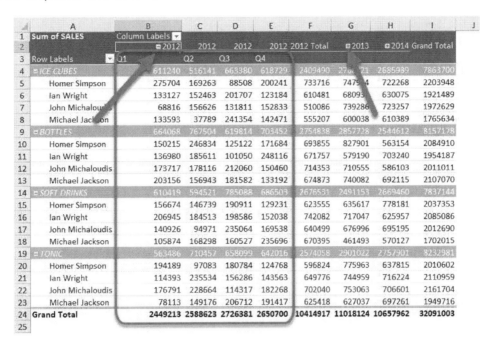

You can now see that we have collapsed the **2012** Column, while expanding the **2013** Column.

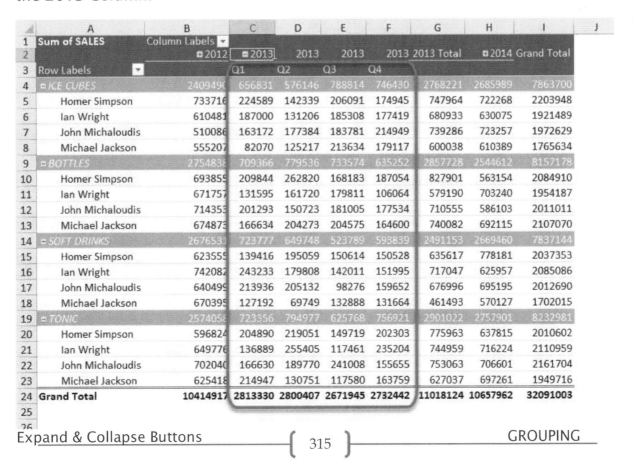

SORTING

Sort by Largest or Smallest

Pivot Tables are sorted based on the contents inside the Row/Column Labels.

- Dates are sorted in chronological order from oldest to newest.
- Text is sorted in alphabetical order.
- Values are sorted by smallest to largest.

If you don't like the default sorting given by a Pivot Table you can easily change this.

Let us start off with this Pivot Table that shows the Sum of SALES for each Year and Quarter.

	A	B
6	Row Labels	Sum of SALES
7	⊟2012	
8	Qtr1	$1,322,504.00
9	Qtr2	$1,676,623.00
10	Qtr3	$2,850,375.00
11	Qtr4	$4,538,744.00
12	⊟2013	
13	Qtr1	$1,523,771.00
14	Qtr2	$3,547,993.00
15	Qtr3	$2,380,031.00
16	Qtr4	$3,566,329.00
17	⊟2014	
18	Qtr1	$1,148,861.00
19	Qtr2	$3,126,441.00
20	Qtr3	$2,021,263.00
21	Qtr4	$4,361,397.00
22	Grand Total	$32,064,332.00

In the example below I will show you how to sort a Pivot Table by Largest or Smallest.

STEP 1: Right click on a **Year** cell in the Pivot Table.

Go to *Sort > Sort Newest to Oldest*

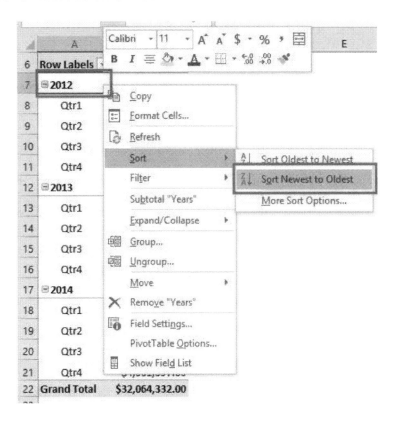

This will sort our Years by descending order. Notice that 2014 was sorted first.

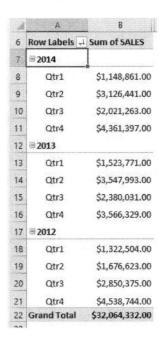

STEP 2: Now let us try to sort by **Quarters**.

Right click on any **Quarter** cell in the Pivot Table.

Go to *Sort > Sort Newest to Oldest*

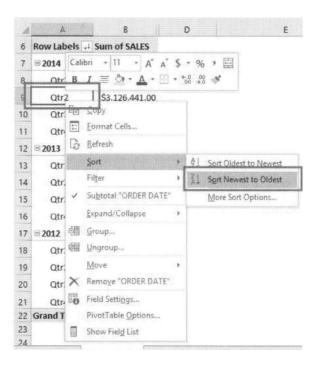

This will sort our Quarters by descending order for each Year. Notice that Quarter 4 was sorted first.

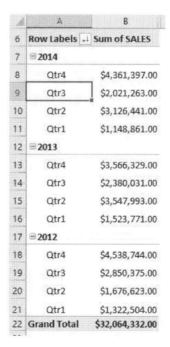

STEP 3: Now let us try sorting the **Sum of SALES**.

Right click on a **Sum** value in the Pivot Table.

Go to *Sort > Sort Largest to Smallest.*

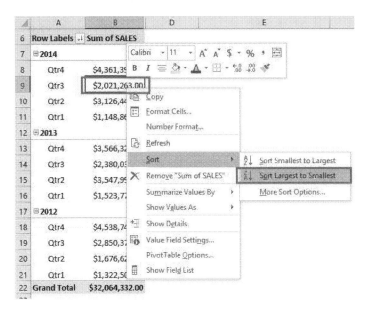

This will sort the Sum of Sales by descending order, regardless of the Quarter.

Sort an Item Row (Left to Right)

You can sort virtually anywhere inside a Pivot Table as well as sort any item from left to right!

Below I have a Pivot Table that consists of Sales Numbers over a three year period.

We want to sort the Pivot Table by the values in the **April** row from **Smallest to Largest**:

Sum of SALES	Column Labels			
Row Labels	2012	2013	2014	Grand Total
January	771,186.00	872,080.00	1,074,820.00	2,718,086.00
February	867,220.00	909,654.00	807,257.00	2,584,131.00
March	784,136.00	1,031,596.00	1,013,466.00	2,829,198.00
April	908,666.00	968,855.00	836,559.00	2,714,080.00
May				2,534,636.00
June	786,918.00	981,050.00	771,976.00	2,539,944.00
July	1,056,573.00	854,835.00	873,543.00	2,784,951.00
August	806,719.00	1,002,597.00	599,246.00	2,408,562.00
September	863,089.00	814,513.00	1,011,288.00	2,688,890.00
October	873,208.00	931,193.00	1,059,308.00	2,863,709.00
November	923,402.00	769,352.00	812,659.00	2,505,413.00
December	854,090.00	1,031,897.00	1,006,745.00	2,892,732.00
Grand Total	10,388,246.00	11,018,124.00	10,657,962.00	32,064,332.00

STEP 1: Right click on a Sales Number in the April row. Go to *Sort > More Sort Options*

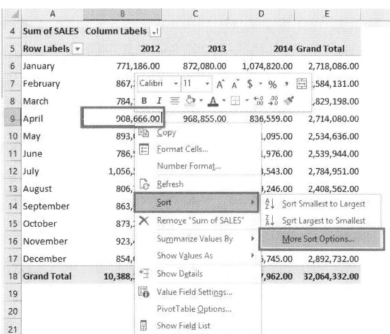

STEP 2: Make sure the following are selected:

Sort options: **Smallest to Largest**

Sort direction: **Left to Right**.

You can see in the **Summary** that it will sort in **ascending order** using the values in the **April row.** Click **OK**.

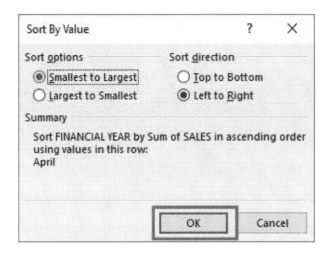

STEP 3: This will sort our Sales values from left to right using the values in the April row.

See that our years are now arranged in this order: 2014, 2012, 2013.

Sum of SALES	Column Labels			
Row Labels	2014	2012	2013	Grand Total
January	1,074,820.00	771,186.00	872,080.00	2,718,086.00
February	807,257.00	867,220.00	909,654.00	2,584,131.00
March	1,013,466.00	784,136.00	1,031,596.00	2,829,198.00
April	836,559.00	908,666.00	968,855.00	2,714,080.00
May				2,534,636.00
June	771,976.00	786,918.00	981,050.00	2,539,944.00
July	873,543.00	1,056,573.00	854,835.00	2,784,951.00
August	599,246.00	806,719.00	1,002,597.00	2,408,562.00
September	1,011,288.00	863,089.00	814,513.00	2,688,890.00
October	1,059,308.00	873,208.00	931,193.00	2,863,709.00
November	812,659.00	923,402.00	769,352.00	2,505,413.00
December	1,006,745.00	854,090.00	1,031,897.00	2,892,732.00
Grand Total	10,657,962.00	10,388,246.00	11,018,124.00	32,064,332.00

Sort Manually

There are a three ways that you can sort a Pivot Table manually...

...Using your mouse, typing over a cell or right clicking.

STEP 1: You can sort by clicking on a cell and **drag the cell's border using your mouse**.

Click on the cell you want to move. Hover over the border of that cell until you see the four arrows.

Left mouse click, **hold and drag it to the position you want.**

Sum of SALES	Column Labels			
Row Labels	2014	2015	2013	Grand Total
123 Warehousing	49,562	75,088	66,826	191,476
ABC Telecom	108,285	14,659	67,320	190,264
Acme, inc.	25,263	113,918	85,030	224,211
Demo Company	13,964	106,826	113,799	234,589
Fake Brothers	164,248	43,216	66,663	274,127
Foo Bars	31,176	85,607	53,522	170,305
Smith and Co.	77,384	41,632	80,369	199,385
Widget Corp	68,797	94,378	129,462	292,637
Grand Total	538,679	575,324	662,991	1,776,994

This is now the sorted result.

Sum of SALES	Column Labels			
Row Labels	2014	2015	2013	Grand Total
Widget Corp	68,797	94,378	129,462	292,637
123 Warehousing	49,562	75,088	66,826	191,476
ABC Telecom	108,285	14,659	67,320	190,264
Acme, inc.	25,263	113,918	85,030	224,211
Demo Company	13,964	106,826	113,799	234,589
Fake Brothers	164,248	43,216	66,663	274,127
Foo Bars	31,176	85,607	53,522	170,305
Smith and Co.	77,384	41,632	80,369	199,385
Grand Total	538,679	575,324	662,991	1,776,994

STEP 2: You can also sort by **typing an existing cell value.**

In our example, we are typing *Widget Corp* (which is currently located at the last row) over *123 Warehousing* (which is currently located at the first row), then pressing Enter.

Sum of SALES	Column Labels			
Row Labels	2014	2015	2013	Grand Total
Widget Corp	49,562	75,088	66,826	191,476
ABC Telecom	108,285	14,659	67,320	190,264
Acme, inc.	25,263	113,918	85,030	224,211
Demo Company	13,964	106,826	113,799	234,589
Foo Bars	31,176	85,607	53,522	170,305
Fake Brothers	164,248	43,216	66,663	274,127
Smith and Co.	77,384	41,632	80,369	199,385
Widget Corp	68,797	94,378	129,462	292,637
Grand Total	538,679	575,324	662,991	1,776,994

123 Warehousing gets pushed down, and *Widget Corp* moves to the top row.

Sum of SALES	Column Labels			
Row Labels	2014	2015	2013	Grand Total
Widget Corp	68,797	94,378	129,462	292,637
123 Warehousing		75,088	66,826	191,476
ABC Telecom		14,659	67,320	190,264
Acme, inc.		113,918	85,030	224,211
Demo Company	13,964	106,826	113,799	234,589
Foo Bars	31,176	85,607	53,522	170,305
Fake Brothers	164,248	43,216	66,663	274,127
Smith and Co.	77,384	41,632	80,369	199,385
Grand Total	538,679	575,324	662,991	1,776,994

> Sum of SALES
> Value: 68,797
> Row: Widget Corp
> Column: 2014

STEP 3: You can also sort by **right clicking.**

Try it on any company name and select **_Sort > Sort A to Z_**

Our Pivot Table will be sorted in alphabetical order based on the company name.

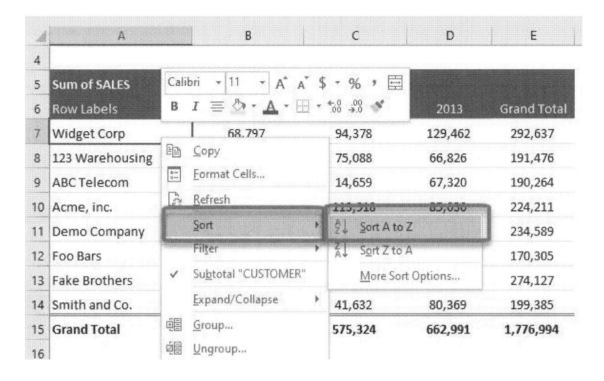

Sort Largest to Smallest Grand Totals

Did you know that you could also sort by the Grand Total? This is a secret tip which I will share with you now.

STEP 1: Insert a new Pivot Table by clicking on your data and going to *Insert > Pivot Table > New Worksheet or Existing Worksheet*

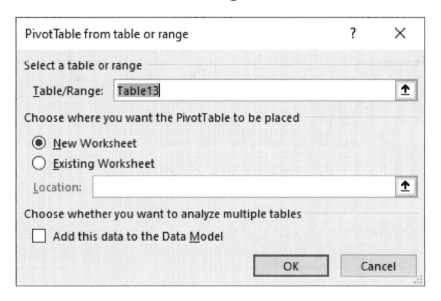

STEP 2: Drag these Pivot Table Fields in the following areas below:

Rows: **SALES MONTH**
Columns: **FINANCIAL YEAR**
Values: **SALES**

STEP 3: Right-click on a Grand Total below at the bottom of the Pivot Table. Go to *Sort > Sort Largest to Smallest.*

	A	B	C	D	E
4	**Sum of SALES**	**Column Labels** ⊡			
5	**Row Labels** ⊡	**2012**	**2013**	**2014**	**Grand Total**
6	January	771,186.00	872,080.00	1,074,820.00	2,718,086.00
7	February	867,220.00	909,654.00	807,257.00	2,584,131.00
8	March	784,136.0		3,466.00	2,829,198.00
9	April	908,666.0		6,559.00	2,714,080.00
10	May	893,039.0		1,095.00	2,534,636.00
11	June	786,918.0			
12	July	1,056,573.0			
13	August	806,719.0			
14	September	863,089.0		1,288.00	2,688,890.00
15	October	873,208.0		9,308.00	2,863,709.00
16	November	923,402.0		2,659.00	2,505,413.00
17	December	854,090.0		6,745.00	2,892,732.00
18	**Grand Total**	**10,388,246.00**	11,018,124.00	10,657,962.00	**32,064,332.00**

Right-click menu (overlaying the table):
- Copy
- Format Cells...
- Number Format...
- Refresh
- Sort ▸
  - Sort Smallest to Largest
  - **Sort Largest to Smallest**
  - More Sort Options...
- Remove "Sum of SALES"
- Summarize Values By ▸
- Show Values As ▸
- Show Details
- Value Field Settings...
- PivotTable Options...
- Hide Field List

If you cannot see the Grand Totals, click in your Pivot Table and go to the ribbon menu. Select the *Design* context ribbon > *Grand Totals > On for Rows and Columns*.

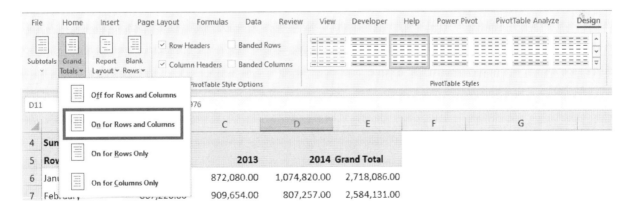

STEP 4: This will sort our Grand Totals by descending order.

Notice that our Years are now arranged based on the largest Grand Total value (2013, 2014, and then 2012).

	A	B	C	D	E
4	Sum of SALES	Column Labels ⬇			
5	Row Labels ▾	2013	2014	2012	Grand Total
6	January	872,080.00	1,074,820.00	771,186.00	2,718,086.00
7	February	909,654.00	807,257.00	867,220.00	2,584,131.00
8	March	1,031,596.00	1,013,466.00	784,136.00	2,829,198.00
9	April	968,855.00	836,559.00	908,666.00	2,714,080.00
10	May	850,502.00	791,095.00	893,039.00	2,534,636.00
11	June	981,050.00	771,976.00	786,918.00	2,539,944.00
12	July	854,835.00	873,543.00	1,056,573.00	2,784,951.00
13	August	1,002,597.00	599,246.00	806,719.00	2,408,562.00
14	September	814,513.00	1,011,288.00	863,089.00	2,688,890.00
15	October	931,193.00	1,059,308.00	873,208.00	2,863,709.00
16	November	769,352.00	812,659.00	923,402.00	2,505,413.00
17	December	1,031,897.00	1,006,745.00	854,090.00	2,892,732.00
18	Grand Total	11,018,124.00	10,657,962.00	10,388,246.00	32,064,332.00

FILTER

Filter a Pivot Table by Dates

Filtering a Pivot Table allows you to drill down on specific data points and to analyze regions, dates or values, just to mention a few examples.

There is an array of different Date filters in a Pivot Table. You can filter by:

Before	Next Week	Next Month	Next Quarter	Next Year	Year To Date
After	This Week	This Month	This Quarter	This Year	All Dates in the Period
Between	Last Week	Last Month	Last Quarter	Last Year	
Tomorrow					
Today					
Yesterday					

Date filters are useful if you want to see what invoices are due to be paid next month or what sales transactions were included in a particular quarter.

This is our current Pivot Table setup with **ORDER DATES** in the Rows area and **SALES** in the Values area.

STEP 1: Select the **Row Labels drop down** and select *Date Filters > Between*

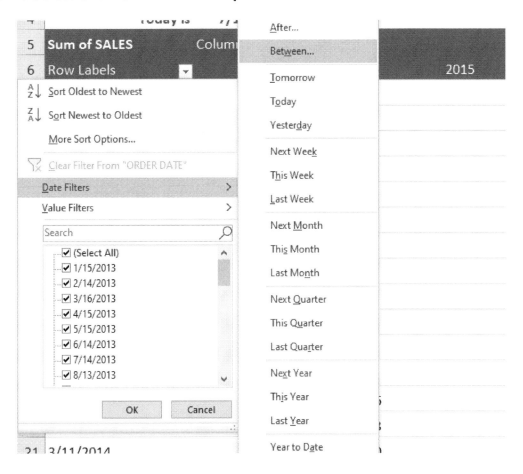

STEP 2: Place a date range manually or using the built in calendar. Click **OK.**

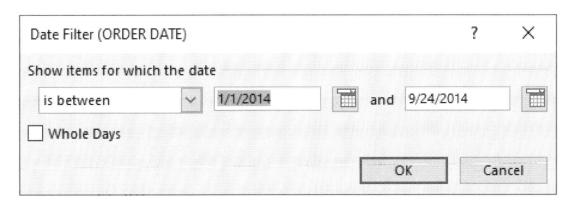

Your Pivot Table is now filtered by the **ORDER DATES** that are between 01/01/2014 and 09/24/2014!

Sum of SALES	Column Labels
Row Labels	2014
1/10/2014	53,586
2/9/2014	14,333
3/11/2014	29,570
4/10/2014	83,468
5/10/2014	25,263
6/9/2014	68,797
7/9/2014	49,562
8/8/2014	13,964
9/7/2014	23,798
Grand Total	**362,341**

Filter by Labels - Text

Pivot Tables offer a lot of filtering options and one of these is filtering based on Text values. Text can be in the form of Months, Customers or Products.

These are the filtering options that are available for Text values:

Equals...	Begins With...	Greater Than...
Does not Equal...	Does Not Begin With...	Greater Than or Equal To...
Between...	Ends With...	Less Than...
Not Between...	Does Not End With...	Less Than or Equal To...
Contains...		
Does Not Contain...		

This is our current Pivot Table setup with **SALES MONTHS** in the Rows area and **SALES** in the Values area.

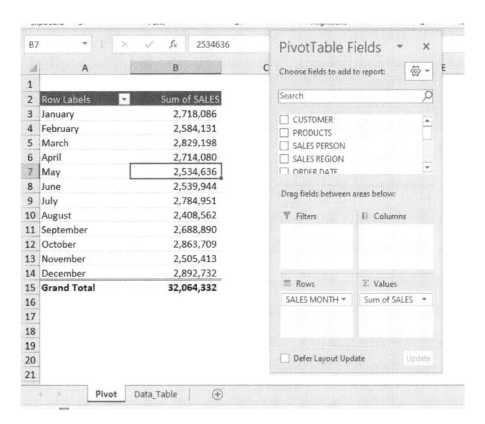

STEP 1: In the **Row Labels**, click on the **Down Arrow** and select **Label Filters.**

You will see that we have a lot of filtering options. Let us try out **Ends With.**

STEP 2: You can see that the Label Filter will be applied to the **SALES MONTH.**

Type in *ber* to get the months ending in *ber*. Click **OK.**

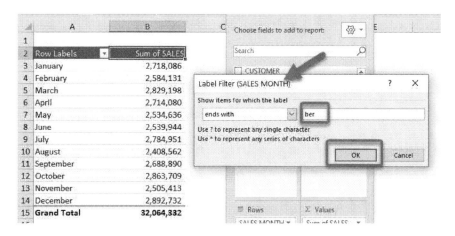

Now we have the filtering applied in a flash and the months of Septem**ber**, Octo**ber**, Novem**ber** and Decem**ber** are showing!

	A	B
1		
2	Row Labels	Sum of SALES
3	September	2,688,890
4	October	2,863,709
5	November	2,505,413
6	December	2,892,732
7	**Grand Total**	**10,950,744**

Filter by Labels - Numerical Text

Pivot Tables allow you to filter based on numerical text, which includes numerical and alphabetical sequences.

This is our current Pivot Table setup with ITEM NUMBERS in the Rows area and SALES in the Values area.

We will be filtering by the ITEM NUMBERS **alphanumeric values**. They come in the format of 3 numbers followed by 3 letters (e.g. 123ABC):

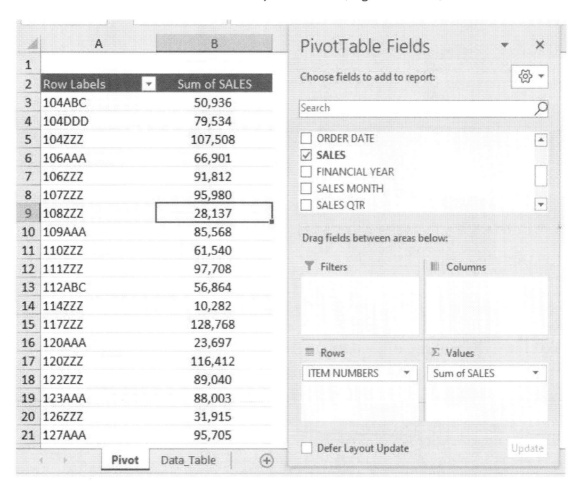

STEP 1: In the **Row Labels**, click on the **Down Arrow** and select **Label Filters.**

You will see that we have a lot of filtering options. Let us try out **Greater Than Or Equal To** filter.

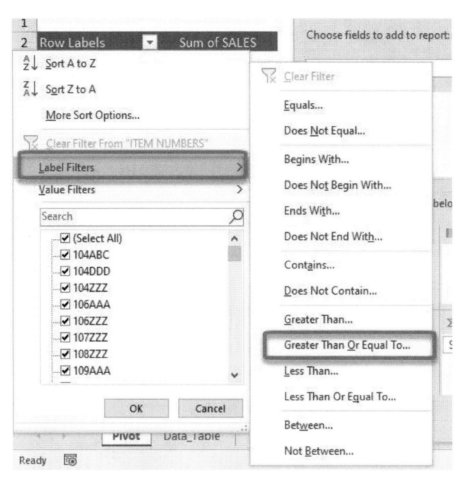

STEP 2: Type in **110aaa** to get the values equal to or above 110aaa. You can see that the Label Filter will be applied to the **ITEM NUMBERS**. Click **OK.**

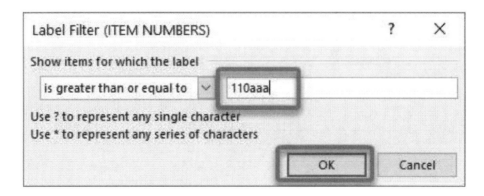

Now we have the filtering applied in a flash!

You can see the values that are greater than or equal to 110AAA like 110ZZZ, 111ZZZ, and 112ABC!

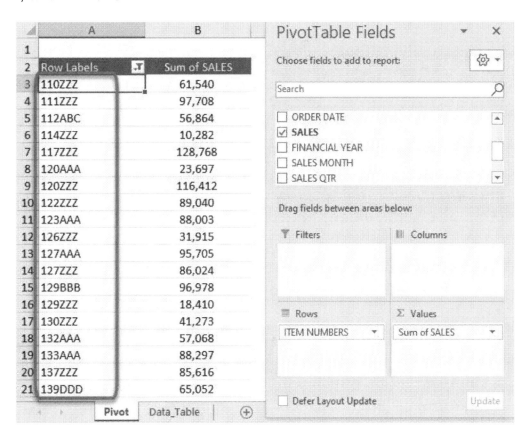

Filter by Values

Pivot Tables allow filtering on numerical values. Values can be in the form of Sales, Units or Phone Numbers, just to name a few examples.

These are the filtering options that are available for Values:

Equals...	Greater Than...	Between...
Does not Equal...	Greater Than or Equal To...	Not Between...
	Less Than...	Top 10...
	Less Than or Equal To...	

This is our current Pivot Table setup with **ORDER DATE** in the Rows area and **SALES** in the Values area.

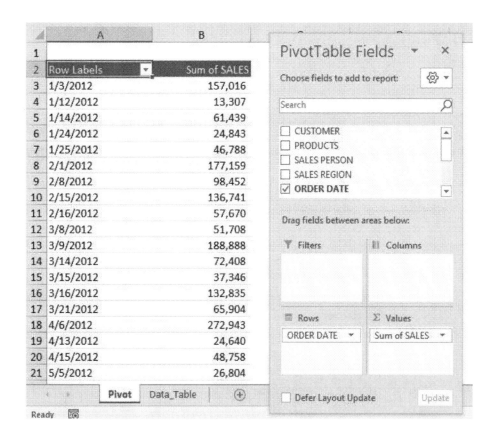

STEP 1: In the **Row Labels**, click on the **Down Arrow** and select **Value Filters.**

You will see that we have a lot of filtering options. Let us try out **Between!**

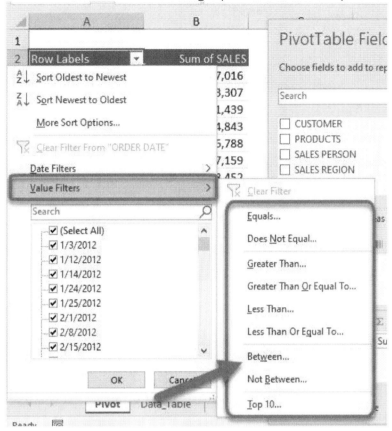

STEP 2: In the Value Filter dialog box, select or input the following into each respective field:

Sum of SALES

Is between

100000 and **200000**

Click **OK.**

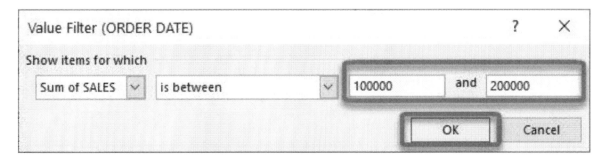

Now we have the filtering applied for any Sum of SALES values between 100,000 and 200,000.

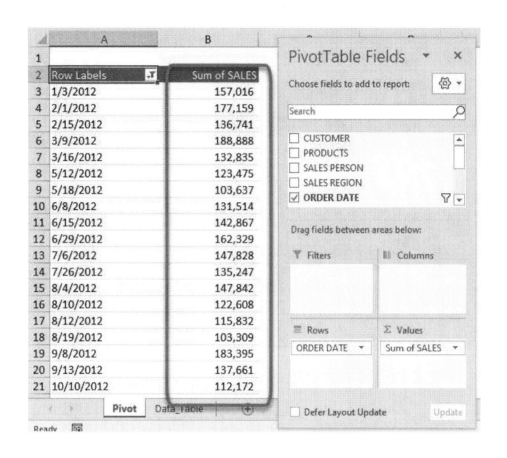

Filter Top or Bottom 5 Customers

You can easily filter your Pivot Table to show the Top or Bottom X Items.

This is great if you want to see your Top/Bottom 5 Performing Customers, Sales Person or Regions, just to name a few examples.

Here is an example of a company's sales data for each customer in an Excel Table:

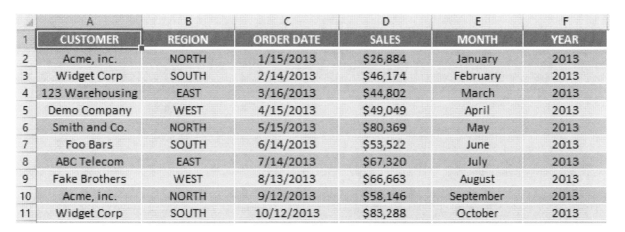

	A	B	C	D	E	F
1	CUSTOMER	REGION	ORDER DATE	SALES	MONTH	YEAR
2	Acme, inc.	NORTH	1/15/2013	$26,884	January	2013
3	Widget Corp	SOUTH	2/14/2013	$46,174	February	2013
4	123 Warehousing	EAST	3/16/2013	$44,802	March	2013
5	Demo Company	WEST	4/15/2013	$49,049	April	2013
6	Smith and Co.	NORTH	5/15/2013	$80,369	May	2013
7	Foo Bars	SOUTH	6/14/2013	$53,522	June	2013
8	ABC Telecom	EAST	7/14/2013	$67,320	July	2013
9	Fake Brothers	WEST	8/13/2013	$66,663	August	2013
10	Acme, inc.	NORTH	9/12/2013	$58,146	September	2013
11	Widget Corp	SOUTH	10/12/2013	$83,288	October	2013

STEP 1: Insert a new Pivot Table by clicking on your data and going to *Insert > Pivot Table > New Worksheet or Existing Worksheet*.

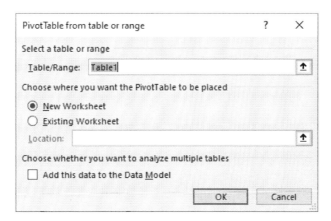

STEP 2: In the PivotTable Fields dialog box, drag the **CUSTOMER Field** to the **Row Area** and **SALES Field** to the **Values Area**.

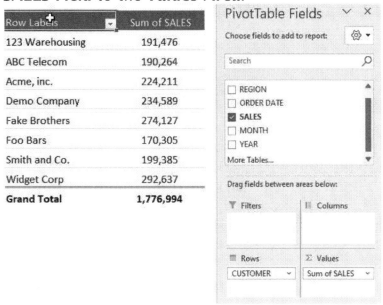

Now we have an entire list of Total Sales for each customer. To find the Top 5 Customers by Total Sales, follow the steps below:

STEP 3: Click on the **drop-down button** next to **Row Labels**.

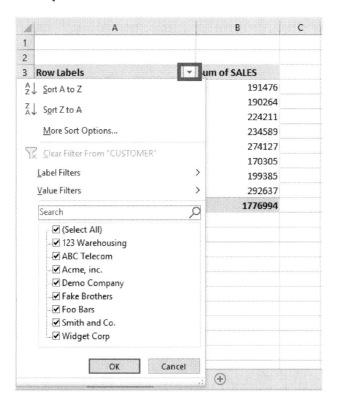

STEP 4: Go to **Value Filters** > **Top 10**.

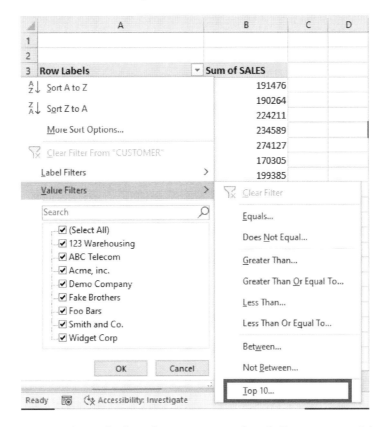

STEP 5: In the Top 10 Filter dialog box, input the following Field items:

Top

5

Items

By Sum of SALES

Click **OK**.

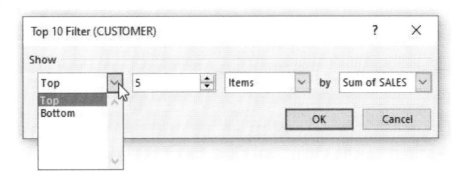

The Pivot Table is now showing the Top 5 customers only!

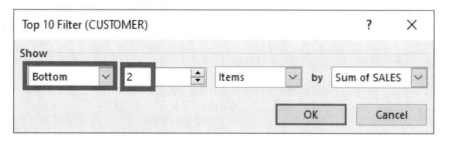

Row Labels	Sum of SALES
Acme, inc.	224211
Demo Company	234589
Fake Brothers	274127
Smith and Co.	199385
Widget Corp	292637
Grand Total	**1224949**

Now that we have a list of the Top 5 customers, we can also find the Bottom 2 customers.

STEP 6: Go to **Value Filters > Top 10**.

In the Top 10 Filter dialog box, input the following field items:

Bottom

2

Items

By Sum of SALES

Click **OK**.

The Pivot Table is now showing the Bottom 2 customers only!

Row Labels	Sum of SALES
ABC Telecom	190264
Foo Bars	170305
Grand Total	**360569**

Filter by Values - Top or Bottom %

You can easily filter your Pivot Table to show the values that make the Top or Bottom X Percentage of the Grand Total.

This is great if you want to see the values that make up the top 25% of the Grand Total.

This is our current Pivot Table setup with **CHANNEL PARTNERS** in the Rows area and **SALES** in the Values area.

We want to find the **Top 25% CHANNEL PARTNERS** by **SALES**.

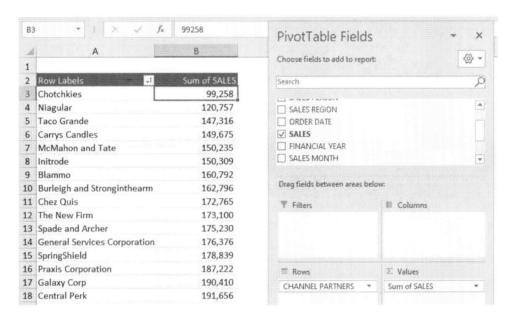

The Grand Total **SALES** for all **CHANNEL PARTNERS** is 32,064,332.

123	Demo Company	403,623
124	The Legitimate Businessmen	428,712
125	ABC Telecom	430,706
126	**Grand Total**	**32,064,332**

STEP 1: In the **Row Labels** click on the **Down Arrow** and select **Value Filters.**

You will see that we have a lot of filtering options. Let us try out the **Top 10.**

STEP 2: In the Top 10 Filter dialog box, select the following from the drop-down options:

Top

25

Percent

By Sum of SALES

Click **OK.**

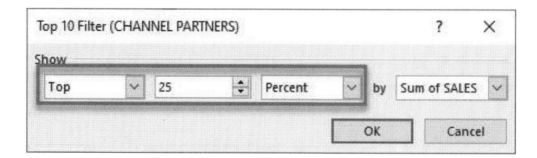

We now have the Top **CHANNEL PARTNERS** that make up 25% of the Grand Total!

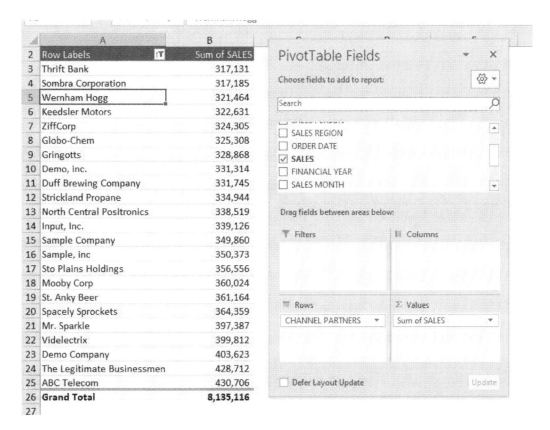

STEP 3: Let's try the Bottom values.

In the Row Labels click on the **Down Arrow** and select **Value Filters** and **Top 10.**

Select the **Bottom 25 Percent** by **Sum of SALES** and click **OK.**

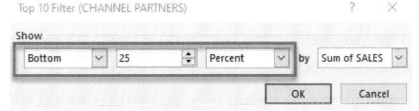

We now have the Bottom CHANNEL PARTNERS that make up 25% of the Grand Total!

Row Labels	Sum of SALES
Chotchkies	99,258
Niagular	120,757
Taco Grande	147,316
Carrys Candles	149,675
McMahon and Tate	150,235
Initrode	150,309
Blammo	160,792
Burleigh and Stronginthearr	162,796
Chez Quis	172,765
The New Firm	173,100
Spade and Archer	175,230
General Services Corporatic	176,376
SpringShield	178,839
Praxis Corporation	187,222
Galaxy Corp	190,410
Central Perk	191,656
The Krusty Krab	193,034
Flowers By Irene	197,257
Compuglobalhypermeganet	197,382
Charles Townsend Agency	198,584
123 Warehousing	204,885
Gadgetron	205,615
Ajax	207,741
Rouster and Sideways	209,216
The Frying Dutchman	209,367
Mammoth Pictures	210,432
Vandelay Industries	210,582
Taggart Transcontinental	212,391
Moes Tavern	212,870
Sirius Cybernetics Corporati	212,907
LexCorp	214,428
Kumatsu Motors	215,098
Osato Chemicals	216,243
C.H. Lavatory and Sons	217,361
Nordyne Defense Dynamics	217,627
Krustyco	218,485
Gizmonic Institute	221,497
Water and Power	223,475
Wentworth Industries	224,072
Widget Corp	224,093
Initech	227,088
U.S. Robotics and Mechanic	227,605
Grand Total	8,116,071

Filter by Values - Top or Bottom Sum

You can easily filter your Pivot Table to show the Top or Bottom Sums.

This is great if you want to see the records that account for the Top/Bottom $1,000,000 of Total Sales.

This is our current Pivot Table setup with **CHANNEL PARTNERS** in the Rows area and **SALES** in the Values area.

We will be filtering the **Top Channel Partners** that account for $1,000,000 of **Total Sales**.

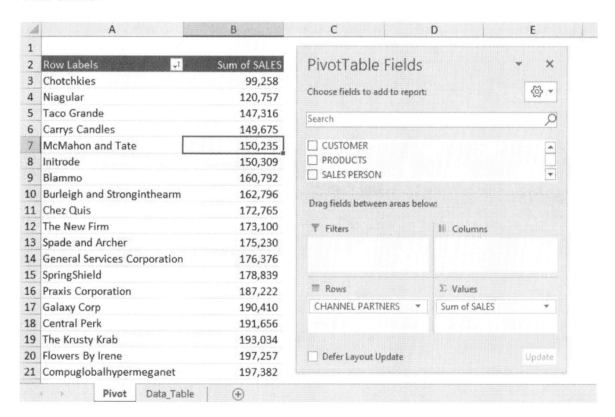

STEP 1: In the **Row Labels** click on the **Down Arrow** and select **Value Filters.**

You will see that we have a lot of filtering options. Let us try out **Top 10.**

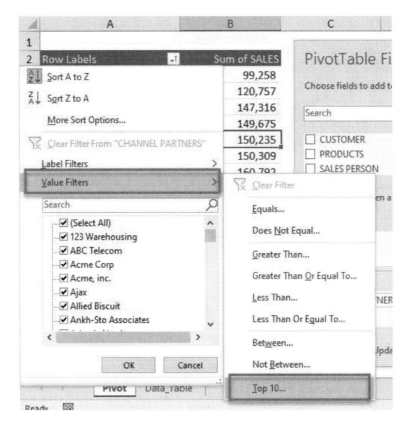

STEP 2: In the Top 10 Filter dialog box, input the following field items:

Top

1,000,000

Sum

By Sum of SALES

Click **OK.**

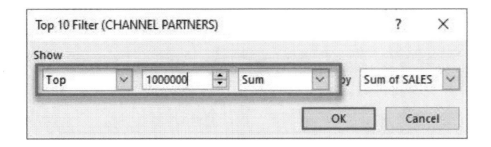

Now we have the **Top CHANNEL PARTNERS** that, when summed up, will give you at least $1,000,000 of the Grand Total value.

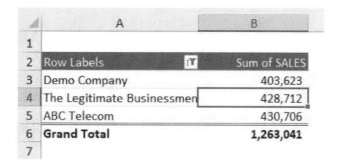

STEP 3: Let's try the Bottom values.

In the Row Labels click on the **Down Arrow** and select **Value Filters** and **Top 10.**

Input **Bottom 1,000,000** and **Sum** and click **OK.**

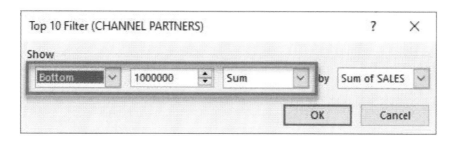

Now we have the **Bottom CHANNEL PARTNERS** that, when summed up, will give you at least $1,000,000 of the Grand Total value.

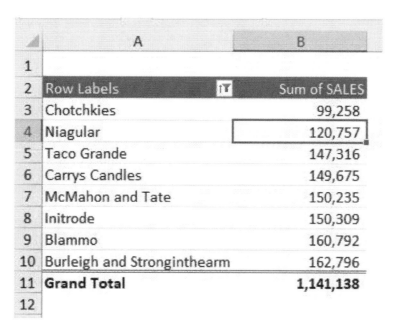

Filter by Text Wildcards

Pivot Table filtering allows you to use wildcard characters to make your filtering dynamic. For example, you can use these wildcard characters:

- *** (Asterisk)** - This returns any series of characters before or after the asterisk.
- **? (Question Mark)** - This returns text that contains one variable.

You can check out a few examples of these wildcards below:

	*	Returns any series of characters before/after the asterisk
Begins with...	Glo*	Globex Corporation
		Globo Gym American Corp
		Globo-Chem

	*tech	
Contains...	*tech	Initech
		Primatech

	inc	
Equals...	*inc*	Acme, inc.
		Demo, inc.
		Incom Corporation
		Input, Inc.
		Sample, inc

	?	Returns text that contains one variable
Contains...	a?c	ABC Telecom
		Monarch Playing Card Co.
		Sombra Corporation
		Spade and Archer

This is our current Pivot Table setup with **CHANNEL PARTNERS** in the Rows area and **SALES** in the Values area.

STEP 1: In the **Row Labels** click on the Down Arrow and select **Label Filters.**

You will see that we have a lot of filtering options. Let us try out **Begins With.**

STEP 2: In the Label Filter dialog box, input the following:

Begins with

Glo*

Click **OK.**

This will give us all the CHANNEL PARTNERS that **start with Glo**, what comes after that could be anything.

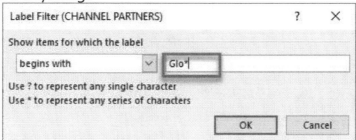

We now have all our CHANNEL PARTNERS **starting with Glo**!

Row Labels	Sum of SALES
Globex Corporation	234,763
Globo Gym American Corp	246,190
Globo-Chem	325,308
Grand Total	**806,261**

STEP 3: In the Row Labels click on the **Down Arrow** and select **Label Filters** and then **Contains.**

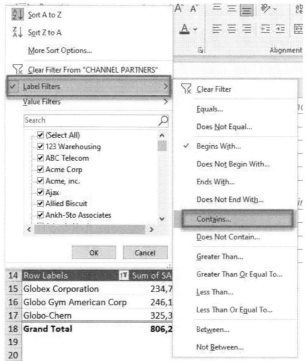

STEP 4: In the Label Filter dialog box, input the following:

contains

a?c

Click **OK.**

This will give us all the CHANNEL PARTNERS that have the following name combination: **a <any character> c**

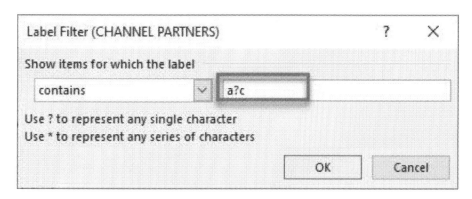

We now have all our CHANNEL PARTNERS that **start with a and end in c**

We can see it matched:

"abc" - **ABC** Telecom

"arc" - Mon**arc**h Playing Card Co.

"a c" - Sombr**a** **C**orporation

"arc" - Spade and **Arc**her

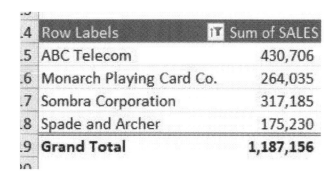

Clear Filters & Clear a Pivot Table

When working with Pivot Table filters, there are times where you have a lot of filters setup and it takes time to reset them one by one.

How about if you don't like your Pivot Table set up and want to start from scratch?

In this tip I will show you how to quickly clear filters as well as clear a Pivot Table.

Here is our current Pivot Table setup. You can see we have 3 Filters for **SALES PERSON**, **SALES QTR** and **ORDER DATE**.

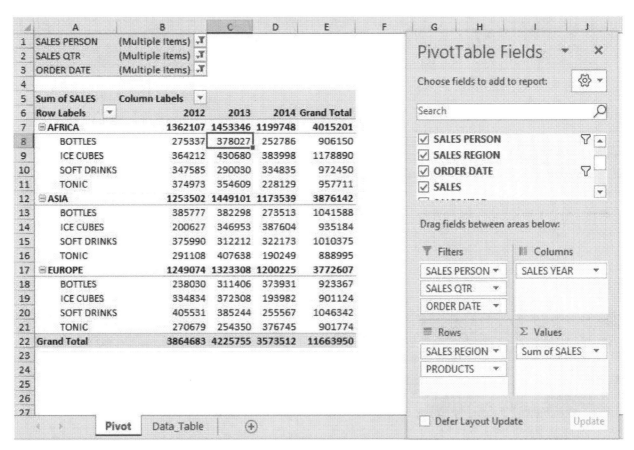

If we open the **SALES PERSON** Filter, you can see we have items filtered out:

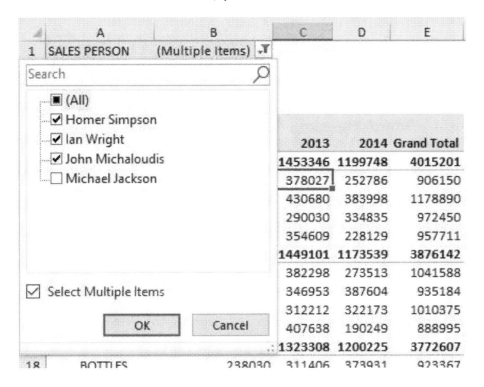

Same goes for the SALES QTR Filter:

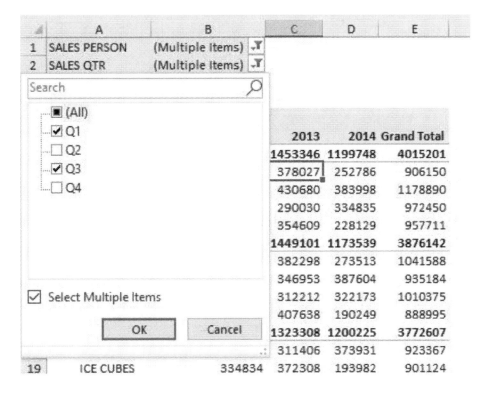

STEP 1: To reset all the filters in one step, go to *PivotTable Analyze > Clear > Clear Filters*

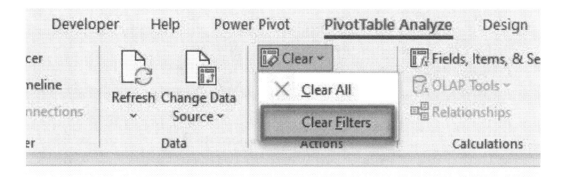

And just like that, all our filters are now reset!

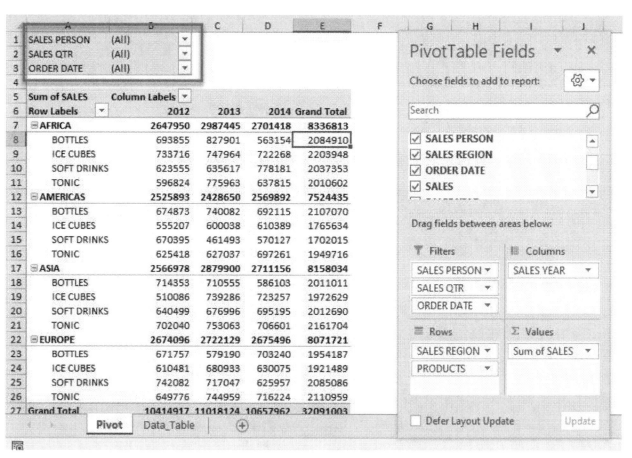

STEP 2: What if you want to reset your PivotTable setup?

Go to *PivotTable Analyze > Clear > Clear All.*

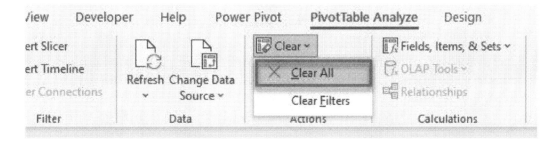

Now you can start again with setting up your Pivot Table Fields!

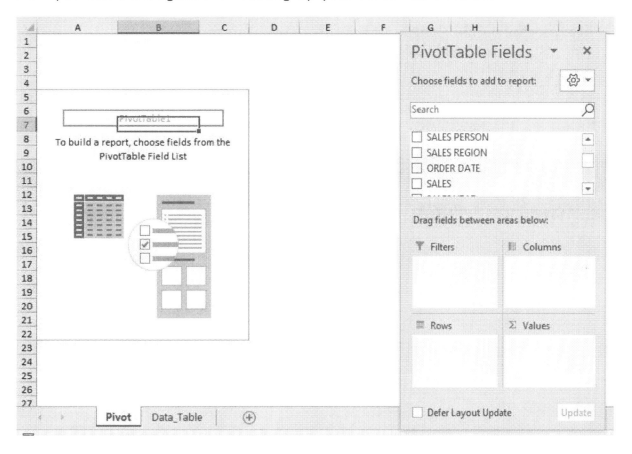

SLICERS

Insert a Pivot Table Slicer

Slicers in Excel are visual filters or interactive buttons that allow you to see what items have been chosen within a Pivot Table.

They were introduced in Excel 2010 and Mac for Excel 2016 and are a must for anyone wanting to wow their boss (and themselves!) by adding interactivity to their reports!

STEP 1: Select your Pivot Table by clicking anywhere inside it.

Sum of SALES	Column Labels		
Row Labels	2013	2014	2015
123 Warehousing	66,826	49,562	75,088
ABC Telecom	67,320	108,285	14,659
Acme, inc.	85,030	25,263	113,918
Demo Company	113,799	13,964	106,826
Fake Brothers	66,663	164,248	43,216
Foo Bars	53,522	31,176	85,607
Smith and Co.	80,369	77,384	41,632
Widget Corp	129,462	68,797	94,378
Grand Total	**662,991**	**538,679**	**575,324**

STEP 2: Go to *PivotTable Analyze > Filter > Insert Slicer.*

Select the **Month** and **Year** Fields. Click **OK**.

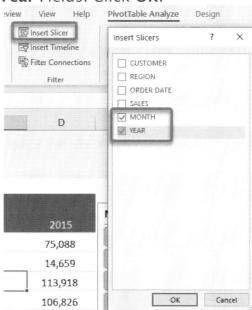

Your Slicers are now ready! Go crazy clicking, slicing and dicing your data!

PRO TIP: Hold down the CTRL key to select multiple items in your Slicer.

Slicer Styles & Settings

There are several different Slicer Styles available for you when you insert a Pivot Table Slicer.

These Slicer Styles add color to a dull Excel workbook and are very eye- catching!

STEP 1: Select your Slicer with your mouse.

STEP 2: Go to *Slicer Tools* > *Options* > *Slicer Styles*

There are 14 Styles you can select ranging from Light to Dark. Select a style you prefer by clicking on it with your mouse.

If you do not like the chosen Style, just follow the process above and choose another color!

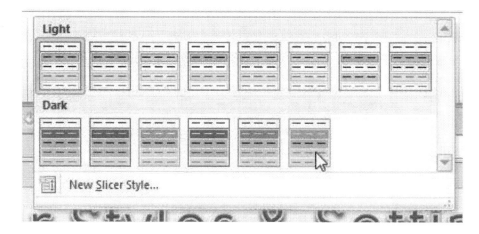

Your Pivot Table Slicer now has come to life!

Customize a Slicer

Pivot Table Slicers are limited in their style & color as there are only 14 different preset Slicer Styles to choose from.

What if you wanted to create your own Slicer with super cool colors and fonts?

Well, you can!

STEP 1: Select the Slicer and go to the **Slicer** tab.

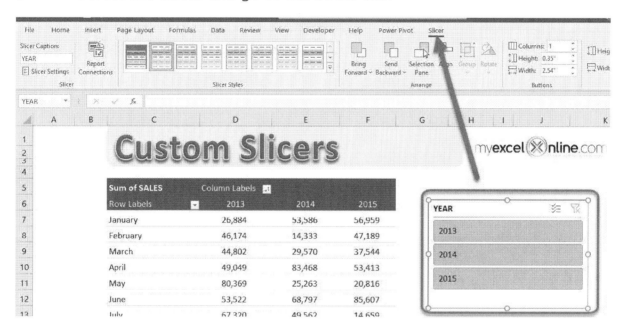

STEP 2: Under the **Slicer Styles** drop down, **right click on a Slicer** and choose **Duplicate.**

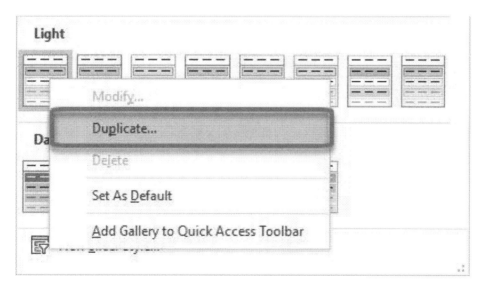

STEP 3: Let's change the Slicer background.

1. In the **Slicer Element** section, select **Whole Slicer**.

2. Click on the **Format** button.

3. Select the **Fill** tab.

4. Select the color **orange**.

5. Press **OK**.

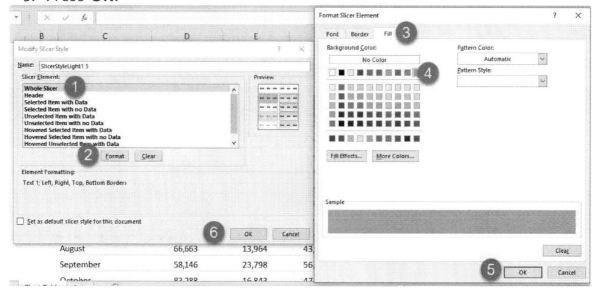

STEP 4: To see the custom changes you need to **select the newly created custom Slicer** from the **Slicer Styles** drop down box.

Below you can see the newly created Slicer!

PRO TIP: There are several Slicer Elements which can become very confusing.

I have tried to explain the different options with images in this Downloadable Workbook: https://www.myexcelonline.com/wp-content/uploads/2015/10/Slicer-Elements1.xlsx

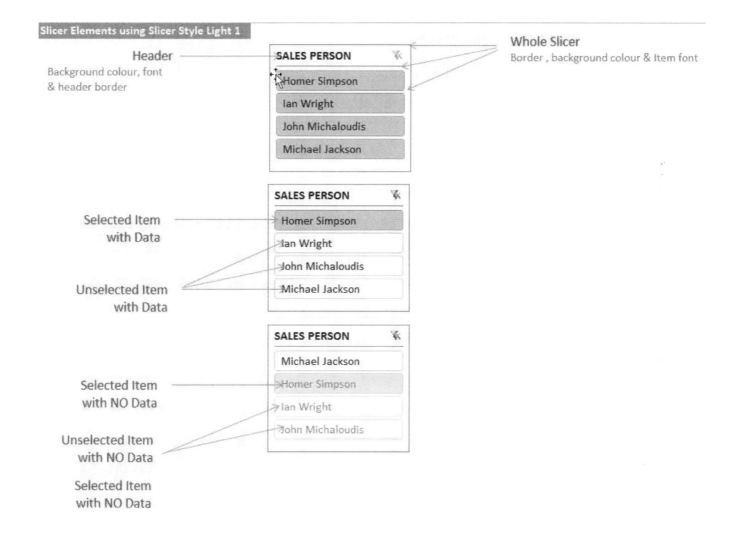

Excel Table Slicers

Pivot Table Slicers were introduced in Excel 2010, and they have been a popular feature as they allow us to filter items with beautiful interactive buttons.

Starting with Excel 2013, Slicers were extended to be used with Excel Tables. WOW!

To insert a Slicer in an Excel Table you must follow these short steps:

STEP 1: Click inside the Excel Table.

STEP 2: Select *Table Design > Tools > Insert Slicer*

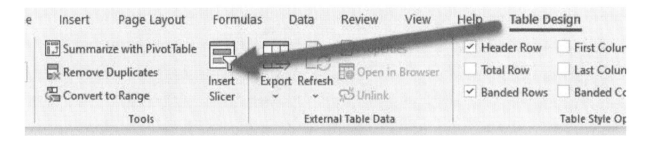

STEP 3: Tick the Table Headers that you want to include in your Slicer and press **OK.**

STEP 4: You can update the look and feel by going to *Slicer > Slicer Styles.*

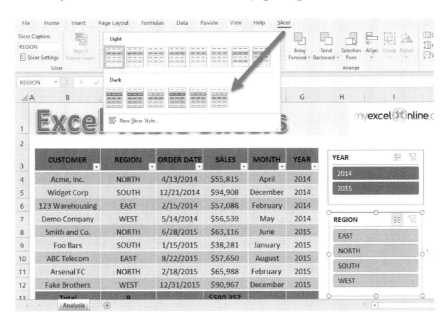

Click on the Slicer buttons and see how your Excel Table gets filtered without needing to select the filter drop down from inside the Excel Table.

Copy a Custom Slicer Style into a New Workbook

Previously in this chapter I showed you how to **Customize a Slicer**!

You can easily copy a custom Slicer Style and reuse it across multiple workbooks.

I have a nifty workaround that you can use, so that you can copy your custom Slicer Style in just a few clicks!

We have **two workbooks** below.

The left side has the **custom Slicer Style** that we created. We want this style to be applied to the Slicers on the workbook to the right.

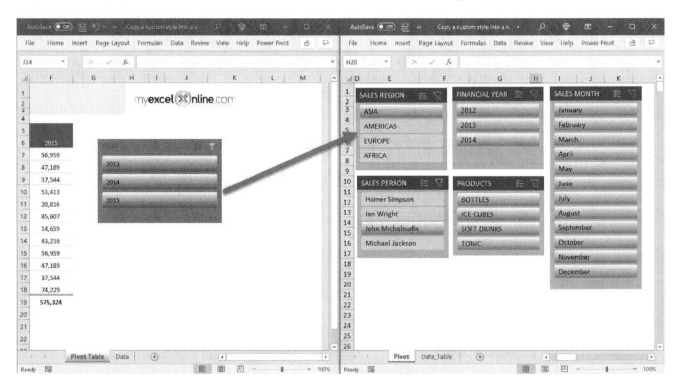

STEP 1: On the workbook that has the custom Slicer Style that we created, **right click on the Slicer** and select **Copy.**

STEP 2: Let us jump over to the second workbook and on any blank space click *Home > Clipboard > Paste*

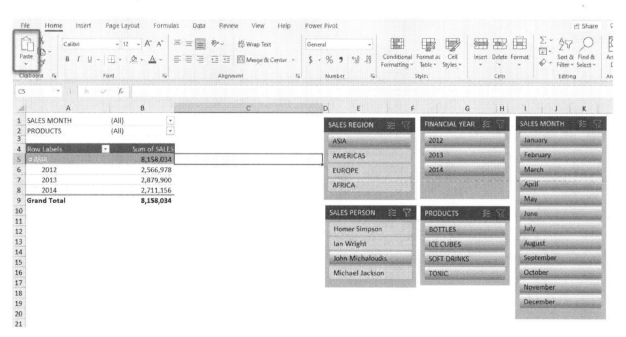

You can see the Slicer with the custom style shows up inside the **Slicer Styles.**

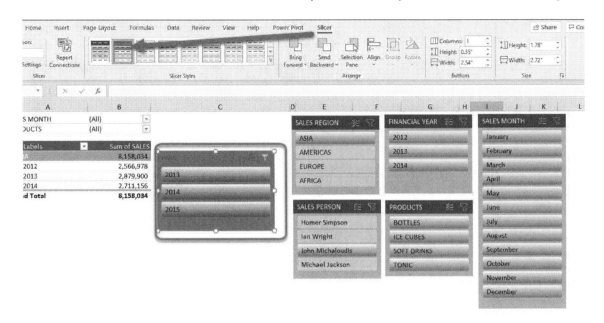

STEP 3: Now select the Slicer that you want to apply the custom style to.

Go to *Slicer > Slicer Styles and select the custom Slicer Style.*

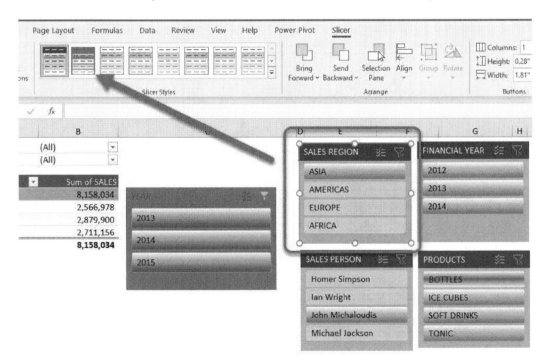

STEP 4: Now we do not need the extra Slicer that we copied. Select that and press **Delete**.

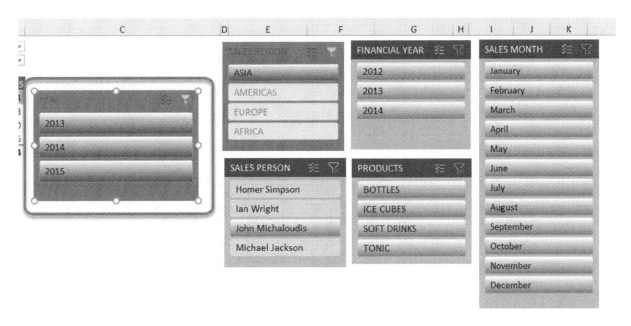

Now you have the custom Slicer Style copied over into another workbook!

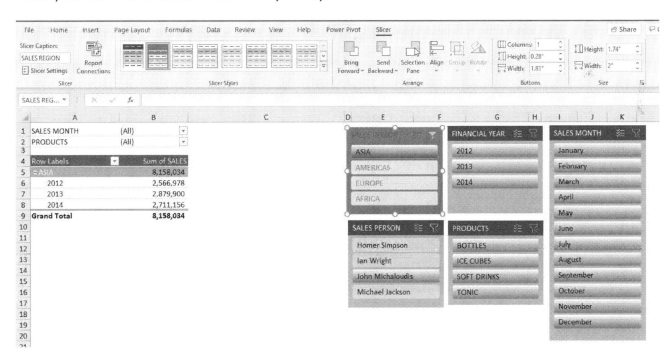

Add Columns to Slicer Buttons

When you insert a Pivot Table Slicer it defaults to a one column Slicer, showing all your items in a vertical layout.

If your Pivot Table Slicer has Months from January to December, you can change the layout of the Slicer buttons to show in 3 separate columns, turning it into a "Quarterly View".

STEP 1: Select your Slicer.

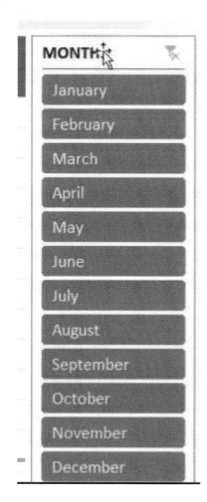

STEP 2: Go to *Slicer > Buttons > Columns*

Select **Columns** to **3.**

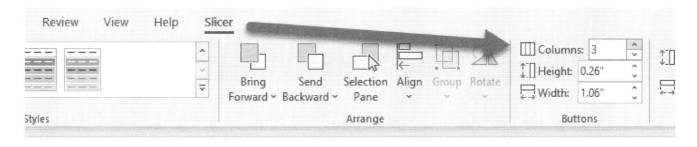

Your slicer now has a 3-column button layout!

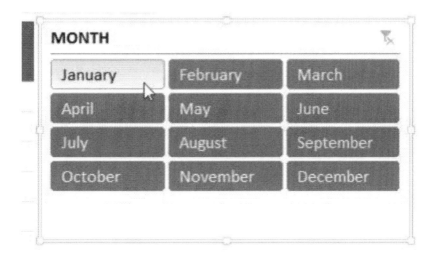

Connect Slicers to Multiple Pivot Tables

When you insert a Pivot Table Slicer, it is only connected to the Pivot Table used to insert it.

What about if you had multiple Pivot Tables from the same data source and wanted to add various Slicers? That way when you press one slicer button all Pivot Tables change in tandem.

This is possible with the **Report Connections** option within the Slicer.

I will show you one of the most popular tips on how to **connect a Slicer to multiple Pivot Tables**.

Let's set up Pivot Table #1!

STEP 1: **Create 2 Pivot Tables** by clicking in your data set and selecting *Insert > Pivot Table > New Worksheet or Existing Worksheet*

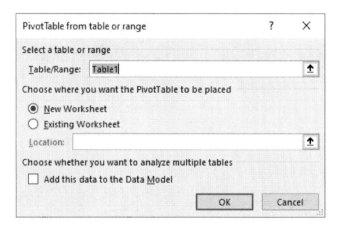

Drag these Pivot Table Fields in the following areas below:
Rows: **REGION**
Values: **SALES**

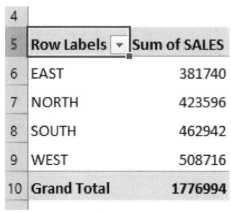

Now, let's set up Pivot Table #2!

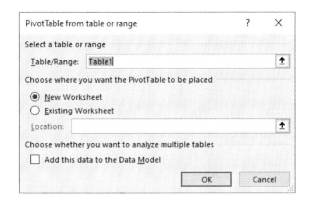

Drag these PivotTable Fields in the following areas below:
Rows: **CUSTOMER**
Values: **SALES**

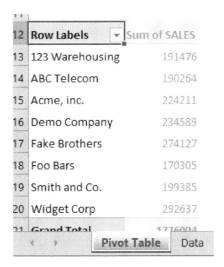

STEP 2: **Click in Pivot Table #1 and insert a MONTH Slicer** by going to
PivotTable Analyze > Filter > Insert Slicer > Month. Press OK.

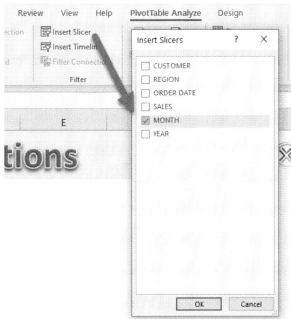

STEP 3: **Click in Pivot Table #2 then insert a YEAR Slicer** by going to *PivotTable Analyze > Filter > Insert Slicer > Year.* Press OK.

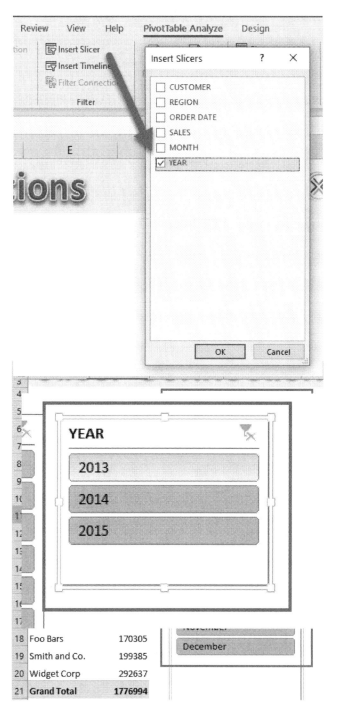

STEP 4: Right Click on Slicer #1 and go to *Report Connections > Check PivotTable2.* Then press **OK**

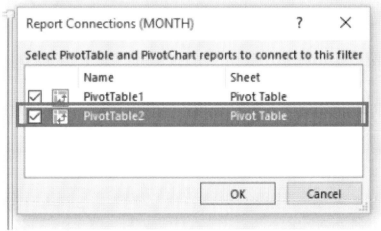

STEP 5: Right Click on Slicer #2 and go to *Report Connections > Check PivotTable2.* Then press **OK.**

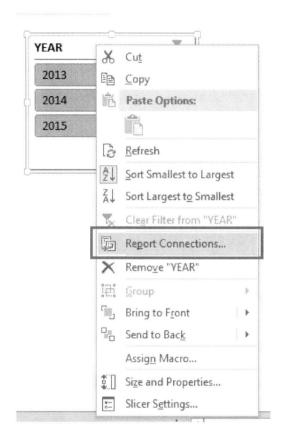

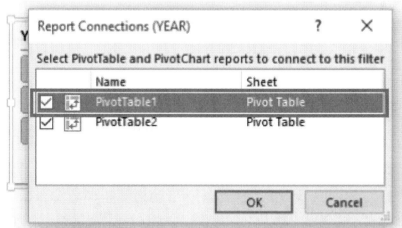

Now as you select each Slicer's items, both Pivot Tables #1 and #2 will cross filter accordingly!

PIVOTTABLE1

Row Labels	Sum of SALES
EAST	381740
NORTH	423596
SOUTH	462942
WEST	508716
Grand Total	**1776994**

SLICER 1

MONTH

January	February	March
April	May	June
July	August	September
October	November	December

PIVOTTABLE2

Row Labels	Sum of SALES
123 Warehousing	191476
ABC Telecom	190264
Acme, inc.	224211
Demo Company	234589
Fake Brothers	274127
Foo Bars	170305
Smith and Co.	199385
Widget Corp	292637
Grand Total	**1776994**

SLICER 2

YEAR

2013
2014
2015

Different Ways to Filter a Slicer

Pivot Table Slicers are the best thing since sliced bread! There are several ways that you can filter a Pivot Table Slicer which I will explain below.

LEFT MOUSE CLICK

You can select Items from the Slicer by using your left mouse button.

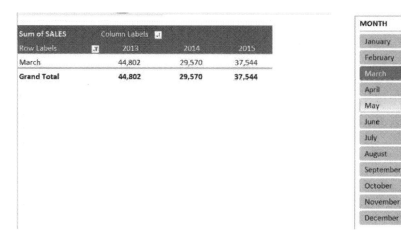

DRAG LEFT MOUSE BUTTON

You can select an array of items by clicking the left mouse button and doing a dragging motion downwards/upwards within the Slicer.

CTRL KEY

You can select multiple items by holding down the CTRL key on your keyboard. Then select the Slicer items with your left mouse button.

SHIFT KEY

Select a Slicer item and hold down the SHIFT key on your keyboard. Then select your two Slicer items. This will select the range between the items!

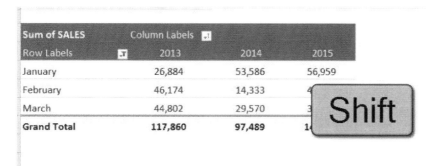

Multi-Select Slicer Items

There is a new way that you can filter a Slicer that was introduced in Excel 2016.

You can now **multi-select Slicer items** without using the CTRL key and your mouse.

This is our data that we will use for our Pivot Table and Slicer.

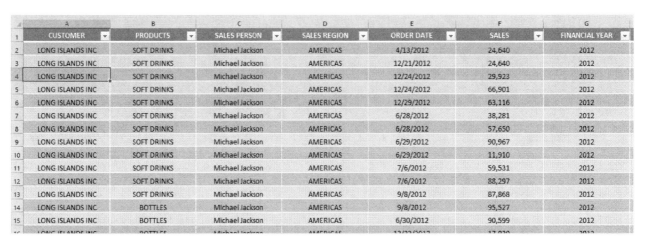

	A	B	C	D	E	F	G
1	CUSTOMER	PRODUCTS	SALES PERSON	SALES REGION	ORDER DATE	SALES	FINANCIAL YEAR
2	LONG ISLANDS INC	SOFT DRINKS	Michael Jackson	AMERICAS	4/13/2012	24,640	2012
3	LONG ISLANDS INC	SOFT DRINKS	Michael Jackson	AMERICAS	12/21/2012	24,640	2012
4	LONG ISLANDS INC	SOFT DRINKS	Michael Jackson	AMERICAS	12/24/2012	29,923	2012
5	LONG ISLANDS INC	SOFT DRINKS	Michael Jackson	AMERICAS	12/24/2012	66,901	2012
6	LONG ISLANDS INC	SOFT DRINKS	Michael Jackson	AMERICAS	12/29/2012	63,116	2012
7	LONG ISLANDS INC	SOFT DRINKS	Michael Jackson	AMERICAS	6/28/2012	38,281	2012
8	LONG ISLANDS INC	SOFT DRINKS	Michael Jackson	AMERICAS	6/28/2012	57,650	2012
9	LONG ISLANDS INC	SOFT DRINKS	Michael Jackson	AMERICAS	6/29/2012	90,967	2012
10	LONG ISLANDS INC	SOFT DRINKS	Michael Jackson	AMERICAS	6/29/2012	11,910	2012
11	LONG ISLANDS INC	SOFT DRINKS	Michael Jackson	AMERICAS	7/6/2012	59,531	2012
12	LONG ISLANDS INC	SOFT DRINKS	Michael Jackson	AMERICAS	7/6/2012	88,297	2012
13	LONG ISLANDS INC	SOFT DRINKS	Michael Jackson	AMERICAS	9/8/2012	87,868	2012
14	LONG ISLANDS INC	BOTTLES	Michael Jackson	AMERICAS	9/8/2012	95,527	2012
15	LONG ISLANDS INC	BOTTLES	Michael Jackson	AMERICAS	6/30/2012	90,599	2012

STEP 1: Insert a new Pivot Table by clicking on your data and going to *Insert > Pivot Table > New Worksheet or Existing Worksheet.*

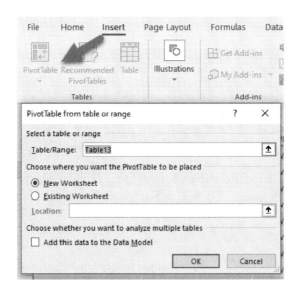

STEP 2: Drag these Pivot Table Fields in the following areas below:

Rows: **PRODUCTS**
Values: **SALES**

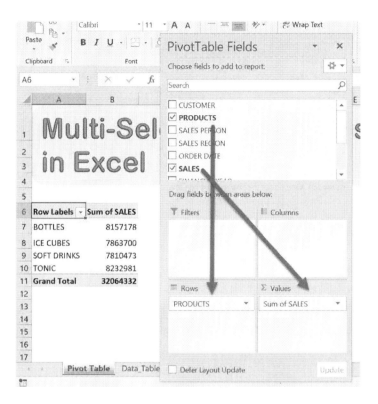

STEP 3: Let us now add our Slicer! Go to *PivotTable Analyze > Filter > Insert Slicer.*

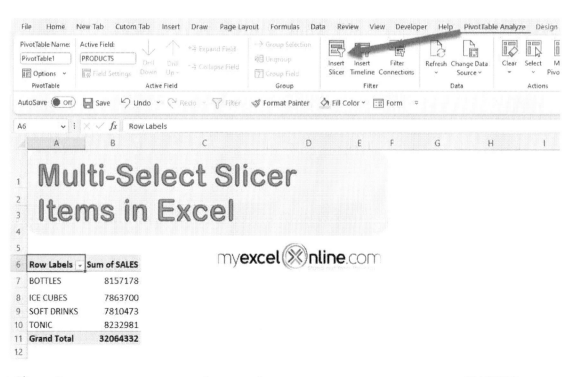

STEP 4: Make sure **SALES REGION** is ticked. Click **OK.**

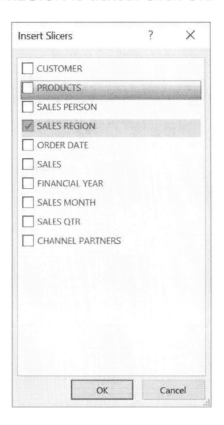

Now we have our **Slicer**! We just need to tick the **Multi-Select button** on the right hand corner of the Slicer to enable this.

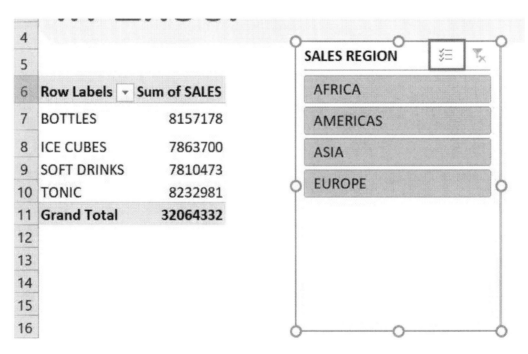

And just like that, you can now **select multiple slicer items with your mouse**! Below we have selected **AMERICAS** and **ASIA**.

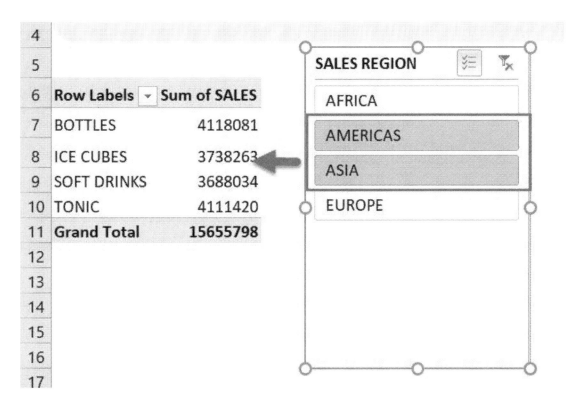

Use One Slicer for Two Pivot Tables

Earlier in this chapter I showed you how to *Connect Slicers to Multiple Pivot Tables* using the Report Connections.

In this tip, you can use a **single slicer for 2 Pivot Tables** without connecting the Slicers.

Here is our current Pivot Table setup.

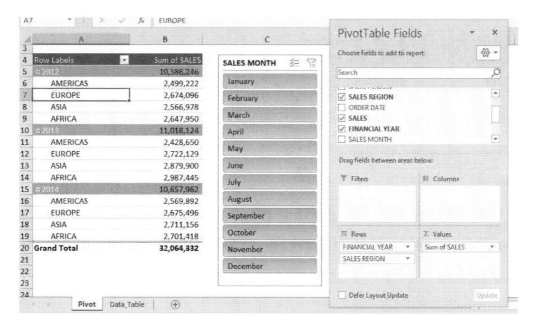

STEP 1: Select any cell inside the Pivot Table and go to *PivotTable Analyze > Select > Entire PivotTable*

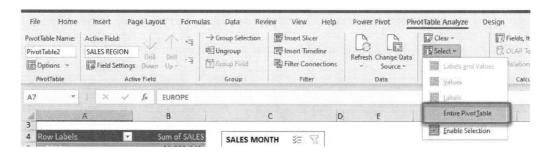

STEP 2: Right click and select **Copy.**

STEP 3: Pick an empty space and select *Home > Paste.*

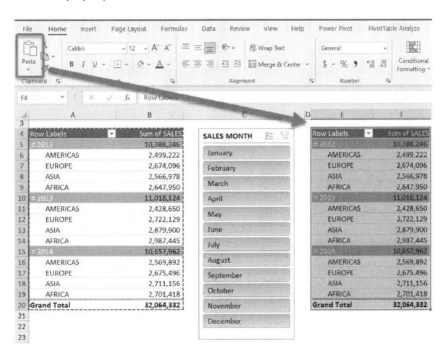

STEP 4: Now setup the second Pivot Table by placing inside the Rows areas the **SALES PERSON** Field and **SALES QTR** Field.

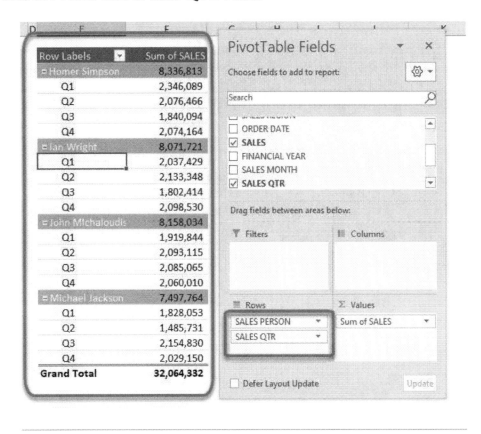

Now let's try out the Slicer! Select **March** and watch both Pivot Tables update at the same time!

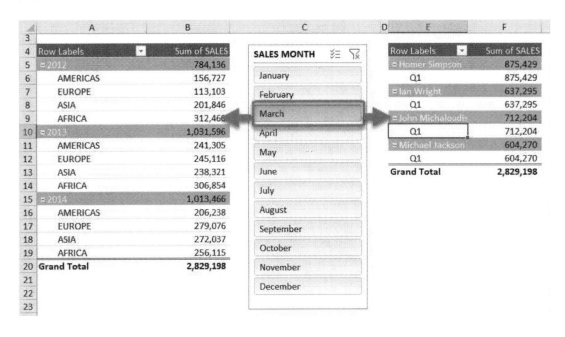

Lock a Pivot Table but not the Slicer

Sometimes when you are sharing a Pivot Table with your colleagues you **do not want the other user(s) to mess with your Pivot Table layout and format**.

What you can do is **lock the Pivot Table** and only allow the user(s) to select the Slicers, making your report interactive and secure from Excel novices like your boss :)

Password to unlock exercise workbook: *myexcelonline*

STEP 1: Click on a Slicer, hold the **CTRL-key** and **select the other Slicer(s)** with your mouse.

STEP 2: Right-click on a Slicer and select **Size & Properties.**

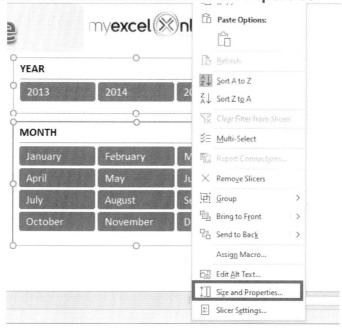

STEP 3: In the **Format Slicer** dialog box, under Properties, ***uncheck* the Locked box**.

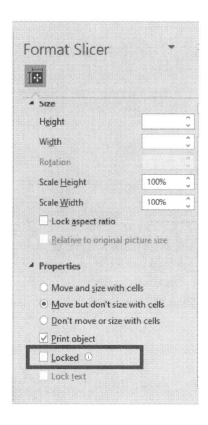

STEP 4: Go to the ribbon menu and select **Review > Protect Sheet.**

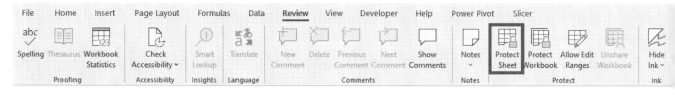

STEP 5: ***Uncheck* the *Select Locked Cells* and *Check* the *Select Unlocked Cells.***

STEP 6: Enter a password (optional) and press **OK.**

STEP 7: Re-enter the password and press **OK.**

The Pivot Table is now locked and a user **can only select the Slicers**!

If they try to mess with your Pivot Table, the following message will appear.

Microsoft Excel

⚠ You cannot use this command on a protected sheet. To use this command, you must first unprotect the sheet (Review tab, Protect group, Unprotect Sheet button). You may be prompted for a password.

OK

Timeline Filter

If your Pivot Table has Dates or Times, you can use a Pivot Table Timeline, which is a dynamic filter option that lets you easily filter by date/time, and zoom in on the period you want with a slider control.

Timelines were introduced in Excel 2013 and are a very cool feature!

Our data source has an ORDER DATE column that we will use for the Timeline.

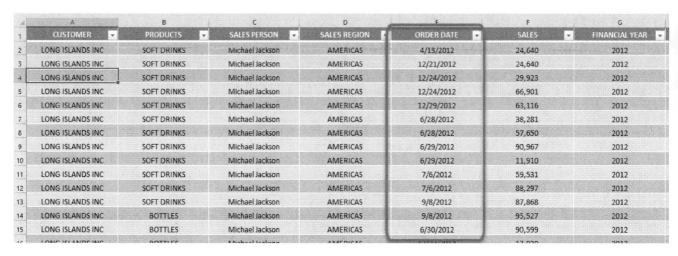

STEP 1: Insert a new Pivot Table by clicking on your data and going to *Insert > Pivot Table > New Worksheet or Existing Worksheet*

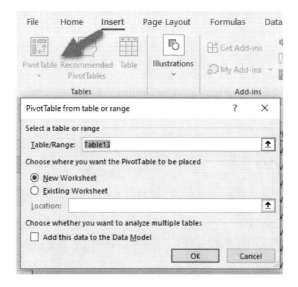

STEP 2: Drag these Pivot Table Fields in the following areas below:

Rows: **SALES REGION**
Values: **SALES**

STEP 3: Let us now add our Timeline! Click in the Pivot Table and go to *PivotTable Analyze > Filter > Insert Timeline.*

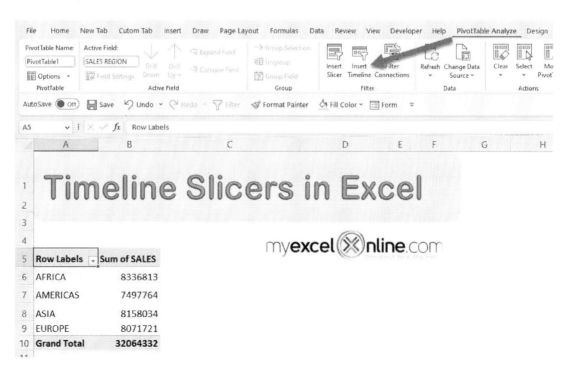

STEP 4: Make sure **ORDER DATE** is ticked. Click **OK.**

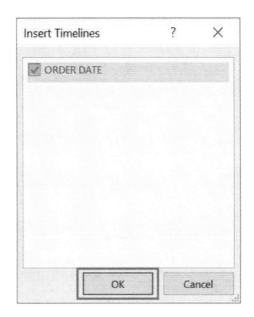

We now you have our **Timeline**!

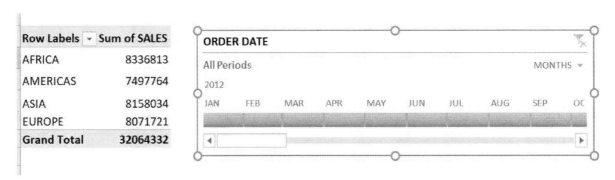

You can play around and set different date ranges. Watch as the Pivot Table data adjusts accordingly.

In the example below we selected Jan 2012 - Mar 2012. On the top right-hand corner, you can also change the periods of your Timeline from the drop down e.g., Years, Quarters, Months and Days.

Slicer Connection Option Greyed Out

Sometimes when you create a Pivot Table and want to insert a Slicer you are unable to do this, as the Slicer button is greyed out.

You try to click on the Slicer button, but nothing

happens. What gives?

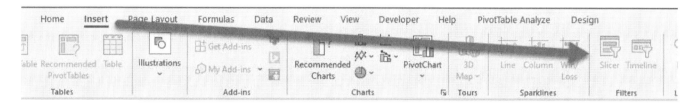

There are two things that can cause your Slicer connection to be greyed out:

1. Your file format is in an **older/incompatible format** (e.g. an *.xls* file extension), OR

2. You can see the text **[Compatibility Mode]** right beside the name of your Excel file:

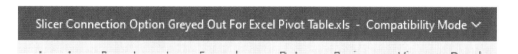

STEP 1: To fix this issue, go to **File > Info > Convert.**

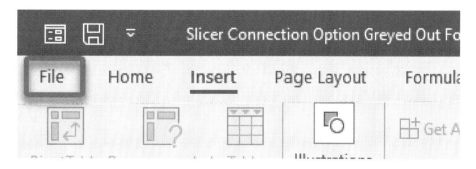

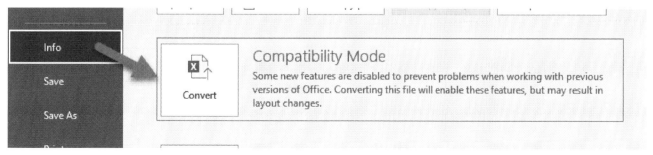

STEP 2: This will convert your Excel file into a more updated version. Click **OK.**

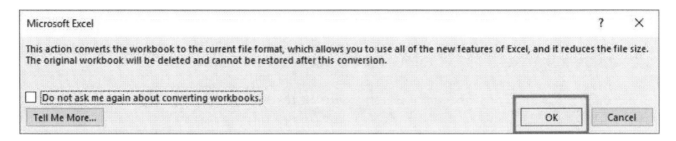

Click **Yes** to reload your workbook.

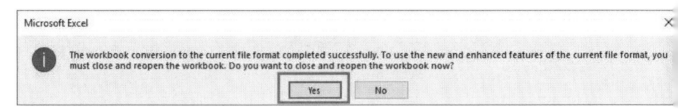

And just like that, you can now insert your Slicer!

PRO TIP: You can also **Save As** your current file as an **.XLSX** file format.

Then close this file and open it again and you will be able to use the Slicer button again!

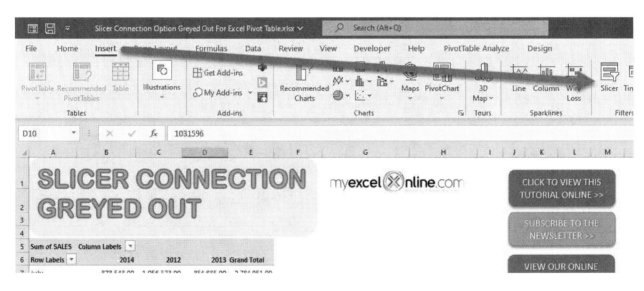

CALCULATED FIELDS & ITEMS

Calculated Field

Pivot Table Calculated Fields allow you to create mathematical calculations with your Field List.

You can use any of the Excel mathematical equations, like: / * + - %

The only limitation is that you cannot reference any cells.

Pivot Table Calculated Fields can be used to calculate Percentage Increases on Sales, Margin Calculations or Cost of Goods sold, as I will show.

Here is our Pivot Table:

| Row Labels | Column Labels | |
| | 2014 | |
	Sum of SALES	Sum of COSTS
123 Warehousing	49,562	7,077
ABC Telecom	108,285	18,477
Acme, inc.	25,263	5,401
Demo Company	13,964	5,124
Fake Brothers	164,248	14,980
Foo Bars	31,176	17,431
Smith and Co.	77,384	15,967
Widget Corp	68,797	9,876
Grand Total	**538,679**	**94,333**

STEP 1: Click on the Pivot Table and go to *PivotTable Analyze > Fields, Items, & Sets > Calculated Field.*

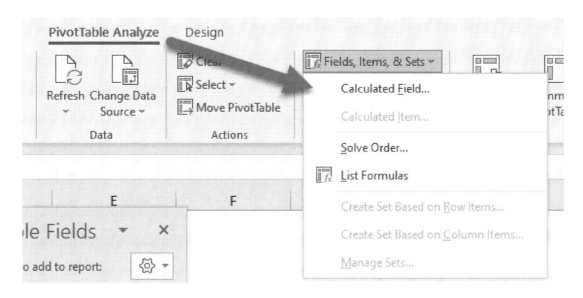

STEP 2: Set the Name to *Cost of Goods Sold*

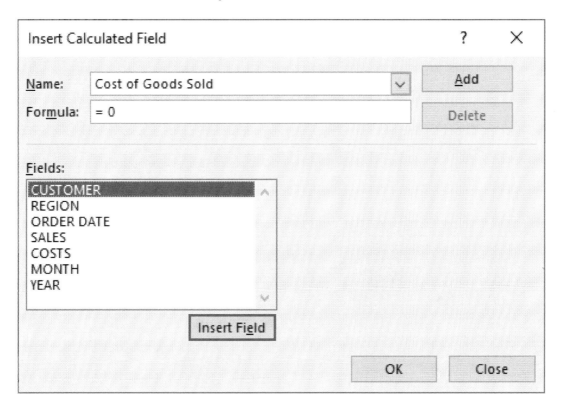

STEP 3: This is the formula to be used for our Calculated Field:

= **COSTS/SALES**

To create this formula:

In the **Formula** area delete the **0** after the = sign.

Select the **COSTS** from the **Fields** area and click on **Insert Field**.

Add the division sign: /

Select the **SALES** from the **Fields** area and click on **Insert Field**.

Press **OK**.

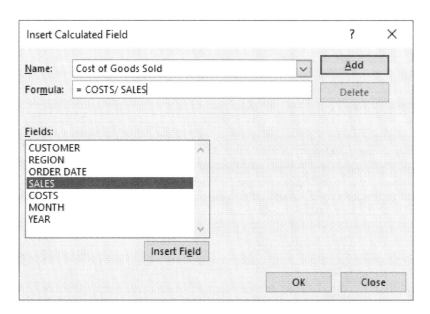

STEP 4: The formatting is still not correct. Right click on the new column and select **Number Format.**

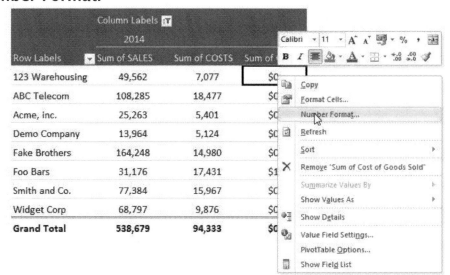

STEP 5: Select **Percentage**. Then click **OK.**

Our new Calculated Field is now ready inside our Pivot Table!

	2014		
Row Labels	Sum of SALES	Sum of COSTS	Sum of Cost of Goods Sold
123 Warehousing	49,562	7,077	14%
ABC Telecom	108,285	18,477	17%
Acme, inc.	25,263	5,401	21%
Demo Company	13,964	5,124	37%
Fake Brothers	164,248	14,980	9%
Foo Bars	31,176	17,431	56%
Smith and Co.	77,384	15,967	21%
Widget Corp	68,797	9,876	14%
Grand Total	**538,679**	**94,333**	**18%**

Editing a Calculated Field

Calculated Fields in Pivot Tables are very flexible to use. However, sometimes making modifications to them is not that straightforward as the interface is not that intuitive.

Let me show it to you so that you can master it in a few steps!

This is our current Pivot Table setup:

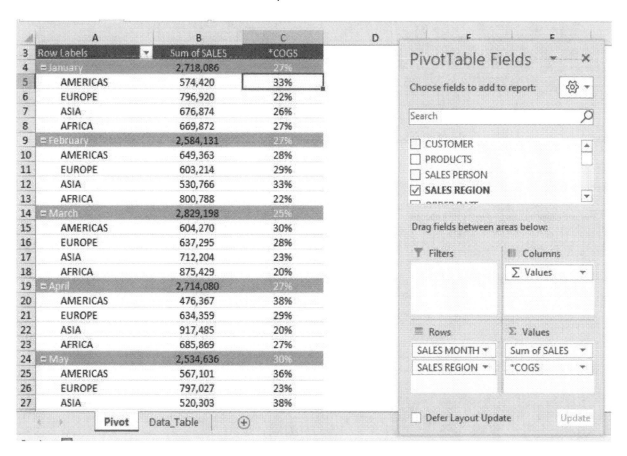

STEP 1: Select anywhere on your Pivot Table. Go to *PivotTable Analyze > Fields, Items, & Sets > Calculated Field.*

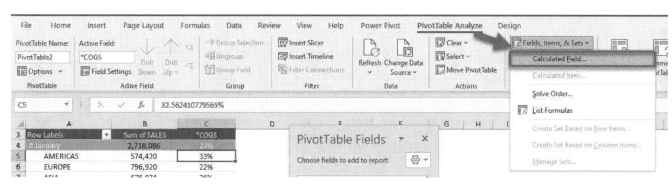

STEP 2: Click on the dropdown list so that you can see all the existing Calculated Fields.

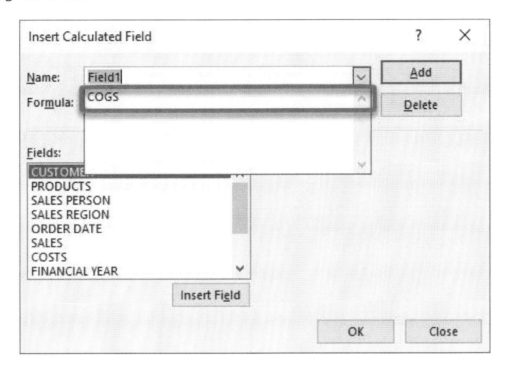

STEP 3: Select **COGS** and now you will see two buttons: **Modify** and **Delete**

If you want to make changes to the Formula, select **Modify**.

If you want to remove it, then select **Delete.**

Let us try out deleting this, click **Delete.**

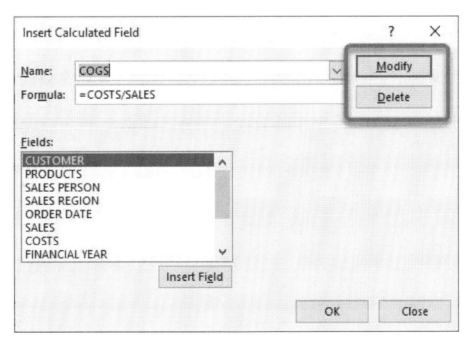

Click **OK**

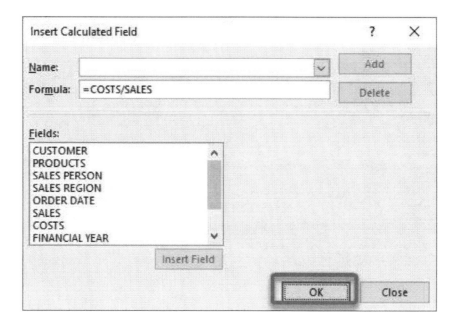

Now you have your updated Pivot Table without the Calculated Field!

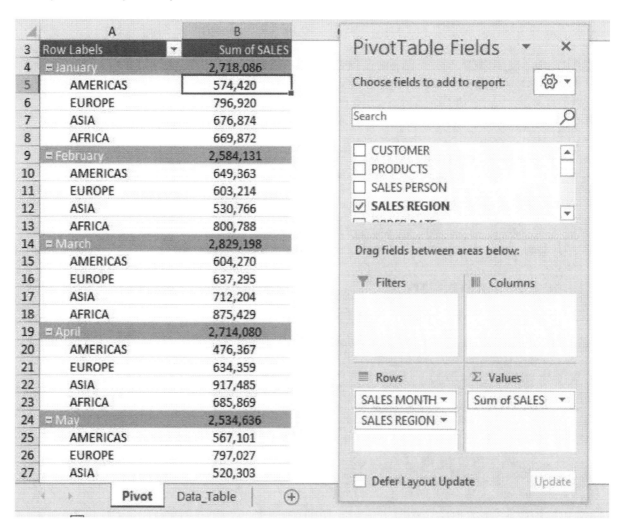

Use Existing Calculated Field in New Calculation

Pivot Table Calculated Fields allows you to create mathematical calculations with your Field List.

Did you know that you can use an existing Calculated Field in a new Calculated Field calculation?

Let me show it to you so that you can master it in a few steps!

This is our current Pivot Table setup. *COGS is an existing Calculated Field:

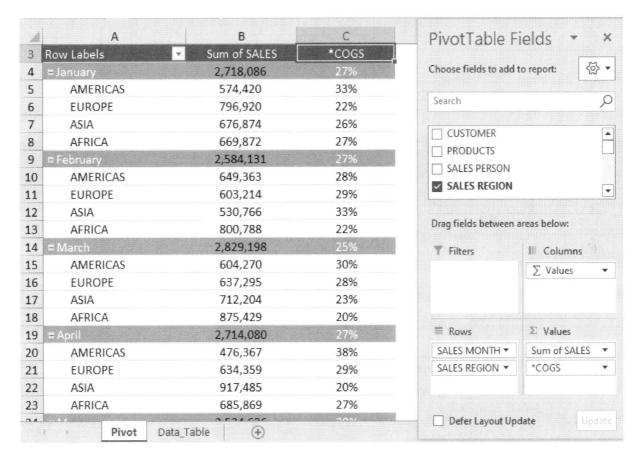

STEP 1: Select anywhere on your Pivot Table. Go to *PivotTable Analyze > Fields, Items, & Sets > Calculated Field.*

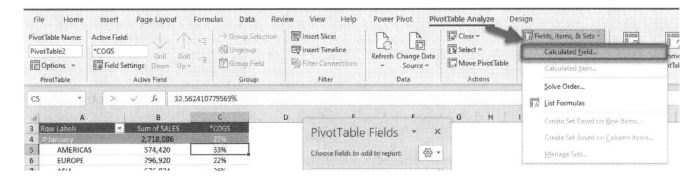

STEP 2: In the **Name** area type in **SALES MARGIN**.

In the **Formula** area delete the **0** after the = sign.

Enter the value **1** followed by the - sign.

Select the **COGS** from the **Fields** area and click on **Insert Field**.

(Notice that we have used the existing **COGS** Calculated Field in our formula).

Click **OK.**

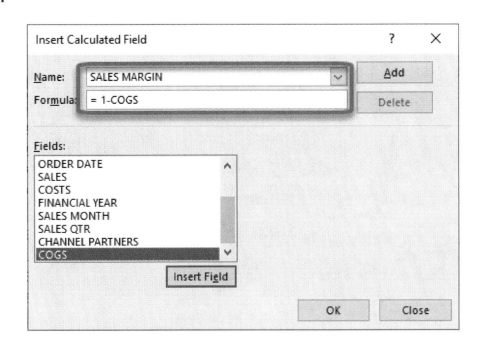

The new Calculated Field has been added. Let us make some formatting changes.

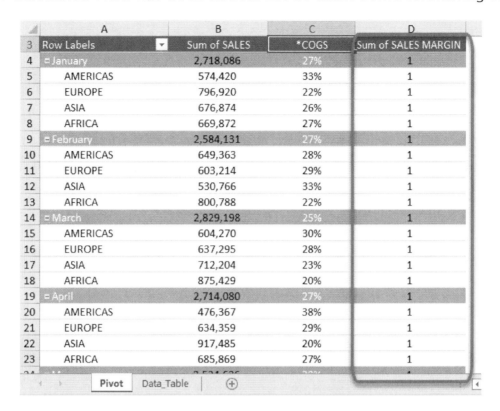

STEP 3: Right click on any **SALES MARGIN** value and select **Number Format.**

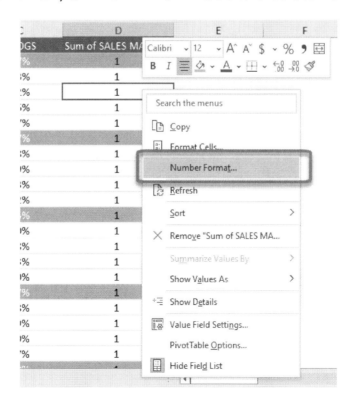

Select **Percentage** and set **Decimal Places** to **1**. Click **OK**.

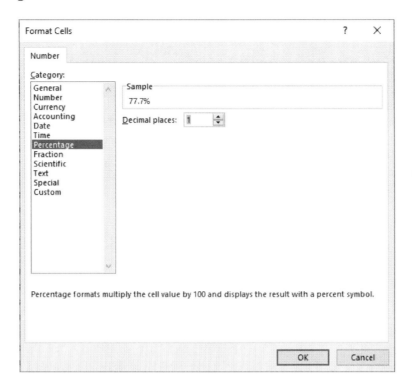

You now have your new Calculated Field based on another Calculated Field!

	A	B	C	D
3	Row Labels	Sum of SALES	*COGS	Sum of SALES MARGIN
4	⊟ January	2,718,086	27%	73.3%
5	AMERICAS	574,420	33%	67.4%
6	EUROPE	796,920	22%	77.7%
7	ASIA	676,874	26%	73.7%
8	AFRICA	669,872	27%	72.6%
9	⊟ February	2,584,131	27%	72.5%
10	AMERICAS	649,363	28%	72.1%
11	EUROPE	603,214	29%	71.2%
12	ASIA	530,766	33%	66.8%
13	AFRICA	800,788	22%	77.7%
14	⊟ March	2,829,198	25%	75.3%
15	AMERICAS	604,270	30%	69.7%
16	EUROPE	637,295	28%	72.1%
17	ASIA	712,204	23%	76.9%
18	AFRICA	875,429	20%	80.3%
19	⊟ April	2,714,080	27%	72.8%
20	AMERICAS	476,367	38%	61.5%
21	EUROPE	634,359	29%	70.9%
22	ASIA	917,485	20%	79.5%
23	AFRICA	685,869	27%	73.5%

Pivot | Data_Table | ⊕

Calculating Actuals VS Plan Using Calculated Fields

We can create various Pivot Table analytical reports using Calculated Fields.

One popular analytical report is to calculate Actual v Plan data for forecasting purposes. This can easily be achieved using a Calculated Field.

We have **ACTUAL $** and **PLAN $** Fields from our data source that we have used to create the Pivot Table below by dragging them in the **Values** area.

We want to calculate the difference between these two Fields by creating a new Calculated Field called **Actual v Plan**:

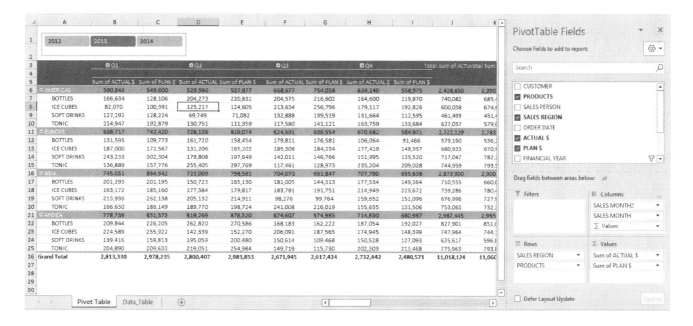

STEP 1: Select anywhere on your Pivot Table. Go to *PivotTable Analyze > Fields, Items, & Sets > Calculated Field.*

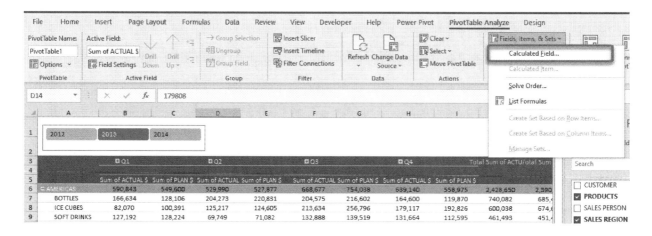

STEP 2: In the **Name** area type in **Actual v Plan**

In the **Formula** area delete the **0** after the = sign.

Select the **ACTUAL $** from the **Fields** area and click on **Insert Field**.

Enter the - sign.

Select the **PLAN $** from the **Fields** area and click on **Insert Field**.

Click **OK.**

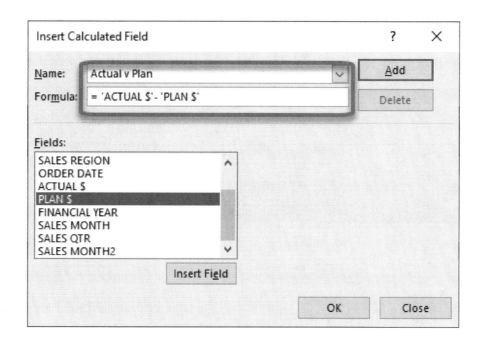

The new Calculated Field has been added and it's called *Sum of Actual v Plan*.

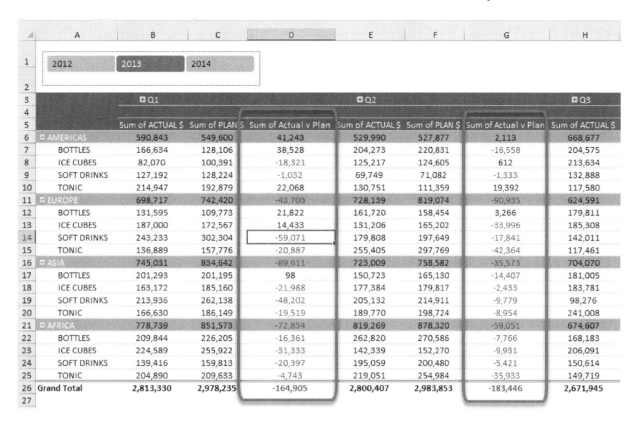

	A	B	C	D	E	F	G	H
1	2012	2013	2014					
2								
3		⊞ Q1			⊞ Q2			⊞ Q3
4								
5		Sum of ACTUAL $	Sum of PLAN $	Sum of Actual v Plan	Sum of ACTUAL $	Sum of PLAN $	Sum of Actual v Plan	Sum of ACTUAL $
6	⊟ AMERICAS	590,843	549,600	41,243	529,990	527,877	2,113	668,677
7	BOTTLES	166,634	128,106	38,528	204,273	220,831	-16,558	204,575
8	ICE CUBES	82,070	100,391	-18,321	125,217	124,605	612	213,634
9	SOFT DRINKS	127,192	128,224	-1,032	69,749	71,082	-1,333	132,888
10	TONIC	214,947	192,879	22,068	130,751	111,359	19,392	117,580
11	⊟ EUROPE	698,717	742,420	-43,703	728,139	819,074	-90,935	624,591
12	BOTTLES	131,595	109,773	21,822	161,720	158,454	3,266	179,811
13	ICE CUBES	187,000	172,567	14,433	131,206	165,202	-33,996	185,308
14	SOFT DRINKS	243,233	302,304	-59,071	179,808	197,649	-17,841	142,011
15	TONIC	136,889	157,776	-20,887	255,405	297,769	-42,364	117,461
16	⊟ ASIA	745,031	834,642	-89,611	723,009	758,582	-35,573	704,070
17	BOTTLES	201,293	201,195	98	150,723	165,130	-14,407	181,005
18	ICE CUBES	163,172	185,160	-21,988	177,384	179,817	-2,433	183,781
19	SOFT DRINKS	213,936	262,138	-48,202	205,132	214,911	-9,779	98,276
20	TONIC	166,630	186,149	-19,519	189,770	198,724	-8,954	241,008
21	⊟ AFRICA	778,739	851,573	-72,834	819,269	878,320	-59,051	674,607
22	BOTTLES	209,844	226,205	-16,361	262,820	270,586	-7,766	168,183
23	ICE CUBES	224,589	255,922	-31,333	142,339	152,270	-9,931	206,091
24	SOFT DRINKS	139,416	159,813	-20,397	195,059	200,480	-5,421	150,614
25	TONIC	204,890	209,633	-4,743	219,051	254,984	-35,933	149,719
26	Grand Total	2,813,330	2,978,235	-164,905	2,800,407	2,983,853	-183,446	2,671,945
27								

STEP 3: We can make some improvements on the Column label.

In the Pivot Table Fields **Values** area, click on the *Sum of Actual v Plan* drop down and select **Value Field Settings.**

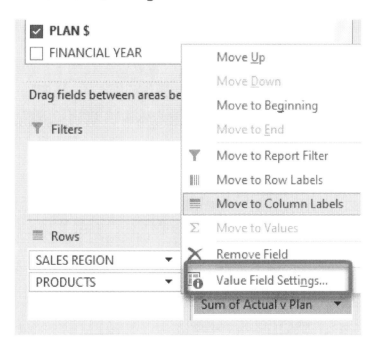

Change the **Custom Name** to *Actual v Plan* to make it more presentable.

Click **OK.**

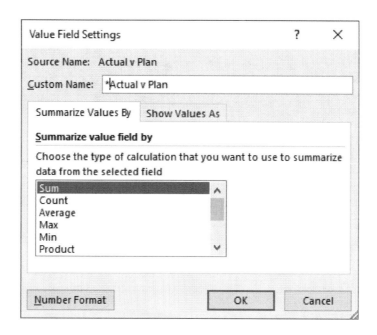

You now have your new Calculated Field!

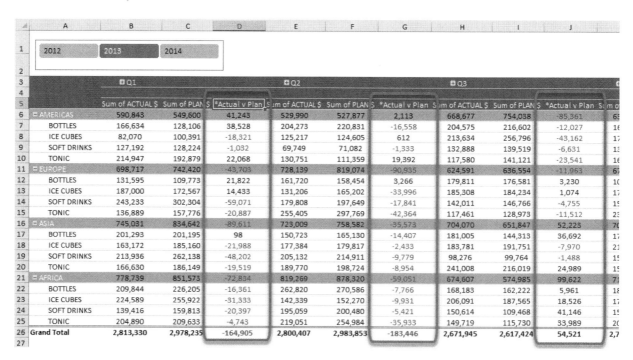

Pro Tip: Add an asterisk at the start of every Calculated Field name so you can avoid conflicts of duplicated calculations with the same name and to easily distinguish a Calculated Field versus a *Summarize Values By* or a *Show Values As* calculation.

Calculated Item

Pivot Table Calculated Items allow you to do mathematical calculations with your Item List.

You can use any of the Excel mathematical equations, like: / * + - %

The only limitation is that you cannot reference any cells.

Pivot Table Calculated Items can be used to calculate variances e.g. Month or Yearly variances, Averages or Summation.

In our example below we are going to create a calculation that shows the variance of the year 2015 with respect to 2014.

STEP 1: Click on the Item inside your Pivot Table that you want to calculate.

These Items are located in the Row Labels or the Column Labels.

Important: We have selected the Year **2015** as we are going to use the YEAR Items for our Calculated Item.

Sum of SALES	Column Labels	
Row Labels	2014	2015
123 Warehousing	49,562	75,088
ABC Telecom	108,285	14,659
Acme, inc.	25,263	113,918
Demo Company	13,964	106,826
Fake Brothers	164,248	43,216
Foo Bars	31,176	85,607
Smith and Co.	77,384	41,632
Widget Corp	68,797	94,378
Grand Total	**538,679**	**575,324**

STEP 2: Click on the Pivot Table and Go to *PivotTable Analyze > Fields, Items, & Sets > Calculated Item*

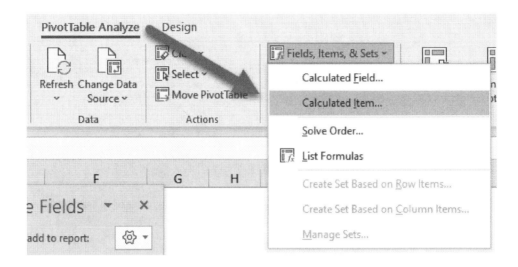

STEP 3: Set the Name to *Year on Year Variance*

STEP 4: This is the formula to be used for our Calculated Item:

= '2015' - '2014'

To create this formula:

Select the **YEAR** from the **Fields** area and then select **2015** from the **Items** area.

Click on **Insert Item**.

Add the minus sign: -

Select the **YEAR** from the **Fields** area and then select **2014** from the **Items** area.

Click on **Insert Item**.

Press **OK**.

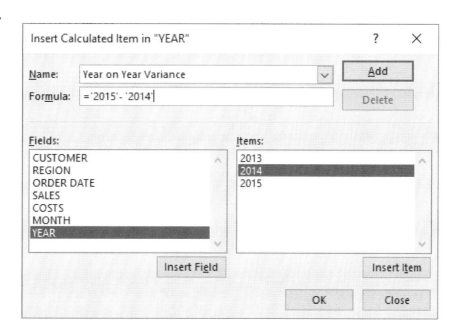

Your **Calculated Item** is now ready!

Sum of SALES	Column Labels		
Row Labels	2014	2015	Year on Year Variance
123 Warehousing	49,562	75,088	25,526
ABC Telecom	108,285	14,659	-93,626
Acme, inc.	25,263	113,918	88,655
Demo Company	13,964	106,826	92,862
Fake Brothers	164,248	43,216	-121,032
Foo Bars	31,176	85,607	54,431
Smith and Co.	77,384	41,632	-35,752
Widget Corp	68,797	94,378	25,581
Grand Total	**538,679**	**575,324**	**36,645**

Editing a Calculated Item

Calculated Items in Pivot Tables are very flexible to use.

However sometimes making modifications to them is not that straightforward as the interface is not that intuitive.

Let me show it to you so that you can master it in a few steps!

This is our current Pivot Table setup:

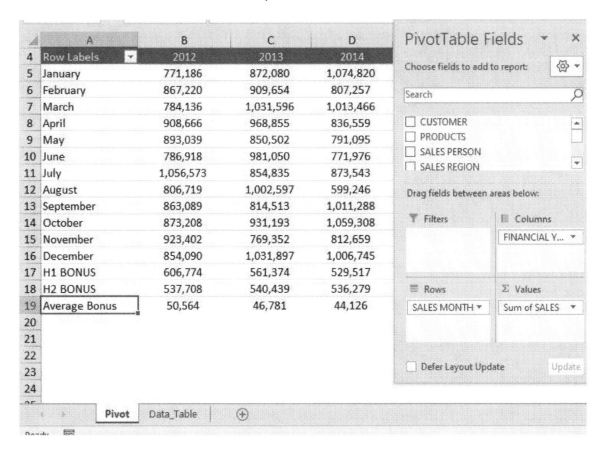

STEP 1: Select anywhere on your Pivot Table Row Labels or Column Labels. Go to *PivotTable Analyze > Fields, Items, & Sets > Calculated Item.*

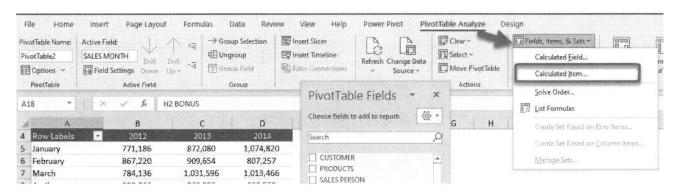

STEP 2: Click on the dropdown list so that you can see all the existing Calculated Items

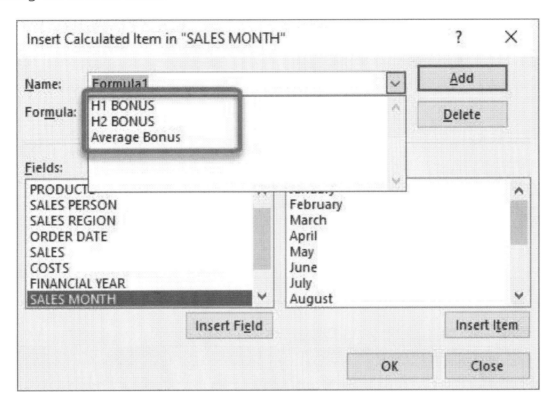

STEP 3: Select **H2 BONUS** and now you will see two buttons: **Modify** and **Delete**

If you want to make changes to the Formula, select **Modify**. If you want to remove it, then select **Delete.**

Let us try out deleting this, click **Delete** and **OK.**

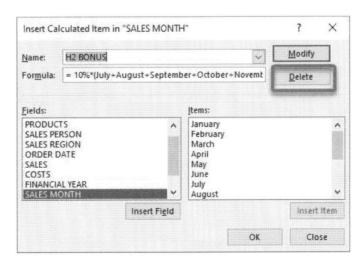

You will see the Calculated Item **H2 BONUS** has now been removed.

Use Existing Calculated Item in New Calculation

Pivot Table Calculated Items allow you to do mathematical calculations with your Item List.

Did you know that you can use an existing Calculated Item in a new Calculated Item calculation? Let me show it to you so that you can master it in a few steps!

This is our current Pivot Table setup. We have two existing Calculated Items called:

- **H1 BONUS** – Bonus calculated on 10% of Total January – June Sales
- **H2 BONUS** – Bonus calculated on 10% of Total July – December Sales

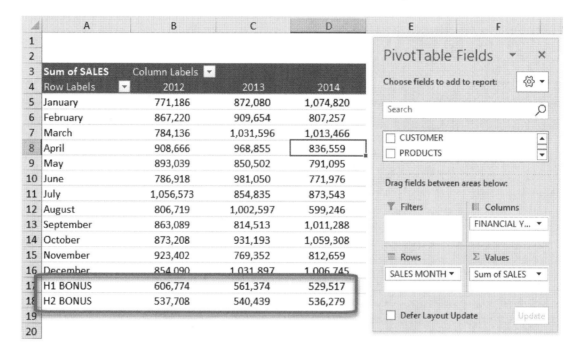

We want to add these two new Calculated Items called:

- **Average H1 BONUS** – H1 Bonus divided by 6 months
- **Average H2 BONUS** – H2 Bonus divided by 6 months

STEP 1: Select anywhere on your Pivot Table Row or Column Labels **(this is important so the Calculated Item can be activated!)**

Go to *PivotTable Analyze > Fields, Items, & Sets > Calculated Item.*

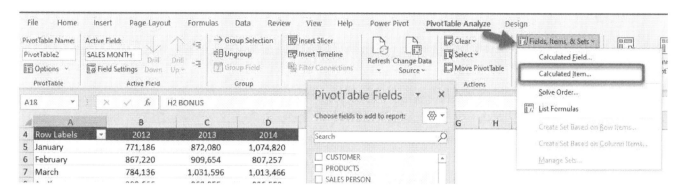

STEP 2:

In the **Name** area type in **AVERAGE H1 BONUS.**

In the **Formula** area delete the **0** after the = sign.

Select the **SALES MONTH** from the **Fields** area and then select the **H1 BONUS** from the **Items** area.

Click on **Insert Item**.

Enter the / sign and then the number **6.**

Click **OK.**

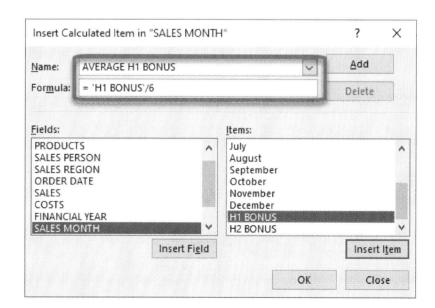

STEP 3:

Now let us enter the second Calculated item.

Select anywhere on your Pivot Table Row or Column Labels **(this is important so the Calculated Item can be activated!)**

Go to *PivotTable Analyze > Fields, Items, & Sets > Calculated Item.*

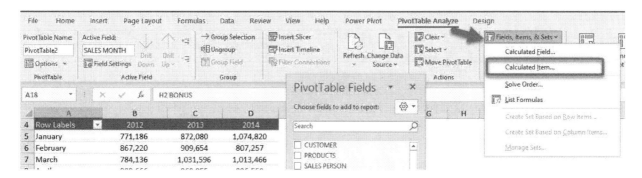

STEP 4:

In the **Name** area type in **AVERAGE H2 BONUS.**

In the **Formula** area delete the **0** after the = sign.

Select the **SALES MONTH** from the **Fields** area and then select the **H2 BONUS** from the **Items** area.

Click on **Insert Item.**

Enter the / sign and then the number **6.**

Click **OK.**

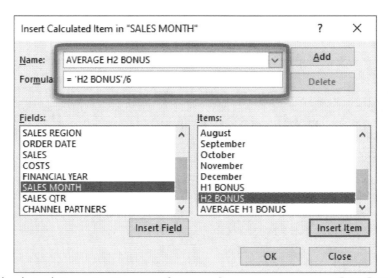

We now have your two new Calculated Items in our Pivot Table!

Sum of SALES	Column Labels		
Row Labels	2012	2013	2014
January	771,186	872,080	1,074,820
February	867,220	909,654	807,257
March	784,136	1,031,596	1,013,466
April	908,666	968,855	836,559
May	893,039	850,502	791,095
June	786,918	981,050	771,976
July	1,056,573	854,835	873,543
August	806,719	1,002,597	599,246
September	863,089	814,513	1,011,288
October	873,208	931,193	1,059,308
November	923,402	769,352	812,659
December	854,090	1,031,897	1,006,745
H1 BONUS	606,774	561,374	529,517
H2 BONUS	537,708	540,439	536,279
AVERAGE H1 BONUS	101,129	93,562	88,253
AVERAGE H2 BONUS	89,618	90,073	89,380

Create a Profit and Loss Report Using Calculated Items

We can create various Pivot Table analytical reports using Calculated Items.

One popular analytical report is to create a Profit & Loss. This can easily be achieved using Calculated Items.

This is our data source that we are going to use to create our Pivot Table.

MONTH	YEAR	P&L TYPE	ITEM	ACTUAL $	PLAN $
JANUARY	2012	REVENUE	CIDER	369,199	430,211
JANUARY	2012	REVENUE	GIN	367,285	230,813
JANUARY	2012	REVENUE	BOTTLES	227,807	298,451
JANUARY	2012	REVENUE	ICE CUBES	136,752	164,194
JANUARY	2012	COGS	Cost Of Goods Sold	33,341	43,476
JANUARY	2012	EXPENSES	ADVERTISING	48,638	34,780
JANUARY	2012	EXPENSES	DEPRECIATION	18,249	9,548
JANUARY	2012	EXPENSES	ELECTRICITY	38,633	48,908
JANUARY	2012	EXPENSES	INSURANCE	44,914	45,574
JANUARY	2012	EXPENSES	INTEREST AND BANK CHARGES	33,386	33,649
JANUARY	2012	EXPENSES	POSTAGE	46,590	63,733
JANUARY	2012	EXPENSES	PRINTING AND STATIONARY	24,552	16,612
JANUARY	2012	EXPENSES	PROFESSIONAL MEMBERSHIPS	41,198	58,027
JANUARY	2012	EXPENSES	RENT FOR PREMISES	47,842	35,866
JANUARY	2012	EXPENSES	REPAIRS AND MAINTENANCE	40,807	37,722
JANUARY	2012	EXPENSES	TRAINING	42,824	30,818
JANUARY	2012	EXPENSES	VEHICLE OPERATING COSTS	49,353	54,961
JANUARY	2012	EXPENSES	WAGES AND SALARIES	16,853	24,777
JANUARY	2012	EXPENSES	WORKERS COMPENSATION	25,159	23,160
FEBRUARY	2012	REVENUE	CIDER	318,233	200,989
FEBRUARY	2012	REVENUE	GIN	144,617	151,662
FEBRUARY	2012	REVENUE	BOTTLES	128,246	183,528
FEBRUARY	2012	REVENUE	ICE CUBES	297,629	257,733

Using our data source, we have created the following Profit & Loss report using a Pivot Table.

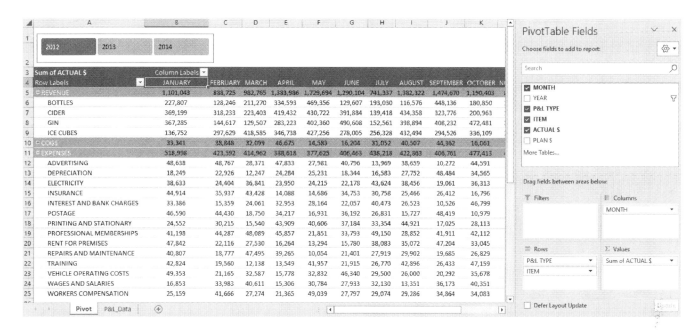

We now want to calculate the following items in our Pivot Table to make it more complete:

- **Gross Profit** = REVENUE – COGS
- **Operating Profit** = Gross Profit - EXPENSES

STEP 1: Select anywhere on your Pivot Table Row Labels that has a P&L TYPE Item i.e., **REVENUE, COGS, EXPENSES**.

This is important as you can only create Calculated Items within each unique Field chosen.

Go to *PivotTable Analyze > Fields, Items, & Sets > Calculated Item.*

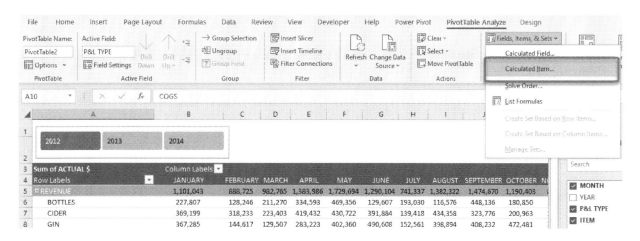

STEP 2:

In the **Name** area type in **Gross Profit.**

In the **Formula** area delete the **0** after the = sign.

Select the **P&L TYPE** from the **Fields** area and then select the **REVENUE** from the **Items** area.

Click on **Insert Item.**

Enter the - sign.

Select the **COGS** from the **Items** area.

Click on **Insert Item.**

Click **OK.**

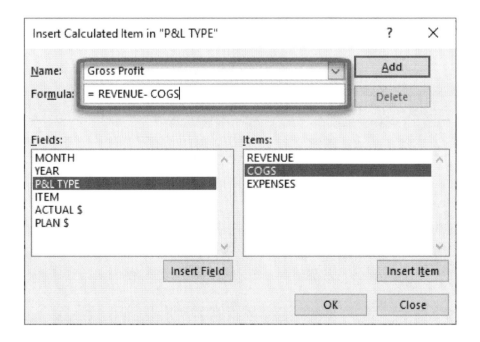

The new Calculated Item **Gross Profit** has been added in our Pivot Table.

Click on the minus icon to collapse this, as we don't need the detailed breakdown.

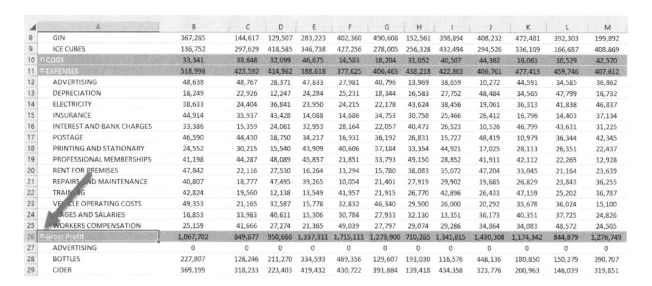

	A	B	C	D	E	F	G	H	I	J	K	L	M
8	GIN	367,285	144,617	129,507	283,223	402,360	490,608	152,561	398,894	408,232	472,481	392,303	199,892
9	ICE CUBES	136,752	297,629	418,585	346,738	427,256	278,005	256,328	432,494	294,526	336,109	166,687	408,869
10	COGS	33,341	38,848	32,099	46,675	14,583	16,204	31,052	40,507	44,362	16,061	10,529	42,570
11	EXPENSES	518,998	423,592	414,962	388,618	377,625	406,463	438,218	422,863	406,761	477,413	459,746	407,612
12	ADVERTISING	48,638	48,767	28,371	47,833	27,981	40,796	13,969	38,659	10,272	44,591	34,585	36,862
13	DEPRECIATION	18,249	22,926	12,247	24,284	25,231	18,344	16,583	27,752	48,484	34,565	47,799	16,732
14	ELECTRICITY	38,633	24,404	36,841	23,950	24,215	22,178	43,624	38,456	19,061	36,313	41,838	46,837
15	INSURANCE	44,914	35,937	43,428	14,088	14,686	34,753	30,758	25,466	26,412	16,796	14,403	37,134
16	INTEREST AND BANK CHARGES	33,386	15,359	24,061	32,953	28,164	22,057	40,473	26,523	10,526	46,799	43,631	31,225
17	POSTAGE	46,590	44,430	18,750	34,217	16,931	36,192	26,831	15,727	48,419	10,979	36,344	42,345
18	PRINTING AND STATIONARY	24,552	30,215	15,540	43,909	40,606	37,184	33,354	44,921	17,025	28,113	26,351	22,437
19	PROFESSIONAL MEMBERSHIPS	41,198	44,287	48,089	45,857	21,851	33,793	49,150	28,852	41,911	42,112	22,265	12,928
20	RENT FOR PREMISES	47,842	22,116	27,530	16,264	13,294	15,780	38,083	35,072	47,204	33,045	21,164	23,639
21	REPAIRS AND MAINTENANCE	40,807	18,777	47,495	39,265	10,054	21,401	27,919	29,902	19,685	26,829	23,843	36,255
22	TRAINING	42,824	19,560	12,138	13,549	41,957	21,915	26,770	42,896	26,433	47,159	25,202	36,787
23	VEHICLE OPERATING COSTS	49,353	21,165	32,587	15,778	32,832	46,340	29,500	26,000	20,292	35,678	36,024	15,100
24	WAGES AND SALARIES	16,853	33,983	40,611	15,306	30,784	27,933	32,130	13,351	36,173	40,351	37,725	24,826
25	WORKERS COMPENSATION	25,159	41,666	27,274	21,365	49,039	27,797	29,074	29,286	34,864	34,083	48,572	24,505
26	Gross Profit	1,067,702	849,877	950,666	1,337,311	1,715,111	1,273,900	710,285	1,341,815	1,430,308	1,174,342	844,879	1,276,749
27	ADVERTISING	0	0	0	0	0	0	0	0	0	0	0	0
28	BOTTLES	227,807	128,246	211,270	334,593	469,356	129,607	193,030	116,576	448,136	180,850	150,379	390,707
29	CIDER	369,199	318,233	223,403	419,432	430,722	391,884	139,418	434,358	323,776	200,963	146,039	319,851

Now right click on **Gross Profit** and go to *Move > Move "Gross Profit" Up*

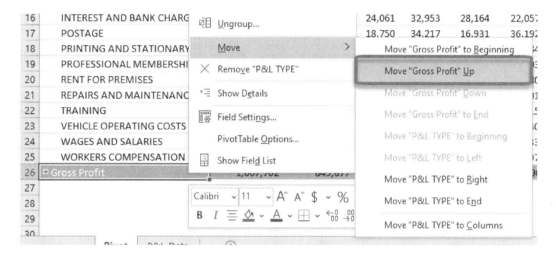

Now we have the **Gross Profit** positioned right after the **COGS**:

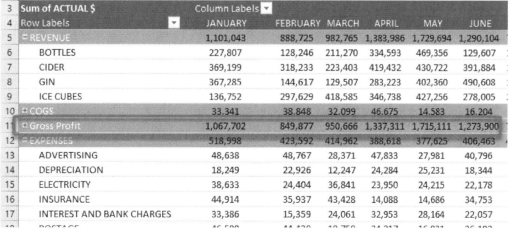

STEP 3: Select anywhere on your Pivot Table Row Labels that has a P&L TYPE Item i.e., **REVENUE, COGS, EXPENSES. This is important as you can only create Calculated Items within each unique Field chosen.**

Go to *PivotTable Analyze > Fields, Items, & Sets > Calculated Item.*

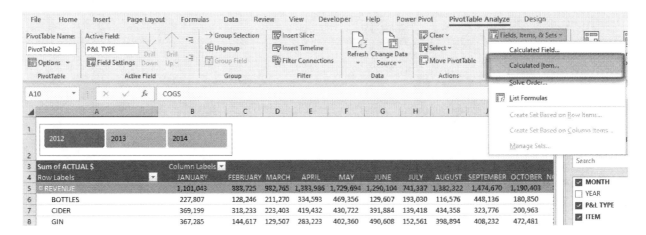

STEP 4:

In the **Name** area type in **OPERATING PROFIT.**

In the **Formula** area delete the **0** after the = sign.

Select the **P&L TYPE** from the **Fields** area and then select the **Gross Profit** from the **Items** area.

Click on **Insert Item**.

Enter the - sign.

Select the **EXPENSES** from the **Items** area.

Click on **Insert Item**.

Click **OK.**

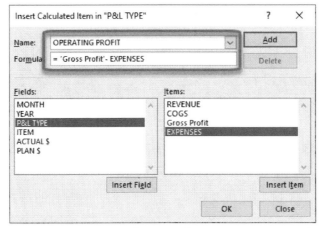

The new Calculated Item **OPERATING PROFIT** has been added.

Click on the minus icon to collapse this, as we don't need the detailed breakdown.

	A	B	C	D	E	F	G
11	⊞ Gross Profit	1,067,702	849,877	950,666	1,337,311	1,715,111	1,273
12	⊟ EXPENSES	518,998	423,592	414,962	388,618	377,625	406,
13	ADVERTISING	48,638	48,767	28,371	47,833	27,981	40,
14	DEPRECIATION	18,249	22,926	12,247	24,284	25,231	18,
15	ELECTRICITY	38,633	24,404	36,841	23,950	24,215	22,
16	INSURANCE	44,914	35,937	43,428	14,088	14,686	34,
17	INTEREST AND BANK CHARGES	33,386	15,359	24,061	32,953	28,164	22,
18	POSTAGE	46,590	44,430	18,750	34,217	16,931	36,
19	PRINTING AND STATIONARY	24,552	30,215	15,540	43,909	40,606	37,
20	PROFESSIONAL MEMBERSHIPS	41,198	44,287	48,089	45,857	21,851	33,
21	RENT FOR PREMISES	47,842	22,116	27,530	16,264	13,294	15,
22	REPAIRS AND MAINTENANCE	40,807	18,777	47,495	39,265	10,054	21,
23	TRAINING	42,824	19,560	12,138	13,549	41,957	21,
24	VEHICLE OPERATING COSTS	49,353	21,165	32,587	15,778	32,832	46,
25	WAGES AND SALARIES	16,853	33,983	40,611	15,306	30,784	27,
26	WORKERS COMPENSATION	25,159	41,666	27,274	21,365	49,039	27,
27	⊟ OPERATING PROFIT	548,704	426,285	535,704	948,693	1,337,486	867,
28	ADVERTISING	-48,638	-48,767	-28,371	-47,833	-27,981	-40,
29	BOTTLES	227,807	128,246	211,270	334,593	469,356	129,
30	CIDER	369,199	318,233	223,403	419,432	430,722	391,
31	Cost Of Goods Sold	-33,341	-38,848	-32,099	-46,675	-14,583	-16,
32	DEPRECIATION	-18,249	-22,926	-12,247	-24,284	-25,231	-18,
33	ELECTRICITY	38,633	24,404	36,841	23,950	24,215	22

We now have our two Calculated Items that complete our Profit & Loss report!

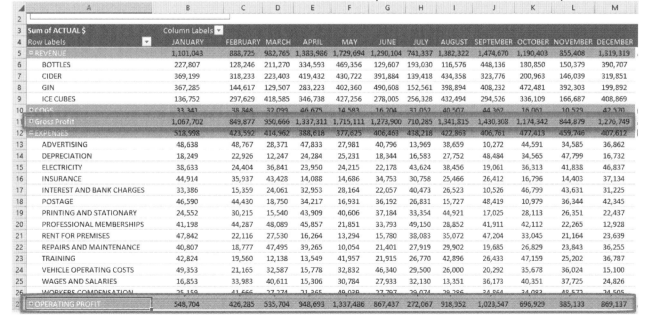

	A	B	C	D	E	F	G	H	I	J	K	L	M
3	Sum of ACTUAL $	Column Labels											
4	Row Labels	JANUARY	FEBRUARY	MARCH	APRIL	MAY	JUNE	JULY	AUGUST	SEPTEMBER	OCTOBER	NOVEMBER	DECEMBER
5	⊟ REVENUE	1,101,043	888,725	982,765	1,383,986	1,729,694	1,290,104	741,337	1,382,322	1,474,670	1,190,403	855,408	1,319,319
6	BOTTLES	227,807	128,246	211,270	334,593	469,356	129,607	193,030	116,576	448,136	180,850	150,379	390,707
7	CIDER	369,199	318,233	223,403	419,432	430,722	391,884	139,418	434,358	323,776	200,963	146,039	319,851
8	GIN	367,285	144,617	129,507	283,223	402,360	490,608	152,561	398,894	408,232	472,481	392,303	199,892
9	ICE CUBES	136,752	297,629	418,585	346,738	427,256	278,005	256,328	432,494	294,526	336,109	166,687	408,869
10	⊟ COGS	33,341	38,848	32,099	46,675	14,583	16,204	31,052	40,507	44,362	16,061	10,529	42,570
11	⊞ Gross Profit	1,067,702	849,877	950,666	1,337,311	1,715,111	1,273,900	710,285	1,341,815	1,430,308	1,174,342	844,879	1,276,749
12	⊟ EXPENSES	518,998	423,592	414,962	388,618	377,625	406,463	438,218	422,863	406,761	477,413	459,746	407,612
13	ADVERTISING	48,638	48,767	28,371	47,833	27,981	40,796	13,969	38,659	10,272	44,591	34,585	36,862
14	DEPRECIATION	18,249	22,926	12,247	24,284	25,231	18,344	16,583	27,752	48,484	34,565	47,799	16,732
15	ELECTRICITY	38,633	24,404	36,841	23,950	24,215	22,178	43,624	38,456	19,061	36,313	41,838	46,837
16	INSURANCE	44,914	35,937	43,428	14,088	14,686	34,753	30,758	25,466	26,412	16,796	14,403	37,134
17	INTEREST AND BANK CHARGES	33,386	15,359	24,061	32,953	28,164	22,057	40,473	26,523	10,526	46,799	43,631	31,225
18	POSTAGE	46,590	44,430	18,750	34,217	16,931	36,192	26,831	15,727	48,419	10,979	36,344	42,345
19	PRINTING AND STATIONARY	24,552	30,215	15,540	43,909	40,606	37,184	33,354	44,921	17,025	28,113	26,351	22,437
20	PROFESSIONAL MEMBERSHIPS	41,198	44,287	48,089	45,857	21,851	33,793	49,150	28,852	41,911	42,112	22,265	12,928
21	RENT FOR PREMISES	47,842	22,116	27,530	16,264	13,294	15,780	38,083	35,072	47,204	33,045	21,164	23,639
22	REPAIRS AND MAINTENANCE	40,807	18,777	47,495	39,265	10,054	21,401	27,919	29,902	19,685	26,829	23,843	36,255
23	TRAINING	42,824	19,560	12,138	13,549	41,957	21,915	26,770	42,896	26,433	47,159	25,202	36,787
24	VEHICLE OPERATING COSTS	49,353	21,165	32,587	15,778	32,832	46,340	29,500	26,000	20,292	35,678	36,024	15,100
25	WAGES AND SALARIES	16,853	33,983	40,611	15,306	30,784	27,933	32,130	13,351	36,173	40,351	37,725	24,826
26	WORKERS COMPENSATION	25,159	41,666	27,274	21,365	49,039	27,797	29,074	29,286	24,864	24,082	49,573	24,505
27	⊟ OPERATING PROFIT	548,704	426,285	535,704	948,693	1,337,486	867,437	272,067	918,952	1,023,547	696,929	385,133	869,137

Formulas & Calculated Items

When working with Calculated Items, you can use Excel Formulas as long as you do not reference any external cells.

The Formulas you can use are the **SUM, IF, OR, AND, AVERAGE, etc.** Let me show you with a quick example!

Here is our current Pivot Table setup:

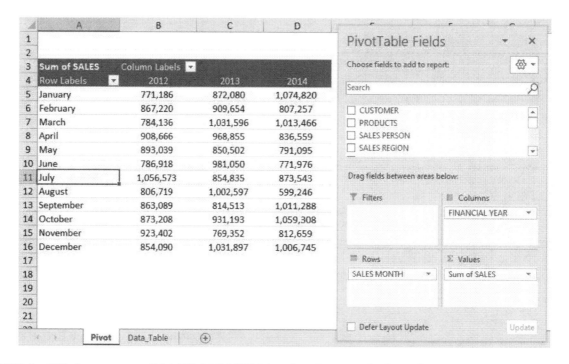

STEP 1: Click on any SALES MONTH in the Row Label and go to *PivotTable Analyze > Fields, Items & Sets > Calculated Item.*

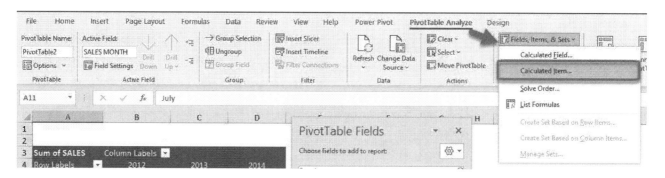

STEP 2: For the Formula we will use the Average Function. The formulas will look like this:

= AVERAGE(January, February, March, April, May, June, July, August, September, October, November, December)

To create this formula:

In the **Name** area, type in: *AVERAGE*

In the **Formula** area enter: = AVERAGE(

In the **Fields** area, click on the **SALES MONTH** Field and in the **Items** area select the **January** Item.

Then select **Insert Item**.

Repeat this process for each month up until December.

After you have entered the December item, close the formula using this parenthesis **)**

Press **OK**.

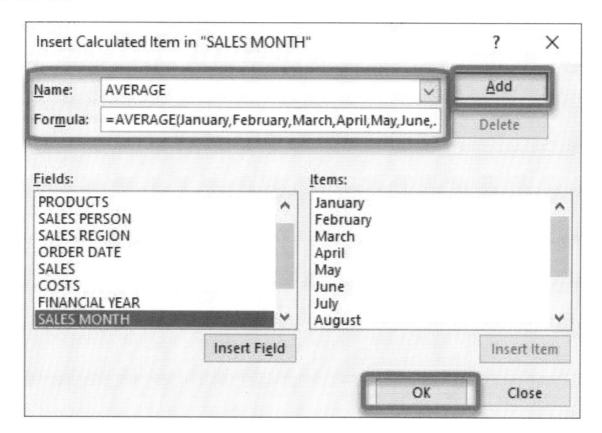

The Average Calculated Item is now ready and it is visible at the bottom of the Pivot Table.

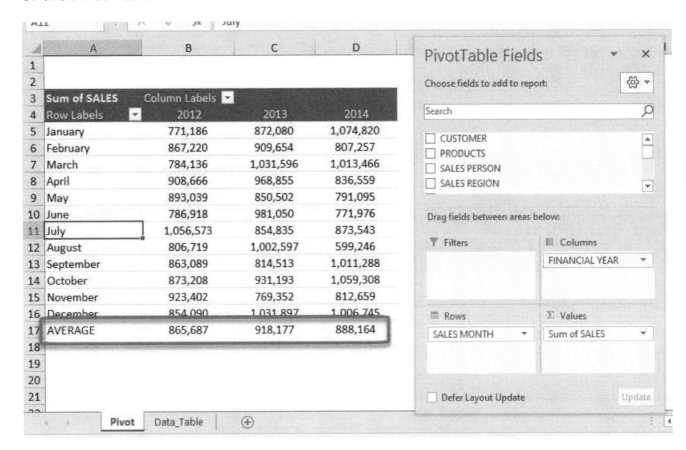

List Calculated Field & Item Formulas

When working with **Calculated Fields and Items** it can sometimes get confusing to keep track of what calculations you have created.

Luckily, there is a feature in Excel that lists all Calculated Fields & Items for you in one place!

Here is our current Pivot Table and our 3 Calculated Items circled in red.

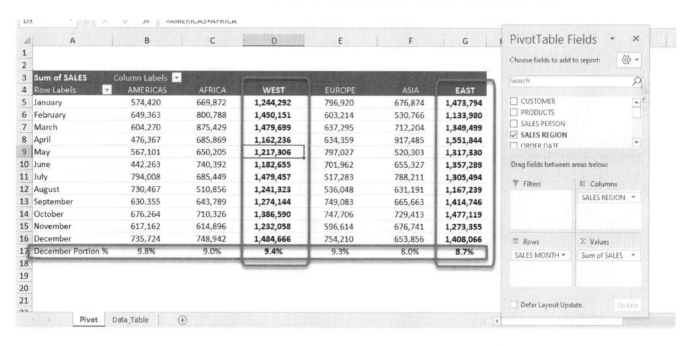

STEP 1: Go to *PivotTable Analyze > Fields, Items & Sets > List Formulas*

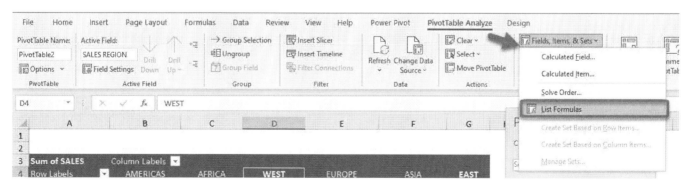

With just one click, all the Calculated Fields and Items are listed
in a new worksheet!

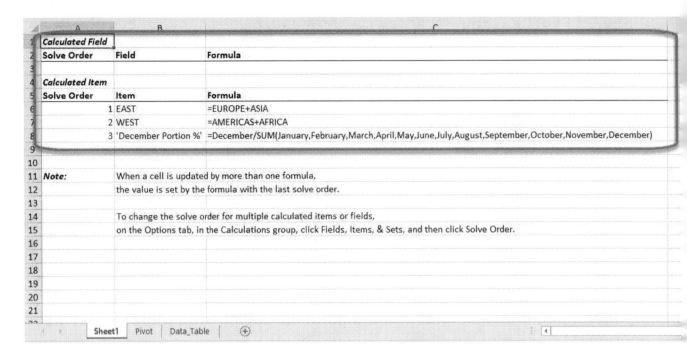

	A	B	C
1	**Calculated Field**		
2	**Solve Order**	**Field**	**Formula**
3			
4	**Calculated Item**		
5	**Solve Order**	**Item**	**Formula**
6	1	EAST	=EUROPE+ASIA
7	2	WEST	=AMERICAS+AFRICA
8	3	'December Portion %'	=December/SUM(January,February,March,April,May,June,July,August,September,October,November,December)
9			
10			
11	**Note:**	When a cell is updated by more than one formula,	
12		the value is set by the formula with the last solve order.	
13			
14		To change the solve order for multiple calculated items or fields,	
15		on the Options tab, in the Calculations group, click Fields, Items, & Sets, and then click Solve Order.	
16			
17			
18			
19			
20			
21			

Sheet1 | Pivot | Data_Table ⊕

Order of Operations

In Excel, the order in which a calculation is performed can affect the return value of the formula, so it's important to understand how the order is determined and how you can change the order to obtain the results you want.

When working with Calculated Fields & Items in a Pivot Table, you need to be aware of this **Order of Operations.**

Here's the list of operations in order of precedence from first to last:

ORDER OF OPERATIONS	
1 BRACKETS	()
2 PERCENTAGES	%
3 EXPONENTS	^
4 DIVISION & MULTIPLICATION	/ *
5 ADDITION & SUBTRACTION	+ -
6 COMPARISONS	=, <>, <=, >=

These are the 2 examples that we want to evaluate step by step using the Order of Operations.

=2+4*5	22
=(2+4)*5	30

STEP 1: Let us check the first example: **=2+4*5**

There are 2 operations here, so based on the Table above, the Order of Operations will be: **Multiplication then addition**

- =2+4*5
- =2+20
- =22

STEP 2: Let us check the second example: **=(2+4)*5**

There are 3 operations here, so based on the Table above, the Order of Operations will be: **Brackets, addition then multiplication**

- =(2+4)*5
- =6*5
- =30

Pro Tip: You can remember the order of operations using the acronym BEDMAS: Brackets, exponents, division, multiplication, addition, subtraction.

PIVOT CHARTS

Pivot Charts

Pivot Charts are a great way to add data visualizations to your data.

Pivot Charts are an extension of a Pivot Table, and they show Pivot Table values in a graphical representation.

When you filter a Pivot Table, the Pivot Chart updates accordingly.

Here is our Pivot Table:

Sum of SALES	Column Labels		
Row Labels	2013	2014	2015
EAST	134,146	157,847	89,747
NORTH	165,399	102,647	155,550
SOUTH	182,984	99,973	179,985
WEST	180,462	178,212	150,042
Grand Total	**662,991**	**538,679**	**575,324**

STEP 1: Click anywhere in your Pivot Table and go to **Insert > PivotChart > PivotChart.**

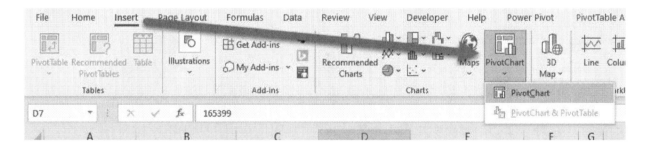

STEP 2: Select a Chart type and click **OK.**

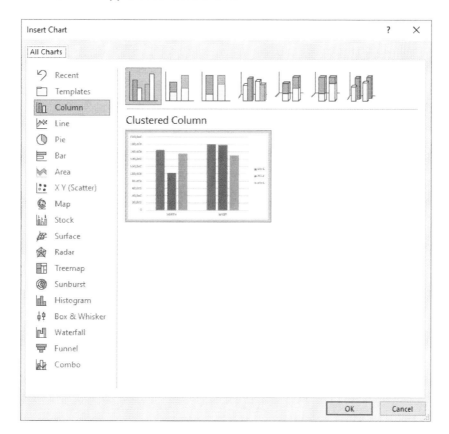

You now have your cool **Pivot Chart**!

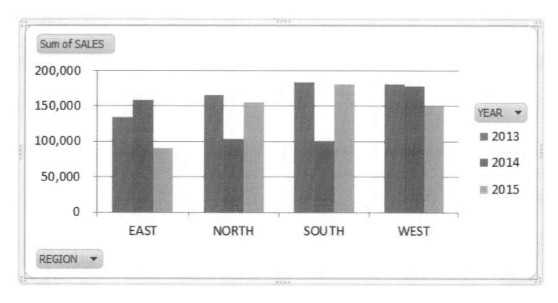

Filtering this Pivot Chart will filter the Pivot Table and vice versa!

Pivot Charts & Slicers

At the start of this chapter, I showed you how to **Insert a Pivot Chart**. Now we will take this concept one step further and insert a Slicer.

The cool thing about this is that the Slicer will control both the Pivot Table and the Pivot Chart.

See how you can start creating some awesome interactive analytical reports in just a couple of steps.

Here we have our Pivot Table and Pivot Chart:

Sum of SALES	Column Labels		
Row Labels	2013	2014	2015
NORTH	165,399	102,647	155,550
WEST	180,462	178,212	150,042
Grand Total	**345,861**	**280,859**	**305,592**

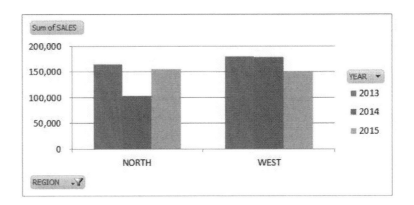

STEP 1: Click in your Pivot Table and go to *PivotTable Analyze > Filter > Insert Slicer*

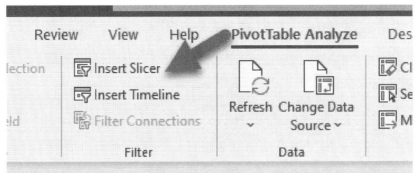

STEP 2: Select **Region** and **Year.** Click **OK.**

We now have our Pivot Table Slicer.

Any Slicer selections will change both the Pivot Table and Pivot Chart.

Give it a go!

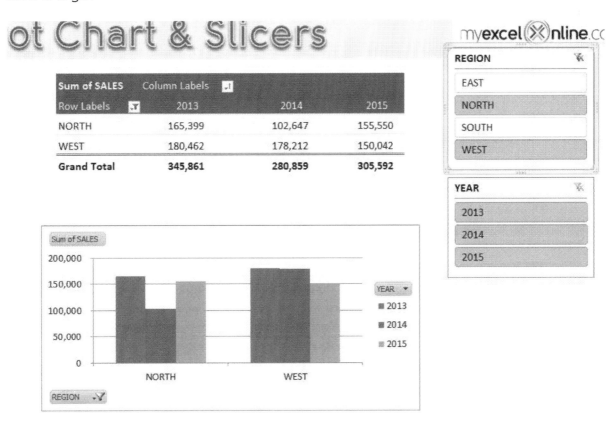

Pivot Chart Settings

When working with **Pivot Charts**, sometimes it gets overwhelming with the number of customizations available.

I will walk you through the different options, so that you can quickly maximize their usage to the fullest!

This is our current Pivot Chart:

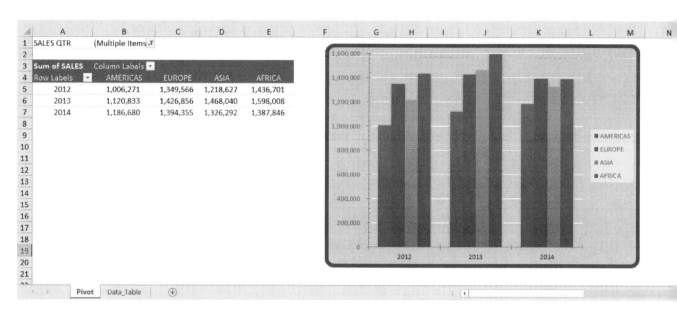

Once you click on the Pivot Chart, you will have two additional ribbon tabs. Let us go over the features found on the **Design** and **Format** ribbons.

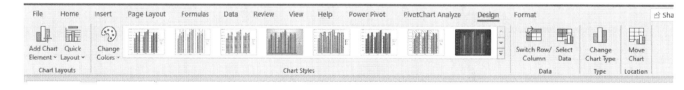

Design Tab

The Design tab has the following settings:

- **Add Chart Element** - if you want to add/remove additional elements to be displayed in your Pivot Chart, you have these settings:

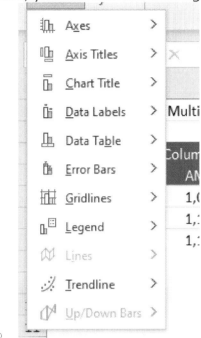

- **Quick Layout** - this is a handy way to have different types of presentation options. Go over them one by one to determine which will be the most appropriate way to visualize your data.

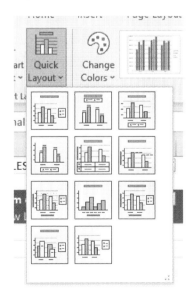

- **Chart Styles** - have fun here by changing the colors and design of your chart

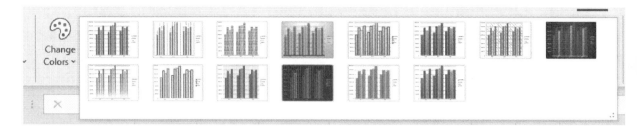

- **Switch Row/Column** - you can swap the data over the axis with this quickly and revert back when needed.

Switch Row/
Column

- **Select Data** - you can change the data source of your Pivot Chart.

Select
Data

- **Change Chart Type** - there are a lot of different chart types that you can change to quickly.

Change
Chart Type

- **Move Chart** - if you need to place the Pivot Chart in a different location.

Move
Chart

Format tab

The Format tab has the following settings:

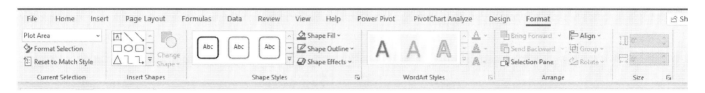

- **Current Selection** - you select a specific element of your Pivot Chart to modify

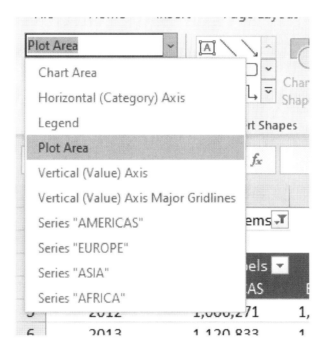

- **Insert Shapes** - add additional shapes on top of your Pivot Chart that will help present your data better such as arrows and boxes

Insert Shapes

- **Shape Styles** - change the color fill, outline, or even add 3D effects

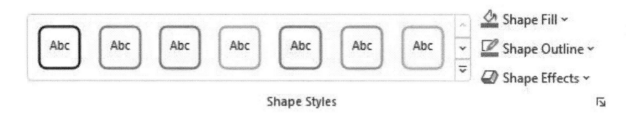

Shape Styles

- **WordArt Styles** - change how the text is formatted and use preset styles

WordArt Styles

- **Arrange** - you can change the display order, set alignment, or even rotate the selected element

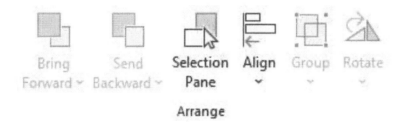

Arrange

- **Size** - set the length and width

Size

Copy a Pivot Chart

If you want to create another Pivot Chart based on the same Pivot Table, you can quickly **copy a Pivot Chart**!

Here we have our Pivot Table and Pivot Chart:

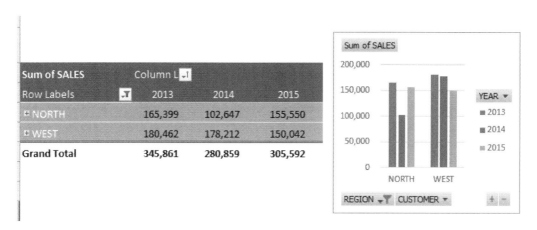

STEP 1: Right Click in your Pivot Chart and select **Copy.**

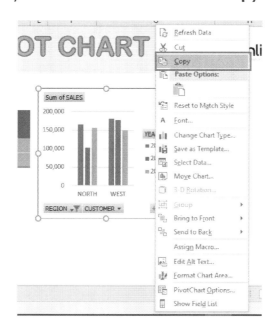

STEP 2: Right click on a blank spot in your worksheet and select the first **Paste Option.**

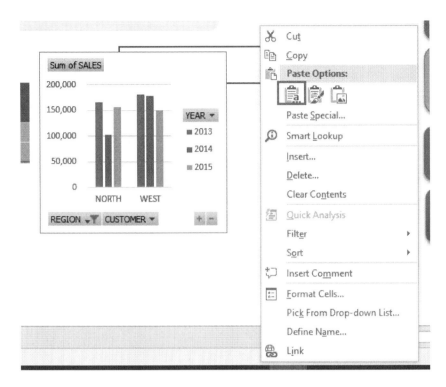

STEP 3: Click on the new Pivot Chart then go to *Design > Type > Change Chart Type.*

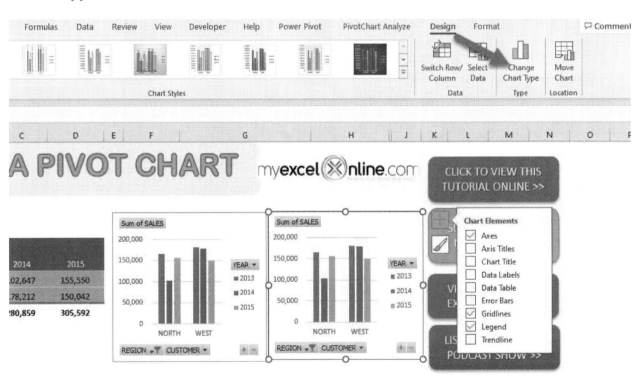

STEP 4: You can select a different chart type. Let's select the 100% Stacked Column. Click OK.

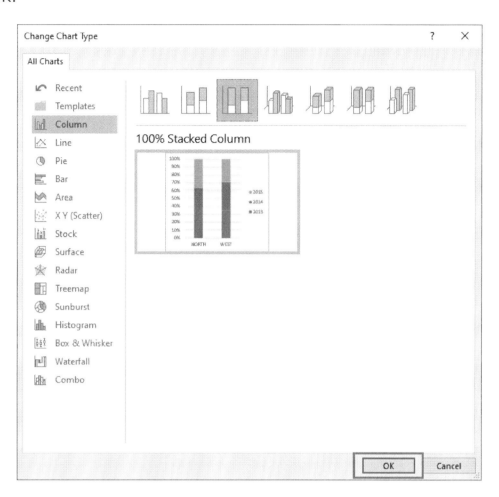

We now have our new Pivot Chart!

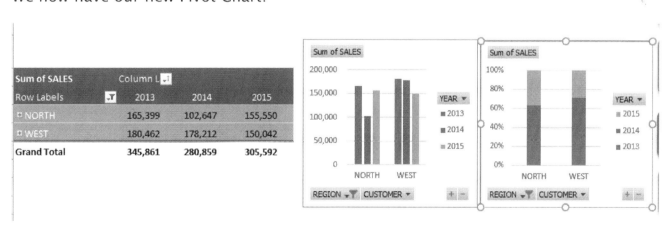

Sum of SALES	Column L		
Row Labels	2013	2014	2015
⊞ NORTH	165,399	102,647	155,550
⊞ WEST	180,462	178,212	150,042
Grand Total	345,861	280,859	305,592

Insert a Pivot Chart Straight from the Data Source

Did you know that you can **insert a Pivot Chart straight from the data source?**

I will show you how you can do this below!

STEP 1: Click anywhere in your data source. Go to *Insert > Charts > PivotChart > PivotChart.*

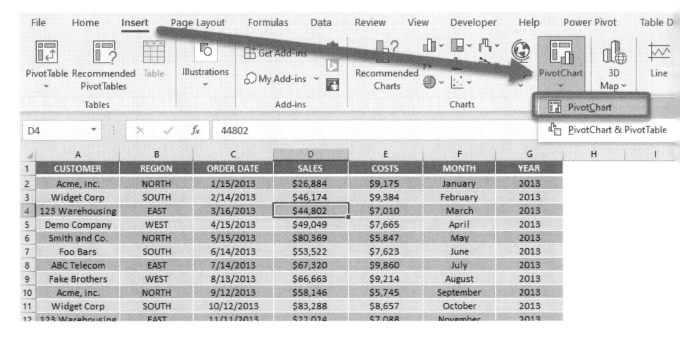

STEP 2: Select **Existing Worksheet** and pick a spot to place your Pivot Chart. Click **OK.**

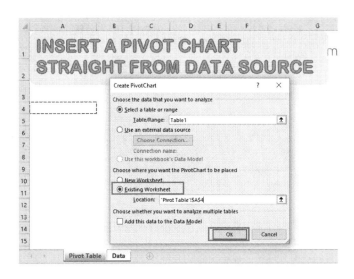

STEP 3: Let us quickly setup our Pivot Chart. Set the following:

Axis: **REGION** and **YEAR**

Values: **SALES**

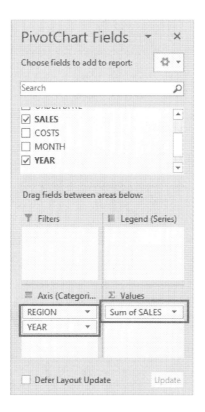

We now have our Pivot Chart straight from the data

source. You can see that it also created a Pivot Table!

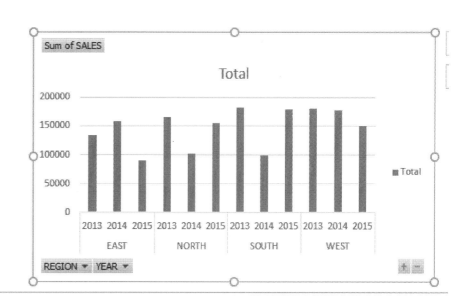

Printing a Pivot Chart

Have you ever thought of printing out your Pivot Chart to present it to your boss?

Excel allows you **print a Pivot Chart** with just a few clicks! We will show you

how to print this out and save as a pdf file.

Here we have our Pivot Table and Pivot Chart ready:

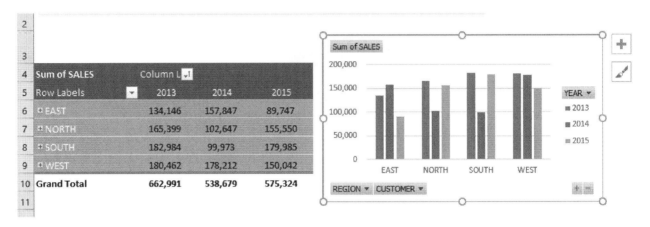

STEP 1: Click on your Pivot Chart and go to *File > Print.*

STEP 2: Change the orientation by selecting **Landscape Orientation.** This ensures our Pivot Chart is shown nicely in the printout.

We have selected **Microsoft Print to PDF** to save this as a pdf file. Click **Print** and **Save the file** to your computer.

Open the pdf file from your computer. You can now see your printout!

Expand & Collapse Fields in a Pivot Chart

Did you know that you can **Expand and Collapse Fields** in your Pivot Chart so that it will control the amount of detail to show in your Chart?

This is our source data.

	A	B	C	D	E	F	G
1	CUSTOMER	REGION	ORDER DATE	SALES	COSTS	MONTH	YEAR
2	Acme, Inc.	NORTH	1/15/2013	$26,884	$9,175	January	2013
3	Widget Corp	SOUTH	2/14/2013	$46,174	$9,384	February	2013
4	123 Warehousing	EAST	3/16/2013	$44,802	$7,010	March	2013
5	Demo Company	WEST	4/15/2013	$49,049	$7,665	April	2013
6	Smith and Co.	NORTH	5/15/2013	$80,369	$5,847	May	2013
7	Foo Bars	SOUTH	6/14/2013	$53,522	$7,623	June	2013
8	ABC Telecom	EAST	7/14/2013	$67,320	$9,860	July	2013
9	Fake Brothers	WEST	8/13/2013	$66,663	$9,214	August	2013
10	Acme, Inc.	NORTH	9/12/2013	$58,146	$5,745	September	2013
11	Widget Corp	SOUTH	10/12/2013	$83,288	$8,657	October	2013
12	123 Warehousing	EAST	11/11/2013	$22,024	$7,088	November	2013
13	Demo Company	WEST	12/11/2013	$64,750	$7,945	December	2013
14	Smith and Co.	NORTH	1/10/2014	$53,586	$6,755	January	2014
15	Foo Bars	SOUTH	2/9/2014	$14,333	$8,045	February	2014
16	ABC Telecom	EAST	3/11/2014	$29,570	$9,277	March	2014
17	Fake Brothers	WEST	4/10/2014	$83,468	$9,533	April	2014

This is our Pivot Table and Pivot Chart.

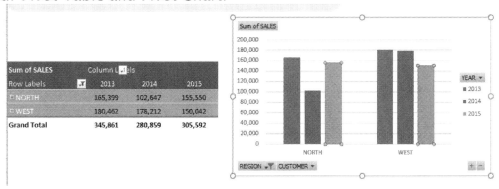

STEP 1: To expand the Fields, right click on a part of the Pivot Chart and go to *Expand/Collapse > Expand Entire Field.*

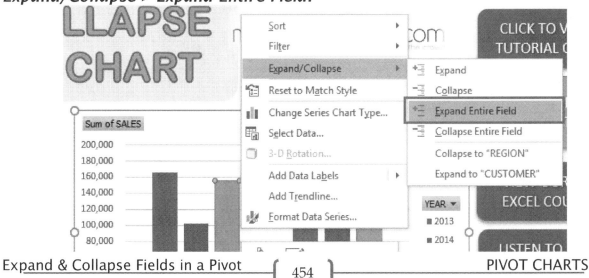

With just that, the Pivot Chart has now expanded to show the Sales per Region and Customer!

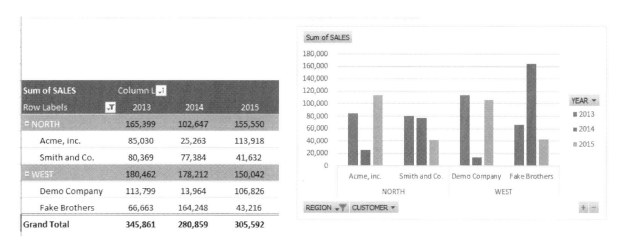

STEP 2: Now let us collapse this back, right click on a part of the Pivot Chart and go to *Expand/Collapse > Collapse Entire Field.*

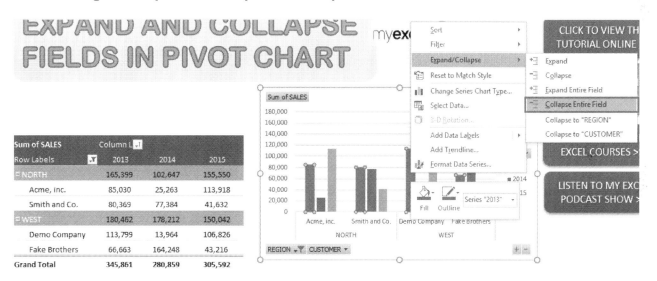

Now the Pivot Chart has gone back to showing the Sales per Region!

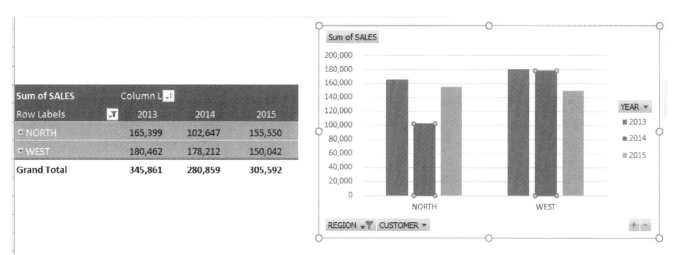

Include a Sparkline with a Pivot Table

A sparkline is a tiny chart in a worksheet cell that provides a visual representation of data.

You can use sparklines to show trends in a series of values, such as seasonal increases or decreases, economic cycles, or to highlight maximum and minimum values.

You can include **a Sparkline with a Pivot Table**!

Here we have our Pivot Table below:

Sum of SALES	Column L		
Row Labels	2013	2014	2015
EAST	134,146	157,847	89,747
123 Warehousing	66,826	49,562	75,088
ABC Telecom	67,320	108,285	14,659
NORTH	165,399	102,647	155,550
Acme, inc.	85,030	25,263	113,918
Smith and Co.	80,369	77,384	41,632
SOUTH	182,984	99,973	179,985
Foo Bars	53,522	31,176	85,607
Widget Corp	129,462	68,797	94,378
WEST	180,462	178,212	150,042
Demo Company	113,799	13,964	106,826
Fake Brothers	66,663	164,248	43,216
Grand Total	662,991	538,679	575,324

STEP 1: Select a spot right beside your Pivot Table. Go to *Insert > Sparklines > Line.*

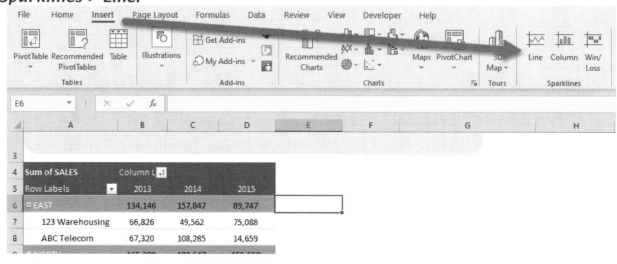

For **Data Range**, select the **Sales values for 2013, 2014 and 2015**. Then click **OK**.

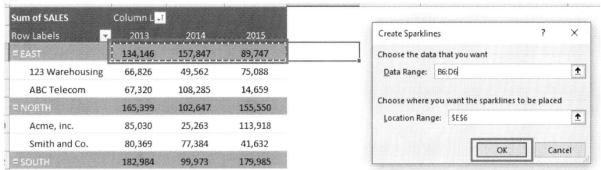

STEP 2: On the lower right corner of the Sparkline cell, drag it all the way down to populate the rest of your Pivot Table with Sparklines.

Sum of SALES	Column L		
Row Labels	2013	2014	2015
EAST	134,146	157,847	89,747
123 Warehousing	66,826	49,562	75,088
ABC Telecom	67,320	108,285	14,659
NORTH	165,399	102,647	155,550
Acme, inc.	85,030	25,263	113,918
Smith and Co.	80,369	77,384	41,632
SOUTH	182,984	99,973	179,985
Foo Bars	53,522	31,176	85,607
Widget Corp	129,462	68,797	94,378
WEST	180,462	178,212	150,042
Demo Company	113,799	13,964	106,826
Fake Brothers	66,663	164,248	43,216
Grand Total	662,991	538,679	575,324

STEP 3: We can change the type as well. Go to *Sparkline > Type > Column.*

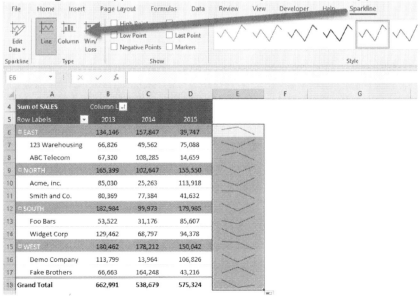

We now have our Column Sparklines for our Pivot Table showing a visual representation of the data trends for each row!

	A	B	C	D	E
4	Sum of SALES	Column L			
5	Row Labels	2013	2014	2015	
6	EAST	134,146	157,847	89,747	
7	123 Warehousing	66,826	49,562	75,088	
8	ABC Telecom	67,320	108,285	14,659	
9	NORTH	165,399	102,647	155,550	
10	Acme, inc.	85,030	25,263	113,918	
11	Smith and Co.	80,369	77,384	41,632	
12	SOUTH	182,984	99,973	179,985	
13	Foo Bars	53,522	31,176	85,607	
14	Widget Corp	129,462	68,797	94,378	
15	WEST	180,462	178,212	150,042	
16	Demo Company	113,799	13,964	106,826	
17	Fake Brothers	66,663	164,248	43,216	
18	Grand Total	662,991	538,679	575,324	

CONDITIONAL FORMATTING

Pivot Table Conditional Formatting

Conditional formatting can help make patterns and trends in your Pivot Table data more apparent. See how easy it is to add some color to your analysis!

STEP 1: We want to create a rule that will **highlight values greater than 100,000.** Select any cell inside the Pivot Table.

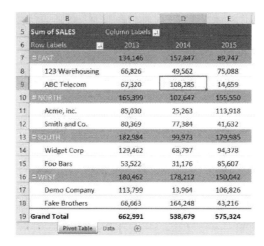

STEP 2: Go to *Home > Conditional Formatting > New Rule*

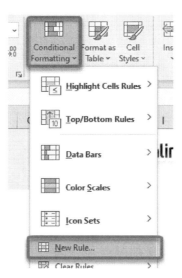

STEP 3: Select the following settings.

Appy Rule to: All cells showing "Sum of SALES" values for "CUSTOMER" and "Year".

Select a Rule Type: Format only cells that contain

Format only cells with:

- **Cell Value**

- **Greater than**

- **100,000**

Click **Format.**

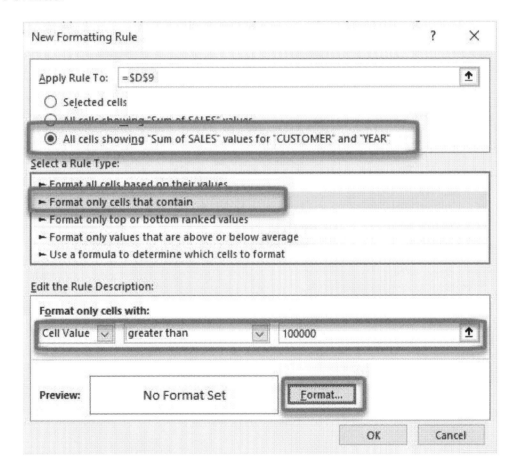

STEP 4: In the Format Cells dialog box, select **Fill** and pick a color of your choice. Click **OK** twice to exit back to the spreadsheet.

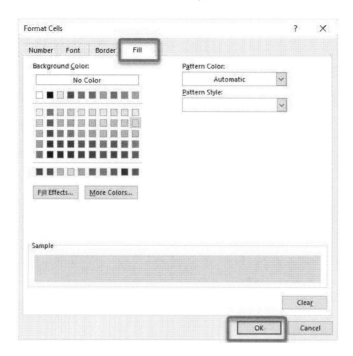

All values that are greater than $100,000 are highlighted in Peach.

	B	C	D	E
5	Sum of SALES	Column Labels		
6	Row Labels	2013	2014	2015
7	EAST	134,146	157,847	89,747
8	123 Warehousing	66,826	49,562	75,088
9	ABC Telecom	67,320	108,285	14,659
10	NORTH	165,399	102,647	155,550
11	Acme, inc.	85,030	25,263	113,918
12	Smith and Co.	80,369	77,384	41,632
13	SOUTH	182,984	99,973	179,985
14	Widget Corp	129,462	68,797	94,378
15	Foo Bars	53,522	31,176	85,607
16	WEST	180,462	178,212	150,042
17	Demo Company	113,799	13,964	106,826
18	Fake Brothers	66,663	164,248	43,216
19	Grand Total	662,991	538,679	575,324

Pivot Table | Data | (+)

Conditionally Format a Cell's Value

A great way to highlight values within your Pivot Table is to use Conditional Formatting rules.

Formatting cells that contain specific criteria, for example, **_greater than X_** or **_less than X_** is a good way to visualize your results.

STEP 1: Select a cell in your Pivot Table.

Sum of SALES	Column Labels		
Row Labels	2013	2014	2015
January	26,884	53,586	56,959
February	46,174	14,333	47,189
March	44,802	29,570	37,544
April	49,049	83,468	53,413
May	80,369	25,263	20,816
June	53,522	68,797	85,607
July	67,320	49,562	14,659
August	66,663	13,964	43,216
September	58,146	23,798	56,959
October	83,288	16,843	47,189
November	22,024	78,715	37,544
December	64,750	80,780	74,229
Grand Total	**662,991**	**538,679**	**575,324**

HIGHLIGHT VALUES
BIGGER THAN...

50,000

STEP 2: Go to **_Home > Conditional Formatting > New Rule_**

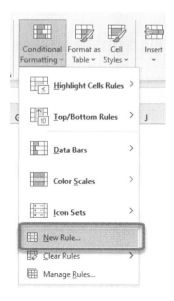

STEP 3: Set **Apply Rule** to the third option:

All cells showing "Sum of SALES" values for "MONTH" and "YEAR"

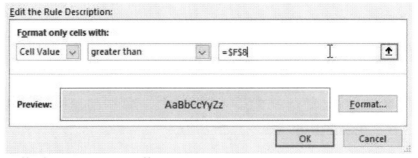

STEP 4: Select the **Rule Type:** *Format Only Cells That Contain*

STEP 5: Select **Format only cells with:**

Cell Value

Greater than

=F8

F8 is a cell we will change manually.

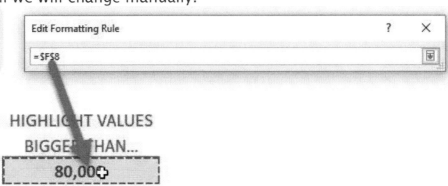

HIGHLIGHT VALUES
BIGGER THAN...
80,000

Click on **Format.**

STEP 6: In the Format Cells dialog box, select a **color** and click **OK.**

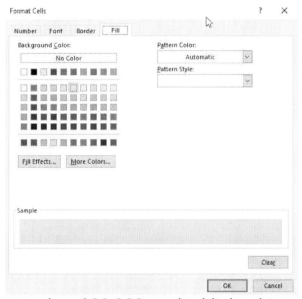

All values that are greater than $80,000 are highlighted in red.

Change cell F8 by entering a different value. Now watch as the conditionally formatted cell colors change dynamically!

Sum of SALES	Column Labels				HIGHLIGHT VALUES
Row Labels	2013	2014	2015		BIGGER THAN...
January	26,884	53,586	56,959		80,000
February	46,174	14,333	47,189		
March	44,802	29,570	37,544		
April	49,049	83,468	53,413		
May	80,369	25,263	20,816		
June	53,522	68,797	85,607		
July	67,320	49,562	14,659		
August	66,663	13,964	43,216		
September	58,146	23,798	56,959		
October	83,288	16,843	47,189		
November	22,024	78,715	37,544		
December	64,750	80,780	74,229		
Grand Total	**662,991**	**538,679**	**575,324**		

Highlight Cell Rules Based on Text Labels

You can also use Conditional Formatting on Pivot Table text labels. Let me show you how easy this is with this example.

This is our current Pivot Table setup. We want to highlight all the **Q1 text** in our **Row Labels**.

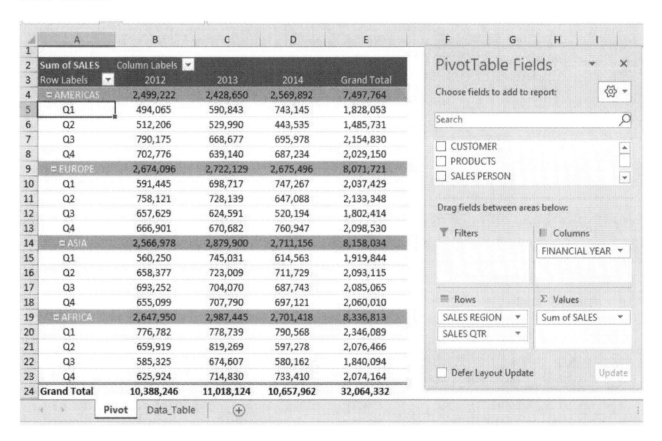

STEP 1: Highlight all the Quarters text by clicking above cell A5.

Sum of SALES	Column Labels			
Row Labels	2012	2013	2014	Grand Total
⊟ AMERICAS	2,499,222	2,428,650	2,569,892	7,497,764
Q1	494,065	590,843	743,145	1,828,053
Q2	512,206	529,990	443,535	1,485,731
Q3	790,175	668,677	695,978	2,154,830
Q4	702,776	639,140	687,234	2,029,150
⊟ EUROPE	2,674,096	2,722,129	2,675,496	8,071,721
Q1	591,445	698,717	747,267	2,037,429
Q2	758,121	728,139	647,088	2,133,348
Q3	657,629	624,591	520,194	1,802,414
Q4	666,901	670,682	760,947	2,098,530
⊟ ASIA	2,566,978	2,879,900	2,711,156	8,158,034
Q1	560,250	745,031	614,563	1,919,844
Q2	658,377	723,009	711,729	2,093,115
Q3	693,252	704,070	687,743	2,085,065
Q4	655,099	707,790	697,121	2,060,010
⊟ AFRICA	2,647,950	2,987,445	2,701,418	8,336,813
Q1	776,782	778,739	790,568	2,346,089
Q2	659,919	819,269	597,278	2,076,466
Q3	585,325	674,607	580,162	1,840,094
Q4	625,924	714,830	733,410	2,074,164
Grand Total	**10,388,246**	**11,018,124**	**10,657,962**	**32,064,332**

STEP 2: Go to *Home > Conditional Formatting > Highlight Cells Rules > Text that Contains....*

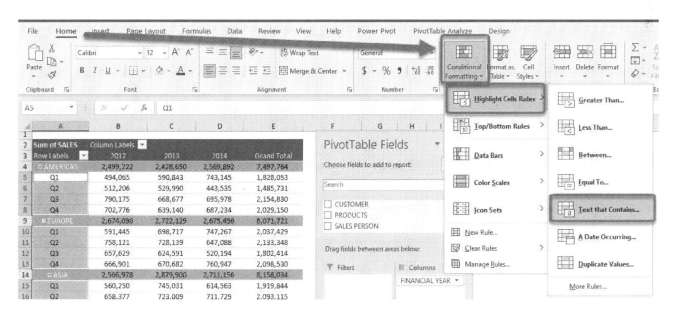

STEP 3: For the **Format cells that contain the text** type **Q1.**

Select the **Light Red Fill with Dark Red Text**.

Select **OK.**

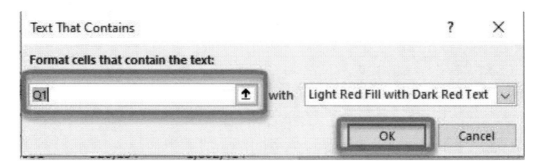

All the Q1's are now highlighted in red!

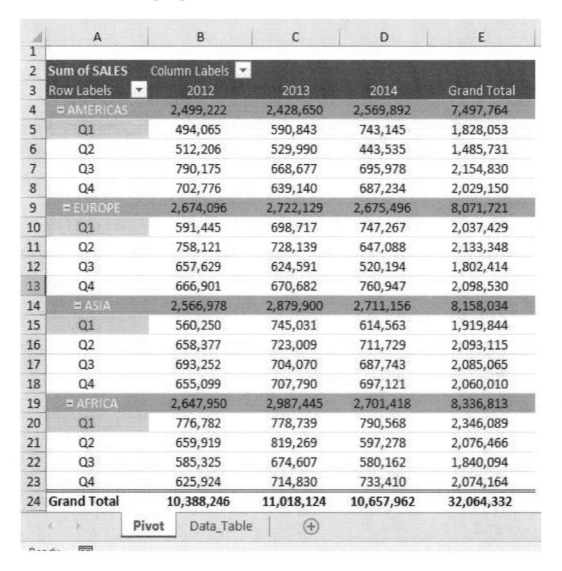

Highlight Cell Rules Based on Date Labels

You can also use Conditional Formatting on Date labels. Let me show you how easy this is with this example.

This is our current Pivot Table setup. We want to highlight all the **dates of the current month (July 2021)** in our **Row Labels**.

For this to work, we are going back in time and are assuming that today is July 2021.

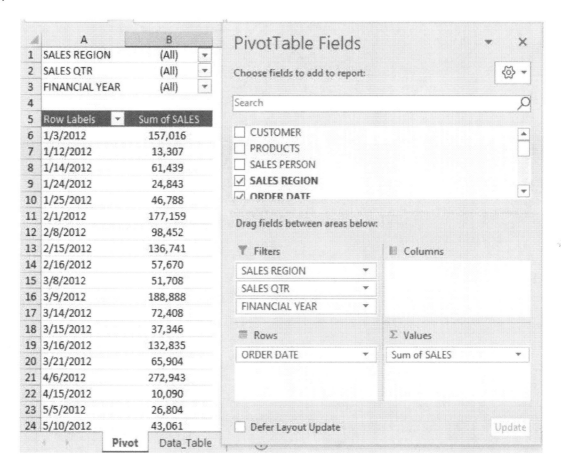

STEP 1: Highlight all the Date labels by clicking above the cell A6.

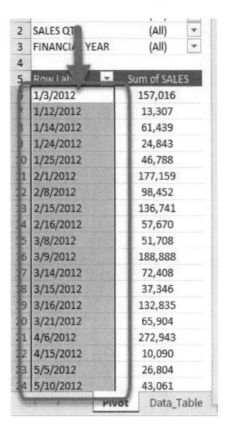

STEP 2: Go to *Home > Conditional Formatting > Highlight Cells Rules > A Date Occurring.*

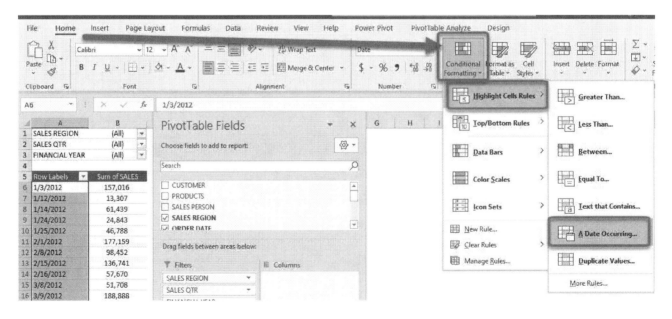

STEP 3: For the **Format cells that contain a date occurring** select **This Month.**

Select the **Light Red Fill with Dark Red Text.**

Select **OK.**

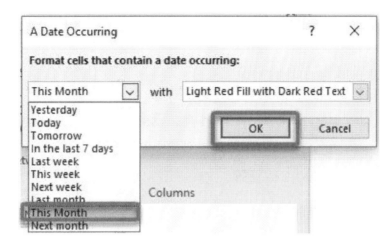

The Dates for this month (assuming we are back in July 2021) are now highlighted!

The best part is this is dynamic, if you open this workbook again next month, the highlighted date values will be for the next month instead!

	A	B
247	11/28/2014	496,575
248	11/29/2014	16,292
249	12/2/2014	741,656
250	12/6/2014	34,696
251	12/8/2014	215,727
252	12/9/2014	135,501
253	12/13/2014	87,319
254	12/14/2014	82,004
255	12/17/2014	162,076
256	12/19/2014	74,283
257	12/20/2014	299,749
258	12/21/2014	65,316
259	12/28/2014	137,310
260	12/30/2014	32,784
261	12/31/2014	53,796
262	4/15/2021	24,640
263	7/15/2021	90,599
264	7/16/2021	17,030
265	7/17/2021	65,026
266	9/15/2022	247,377
267	Grand Total	32,064,332
268		
269		
270		

Pivot   Data_Table

Ready

Data Bars, Color Scales & Icon Sets

DATA BARS

Data Bars are a cool Conditional Formatting feature in Excel, and they add a colored bar to your values.

The length of the data bar represents the value in the cell. A longer bar represents a higher value.

You have a Gradient Fill or a Solid Fill to choose from as well as different pre- determined colors.

If you select the *More Rules* option, then you can select more colors as well as many different values types to format.

STEP 1: Select any value inside the Pivot Table. Go to ***Home > Conditional Formatting > Data Bars > Any Gradient Fill.***

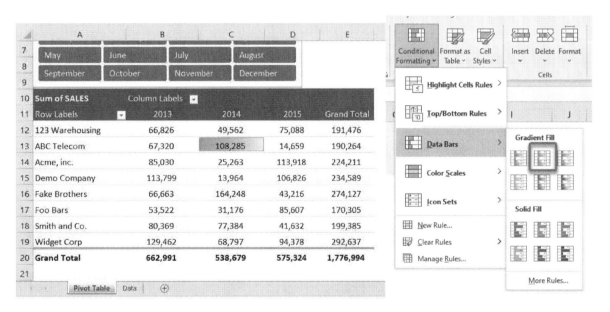

STEP 2: Go to the **Formatting Options Icon** and **select the second option** to apply the data bar formatting to the entire Pivot Table.

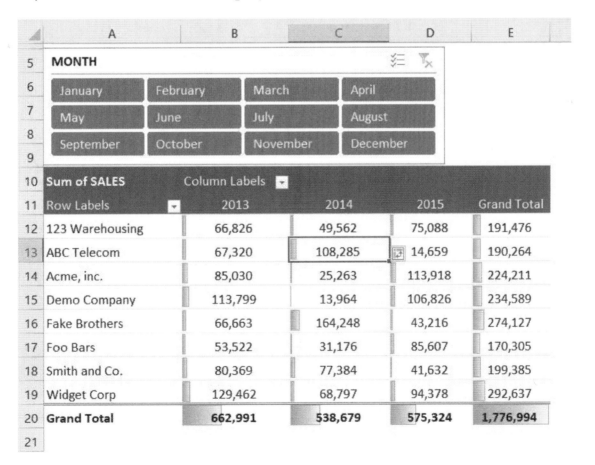

Now you have data bars showing up for the entire Pivot Table.

STEP 3: Go to the **Formatting Options Icon** and **select the third option** to apply the data bar formatting to the entire Pivot Table while excluding the Grand Totals.

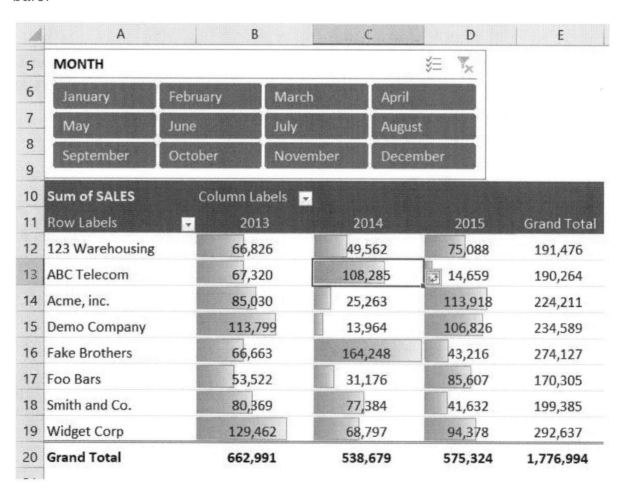

Sum of SALES	Column Labels			
Row Labels	2013	2014	2015	Grand Total
123 Warehousing	66,826	49,562	75,088	191,476
ABC Telecom	67,320	108,285	4,659	190,264
Acme, inc.	85,030	25,263		
Demo Company	113,799	13,964		
Fake Brothers	66,663	164,248		
Foo Bars	53,522	31,176	85,607	170,305
Smith and Co.	80,369	77,384	41,632	199,385
Widget Corp	129,462	68,797	94,378	292,637
Grand Total	662,991	538,679	575,324	1,776,994

Apply formatting rule to ...
- Selected cells
- All cells showing "Sum of SALES" values
- All cells showing "Sum of SALES" values for "CUSTOMER" and "YEAR"

You get better visual representation as the Grand Totals do not affect the data bars!

	A	B	C	D	E
5	**MONTH**				
6	January	February	March	April
7	May	June	July	August
8	September	October	November	December
9					
10	**Sum of SALES**	Column Labels			
11	Row Labels	2013	2014	2015	Grand Total
12	123 Warehousing	66,826	49,562	75,088	191,476
13	ABC Telecom	67,320	108,285	14,659	190,264
14	Acme, inc.	85,030	25,263	113,918	224,211
15	Demo Company	113,799	13,964	106,826	234,589
16	Fake Brothers	66,663	164,248	43,216	274,127
17	Foo Bars	53,522	31,176	85,607	170,305
18	Smith and Co.	80,369	77,384	41,632	199,385
19	Widget Corp	129,462	68,797	94,378	292,637
20	**Grand Total**	662,991	538,679	575,324	1,776,994

COLOR SCALES

Color Scales were introduced in Excel 2010 and they highlight the smallest and largest data points within your Pivot Table.

It works like a heat map, in that it gives the highest number a shade of color and the lowest number a different shade of color, so your numbers can stand out at a glance.

STEP 1: Select the range of cells that you want to apply the **Color Scale** to.

MONTH			
January	February	March	April
May	June	July	August
September	October	November	December

Sum of SALES	Column Labels			
Row Labels	2013	2014	2015	Grand Total
123 Warehousing	66,826	49,562	75,088	191,476
ABC Telecom	67,320	108,285	14,659	190,264
Acme, inc.	85,030	25,263	113,918	224,211
Demo Company	113,799	13,964	106,826	234,589
Fake Brothers	66,663	164,248	43,216	274,127
Foo Bars	53,522	31,176	85,607	170,305
Smith and Co.	80,369	77,384	41,632	199,385
Widget Corp	129,462	68,797	94,378	292,637
Grand Total	662,991	538,679	575,324	1,776,994

STEP 2: Go to *Home > Styles > Conditional Formatting > Color Scales.*

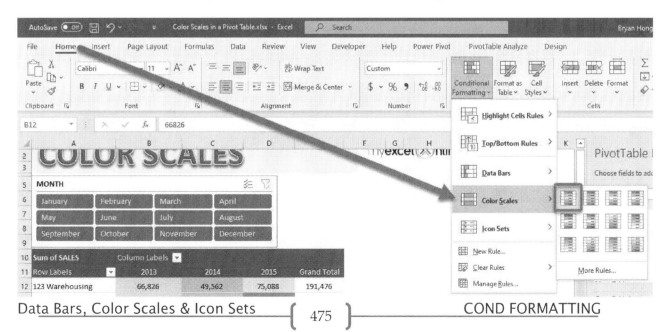

Data Bars, Color Scales & Icon Sets ⎨ 475 ⎬ COND FORMATTING

STEP 3: You now have a **Color Scale** applied to your selection!

Sum of SALES	Column Labels			
Row Labels	2013	2014	2015	Grand Total
123 Warehousing	66,826	49,562	75,088	191,476
ABC Telecom	67,320	108,285	14,659	190,264
Acme, inc.	85,030	25,263	113,918	224,211
Demo Company	113,799	13,964	106,826	234,589
Fake Brothers	66,663	164,248	43,216	274,127
Foo Bars	53,522	31,176	85,607	170,305
Smith and Co.	80,369	77,384	41,632	199,385
Widget Corp	129,462	68,797	94,378	292,637
Grand Total	**662,991**	**538,679**	**575,324**	**1,776,994**

MONTH: January, February, March, April, May, June, July, August, September, October, November, December

STEP 4: Let us have some fun with the Slicers.

Select any month in the slicer. Notice your **Color Scale** is still applied.

MONTH: January, February, March, April, May, June (selected), July, August, September, October, November, December

Sum of SALES	Column Labels			
Row Labels	2013	2014	2015	Grand Total
Foo Bars	53,522		85,607	139,129
Widget Corp		68,797		68,797
Grand Total	**53,522**	**68,797**	**85,607**	**207,926**

ICON SETS

An Icon Set is a Conditional Formatting icon/graphic that you can include in your cells or Pivot Tables.

The icon will depend on the cell's value so you can highlight key variances or trends. There are a few sets that you can include, like:

DIRECTIONAL (Change in values)

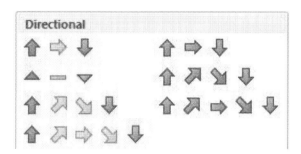

SHAPES (Milestones)

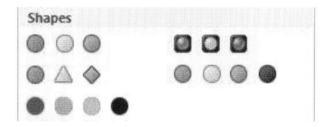

INDICATORS (Positive/Negative)

RATINGS (Scores)

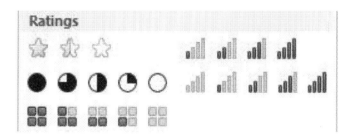

I will show you how easy it is to insert an Icon Set within a Pivot Table that will show a "directional icon" depending on the change of the Monthly Sales values.

So, when Monthly Sales increase from the previous month, a green up arrow is shown and when Monthly Sales decrease, a red down arrow is shown.

STEP 1: Place the **SALES** Field in the **Values area a second time.**

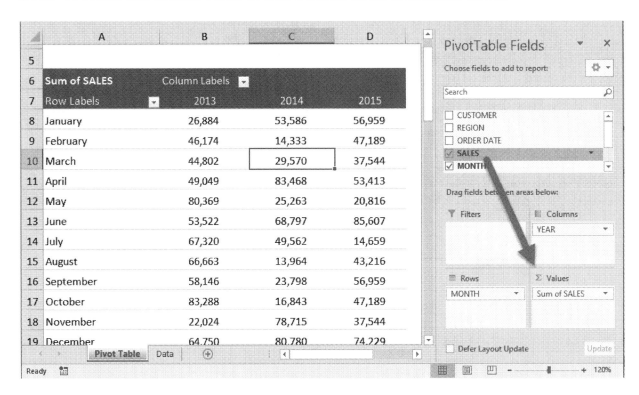

STEP 2: Click on the **Sum of SALES2** Field and Select **Value Field Settings.**

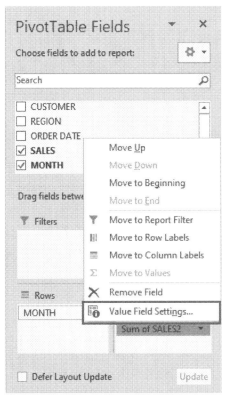

Go to *Show Values as > Difference From > (previous)* to get the difference from the previous month.

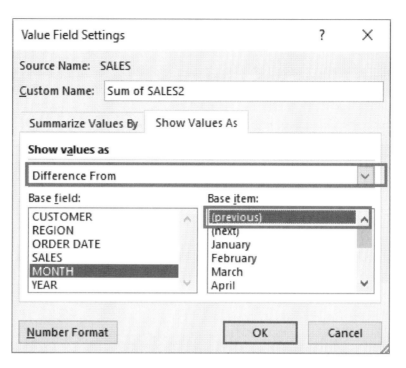

STEP 3: Click in a Sum of SALES2 cell. Go to *Home > Styles > Conditional Formatting > Icon Sets > The First Icon Set.*

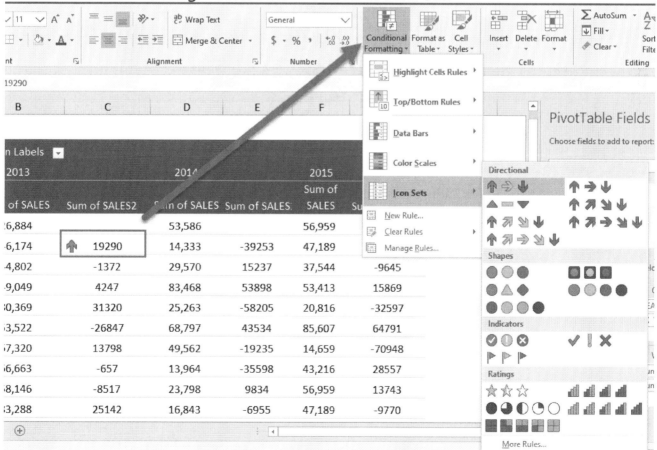

STEP 4: Make sure to select the third option. This excludes the Subtotals and Grand Totals.

Row Labels	2013 Sum of SALES	Sum of SALES2	2014 Sum of SALES	Sum of SALES	2015 Sum of SALES	Sum of SALES2
January	26,884		53,586		56,959	
February	46,174	⬆ 19290	▣▾ 4,333	-39253	47,189	-9770
March	44,802	-1372				
April	49,049	4247				
May	80,369	31320				
June	53,522	-26847	68,797	43534	85,607	64791
July	67,320	13798	49,562	-19235	14,659	-70948
August	66,663	-657	13,964	-35598	43,216	28557
September	58,146	-8517	23,798	9834	56,959	13743
October	83,288	25142	16,843	-6955	47,189	-9770

Apply formatting rule to ...
- ○ Selected cells
- ○ All cells showing "Sum of SALES2" values
- ○ All cells showing "Sum of SALES2" values for "MONTH" and "YEAR"

STEP 5: Go to *Home > Styles > Conditional Formatting > Manage Rules.*

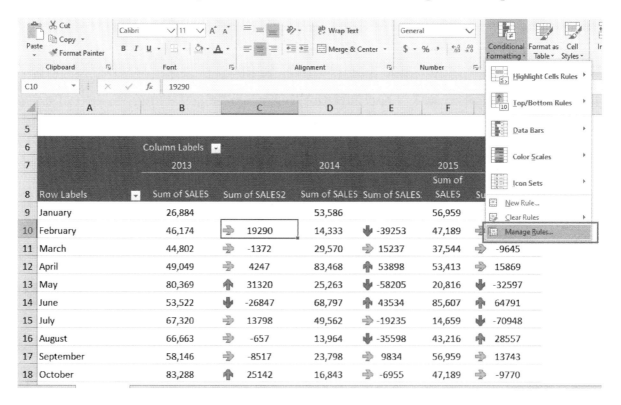

Select **Edit Rule.**

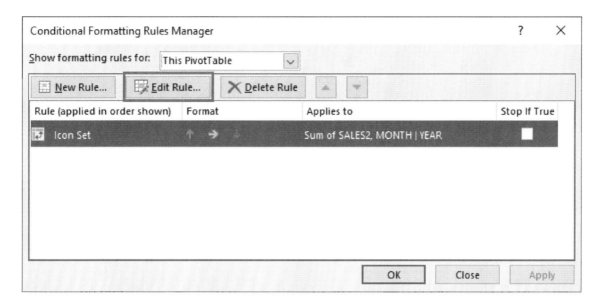

Set the settings to the ones shown below. This will only show the **arrow icons** in the Pivot Table.

Our icon sets are now ready in our Pivot Table!

Row Labels	2013 Sum of SALES	Sum of SALES2	2014 Sum of SALES	Sum of SALES	2015 Sum of SALES	Sum of SALES2
January	26,884		53,586		56,959	
February	46,174	⬆	14,333	⬇	47,189	⬇
March	44,802	⬇	29,570	⬆	37,544	⬇
April	49,049	⬆	83,468	⬆	53,413	⬆
May	80,369	⬆	25,263	⬇	20,816	⬇
June	53,522	⬇	68,797	⬆	85,607	⬆
July	67,320	⬆	49,562	⬇	14,659	⬇
August	66,663	⬇	13,964	⬇	43,216	⬆
September	58,146	⬇	23,798	⬆	56,959	⬆
October	83,288	⬆	16,843	⬇	47,189	⬇
November	22,024	⬇	78,715	⬆	37,544	⬇
December	64,750	⬆	80,780	⬆	74,229	⬆
Grand Total	662,991		538,679		575,324	

BONUS TIPS

Clear & Delete Old Pivot Table Items

You might have come across this issue before.

You have deleted or replaced old data from your data source but even after refreshing the Pivot Table, **the data is still visible**.

This is because the old data is **stored in the cache memory** and displayed in filter selections even if there is no data for it at all. This can be confusing as well as annoying.

Let's look at an example and understand How to Clear the Pivot Table Cache Memory!

So, you have created a Pivot Table using the original data source containing the Years 2012, 2013, and 2014. The Pivot Table will look like this:

Sum of SALES	Column Labels			
Row Labels	2014	2012	2013	Grand Total
July	873,543.00	1,056,573.00	854,835.00	2,784,951.00
January	1,074,820.00	53,089,979.00	872,080.00	55,036,879.00
February	807,257.00	867,220.00	909,654.00	2,584,131.00
March	1,013,466.00	784,136.00	1,031,596.00	2,829,198.00
April	836,559.00	908,666.00	968,855.00	2,714,080.00
May	791,095.00	893,039.00	850,502.00	2,534,636.00
June	771,976.00	786,918.00	981,050.00	2,539,944.00
August	599,246.00	806,719.00	1,002,597.00	2,408,562.00
September	1,011,288.00	863,089.00	814,513.00	2,688,890.00
October	1,059,308.00	873,208.00	931,193.00	2,863,709.00
November	812,659.00	923,402.00	769,352.00	2,505,413.00
December	1,006,745.00	854,090.00	1,031,897.00	2,892,732.00
Grand Total	10,657,962.00	62,707,039.00	11,018,124.00	84,383,125.00

Now, you change the year 2012 in your data source to 2013 and the same is reflected in the Pivot Table as well after a Refresh.

But the year 2012 is **still visible in the Pivot Table's filter** selection.

This is because the old item is still saved in the Pivot Table cache memory. Let's learn how to fix it!

STEP 1: Below is our data source and we want to replace the year 2012 with 2013, effectively only showing the years 2014 & 2013.

Go to *Home > Find & Select > Replace.*

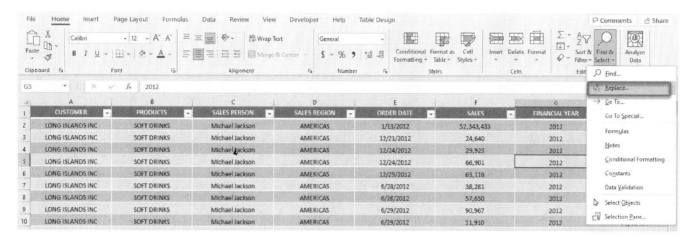

Let us **replace** the year **2012** with the year **2013.** Click **Replace All.**

STEP 2: Go back to your Pivot Table. **Right click** and select **Refresh.**

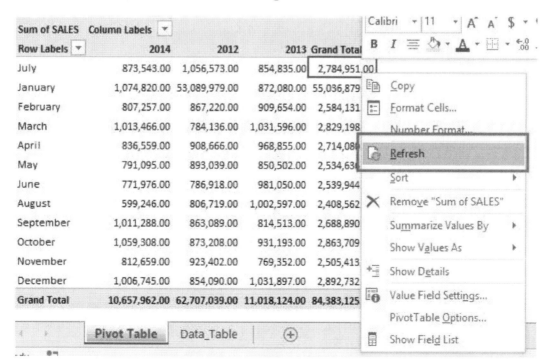

We have technically deleted the year 2012 records, so they should be gone from our Pivot Table, right?

Hmm.. Looking good, the **year 2012** is now gone from our Pivot Table!

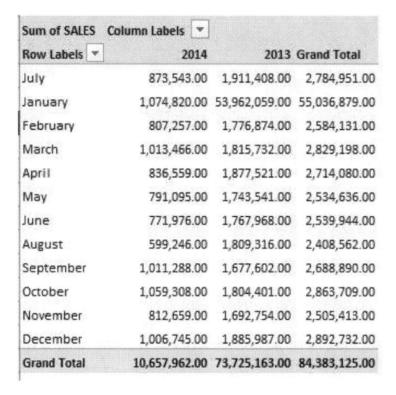

BUT WAIT!

Clicking on the **Column Labels** drop-down list, the **Year 2012** is still there!

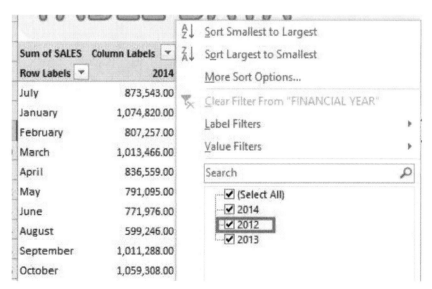

STEP 3: Let us fix this! Go back to your Pivot Table > **Right click** and select **PivotTable Options.**

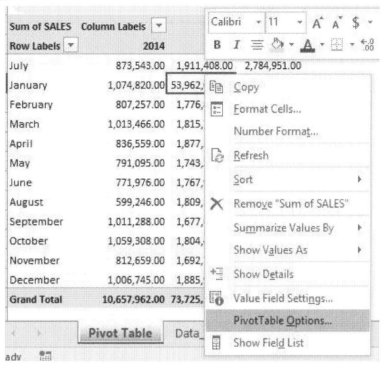

STEP 4: Go to *Data > Number of items to retain per Field.*

Select **None** then **OK.**

This will stop Excel from retaining deleted data!

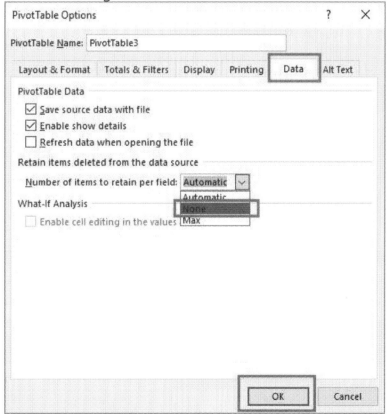

STEP 5: Go back to your Pivot Table. **Right-click** and select **Refresh.**

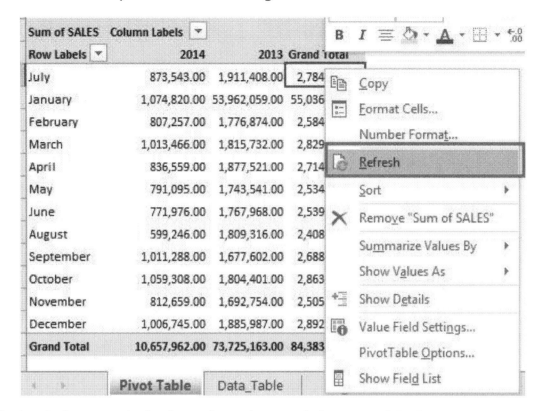

Click the **Column Labels** drop-down list, and the **Year 2012** is now gone. Problem fixed!

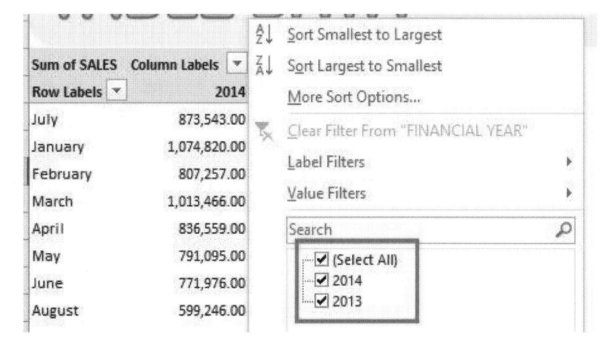

Change Default setting of Retain Items

By default, the number of Pivot items to retain per Field is set to **"Automatic"**.

If you want, you can change the **default setting to None.** Then this setting is reflected in all the Pivot Tables you create. To do that, follow the steps below (this is applicable for **Microsoft 365 and Excel 2019** only):

STEP 1: Click on the **File Tab** at the top-left corner of Excel

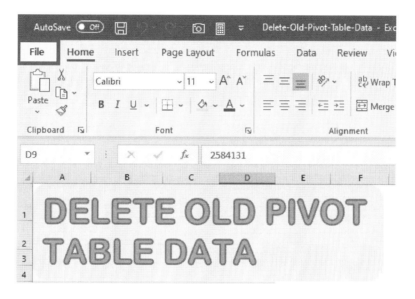

STEP 2: From the left panel, select **Options**.

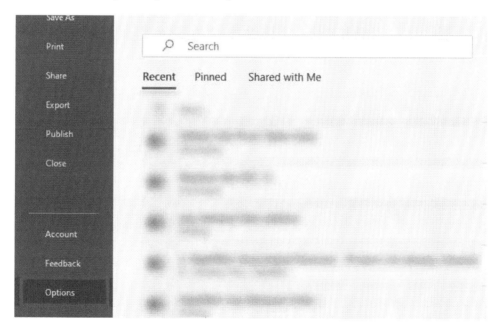

STEP 3: In the Excel Options dialog box, click on the **Data** and select **Edit Default Layout** button.

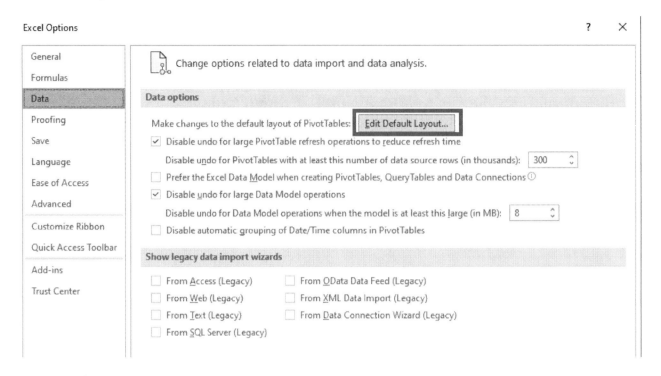

STEP 4: In the Edit Default Layout dialog box, click on **PivotTable options** button.

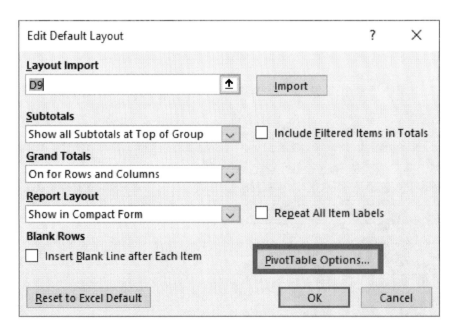

STEP 5: In the PivotTable Options dialog box, click on the **Data tab**,

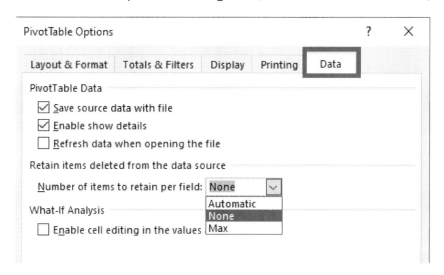

STEP 6: Under the **Data tab**, select **None** from the drop-down list in the **Retain Items** section.

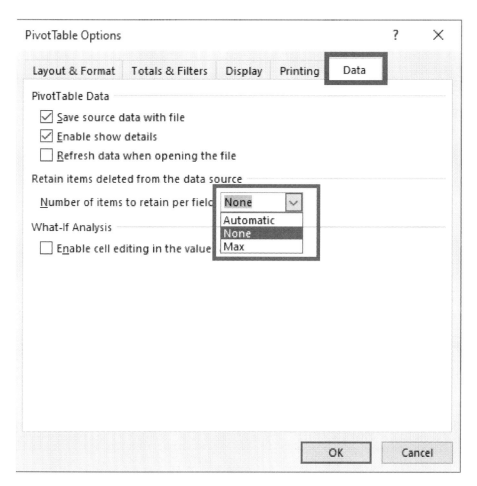

Click **Ok** three times and voila it's done!

The old deleted items from the data source will **not be shown in the Pivot Table's filter selection** anymore.

GETPIVOTDATA Function

What does it do?

A formula that extracts data stored in a Pivot Table

Formula breakdown:

=GETPIVOTDATA(data_Field, Pivot_Table, [Field1, item1], [Field2,item2],...)

What it means:

=GETPIVOTDATA(return me this value from the Values Area, any cell within the Pivot Table, [and return me the value that pertains to this Field name, and this Field item],...)

The GETPIVOTDATA function in Excel returns data stored in a Pivot Table. So essentially it extracts the Pivot Table data to enable a user to create customized reports.

Think of the Pivot Table like your data source, so anything you see in the Pivot Table report can be extracted with the GETPIVOTDATA function and put into a cell within your worksheet.

The GETPIVOTDATA function becomes powerful when you reference cells to create shell reports, which you can see from the tutorial below.

Pro tip: *Only the Fields and Items that are included in the Pivot Table report (Row/Column Labels and Values area) can be used to extract their values.*

This is our Pivot Table report with **SALES QTR** and **SALES REGION** in the Rows area, **FINANCIAL YEAR** in the Columns area and **SALES** in the Values area.

Sum of SALES	Column Labels		
Row Labels	2012	2013	2014
☐ Q1	2,422,542	3,786,643	2,895,543
AMERICAS	494,065	1,564,156	743,145
EUROPE	591,445	698,717	747,267
ASIA	560,250	745,031	614,563
AFRICA	776,782	778,739	790,568
☐ Q2	2,588,623	2,800,407	2,399,630
AMERICAS	512,206	529,990	443,535
EUROPE	758,121	728,139	647,088
ASIA	658,377	723,009	711,729
AFRICA	659,919	819,269	597,278
☐ Q3	2,726,381	2,671,945	2,484,077
AMERICAS	790,175	668,677	695,978
EUROPE	657,629	624,591	520,194
ASIA	693,252	704,070	687,743
AFRICA	585,325	674,607	580,162
☐ Q4	2,650,700	2,732,442	2,878,712
AMERICAS	702,776	639,140	687,234
EUROPE	666,901	670,682	760,947
ASIA	655,099	707,790	697,121
AFRICA	625,924	714,830	733,410

STEP 1: We need to **enter the *GETPIVOTDATA* function**:

=GETPIVOTDATA(

⁄	A	B	C	D	E	F
25		2013	2013	2013	2013	**2013**
26		Q1	Q2	Q3	Q4	**ACTUAL**
27		=GETPIVOTDATA(				0
28	EUROPE	GETPIVOTDATA(**data_field**, pivot_table, [field1, item1], ...)				0
29	ASIA					0
30	AFRICA					0
31	**TOTALS**	0	0	0	0	0

STEP 2: The GETPIVOTDATA arguments:

data_Field
What is the value that we want to return?
Type in **"SALES"** as we want to return the sales value:

=GETPIVOTDATA("SALES",

	A	B	C	D	E	F
25		2013	2013	2013	2013	**2013**
26		Q1	Q2	Q3	Q4	**ACTUAL**
27		=GETPIVOTDATA("SALES"				0
28	EURO	GETPIVOTDATA(**data_field**, pivot_table, [field1, item1], ...)				0
29	ASIA					0
30	AFRICA					0
31	**TOTALS**	0	0	0	0	0

Pivot_Table
From which Pivot Table?

We can reference any cell in the Pivot Table. Let's type in **A1**

=GETPIVOTDATA("SALES", A1,

	A	B	C	D	
1	Sum of SALE	olumn La ▼			3
2	Row Label ▼	2012	2013	2014	UAL
3	= Q1	2,422,542	3,786,643	2,895,543	
4	AMERICAS	494,065	1,564,156	743,145	
5	EUROPE	591,445	698,717	747,267	
6	ASIA	560,250	745,031	614,563	
7	AFRICA	776,782	778,739	790,568	
8	= Q2	2,588,623	2,800,407	2,399,630	
9	AMERICAS	512,206	529,990	443,535	
10	EUROPE	758,121	728,139	647,088	
11	ASIA	658,377	723,009	711,729	
12	AFRICA	659,919	819,269	597,278	

[Field1, item1]
What are the Fields that would serve as our filtering criteria?

To get our target sales figure, we will need: Sales Region, Financial Year and

Sales Quarter. To do this we will need 3 Field-item pairs:

=GETPIVOTDATA("SALES", A1, "SALES REGION", $A27, "FINANCIAL YEAR", B$25, "SALES QTR", B$26)

	A	B	C	D	E	F
25		2013	2013	2013	2013	**2013**
26		Q1	Q2	Q3	Q4	**ACTUAL**
27	=GETPIVOTDATA("SALES", A1, "SALES					1,564,156
28	REGION", $A27, "FINANCIAL YEAR",					0
29	B$25, "SALES QTR", B$26)					0
30	GETPIVOTDATA(**data_field**, pivot_table, [field1, item1], [field2, item2], [field3, item3], [field4, item4					
31	**TOTALS**	**1,564,156**	**0**	**0**	**0**	**1,564,156**

Press **ENTER**.

	A	B	C	D	E	F
25		2013	2013	2013	2013	**2013**
26		Q1	Q2	Q3	Q4	**ACTUAL**
27	AMERICAS	1,564,156				1,564,156
28	EUROPE					0
29	ASIA					0
30	AFRICA					0
31	**TOTALS**	**1,564,156**	**0**	**0**	**0**	**1,564,156**

STEP 3: Do the same for the rest of the cells by copying the **GETPIVOTDATA** formula to the rest of the cells.

	A	B	C	D	E	F
25		2013	2013	2013	2013	2013
26		Q1	Q2	Q3	Q4	ACTUAL
27	AMERICAS	1,564,156				1,564,156
28	EUROPE					0
29	ASIA					0
30	AFRICA					0
31	TOTALS	1,564,156	0	0	0	1,564,156

We have successfully imported data from the Pivot Table to a separate area of the worksheet so we can do further analysis.

	A	B	C	D	E	F
25		2013	2013	2013	2013	2013
26		Q1	Q2	Q3	Q4	ACTUAL
27	AMERICAS	1,564,156	529,990	668,677	639,140	3,401,963
28	EUROPE	698,717	728,139	624,591	670,682	2,722,129
29	ASIA	745,031	723,009	704,070	707,790	2,879,900
30	AFRICA	778,739	819,269	674,607	714,830	2,987,445
31	TOTALS	3,786,643	2,800,407	2,671,945	2,732,442	11,991,437

Reducing File Memory

When working with Pivot Tables, each time you create a brand new Pivot Table, the size of the workbook also grows.

If your Excel workbook is running slowly, what should you do?

I have a couple of quick tips for you on how to reduce the file size of your workbook!

Let us go over our current setup first. Here is our Pivot Table:

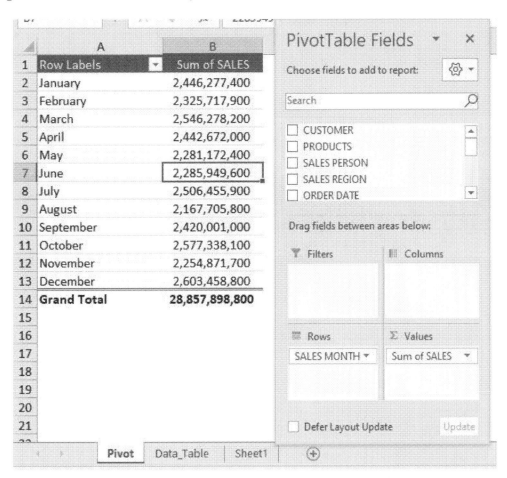

And here is our data source. It's a big Excel Table!

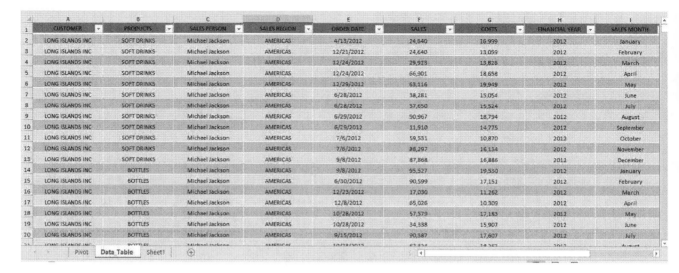

Now go to **File > Info** so that we can quickly check the original file size.

It's **45.7 MB**. Let's get to work!

Saving as a Binary Workbook

STEP 1: One quick way is to convert this file into a **Binary Workbook**. Storing this in the binary format is useful for large spreadsheets.

Go to *File > Save As.*

Select **Excel Binary Workbook (*.xlsb)** as the **File type**. Click **Save.**

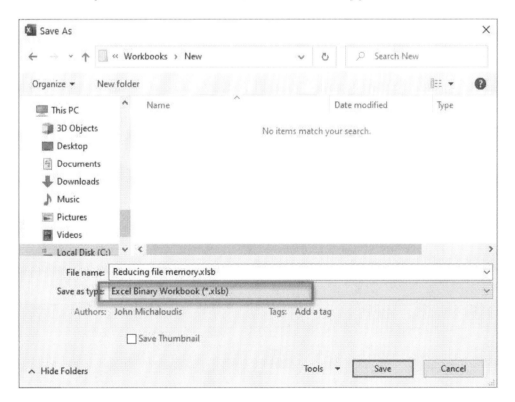

After you do that, go to **File > Info** and you will be surprised! It is now **25.9 MB!**

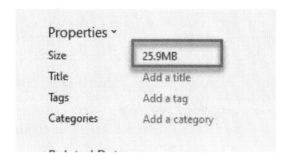

Deleting the original Table

STEP 2: If you prefer to keep the original **.xlsx** format, there is another workaround! Make sure to use the original Excel workbook file (.xlsx) with the big data Excel Table.

Right-click on the Excel Table data source worksheet and select **Delete.**

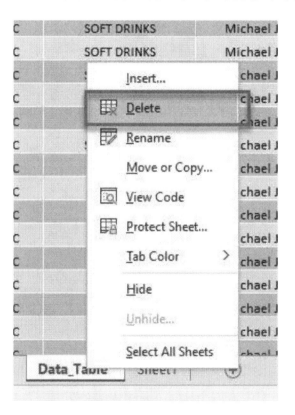

Click **Delete.** The drawback with this approach is we will not be able to Refresh the Pivot Table.

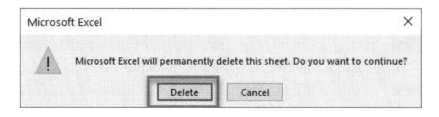

STEP 3: Even without the Excel Table data source, the Pivot Table will still work! It is all thanks to the Pivot cache.

Drag the **SALES REGION** to **Columns area.**

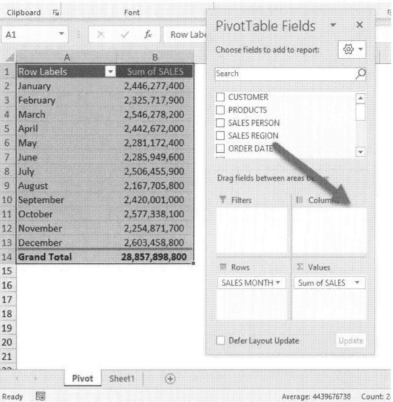

It is working as expected, amazing!

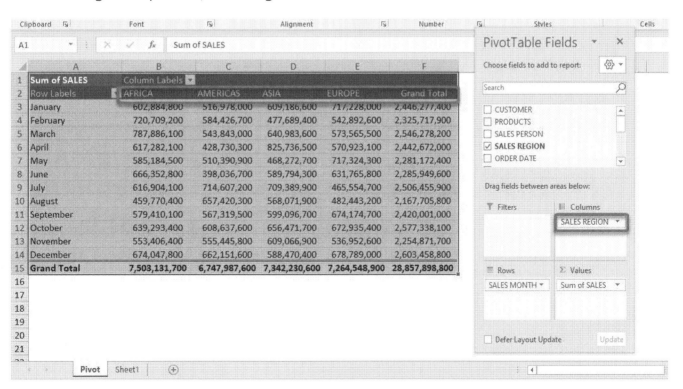

Make sure to save the workbook.

Now go to **File > Info** and it's now only **11.3 MB**!

Properties ⌄	
Size	11.3MB
Title	Add a title
Tags	Add a tag
Categories	Add a category

STEP 4: What if you need the Excel Table data source again? There is a cool trick by **double-clicking** on the **Grand Total.**

	A	B	C	D	E	F
1	Sum of SALES	Column Labels				
2	Row Labels	AFRICA	AMERICAS	ASIA	EUROPE	Grand Total
3	January	602,884,800	516,978,000	609,186,600	717,228,000	2,446,277,400
4	February	720,709,200	584,426,700	477,689,400	542,892,600	2,325,717,900
5	March	787,886,100	543,843,000	640,983,600	573,565,500	2,546,278,200
6	April	617,282,100	428,730,300	825,736,500	570,923,100	2,442,672,000
7	May	585,184,500	510,390,900	468,272,700	717,324,300	2,281,172,400
8	June	666,352,800	398,036,700	589,794,300	631,765,800	2,285,949,600
9	July	616,904,100	714,607,200	709,389,900	465,554,700	2,506,455,900
10	August	459,770,400	657,420,300	568,071,900	482,443,200	2,167,705,800
11	September	579,410,100	567,319,500	599,096,700	674,174,700	2,420,001,000
12	October	639,293,400	608,637,600	656,471,700	672,935,400	2,577,338,100
13	November	553,406,400	555,445,800	609,066,900	536,952,600	2,254,871,700
14	December	674,047,800	662,151,600	588,470,400	678,789,000	2,603,458,800
15	Grand Total	7,503,131,700	6,747,987,600	7,342,230,600	7,264,548,900	28,857,898,800
16						
17						
18						

Now the data Table is back again!

	A	B	C	D	E	F	G	H	I	J	K	L
1	CUSTOMER	PRODUCTS	SALES PERSON	SALES REGION	ORDER DATE	SALES	COSTS	FINANCIAL YEAR	SALES MONTH	SALES QTR	CHANNEL PARTNERS	
2	GIN ON THE RISOFT DRINKS	Homer Simpson	AFRICA	3/9/2012	44719	15139	2012	January	Q1	Zevo Toys		
3	GIN ON THE RIBOTTLES	Homer Simpson	AFRICA	11/28/2012	24997	10940	2012	January	Q1	Krustyco		
4	GIN ON THE RIICE CUBES	Homer Simpson	AFRICA	9/7/2012	90340	15531	2012	January	Q1	Nordyne Defense Dynamics		
5	GIN ON THE RITONIC	Homer Simpson	AFRICA	4/15/2012	10090	19174	2012	January	Q1	SpringShield		
6	GIN ON THE RISOFT DRINKS	Homer Simpson	AFRICA	7/6/2013	14169	17210	2013	January	Q1	Chotchkies		
7	GIN ON THE RIBOTTLES	Homer Simpson	AFRICA	5/18/2013	98852	10634	2013	January	Q1	Acme, inc.		
8	GIN ON THE RIICE CUBES	Homer Simpson	AFRICA	12/8/2013	61233	15918	2013	January	Q1	Acme Corp		
9	GIN ON THE RITONIC	Homer Simpson	AFRICA	9/14/2013	41975	15396	2013	January	Q1	Praxis Corporation		
10	GIN ON THE RISOFT DRINKS	Homer Simpson	AFRICA	12/20/2014	92590	16749	2014	January	Q1	Western Gas & Electric		
11	GIN ON THE RIBOTTLES	Homer Simpson	AFRICA	10/26/2014	15201	10729	2014	January	Q1	Kumatsu Motors		
12	GIN ON THE RIICE CUBES	Homer Simpson	AFRICA	4/1/2014	97314	17060	2014	January	Q1	Input, Inc.		
13	GIN ON THE RITONIC	Homer Simpson	AFRICA	12/20/2014	78392	19215	2014	January	Q1	Dunder Mifflin		
14	GIN ON THE RISOFT DRINKS	Homer Simpson	AFRICA	3/9/2012	44719	15139	2012	January	Q1	Zevo Toys		
15	GIN ON THE RIBOTTLES	Homer Simpson	AFRICA	11/28/2012	24997	10940	2012	January	Q1	Krustyco		
16	GIN ON THE RIICE CUBES	Homer Simpson	AFRICA	9/7/2012	90340	15531	2012	January	Q1	Nordyne Defense Dynamics		
17	GIN ON THE RITONIC	Homer Simpson	AFRICA	4/15/2012	10090	19174	2012	January	Q1	SpringShield		
18	GIN ON THE RISOFT DRINKS	Homer Simpson	AFRICA	7/6/2013	14169	17210	2013	January	Q1	Chotchkies		
19	GIN ON THE RIBOTTLES	Homer Simpson	AFRICA	5/18/2013	98852	10634	2013	January	Q1	Acme, inc.		
20	GIN ON THE RIICE CUBES	Homer Simpson	AFRICA	12/8/2013	61233	15918	2013	January	Q1	Acme Corp		
21	GIN ON THE RITONIC	Homer Simpson	AFRICA	9/14/2013	41975	15396	2013	January	Q1	Praxis Corporation		

Sheet2 | Pivot | Sheet1 | ⊕

Ready

Average: 28563.89193 Count: 5702411 Numerical Count: 2073600 Min: 2012 Max: 99878 Sum: 59230086300

Frequency Distribution

With Pivot Tables you can do a lot of creative analytical reports with your data!

Did you know that you can create a **Frequency Distribution Table**?

I'll show you how easy it is to create your own Frequency Distribution Chart! We will create a Chart based on this Excel Table with Sales values:

CUSTOMER	PRODUCTS	SALES PERSON	SALES REGION	ORDER DATE	SALES	FINANCIAL YEAR	SALES MONTH
LONG ISLANDS INC	SOFT DRINKS	Michael Jackson	AMERICAS	1/13/12	34,324	2012	January
LONG ISLANDS INC	SOFT DRINKS	Michael Jackson	AMERICAS	12/21/12	24,640	2012	February
LONG ISLANDS INC	SOFT DRINKS	Michael Jackson	AMERICAS	12/24/12	29,923	2012	March
LONG ISLANDS INC	SOFT DRINKS	Michael Jackson	AMERICAS	12/24/12	66,901	2012	April
LONG ISLANDS INC	SOFT DRINKS	Michael Jackson	AMERICAS	12/29/12	63,116	2012	May
LONG ISLANDS INC	SOFT DRINKS	Michael Jackson	AMERICAS	6/28/12	38,281	2012	June
LONG ISLANDS INC	SOFT DRINKS	Michael Jackson	AMERICAS	6/28/12	57,650	2012	July
LONG ISLANDS INC	SOFT DRINKS	Michael Jackson	AMERICAS	6/29/12	90,967	2012	August

STEP 1: Let us insert a new Pivot Table. Select your data and Go to *Insert > PivotTable*

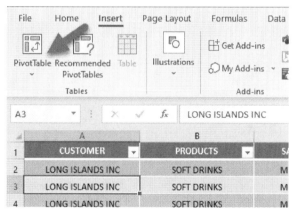

Select **Existing Worksheet** and pick an empty space to place your **Pivot Table.** Click **OK.**

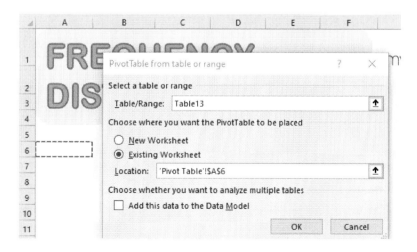

STEP 2: Drag these Pivot Table Fields in the following areas below: Rows:

SALES
Values: **SALES**

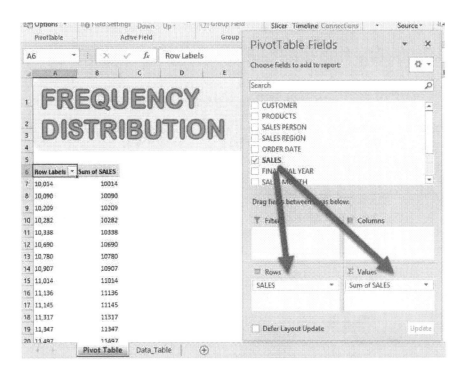

Click on *Sum of SALES* in the Values area and select *Value Field Settings.*

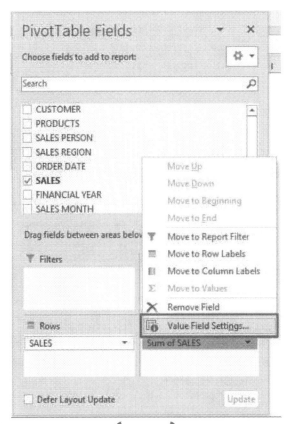

Select **Count** and click **OK.**

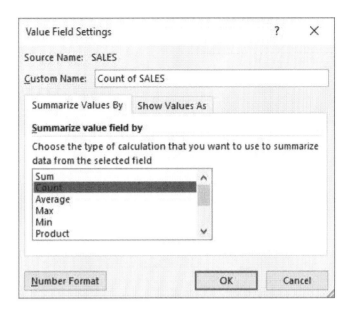

STEP 3: We are almost there! Right click on a SALES cell in the Row Labels and select **Group.**

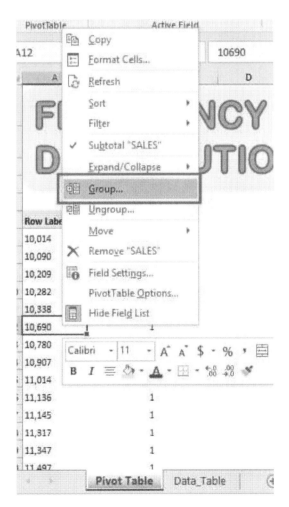

Accept the suggested values. It will group our SALES values by ranges of 10,000. Click **OK.**

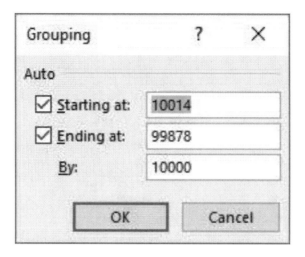

Now our SALES values are grouped together!

Row Labels ▼	Count of SALES
10014-20013	67
20014-30013	56
30014-40013	61
40014-50013	60
50014-60013	65
60014-70013	67
70014-80013	71
80014-90013	67
90014-100013	62
Grand Total	**576**

STEP 4: Go to *PivotTable Analyze > Tools > PivotChart*

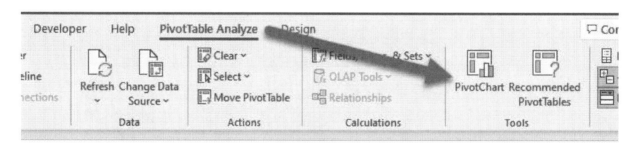

Ensure **Clustered Column** is selected. Click **OK.**

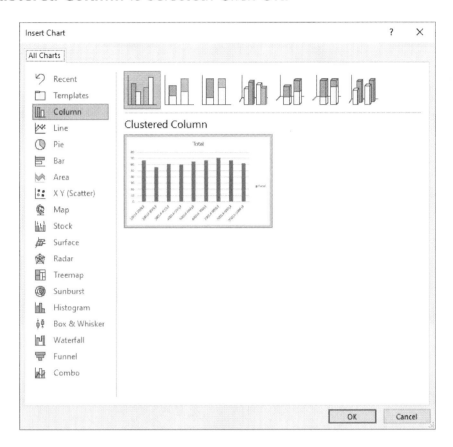

Our awesome **Frequency Distribution Chart** is now ready!

Row Labels	Count of SALES
10014-20013	67
20014-30013	56
30014-40013	61
40014-50013	60
50014-60013	65
60014-70013	67
70014-80013	71
80014-90013	67
90014-100013	62
Grand Total	**576**

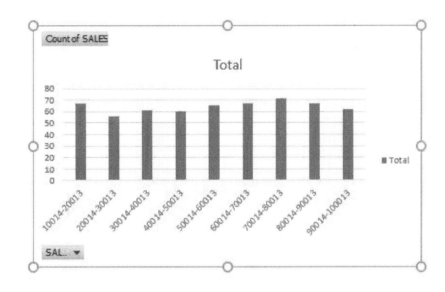

Recommended Pivot Tables

Did you know that Excel can **automatically generate Pivot Tables** for you?

You heard that right! There are **Recommended Pivot Tables** in Excel that you can use from the Ribbon Menu.

This is a new feature introduced in Excel 2013.

STEP 1: Make sure you have selected your data source. Go to *Insert > Recommended Pivot Tables.*

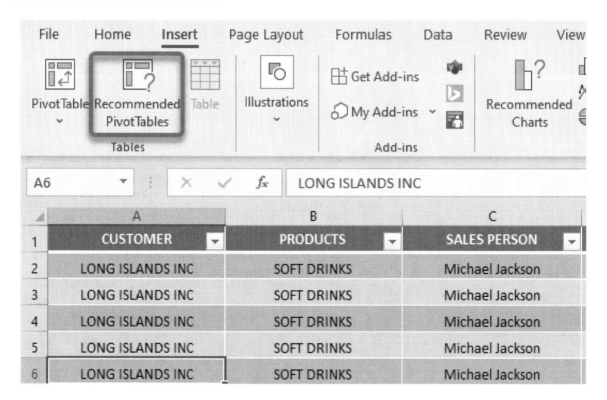

STEP 2: You will see the Recommended Pivot Tables and you also get a live preview.

Let us select the **Count of SALES by PRODUCTS.** Click **OK.**

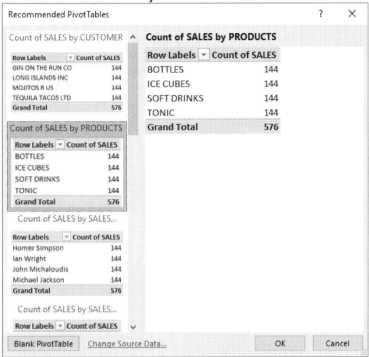

STEP 3: The Recommended Pivot Table is now in a new sheet!

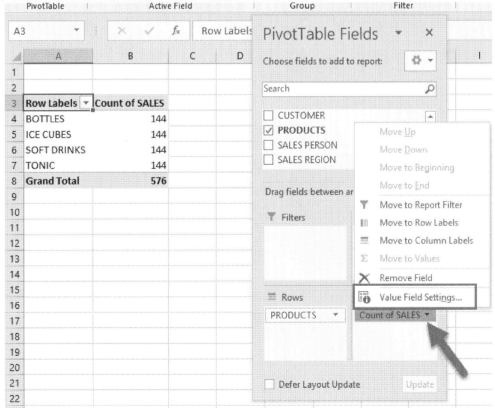

Data Model & Relationships

Ever had multiple related Excel Tables and wondered how to create a report that connects them together in a single Pivot Table?

We have just the thing with **Data Model and Relationships!**

Below is our data that we will be using to create our relationships.

What we want to do is create a report that shows the First Name of the student and the Number of Classes that the student has taken.

The tricky part here is the First Name is in the **Students Table,** whilst the number of classes can be retrieved from the **Classes Table**.

Both Tables are linked by the **StudentId column**.

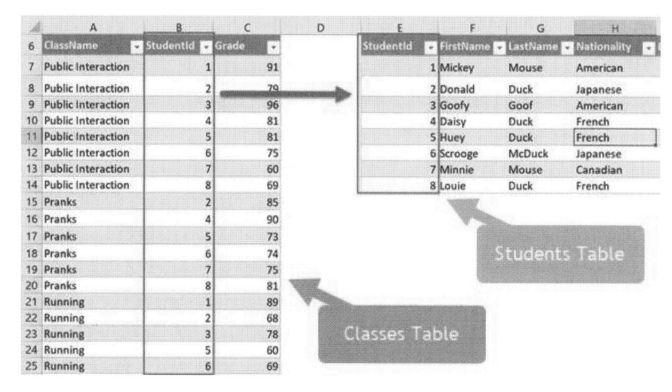

STEP 1: Select the *Classes Table.* Go to *Insert > Pivot Table > New Worksheet.*

Make sure to tick **Add this data to the Data Model.** Click **OK.**

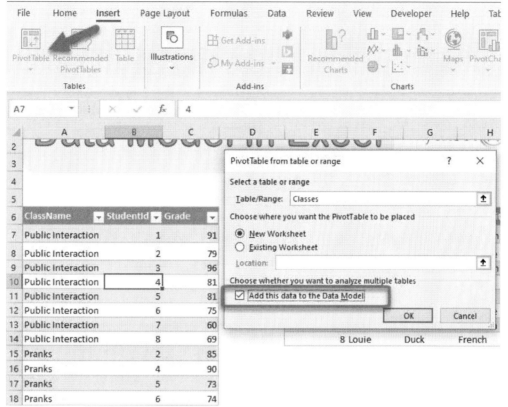

STEP 2: Select the *Students Table.* Go to *Insert > Pivot Table > New Worksheet.*

Make sure to tick **Add this data to the Data Model.** Click **OK.**

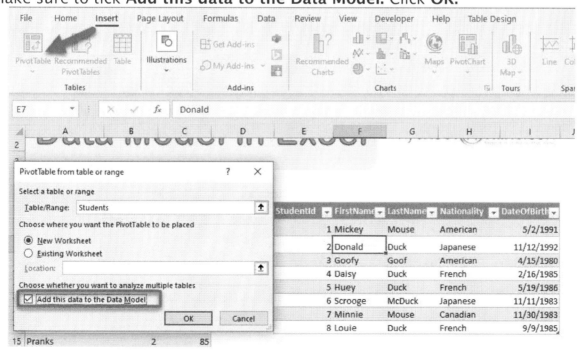

STEP 3: Click All in the **PivotTable Fields** and you should see both Tables there.

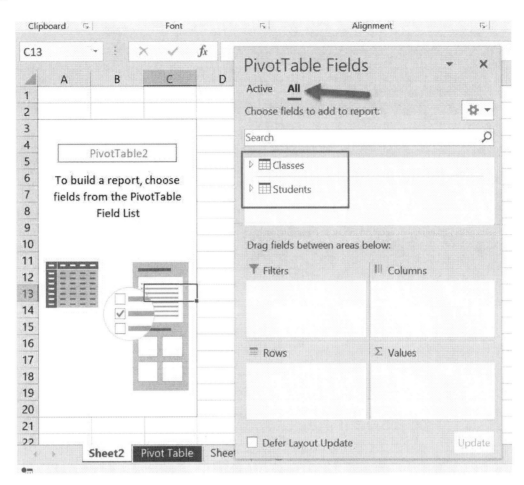

STEP 4: Now we need to link them together! Go to *PivotTable Analyze > Calculations > Relationships*

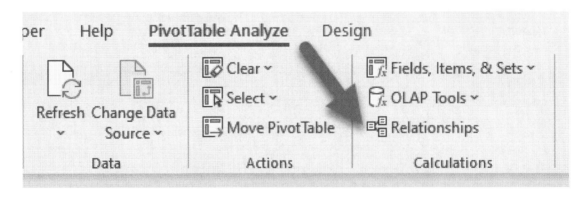

Click New.

STEP 5: There are two sides of a Relationship when linking data together.

The rule of thumb is that the **Primary Table should have no duplicates**. This is the **Students Table** as it does not have duplicate **Student Ids**.

Set the following then Click OK:

Table: **Classes**

Column (Foreign) - **StudentId**

Related Table – **Students**

Related Column (Primary) - **StudentId**

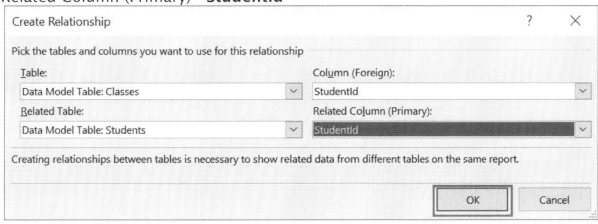

PRO TIP: For relationships to work correctly, the Related Column (Primary) has to have unique values and no duplicates.

The Column (Foreign) can have duplicate values.

Click Close.

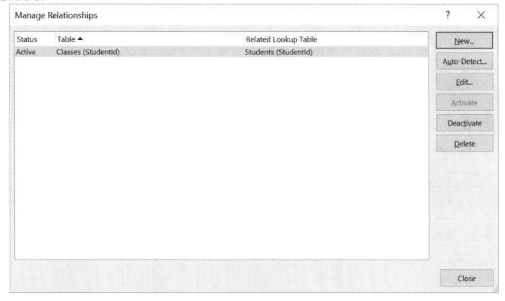

STEP 6: Drag these PivotTable Fields in the following areas below:

Rows: **Students (FIRSTNAME)**
Values: **Classes (CLASSNAME)**

You can see that Excel was able to show the results in a **merged fashion!**

You can see **Daisy has 2 classes enrolled** pulling from the individual Excel Tables. We would not have that information readily available unless we used a VLOOKUP or XLOOKUP Formula.

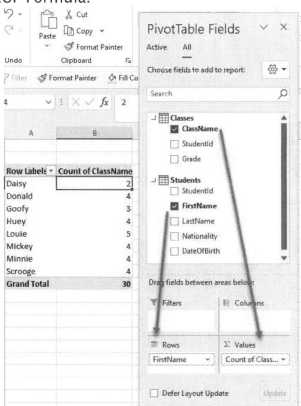

New Features in Excel Microsoft 365

The best thing with Pivot Tables is that more features are being added with Excel updates.

I will give you my top 4 picks on the new features that can be used in Excel for Microsoft 365:

1. Personalize the Default Pivot Table Layout

2. Automatic Relationship detection

3. Automatic Time Grouping

4. Search In The Pivot Table Fields List

Personalize the Default Pivot Table Layout

If you have an existing PivotTable laid out the way you like, you can import those settings, and use them for any newly created Pivot Tables.

Existing PivotTables aren't impacted by changes to the default layout.

Below we have selected a Pivot Table Style and Color that we like.

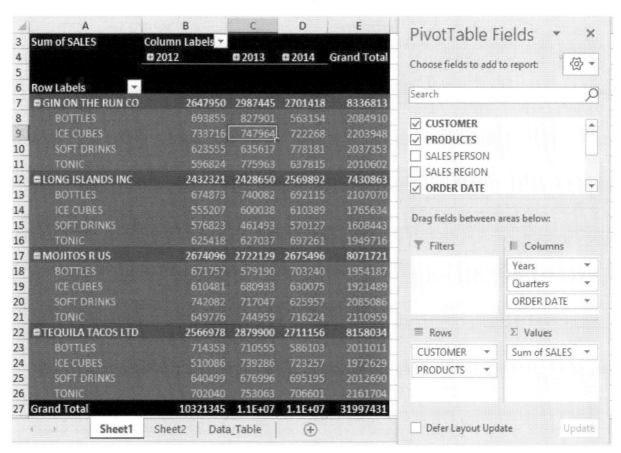

STEP 1: Go to **File** > **Options**

STEP 2: Select **Data** > **Data options** > **Edit Default Layout**

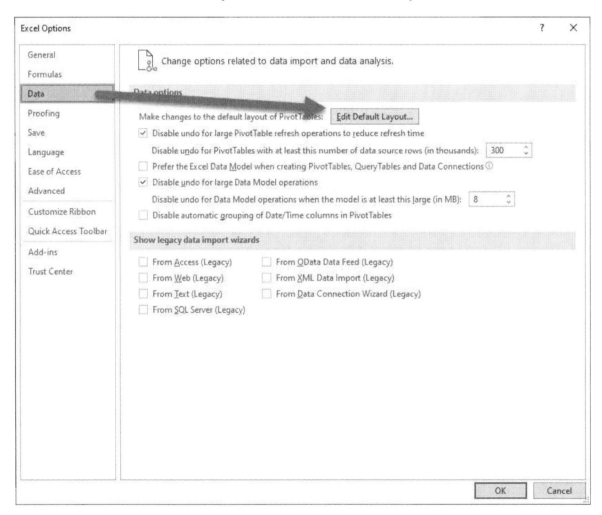

STEP 3: Let us have some fun! Try out the following:

- **Subtotals** - Show all Subtotals at Bottom of Group

- **Report Layout** - Show in Tabular Form

- **Blank Rows** - Tick Insert Blank Line after Each Item

You can explore more options inside **PivotTable Options**. Click **OK**.

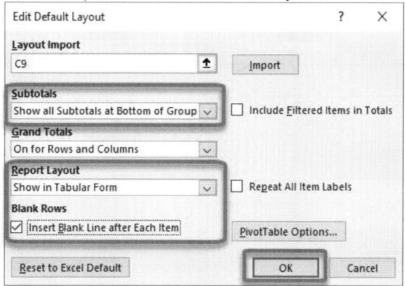

STEP 4: Let us insert a new Pivot Table to see our new default layout!

Open our Excel Table data source. Go to *Insert > Tables > PivotTable.*

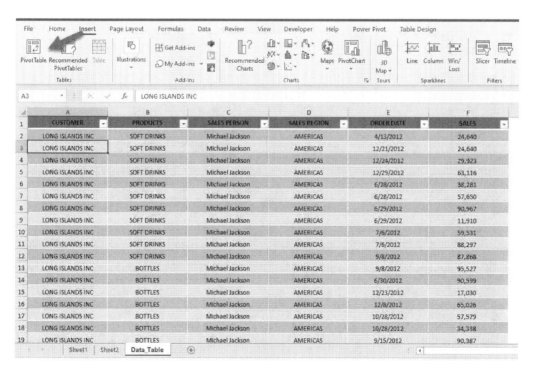

STEP 5: Click **OK.**

PivotTable from table or range   ?   ✕

Select a table or range

Table/Range: Table1   ⬆

Choose where you want the PivotTable to be placed

◉ New Worksheet

○ Existing Worksheet

Location: ⬆

Choose whether you want to analyze multiple tables

☐ Add this data to the Data Model

OK   Cancel

STEP 6: Drag these PivotTable Fields in the following areas

below: Rows: **CUSTOMER** and **PRODUCTS**
Columns: **ORDER DATE**
Values: **SALES**

And you will now see the new layout!

The **PRODUCTS Field** is in a separate column as we selected a Tabular Form Report Layout.

The **Subtotals** are now at the bottom of each group, and there is an **empty row** after each item!

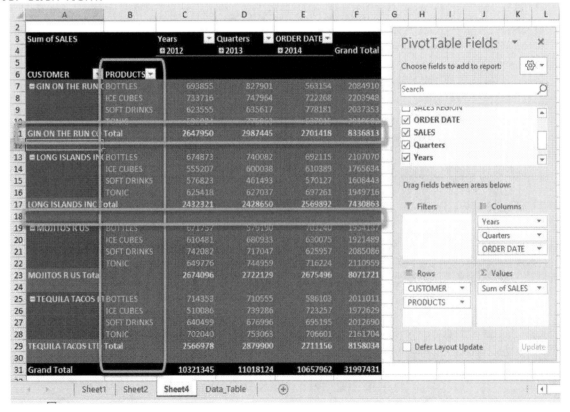

Automatic Relationship detection

To better understand how the data model and relationships work for Pivot Tables, have a look at the **Data Model & Relationships** tip earlier in this chapter.

We have 3 data Tables that are related to each other: **Product**, **Customer** and **Sales.**

What connects these Tables together are related columns, as shown below:

Product Table > Product Key

Product Key	Product Name	Product Cost	List Price
1	Skittles	0.69	1.72
2	Smarties	0.52	1.30
3	Galaxy	0.94	2.35
4	minstrels	0.58	1.46
5	Galaxy counters	0.10	0.24
6	Toffee crisp	0.97	2.42
7	Mars Bar	0.23	0.58
8	Cadbury wispa	0.57	1.43
9	Cadbury egg	0.97	2.41
10	Cadbury buttons	0.17	0.43
11	Starburst	0.68	1.69
12	Jelly tots	0.17	0.42
13	Kinder surprise	0.67	1.67
14	Kinder bueno	0.94	2.35
15	Kinder bars	0.98	2.46
16	Haribo starmix	0.36	0.90
17	Haribo tangfastics	0.65	1.61
18	Haribo bears	0.33	0.83
19	Fruit pastilles	0.55	1.38
20	Chupa chups	0.26	0.64

Sales | Customer | **Product** | ⊕

Customer Table > Customer Number

Sales Table > Product Key & Customer Number

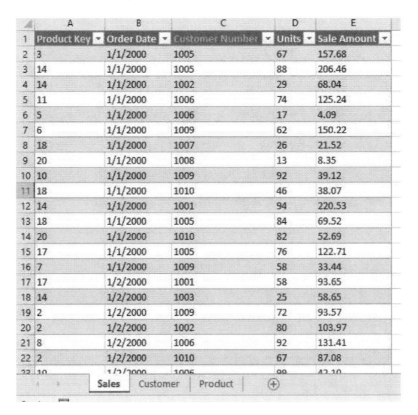

STEP 1: The cool thing is once we add this to our data model, Excel is able to auto-detect the relationships when we work on the Pivot Table.

Select anywhere in one of our Excel Tables. Go to *Insert > Tables > PivotTable.*

Make sure **Add this data to the Data Model** is ticked. Click **OK**

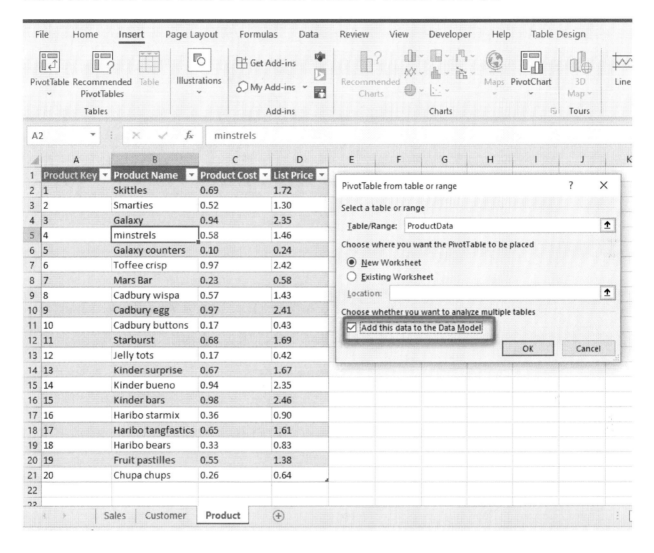

STEP 2: You will see that all the Tables are added to the Data Model.

Select **All** and you will see all 3 Tables are listed there.

STEP 3: Let us see how Excel works its magic! Drag these PivotTable Fields in the following areas below:

Columns: **PRODUCT NAME**
Values: **SALE AMOUNT**
Click **Auto-Detect**

STEP 4: Select **Manage Relationships** to see what was created automatically.

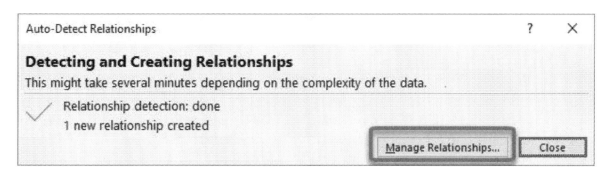

Click **Edit.**

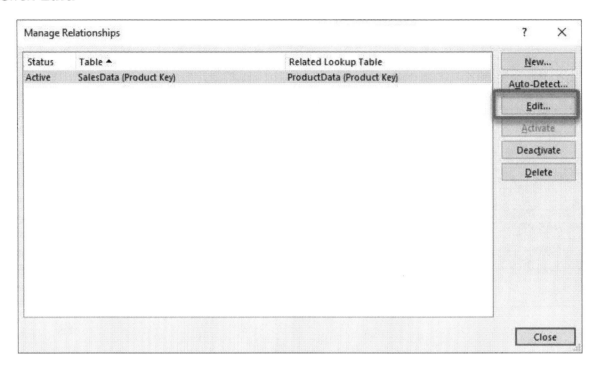

STEP 5: This is cool as the relationship between **Sales** and **Product Tables** is correct!

Excel can link these Tables together via the **Product Key**

columns. Click **OK.**

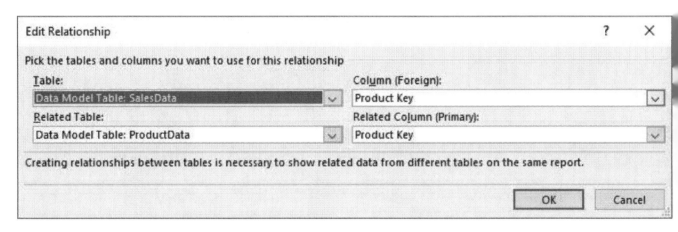

STEP 6: Now set up the following:

Rows: **COUNTRY**
Click **Auto-Detect**

STEP 7: Select **Manage Relationships** to see what was created automatically

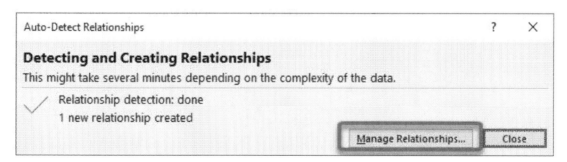

Click **Edit.**

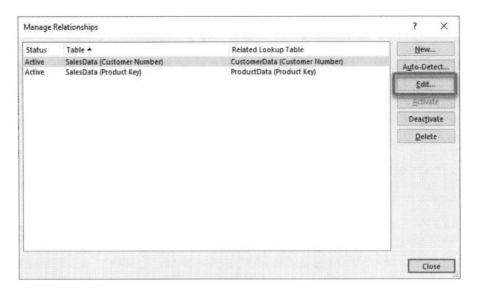

STEP 8: This is cool as the relationship between **Sales** and **Customer Tables** is correct!

Excel can link these Tables together via the **Customer Number**

columns. Click **OK.**

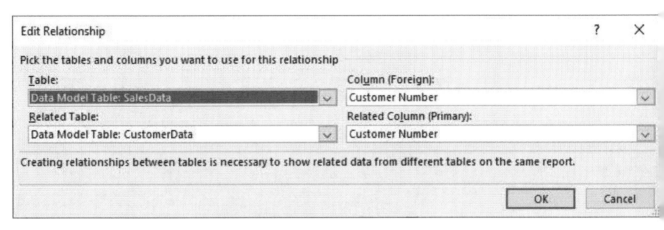

Our Pivot Table is all setup thanks to the automatic creation of the relationships between the 3 Excel Tables.

We can now create more robust Pivot Table reports without having to use the VLOOKUP or XLOOKUP formulas.

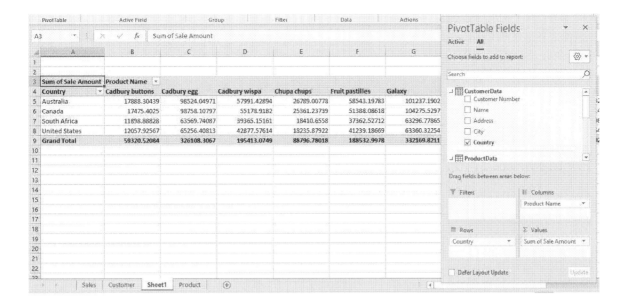

PRO TIP: For relationships to work correctly, the Related Column (Primary) has to have unique values and no duplicates.

The Column (Foreign) can have duplicate values.

Automatic Time Grouping

With time grouping, relationships across time-related fields are automatically detected and grouped together when you add rows of time fields to your PivotTables.

Once grouped together, you can drag the group to your Pivot Table and start your analysis.

Have a look at our Excel Table data source.

You can see the **TIME OF ORDER** column. Once we create the Pivot Table, Excel will group by time periods automatically.

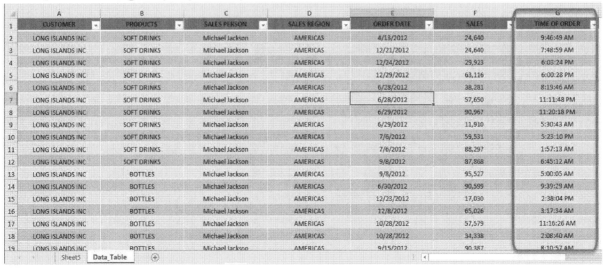

STEP 1: Drag these PivotTable Fields in the following areas below:

Rows: **TIME OF ORDER**
Values: **SALES**

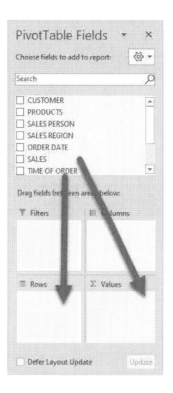

And just like that, our Sales amounts are **grouped by the hour**!

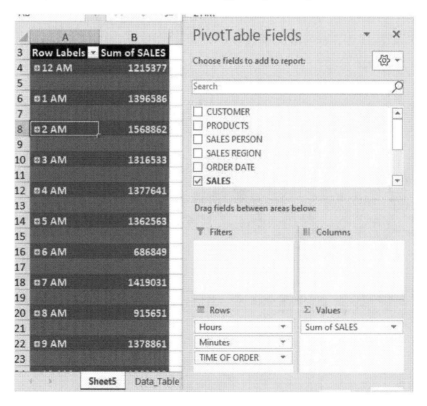

Search In the Pivot Table Fields List

You can quickly find the Pivot Table Fields you are looking for in long lists of fields without scrolling, using the new search in PivotTable functionality.

Here is our Field list:

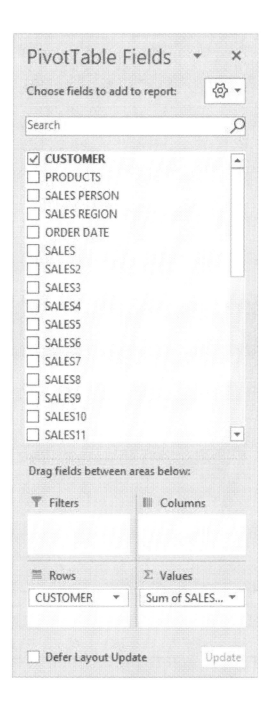

STEP 1: Let us say we want to get the **SALES30** Field.

Just type in **30** in the search box and you have the Field right away for selection!

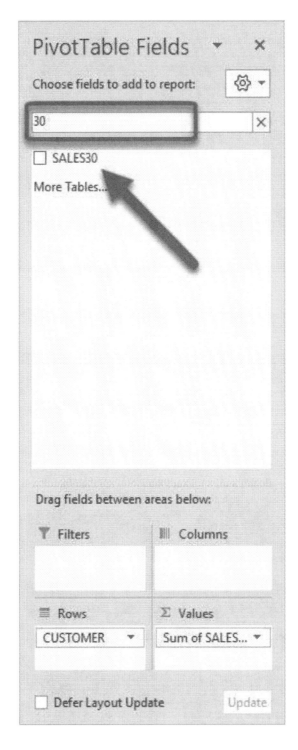

Insert a Pivot Table in Excel Web

With Excel Online, you can easily create Pivot Tables on your web browser!

I will show you how easily this can be created with the following steps.

STEP 1: First you need to have a paid Microsoft 365 account.

Once you have a Microsoft 365 account, on your web browser type in **www.office.com** and click on the **Excel** icon.

Select **New blank workbook.**

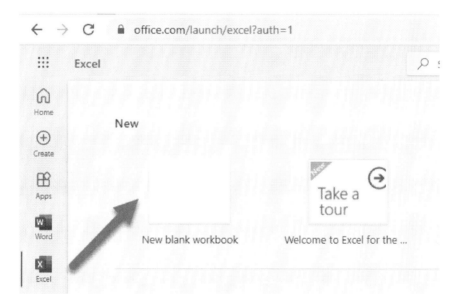

Let us create a quick table of random data:

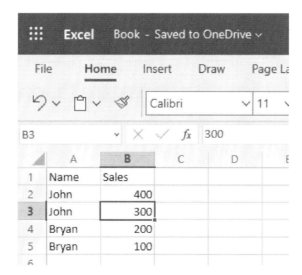

STEP 2: Click on any cell that has your data and go to *Insert > PivotTable.*

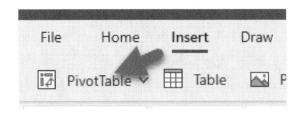

STEP 3: Excel Online will know to select the data table that we have created in the **Source** area.

Select **New sheet**.

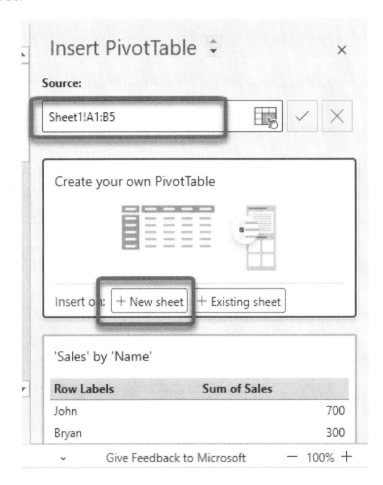

STEP 4: We can now set up our Pivot Table by dragging the **Name** Field in the *Rows* area and **Sales** Field in the *Values* area (just like in desktop Excel).

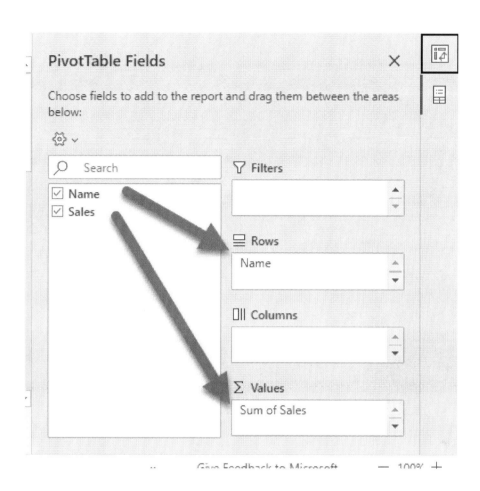

We now have our Pivot Table using the web version of Excel!

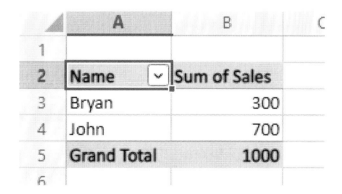

FREE EXCEL WORKSHOP

If you want to dramatically **reduce repetition, stress, and at least 2 Hours of daily overtime**...

...And exponentially **increase your chances of a promotion, pay raise or new job**...

...Then join me in this FREE Excel Online Masterclass Training where I will cover the *Top 10 Secret Excel Productivity Tips*...

...**Covering Formulas, Pivot Tables, Dashboards, Flash Fill, Shortcuts PLUS MORE!**

Go to the link below to register for FREE and ADVANCE your Excel skills today:

👉 https://www.myexcelonline.com/tips-webinar

101 EXCEL BOOK SERIES

Check out our best selling Excel eBooks at discounted prices now! Learn the 101 Most Popular Excel Formulas, 101 Ready To Use Excel Macros and 101 Best Excel Tips and Tricks!

👉 View All Our Excel eBooks: https://ebooks.myexcelonline.com/

We have also created paperback book versions of our 101 Book Series which you can have delivered to your home via Amazon:

👉 View Our Amazon Paperback: 101 Most Popular Excel Formulas:
   https://www.myexcelonline.com/101FormulasPaperback

👉 View Our Amazon Paperback: 101 Ready To Use Excel Macros:
   https://www.myexcelonline.com/101MacrosPaperback

👉 View Our Amazon Paperback: 101 Best Excel Tips and Tricks:
   https://www.myexcelonline.com/101TipsPaperback

MYEXCELONLINE ACADEMY COURSE

Access a library of 1,000+ Microsoft Excel & Office video training tutorials, support and certification covering all levels and features like:

Formulas, Macros, VBA, Pivot Tables, Power Pivot, Power Query, Power BI, Charts, Analysis, Financial Modeling, Dashboards & MORE!

Plus, all of the following Microsoft Office 365 courses on:

Word, Outlook, PowerPoint, Access, Teams, OneNote, Project, Visio, Power Apps, Power Automation, SQL, SharePoint, Forms & MORE!

👉 https://join.myexcelonline.com/

EXCEL EXPERT CONSULTATIONS

Need help with your Excel workbook?

We offer fast, expert consulting help to solve your Excel problems quickly on:

Formulas, Macros, VBA, Pivot Tables, Charts, Dashboards, Power BI, Power Query, Modifying Templates, Recovering Corrupt Files, Access, Microsoft Office plus More!

👉 https://www.myexcelonline.com/consulting

FREE GOODWILL

"He who said money can't buy happiness, hasn't given enough away."

- Unknown

People who help others (with zero expectation) experience higher levels of fulfillment, live longer, *and* make more money. We'd like to create the opportunity to deliver this value to you during your reading experience. To do so, we have a simple question for you...

Would you help someone you've never met, if it didn't cost you money, but you never got credit for it?

If so, I have an 'ask' to make on behalf of someone you do not know. And likely, never will.

They are just like you, or like you were a few years ago: less experienced, full of desire to help the world, seeking information but unsure where to look... this is where you come in.

The only way for us at MyExcelOnline.com to accomplish our mission of helping professionals is, first, by reaching them. And most people do, in fact, judge a book by its cover (and its reviews). If you have found this book valuable thus far, would you please take a brief moment right now and leave an honest review of the book and its contents? It will cost you zero dollars and less than 60 seconds.

Your review will help...

...one more professional support his or her family.

...one more client experience a transformation they otherwise would never have encountered.

...one more life change for the better.

To make that happen...all you have to do is... and this takes less than 60 seconds...leave a review.

You can go to the book page on Amazon (or go to www.myexcelonline.com/goodwill) and leave a review right on the page.

P.S. – If you feel good about helping a faceless professional, you are our kind of people. We are that much more excited to help you crush it in the world of Excel.

Thank you from the bottom of our hearts.

Your biggest fans, John and Bryan

Thank You!

Here is the **download link** that has all the workbooks covered in this book (type this URL to your web browser):

👉 https://www.myexcelonline.com/Pivot-Table-download-paperback

Here is the link and password to the Free 20-Hour Microsoft Excel Course (type this URL to your web browser):

👉 https://www.myexcelonline.com/free-excel-course

👉 Password: **101excel**

We would like to thank you again for taking the time to check out our Excel Pivot Table Book! We hope you've found value in it and can use it as a guide to help you gain more Excel knowledge which will make you more productive, give you more confidence and ultimately make you stand out from the crowd!

You can also go directly to other Excel services & products here:

www.MyExcelOnline.com/webinars to get free online Excel training!

https://join.myexcelonline.com/ to enroll in our Flagship Excel & Office Course and ADVANCE your level!

ebooks.MyExcelOnline.com to get our bestselling Excel Books!

www.MyExcelonline.com/blog to get daily tutorials on Formulas, Pivot Tables, Charts, Analysis, Macros & Power BI!

Feel free to email us regarding anything Excel related, improvements and additions to this book at support@myexcelonline.com

To Your Success!

John Michaloudis & Bryan Hong

MyExcelOnline.com

Made in the USA
Middletown, DE
18 June 2025

77226442R00300